"THERE ARE TWO GOVERNMENTS IN THE UNITED STATES TODAY. ONE IS VISIBLE. THE OTHER IS INVISIBLE.

"THE FIRST IS THE GOVERNMENT THAT CITIZENS READ ABOUT IN THEIR NEWSPAPERS AND CHILDREN STUDY ABOUT IN THEIR CIVICS BOOKS. THE SECOND IS THE INTERLOCKING, HIDDEN MACHINERY THAT CARRIES OUT THE POLICIES OF THE UNITED STATES IN THE COLD WAR."

David Wise and Thomas B. Ross

THE INVISIBLE GOVERNMENT

"Reads like a spy novel . . . Will give most Americans their first good look at a vastly expensive, highly important and extremely risky sector of government operations."

Minneapolis Tribune

"Forces attention on a painful and perilous dilemma we have been avoiding too long."

The New York Times

"Startling . . . Disturbing . . . Highly informative."

Chicago Tribune

Also by David Wise and Thomas B. Ross

❦ THE U-2 AFFAIR

❦ Published by Bantam Books

THE INVISIBLE GOVERNMENT
by DAVID WISE and THOMAS B. ROSS

BANTAM BOOKS
TORONTO · NEW YORK · LONDON

*This low-priced Bantam Book
has been completely reset in a type face
designed for easy reading, and was printed
from new plates. It contains the complete
text of the original hard-cover edition.*
NOT ONE WORD HAS BEEN OMITTED.

THE INVISIBLE GOVERNMENT

*A Bantam Book / published by arrangement with
Random House, Inc.*

PRINTING HISTORY

Random edition published June 1964
2nd printing .... June 1964
3rd printing .... June 1964
4th printing .... August 1964
5th printing .... September 1964

Kiplinger Book Service edition published July 1964

Serialized, in condensed form, by ST. LOUIS POST DISPATCH, BOSTON
GLOBE, *and* CHICAGO SUN-TIMES *July–August 1964*

Book Find Club edition published August 1964

Book-of-the-Month Club edition published February 1965

Bantam edition published March 1965

Quotations from the following are reprinted by permission:
Six Crises, *Richard M. Nixon.* © *Copyright, 1962, by Richard M.
Nixon. Doubleday & Company, Inc.*
The White House Years, Mandate for Change 1953–1956, *Dwight
D. Eisenhower.* © *Copyright, 1963, by Dwight D. Eisenhower.
Doubleday & Company, Inc.*
Memoirs, Volume II, Harry S Truman. © *Copyright, 1956, Time
Inc.*
My War With Communism, *Miguel Ydigoras Fuentes with Mario
Rosenthal.* © *Copyright, 1963, by Prentice-Hall, Inc.*
The Bridge at Andau, *James A. Michener.* © *Copyright, 1957, by
James A. Michener. Random House, Inc.*
*Excerpts from copyrighted interview with Robert F. Kennedy,
January 28, 1963.* U.S. NEWS & WORLD REPORT.

Published simultaneously in the United States and Canada.

*Bantam Books are published by Bantam Books, Inc., a subsidiary
of Grosset & Dunlap, Inc. Its trade-mark, consisting of the words
"Bantam Books" and the portrayal of a bantam, is registered in the
United States Patent Office and in other countries. Marca Registrada.
Bantam Books, Inc., 271 Madison Avenue, New York 16, New York.*

PRINTED IN THE UNITED STATES OF AMERICA

FOR
Joan
AND
Gunilla

Contents

The Invisible Government

THERE ARE two governments in the United States today. One is visible. The other is invisible.

The first is the government that citizens read about in their newspapers and children study about in their civics books. The second is the interlocking, hidden machinery that carries out the policies of the United States in the Cold War.

This second, invisible government gathers intelligence, conducts espionage, and plans and executes secret operations all over the globe.

The Invisible Government is not a formal body. It is a loose, amorphous grouping of individuals and agencies drawn from many parts of the visible government. It is not limited to the Central Intelligence Agency, although the CIA is at its heart. Nor is it confined to the nine other agencies which comprise what is known as the intelligence community: the National Security Council, the Defense Intelligence Agency, the National Security Agency, Army Intelligence, Navy Intelligence, Air Force Intelligence, the State Department's Bureau of Intelligence and Research, the Atomic Energy Commission and the Federal Bureau of Investigation.

The Invisible Government includes, also, many other units and agencies, as well as individuals, that appear outwardly to be a normal part of the conventional government. It even encompasses business firms and institutions that are seemingly private.

To an extent that is only beginning to be perceived, this shadow government is shaping the lives of 190,000,000 Americans. Major decisions involving peace or war are taking place out of public view. An informed citizen might come to suspect that the foreign policy of the United States often works publicly in one direction and secretly through the Invisible Government in just the opposite direction.

This Invisible Government is a relatively new institution. It came into being as a result of two related factors: the rise of the United States after World War II to a position of pre-eminent world power, and the challenge to that power by Soviet Communism.

It was a much graver challenge than any which had previously confronted the Republic. The Soviet world strategy threatened the very survival of the nation. It employed an espionage network that was dedicated to the subversion of the power and ideals of the United States. To meet that challenge the United States began constructing a vast intelligence and espionage system of its own. This has mushroomed to extraordinary proportions out of public view and quite apart from the traditional political process.

By 1964 the intelligence network had grown into a massive, hidden apparatus, secretly employing about 200,000 persons and spending several billion dollars a year.

"The National Security Act of 1947," in the words of Allen W. Dulles, ". . . has given Intelligence a more influential position in our government than Intelligence enjoys in any other government of the world." [1]

Because of its massive size and pervasive secrecy, the Invisible Government became the inevitable target of suspicion and criticism. It has been accused by some knowledgeable congressmen and other influential citizens, including a former President, Harry S. Truman, of conducting a foreign policy of its own, and of meddling deeply in the affairs of other countries without presidential authority.

The American people have not been in a position to

2

assess these charges. They know virtually nothing about the Invisible Government. Its employment rolls are classified. Its activities are top-secret. Its budget is concealed in other appropriations. Congress provides money for the Invisible Government without knowing how much it has appropriated or how it will be spent. A handful of congressmen are supposed to be kept informed by the Invisible Government, but they know relatively little about how it works.

Overseas, in foreign capitals, American ambassadors are supposed to act as the supreme civilian representatives of the President of the United States. They are told they have control over the agents of the Invisible Government. But do they? The agents maintain communications and codes of their own. And the ambassador's authority has been judged by a committee of the United States Senate to be a "polite fiction."

At home, the intelligence men are directed by law to leave matters to the FBI. But the CIA maintains more than a score of offices in major cities throughout the United States; it is deeply involved in many domestic activities, from broadcasting stations and a steamship company to the university campus.

The Invisible Government is also generally thought to be under the direct control of the National Security Council. But, in fact, many of its major decisions are never discussed in the Council. These decisions are handled by a small directorate, the name of which is only whispered. How many Americans have ever heard of the "Special Group"? (Also known as the "54/12 Group.") The name of this group, even its existence, is unknown outside the innermost circle of the Invisible Government.

The Vice-President is by law a member of the National Security Council, but he does not participate in the discussions of the Special Group. As Vice-President, Lyndon B. Johnson was privy to more government secrets than any of his predecessors. But he was not truly involved with the Invisible Government until he was sworn in as the thirty-sixth President of the United States.

On November 23, 1963, during the first hour of his first

3

full day in office, Johnson was taken by McGeorge Bundy—who had been President Kennedy's personal link with the Special Group—to the Situation Room, a restricted command post deep in the White House basement.

There, surrounded by top-secret maps, electronic equipment and communications outlets, the new President was briefed by the head of the Invisible Government, John Alex McCone, Director of Central Intelligence and a member of the Special Group. Although Johnson knew the men who ran the Invisible Government and was aware of much of its workings, it was not until that morning that he began to see the full scope of its organization and secrets.

This book is an attempt, within the bounds of national security, to reveal the nature, size and power of the Invisible Government. It is not intended to be an exposé, although much of the material has never been printed anywhere else before. It is an attempt to describe a hidden American institution which the American people, who finance it, have a right to know about.

The premise of this book is that even in a time of Cold War, the United States Government must rest, in the words of the Declaration of Independence, on "the consent of the governed." And there can be no meaningful consent where those who are governed do not know to what they are consenting.

In the harsh conditions of the mid-twentieth century, the nation's leaders have increasingly come to feel that certain decisions must be made by them alone without popular consent, and in secret, if the nation is to survive. The area of this secret decision-making has grown rapidly and the size of the Invisible Government has increased proportionately.

To what extent is this secret government compatible with the American system, or necessary to preserve it? Will it gradually change the character of the institutions it seeks to preserve? If the American people are to try to answer these questions they must first achieve a greater level of understanding about the secret government itself.

"I know no safe depository of the ultimate powers of

the society but the people themselves," said Thomas Jefferson, "and if we think them not enlightened enough to exercise their control with a wholesome discretion, the remedy is not to take it from them, but to inform their discretion."

This book is an effort to thus inform the American people. It traces the history of the Invisible Government: how it was created by President Truman and how it has functioned under President Eisenhower, President Kennedy and President Johnson. It discloses how the Invisible Government has operated in Washington to expand and consolidate its power, and how it has operated overseas in attempts to bolster or undermine foreign governments. For beyond the mere gathering of intelligence, the secret government has engaged in "special operations," ranging from political warfare to para-military activities and full-scale invasion.

Under certain conditions, and on a limited, controlled basis, such special operations may sometimes prove necessary. But they cannot become so unwieldy that they are irreconcilable with the kind of society that has launched them. When that happens, the result is disaster. This was nowhere better illustrated than on the beaches of Cuba.

Because it has now passed into history and because it is a deeply revealing example of how the Invisible Government works, we shall begin with the story of the Bay of Pigs.

48 Hours

THE STARS sparkled against the blue-black tropical sky overhead and the warm night air carried as yet no hint of dawn. Mario Zuniga edged his B-26 bomber onto the runway at the edge of the Caribbean Sea.

Only the sound of the twin engines broke the stillness of the darkened airfield at Puerto Cabezas, Nicaragua. The tall, thirty-five-year-old Cuban exile pilot sat alone in the cockpit of the big bomber. He would have no co-pilot for this mission. On the nose of his plane the number 933 had been painted in black letters. On the tail, the letters FAR—the markings of Fidel Castro's air force, the "Fuerza Aerea Revolucionaria."

But Mario Zuniga was not a Castro pilot. He was flying on an extraordinary top-secret mission for the Central Intelligence Agency of the United States Government.

Earlier, the CIA had trundled the bomber out onto the runway and fired a machine gun at it. There were bullet holes in the fuselage now. These were some of the stage props for Zuniga's masquerade. In his pocket he carried a pack of Cuban cigarettes, borrowed from a fellow pilot at the last moment to lend a final authentic touch. In his mind was a carefully memorized story. His destination was Miami International Airport, 834 miles and more than four hours to the northeast.

At a signal, Zuniga took off, his bomber roaring down the 6,000-foot runway. It was April 15, 1961, and perfect flying weather. His mission, upon which hinged the success or failure of the most ambitious operation in the history of the Central Intelligence Agency, was under way.

Beginning at 1:40 A.M., shortly before Zuniga's take-off, eight other CIA B-26s had roared into the night from the same airstrip, their engines straining with the weight of extra fuel and the ten 260-pound bombs they each carried. Their pilots were Cuban exiles, trained and employed by the CIA. Their target was Cuba, and their mission—to smash Castro's air force before it could get off the ground.

These planes, too, bore a replica of the FAR insignia of Castro's air force. Flying in three formations, under the code names of "Linda," "Puma" and "Gorilla," the eight B-26s were to strike at dawn in a surprise raid. It was to be the first of two strikes at Castro's air bases, to pave the way for the secret invasion of Cuba scheduled to take place forty-eight hours later at the Bahia de Cochinos, the Bay of Pigs. The operation had the approval of the CIA, the Joint Chiefs of Staff and the President of the United States.

Zuniga was to land in Miami shortly after the bombing raid. He was to announce to the world that the attack had been carried out from bases inside Cuba by himself and other pilots who had defected from Castro's air force. In reality, of course, all nine planes had left from Happy Valley, the CIA code name for the air base at Puerto Cabezas. The Nicaraguan Government had secretly agreed to let the United States use the air base and port as a staging area for the invasion.

As he flew northward through the night to Miami, Zuniga had time to go over the prepared story once more in his mind. He had been especially selected by the CIA's American instructors from among the Cuban exile pilots. A CIA agent known simply as "George" had asked for volunteers for a special mission. Three men offered to go. The CIA fired questions at them to test their reactions under stress. Mario was then selected for his intelligence and quick thinking. There followed endless rehearsals of the cover story that Zuniga came to know almost in his sleep. He was instructed not to reveal the truth about his mission, even years afterward.

As his plane carried him toward Florida, Zuniga was flying also toward his wife Georgina, his two young sons, Eduardo and Enrique, and his daughters, Beatriz and Maria Cristina. He had left them behind in the safety of Miami, in an apartment on South West 20th Avenue, when he had joined the exiles who were training in Central America to invade their homeland.

To the southeast, the strike force droned onward toward Cuba and the new day. The attack was to be led by Luis Cosme, a wiry, crew-cut former Cuban Air Force and Cubana Airlines pilot who had fled Cuba eight months before. At the controls of the other two planes in Cosme's "Linda" wing were Alfredo Caballero, a stocky twenty-five-year-old, and Rene Garcia. They, too, were Cuban Air Force veterans. Their target was San Antonio de los Banos, the vital military airfield twenty-five miles southwest of Havana.

Jose Crespo, short and handsome, led the "Puma" flight that was to strike at Camp Libertad airfield on the outskirts of Havana. The other two B-26s in Crespo's wing were flown by Daniel Fernandez Mon, Spanish-born and the only bachelor in the flight, and "Chirrino" Piedra, at twenty-five one of the youngest and best-liked of the exile pilots. None of these three pilots or their co-pilots survived the Bay of Pigs. All six men in the "Puma" wing had less than forty-eight hours to live.

Two planes comprised the third, "Gorilla," wing. They were flown by Gustavo Ponzoa and Gonzalo Herrera. Their target was the airport at Santiago de Cuba, in Oriente Province, where Castro had begun his climb to power in the Sierra Maestra five years earlier.

The invasion fleet of half a dozen ships was already steaming toward Cuba under the escort of U.S. warships. Unable to sleep on the crowded deck of the *Houston*, nineteen-year-old Mario Abril, a private in E Company, 2nd Infantry Battalion of the exile brigade, heard the drone of the bomber fleet overhead.

He looked up and saw the B-26 formation against the night sky. Two months before he had been in Miami, preparing to leave for the training camp in Guatemala. He had told no one of his decision. And yet, when his mother had awakened him on February 26, his nineteenth birthday, instead of the present he expected she gave him a rosary. She had said it was all she could give him.

Now, aboard the *Houston* in battle dress, the slender youth switched on his transistor radio to hear whether Havana would describe the bombing raids. Tomorrow he would still be at sea. The day after he would face his first trial in battle.

In Washington, Richard M. Bissell, Jr., an urbane, six-foot-four former economics professor, waited anxiously for word of the bombing strike and for news of Zuniga's arrival in Miami. Bissell was the CIA's deputy director for plans (DDP), "plans" being a cover name for covert foreign operations. In intelligence parlance, "black" means secret, and Bissell directed the blackest of the black operators. He was the CIA man in charge of the clandestine Bay of Pigs operation from the beginning. From a secret office near the Lincoln Memorial, across the reflecting pool from the White House, he was linked by high-speed coded teletype circuits to Happy Valley.

On this Saturday, April 15, Bissell's boss, the CIA director, Allen W. Dulles, was in Puerto Rico. He had gone there that day to keep a long-standing engagement to speak at a convention of young businessmen Monday morning. The CIA chief decided that to cancel it would look peculiar and might attract attention. Moreover, Dulles reasoned, his presence in Puerto Rico would be good cover. The public appearance of the head of the CIA in San Juan, rather than in Washington, might divert any suspicion that the CIA was directing the drama which was now unfolding.

Partly for similar reasons, President John F. Kennedy had decided to spend the weekend as usual at Glen Ora, his rented estate in Middleburg, Virginia. At 11:37 A.M. he spoke at an African Freedom Day celebration at the

9

State Department. Early in the afternoon he got into a helicopter and flew to Middleburg.

The largest secret operation in American history was already beginning. But neither the President of the United States nor the director of the Central Intelligence Agency was in Washington.

At 6:00 A.M. in Havana, it sounded at first like thunder. But then anti-aircraft guns opened up and the sleepy residents of the Cuban capital realized that an air raid was in progress. From their windows and balconies, Cubans could see tracers from the anti-aircraft shells shooting in great arcs across the sky. In Miramar, a suburb near Camp Libertad, early risers watched as the three B-26s in Jose Crespo's "Puma" wing attacked with bombs, machine guns and rockets. Some of the bombs struck an ammunition dump and flames leaped skyward. A series of explosions followed and continued intermittently for forty minutes. Bomb fragments hit the administration building and gouged huge holes in the airport runways. The attack lasted only fifteen minutes, but the guns kept firing for an hour.

Simultaneously, Luis Cosme's "Linda" flight of three B-26s was bombing San Antonio de los Banos. One of Castro's T-33 American-made jet trainers sitting on the end of Runway 11 blew up and some Castro B-26s were caught on the ground.

At Antonio Maceo Airport in Santiago de Cuba, on the eastern end of the island, the "Gorilla" wing destroyed a hangar containing one British-built Sea Fury and two smaller planes. A Cubana Airlines C-47 parked in front of the administration building was also demolished.

Less actual damage to aircraft was inflicted at Camp Libertad by the "Puma" flight. And the exile air force lost its first plane. The B-26 piloted by Daniel Fernandez Mon, mortally crippled in the raid over Havana, wheeled out to sea north of the city and burst into flames. It crashed into the ocean within sight of Havana's Commodoro Hotel. The red-haired bachelor pilot had pleaded for five days to be allowed to take part in the first raid. He was twenty-nine when he died. His co-pilot, Gaston Perez, perished with him. Perez would have celebrated his twenty-sixth birthday in thirteen days.

Now a tiny crack, the first of several things that went wrong, appeared in the carefully polished CIA plans. Jose Crespo, leader of the "Puma" wing, developed engine trouble. He decided he could not make it back to Happy Valley, and nosed his bomber north to Key West.

At 7:00 A.M. Crespo and his co-pilot, Lorenzo Perez, made an emergency landing at the Boca Chica Naval Air Station in Key West, to the consternation of Navy officials there. Key West high schools were to have held an Olympics Day at Boca Chica, with track events, bands and parades, and the public invited. The Navy hastily closed the field without explanation. Olympics Day was canceled.

In "Linda" flight, Alfredo Caballero discovered, after dropping his bombs on San Antonio de los Banos, that one fuel tank was not feeding. He headed south and landed on Grand Cayman Island with his co-pilot, Alfredo Maza. It caused another small complication for the CIA. Grand Cayman was British territory.

Shortly after 8:00 A.M. the Federal Aviation Agency control tower at Miami International Airport picked up a mayday distress signal from a B-26 bomber. Mario Zuniga was on the last leg of his cover mission. He called the tower at a point twenty-five miles south of Homestead, Florida, or about twelve minutes from Miami. At 8:21 A.M. he landed, his right engine feathered as if it had been put out of action by gunfire. Zuniga, wearing a white T-shirt and green fatigue trousers, climbed out.

Whisked into Immigration Headquarters and "questioned" for four hours, Zuniga was successfully kept from reporters. Edward Ahrens, the district director of the United States Immigration and Naturalization Service, solemnly announced that the pilot's name was being withheld to prevent reprisals against his family still in Cuba.

But, oddly, in view of the tight security measures that surrounded Zuniga's arrival, photographers were allowed to take pictures of the unidentified pilot and of his bullet-pocked bomber. Across the nation the next morning, newspapers carried photographs of the mysterious pilot, a tall, mustached man wearing dark glasses and a baseball cap.

Ahrens released a statement from the nameless pilot. Now the CIA's cover story was clattering out over the news wires around the world:

"I am one of the twelve B-26 pilots who remained in the Castro air force after the defection of Pedro Luis Diaz Lanz * and the purges that followed.

"Three of my fellow pilots and I have planned for months how we could escape from Castro's Cuba.

"Day before yesterday I heard that one of the three, Lieutenant Alvara Galo, who is the pilot of the B-26 No. FAR915, had been seen talking to an agent of Ramiro Valdes, the G-2 chief.

"I alerted the other two and we decided that probably Alvara Galo, who had always acted like somewhat of a coward, had betrayed us. We decided to take action at once.

"Yesterday morning I was assigned the routine patrol from my base, San Antonio de los Banos, over a section of Pinar del Rio and around the Isle of Pines.

"I told my friends at Campo Libertad and they agreed that we must act. One of them was to fly to Santiago. The other made the excuse that he wished to check out his altimeter. They were to take off from Campo Libertad at 06:00. I was airborne at 06:05.

"Because of Alvara Galo's treachery, we had agreed to give him a lesson, so I flew back over San Antonio, where his plane is stationed, and made two strafing runs at his plane and three others parked nearby.

"On the way out I was hit by some small-arms fire and took evasive action. My comrades had broken off earlier, to hit airfields which we agreed they would strike. Then, because I was low on gas, I had to go into

* Former head of the Cuban Air Force.

Miami, because I could not reach our agreed destination.

"It may be that they went on to strafe another field before leaving, such as Playa Baracoa, where Fidel keeps his helicopter."

In New York, Dr. Jose Miro Cardona, the professorial, soft-spoken president of the Cuban Revolutionary Council, could not resist issuing a flowery Latin statement. From his headquarters at the Hotel Lexington, Cardona hailed the "heroic blow for Cuban freedom . . . struck this morning by certain members of the Cuban Air Force." He said it came as no surprise because "the Council has been in contact with and has encouraged these brave pilots." Cardona's announcement was a bad move, as events later proved.

Not until 9:00 A.M., three hours after the attack, did the Cuban radio in Havana announce the bombings. But at 7:00 A.M. the Soviet Ambassador to Cuba, Sergei M. Kudryavtsev, an old hand in the KGB, the Soviet intelligence network, was seen hurriedly leaving his official residence in a Cuban military car with two Cuban Army officers. Newsmen were unable to find out where he was going. But at noon, with militiamen armed with Czechoslovak automatic weapons stalking the streets of Havana, and others posted on roofs, the foreign diplomatic corps was summoned to the Foreign Ministry and told that Cuba had proof that the United States had "directed" the attack. Fidel Castro issued a communiqué saying he had ordered his United Nations delegation "to accuse the United States government directly of aggression. . . . If this air attack is a prelude to an invasion, the country, on a war basis, will resist . . . the fatherland or death!" He called on U.S. news agencies to "report the truth."

That was no easy task. At Key West, Rear Admiral Rhodam Y. McElroy, the commander of the Boca Chica Naval Air Station, announced: "One of the stolen B-26 bombers that was involved in the blasts against Havana this morning landed here."

At the White House, presidential press secretary Pierre

Salinger denied any knowledge of the bombing. He said the United States was seeking information.

Alongside the East River in New York, in the United Nations Building, the drama that had begun at the jungle airstrip in Nicaragua before daylight now moved into the full glare of the world stage.

Raul Roa, the excitable Cuban representative, marched to the speaker's rostrum at the start of the General Assembly session that was meeting on the Congo crisis.

Roa began: "At 6:30 A.M. in the morning, North American aircraft—"

The sharp rap of a gavel, wielded by the Assembly's president, Frederick H. Boland of Ireland, cut off the bespectacled Cuban. Boland reminded Roa that the item was not on the Assembly's agenda. Valerian Zorin, the Soviet representative, then proposed an emergency session of the Assembly's political committee to hear the Cuban complaint. The meeting was scheduled for that afternoon.

At 3:00 P.M. Roa rose to charge the United States with launching a "cowardly, surprise attack" on Cuba with "mercenaries" trained on United States territory, and in Guatemala, by "experts of the Pentagon and the Central Intelligence Agency." Seven persons had been killed and many wounded, he said. The United States, he added, was "cynically attempting" to assert the attack was carried out by Cuban Air Force defectors. Dr. Cardona's statement that he had been in touch with those who did the bombing was in itself a violation of United States neutrality laws, Roa said.

It was an awkward moment for Adlai E. Stevenson, the United States representative to the UN. (The man who had run twice as the Democratic candidate for President, only to see John F. Kennedy win in 1960, now rose to defend the administration.) Only his closest advisers were aware of exactly how delicate and difficult a position Stevenson was in. Although the idea later gained currency that Stevenson had been totally unaware of the Bay of Pigs operation, they knew the real background:

Initially, Stevenson had become aware of Cuban exile

training from newspaper stories. Some time before the invasion, he had expressed some misgivings about these published reports in an informal conversation with President Kennedy, which took place in the White House living quarters. Kennedy assured Stevenson on that occasion that whatever happened, United States armed forces would not be used in any Cuban operation.

A couple of days before the April 15 raid, a high CIA official had come to see Stevenson in New York. He was Tracy Barnes, the CIA man assigned to keep the State Department informed of the Bay of Pigs plans as they progressed.

Barnes, in briefing Stevenson, indicated vaguely that the United States would not be involved in any Cuban exile operation. Barnes talked on about how the Cubans were operating from abandoned airfields; he mentioned the exile (CIA) radio on Swan Island in the Caribbean. Stevenson was aware that Barnes was from the CIA; and the more he listened to Barnes's ambiguous assurances, the more convinced he became that the United States *was* involved.

Barnes did not mention that an invasion was about to begin over the weekend. Nor did he indicate that one was imminent. As a result, it is possible that Stevenson did not immediately connect the April 15 bombings with the CIA man's briefing of two days earlier. Nevertheless, he chose his words carefully:

Two aircraft had landed in Florida that morning. "These pilots, and certain other crew members," said Stevenson, "have apparently defected from Castro's tyranny.

"No United States personnel participated. No United States Government airplanes of any kind participated. These two planes, to the best of our knowledge, were Castro's own air-force planes, and according to the pilots, they took off from Castro's own air-force fields."

Stevenson then held aloft a UPI photograph of Zuniga's plane. "I have here a picture of one of these planes. It has the markings of the Castro air force right on the tail, which everyone can see for himself. The Cuban star and the initials FAR—Fuerza Aerea Revolucionaria—are clearly visible.

"Let me read the statement which has just arrived over the wire from the pilot who landed in Miami," Stevenson said. He then repeated Zuniga's cover story in its entirety.

Steps had been taken to impound the Cuban planes that had landed in Florida, he added; they would not be permitted to take off.

The UN meeting broke up at 4:05 P.M.

Spring is in many ways the loveliest time of the year in the rolling hills of the Virginia hunt country. But on Sunday, April 16, President Kennedy had little time to appreciate it. At his Glen Ora estate in Middleburg, the President was deeply worried. And he did not like what he saw in his Sunday *New York Times*.

He and his advisers had not anticipated the volume and nature of the publicity that was being given to the bombing raids and to the story of the mysterious "defecting" pilot who had landed in Miami.

Across the nation, the morning papers had played the story of the bombing raids with varying degrees of caution.

Many papers ran the Associated Press lead out of Cuba, which said flatly:

> HAVANA, April 15—Pilots of Prime Minister Fidel Castro's air force revolted today and attacked three of the Castro regime's key air bases with bombs and rockets.

But the influential *New York Times* was not buying the story completely. Tad Szulc's lead story from Miami was carefully qualified. He wondered, for example, how the Cuban Revolutionary Council had advance notice of the flier's defection, since the pilot who landed in Miami said their escape was hasty. Ruby Hart Phillips filed a similar carefully worded story from Havana.

And the *Times* Washington Bureau this Sunday was trying to reach administration officials at their homes. The bureau was busily putting together a story pointing out "puzzling circumstances." Besides the question of how Cardona knew about the defections in advance, the *Times* wanted to know why the pilot's name had been withheld in

Miami, since pictures were allowed which clearly showed his face and the number 933 on the nose of his bomber.* Furthermore, the *Times* asked whether Havana would not quickly know the identity of a Cuban Air Force pilot who waltzed off with a B-26 bomber.

Other newsmen in Washington and Miami were asking where the third plane was if three pilots had defected. A reporter in Miami saw the bullet holes but noted that dust and grease covered the bomb-bay fittings of B-26 933 and that the plane's guns did not appear to have been fired. Further, while the B-26s in Castro's air force had plexiglass transparent noses and guns in the wing pods, this B-26 had eight .50-caliber machine guns in a solid nose.

The Bay of Pigs operation was already foundering. What had occurred was the inevitable collision between the secret machinery of the government and a free press. It was at this point of contact between the Invisible Government and the outside, real world, that the Bay of Pigs plan began to deteriorate. As President Eisenhower had discovered during the U-2 fiasco a year earlier, and as President Kennedy was now finding out, it is an extremely difficult and precarious business for the government to try to deceive the press and the country to protect a covert operation.

In Havana, Fidel Castro exploited the situation for all it was worth. At a military funeral for the "Cuban heroes" killed by the bombing raids, he compared the attack to the raid on Pearl Harbor. He said the Japanese had at least assumed full responsibility for their raid, but "the President of the United States is like a cat . . . which throws a rock and hides its hand." Of the pilot's tale, he said, "even Hollywood would not try to film such a story."

But in Miami, Immigration Director Ahrens was sticking to the scenario. He announced that the three fliers who had landed in Florida had been granted political asylum. Ahrens was still silent about their identities, however.

* When the *Times* story appeared the next day, it particularly irritated President Kennedy. He was angered because he felt it had systematically listed flaws in the CIA cover.

"These men don't want their names released," he told UPI, "or any other information about them." *

Nine B-26s had left Nicaragua. One was shot down, and three had landed, respectively, at Key West, Grand Cayman and Miami. Two pilots were dead. But five of the bombers returned to Happy Valley.

Despite the heavy air losses, the trouble over Zuniga's cover story and the UN debate, Richard Bissell was encouraged by the partial success of the April 15 raid. From the beginning the CIA understood the rather elementary military principle that no amphibious landing can take place without either (1) air cover at the beaches or (2) complete destruction of the opposing air force on the ground.

In the case of the Bay of Pigs, the latter course was chosen. Castro's air force would be destroyed on the ground by the exile B-26 force, so that air cover at the beaches would be unnecessary. Originally, three full-strength strikes by the B-26s were planned. This was cut down to two strikes of moderate strength. The second strike was scheduled to take place at dawn, Monday, April 17, as the 1,400-man exile invasion force fought its way ashore.

The CIA had estimated before the first raid that Castro's air force included at least four T-33 jet trainers, six to eight B-26s and several British Sea Furies, fast propeller-driven fighters. Estimates by the returning exile fliers of how many of Castro's planes were destroyed varied. They claimed they had destroyed twenty-two to twenty-four planes. Pilot claims are often inflated, but Bissell knew that at least a number of Castro's B-26s were destroyed.

* The names of Mario Zuniga, Jose Crespo and Lorenzo Perez, the three pilots who landed in Florida, April 15, 1961, had not been released by the government as of the beginning of 1964. In actual fact, the pilots flew back to Happy Valley in a C-54 on April 16, and participated in the air operations during the invasion. Zuniga survived, but Crespo and Perez died on April 17. Alfredo Caballero, who had landed on Grand Cayman Island, was flown to Miami, and then to Retalhuleu, the CIA's Guatemalan air base. Through a mix-up, he remained there until April 19, out of action.

Hopefully, the next raid, on Monday, would finish the job of demolishing Castro's air force.

But political and foreign policy considerations began to outweigh the tactical plan. The cover story crumbled as Sunday wore on. United States participation was surfacing rapidly. The CIA plan had hinged on the assumption that Zuniga's cover story would hold for at least forty-eight hours. In that event, the second air strike would either seem like the work of the rebelling Castro pilots, or would be overlooked in the general confusion of the invasion.

The CIA reasoned that if the airstrip at the Bay of Pigs could be captured and held, photographs could be released by Tuesday, April 18, showing exile B-26s operating from inside Cuba. This, the CIA assumed, would divert attention from the question of where the bombers had taken off from on April 15 and 17. The problem was to get by with the "defecting" pilots' tale from Saturday to Tuesday. After that, the cover story told by Zuniga would not matter; it would be overtaken by events.

Now the situation had changed radically. All had hinged on the Zuniga story. With that story fast unraveling at the edges, could the President permit another B-26 strike on Monday and still convince the world that somehow a new covey of Castro pilots had defected from the Cuban Air Force? The President decided he could not.

With Allen Dulles in Puerto Rico, Bissell was the CIA's man in charge. At 9:00 P.M. on Sunday, April 16, his telephone rang. It was McGeorge Bundy, the patrician Assistant to the President for National Security Affairs. Bundy had been a student of Bissell's at Yale.* Now he was calling to instruct Bissell that the President had decided to cancel tomorrow's D-Day B-26 strike against Castro's air bases.

Alarmed by the President's eleventh-hour decision, Bissell and General Charles P. Cabell, the CIA's deputy

* He had also worked for Bissell in the Marshall Plan from April–September, 1948.

director, hurried to the State Department to appeal to Secretary of State Dean Rusk.

The air strike was vital to the invasion plan and should be reinstated, Bissell and Cabell argued, otherwise Castro would have jets and other planes to attack the invaders. It was now 10:00 P.M. From his office at the State Department, Rusk telephoned Kennedy at Glen Ora. He told him that Cabell and Bissell were there and believed the strike should go ahead as planned. The President said no. Rusk asked whether Cabell wished to say anything to the President directly, but Cabell declined. Bissell did not talk to Kennedy either. Twelve hundred miles away, the invasion fleet was already approaching the beaches.

In retrospect, some CIA officials felt Bissell should have hopped into a car and driven to Glen Ora to plead with the President; because the operation was secret he would have been able to speak more freely in person than he could have over a telephone wire, and he might have been able to present his case more fully. But it would have been close to midnight before he could have arrived at Middleburg, and D-Day would then have been at hand.

Or Bissell and Cabell might have gotten on the telephone in Rusk's office and pleaded with the President directly at this point. They did not.

Bissell returned to his office from the State Department, and about 11:00 P.M. he flashed the word to Happy Valley that the B-26s were not to strike at Castro's air bases. Messages flowed back and forth between Nicaragua and Washington, and as it was finally resolved, the bombers were only to try to fly support missions over the beaches. At Happy Valley the change in orders caused dismay and considerable confusion.

So secret was the Bay of Pigs operation that many high officials of the government were not let in on it. Robert Amory, Jr., the CIA's deputy director for intelligence (DDI), had not been officially informed of the plan even though on this Sunday he was the senior staff duty officer at the CIA. Roger Hilsman, the director of the State Department's Bureau of Intelligence and Research, had also been kept in the dark. But the Joint Chiefs of Staff, headed by General Lyman L. Lemnitzer, had been consulted and had given their qualified approval. The second air strike was a vital part of the plan that had been approved by the Joint Chiefs. Now that element was being suddenly removed by the President, acting in the isolation of Glen Ora; and Admiral Arleigh Burke, Chief of Naval Operations, whose ships were deployed off the Bay of Pigs, did not learn of the cancellation of the second air strike until ten hours later, at 7:00 A.M. Monday.

As the first tense hours of April 17 slipped by, Bissell and Cabell remained in touch with Happy Valley and waited uncertainly for the dawn. At 4:00 A.M. Cabell could stand it no longer. He decided to appeal again to Rusk.

Cabell drove through the darkened capital to Rusk's hotel. (Rusk, Secretary of State for less than three months, had not yet moved into a home in Washington; he had an apartment at the Sheraton Park Hotel on upper Connecticut Avenue.) In Rusk's apartment he again expressed his fears over the cancellation of the air strike. Despite the hour the Secretary of State called the President once more in Middleburg. This time Cabell did speak directly to him. In answer to the CIA official's pleadings, the President's reply was still negative.

The light burned late in Rusk's suite K-608 in the otherwise quiet Sheraton Park. Outside, the capital's streets were deserted as the city slept. A light spring breeze caressed the pale, new green leaves on the trees. In the Bahia de Cochinos the men were now going ashore. But Castro still had planes, and they were about to raise havoc with the exile brigade on the beaches.

It was forty-eight hours since Mario Zuniga had taken off from Happy Valley. The invasion was just beginning. In reality, it was already over.

3

Build-Up

It HAD BEGUN one day early in April, 1960, when two visitors walked into the office of Roberto Alejos in the Edificio Townson in Guatemala City.

Alejos, a handsome, athletic businessman, was one of the wealthiest coffee-growers in Guatemala. His brother, Carlos, was Guatemala's Ambassador to Washington. But there were two other facts about Roberto Alejos that interested his visitors this day: He owned two huge *fincas*, plantations, in Guatemala, both in remote areas. And he was the closest friend, backer and adviser of Miguel Ydigoras Fuentes, the highly individualistic and unpredictable President of that Central American Republic.

The visitors were Americans. One was Robert Kendall Davis, a close friend of Alejos. Davis bore the title of First Secretary of the American Embassy in Guatemala City. A charming Californian of forty-three, graying at the temples, he looked the part of a diplomat. But it was an open secret in sophisticated political and diplomatic circles in Guatemala City that Davis was the CIA station chief in Guatemala. The CIA agent who accompanied him was less well known; he had recently returned to Guatemala after a three-year absence.

Davis and his companion had no small request. They wanted to know if Alejos would help arrange secret training sites in Guatemala for Cuban anti-Castro exiles. They also wanted to know whether Alejos could fix it for them to talk to President Ydigoras.

The CIA had good reason to approach Ydigoras gingerly. They were aware that he felt the United States regarded him as politically erratic. His election two years before had been greeted by Washington with less than enthusiasm, and Ydigoras knew it. Late in January, 1958, according to Ydigoras, a mysterious visiting American had called on him at his suite at the Maya Excelsior Hotel in Guatemala City. At this point, the Guatemalan Congress had not yet officially chosen him to be President.

As Ydigoras later related the story on nation-wide television, the visitor, who gave his name as "Mr. Karr," opened a suitcase containing $500,000 in United States currency and offered it to Ydigoras if he would withdraw. The CIA knew that rightly or wrongly Ydigoras, who declined the money, became convinced that "Mr. Karr" was a CIA agent, although he possessed no evidence of that.

Now the CIA was asking Ydigoras to risk his political career by permitting the United States to establish secret training camps in Guatemala. Nevertheless, when Alejos approached him, Ydigoras agreed to meet discreetly with Davis at the President's private residence, the Casa Crema, located on the grounds of a military school. (Ydigoras, understandably, had declined to live in the Presidential House where President Carlos Castillo-Armas had been murdered on July 26, 1957. Castillo-Armas had come to power in 1954 in a CIA-engineered coup that overthrew President Jacobo Arbenz Guzman, whose regime was honeycombed with Communists.)

When Davis, Alejos and Ydigoras got together, the Guatemalan President, who had no use for Communism or Castro, agreed to allow the Cuban exiles to train in his country. He designated Roberto Alejos to handle the details of the project for him.

Now Guatemala was to become the staging area for the overthrow of Fidel Castro's regime in Cuba.

The CIA told Alejos that it would like to find privately owned land, with trustworthy owners, for use as training sites. Alejos suggested his own plantations. CIA, after looking over several other possible sites, selected as its main base Helvetia, the Alejos coffee ranch in the Boca Costa, the Pacific slope region of southwestern Guatemala.

Helvetia was particularly suitable for the CIA's purpose. It had no access roads, and was a self-contained city with 100 kilometers of private roads winding through 5,000 acres. The estate rose to 8,000 feet along the slopes of Santiago Volcano, which had erupted in 1928 and was still active. The training area, or "Trax Base," as the camp came to be known, was at 4,000 feet. It was well above and out of view of the main ranch building. The nearest habitation was the remote village of San Felipe. Retalhuleu, the other town in the area, was twenty-five kilometers from Helvetia. Guns could be fired and military maneuvers held at the ranch with complete security and safety.

The entire plantation was heavily guarded, so there was little chance that any curious outsider would stumble into the Cuban exile camp, or penetrate its secrets. If the volcano behaved, the CIA would have an ideal mountain hideaway to begin training the exiles who would topple Fidel Castro. It would be Guatemala, 1954, all over again.

The Americans who called on Roberto Alejos in the Edificio Townson that day in April, 1960, were acting on the authority of the President of the United States. Their visit was a direct result of an order given by President Dwight D. Eisenhower on March 17, 1960.* On that day Eisenhower authorized the secret training and arming of the Cuban rebels.

The President turned over the task of arming and training the Cuban exiles to Allen Dulles. Dulles in turn placed the project in the hands of Bissell.

A highly articulate, highly intelligent man, Richard Mervin Bissell did not fit the popular conception of a master spy, any more than did Dulles. Bissell liked to refer to him-

---

* The date was revealed by Eisenhower at a Cincinnati press conference June 13, 1961, following the Bay of Pigs disaster. The former chief executive said he had issued orders when President to "take measures to help these people organize and to help train them and equip them."

self as a "high risk man," and it was he who ran the U-2 spy plane program.

Bissell was graduated from Groton, Yale and the London School of Economics. He took his Ph.D. at Yale in 1939, taught economics there and at Massachusetts Institute of Technology, and worked in the War Shipping Administration during World War II. In 1948 he joined the Marshall Plan, rising to the post of Acting Administrator. He entered the CIA in 1954.

The CIA's original plan, as it evolved under Bissell's direction, was to build up the underground within Cuba through a long, slow period of guerrilla infiltration by exiles trained in Guatemala.

The CIA designated one of its most energetic agents, with the cover name of Frank Bender, to be the top agency representative in dealing with the fragmented Cuban exile groups. Bender, whose real identity was carefully protected, became an almost mythical figure to the Cuban refugees. He was rumored to be everywhere—in New York, Miami and Guatemala—during the months that followed. After the Bay of Pigs, he was said to have been spotted in the Congo.

Most of the exiles believed Bender was a European who had fought with the French Maquis during World War II. Another account had Bender as an assistant to top Allied planners during the North African invasion in 1942.

Those who met him described the CIA field chief as a man in his fifties, perhaps 185 pounds, of medium build. He smoked a pipe, wore glasses, was well mannered and displayed a good knowledge of history. Bender established headquarters in New York, which with Washington, Miami and Retalhuleu became the four key centers of the operation.

The CIA's first task was to try to weld the squabbling and emotional exile groups into some semblance of cohesion, and to select promising leaders. The Cuban who looked most promising was Manuel Artime Buesa, a young firebrand orator who had fought in the hills with Castro in 1958. Artime accepted a job with the Institute of Agrarian Reform when Castro overthrew Dictator Fulgen-

cio Batista on New Year's Day, 1959, and became Premier.
But Artime broke with Castro later that year and fled
Cuba in a boat. Now, at twenty-eight and violently anti-
Castro, he was the secretary general in Miami of the Movi-
miento de Recuperacion Revolucionario, the MRR.

Another Cuban leader contacted by the CIA early in the
planning stage was Manuel Antonio de Varona, former
Premier of Cuba under President Carlos Prio Socarras, the
man Batista had overthrown.

By the end of May, 1960, five exile groups had been organized as a revolutionary *frente*, or front, with Varona as
co-ordinator.*

At a meeting in New York, the CIA promised financial
support to the newly formed *frente*. Bender dispatched
agents into Miami. The CIA began pumping what eventually became millions of dollars into the *frente* and its
successor, the Cuban Revolutionary Council. The CIA
funds were deposited in a Miami bank and drawn by the
frente through checks signed by an accountant named
Juan Paula.

The first exiles were being recruited for the training
camps. In the back streets of downtown Miami, in the
bars, hotels, old rooming houses and apartments of the
Cuban refugee community, the exciting word began to
spread that something big was afoot.

Sometimes their leaders flew to New York for conferences with the CIA. When there was a crisis, Bender
would fly to Miami.

The news would pass among the exile community: "Mr.
B. is coming."

In May of 1960, less than a month after Davis had approached Alejos, the first Cubans arrived at Helvetia. The
detachment of thirty-two men had entered Guatemala as

* Besides Artime's MRR and Varona, who headed the Movimiento
de Rescate Revolucionario, the *frente* members were Jose Ignacio
Rasco of the Movimiento Democratico Cristiano; Justo Carrillo of
the Asociacion Montecristi; and Aureliano Sanchez Arango, former
Foreign Minister of Cuba and head of the Triple A, which later
pulled out of the *frente*.

"surveying engineers." At Helvetia they were trained as communications experts.

Alejos already had radio facilities for communication with the rest of the ranch; these were now greatly expanded by the CIA and installed in a warehouse near the main building.

The first group of Cubans lived comfortably in the Alejos guest house. But as more trainees flowed into Helvetia, the Trax Base was built on the mountainside, with barracks completed in June. The base was also known by its code name, "Vaquero," which means cowboy in Spanish. As cover for the entire operation, the Guatemalan Army allowed Alejos to train 400 Guatemalan troops at the ranch. They doubled as armed guards to keep potential snoopers and the 1,300 coffee workers out of the Trax area. CIA instructors, as well as logistics and accounting officials from the agency, were also housed at the base.

In addition to Helvetia, training took place at two other sites. Alejos owned a sugar plantation at San Jose Buena Vista, halfway between Retalhuleu and Guatemala City. The terrain proved excellent for parachute jump training and mass maneuvers. Amphibious landings were practiced on the Pacific coast below Retalhuleu.

In July the CIA began construction of a secret airstrip at Retalhuleu. The existing strip there was inadequate for the C-46s, C-54s and B-26s that would be brought in. The airstrip contract was awarded to Thompson-Cornwall, Inc., a big American construction firm with offices in the Chrysler Building in New York. The firm, already in operation in Guatemala, had the necessary heavy equipment available in the area.

Alejos fronted for CIA on all financial transactions in Guatemala, and it was he who signed the airstrip contract.* The initial payment for paving was $450,000. Before it was over, the airstrip and air-base facilities at Retalhuleu cost the CIA $1,200,000.

* Davis continued to co-ordinate the Cuban operation for CIA from the embassy at Guatemala City. U. S. Ambassador John J. Muccio was generally aware of what was going on at Helvetia but did not become officially involved, since the operation was "black."

In August the crash job of constructing the airstrip was completed. Since there had to be some explanation for the existence of a modern airstrip in the middle of nowhere, foreign diplomats in Guatemala were told it had been built for exporting "fruit and frozen shrimp." President Ydigoras, his son and adviser, Miguelito Ydigoras, and the foreign diplomatic corps journeyed to Retalhuleu to cut the ribbon.

But the CIA overlooked one detail. A few of the more observant diplomats noticed that, curiously, there were no markings at all on the planes that were to transport the fruit and seafood delicacies. Miguelito had to talk fast. "The planes," he explained soothingly, "are waiting here to have markings painted on them."

The training of exiles also moved forward in the United States. In Miami the CIA instructed them in weapons handling and guerrilla tactics. The training took place in the Everglades and even in Miami hotels. In Louisiana one group trained under the leadership of Higinio "Nino" Diaz, an MRR leader.

Once the airstrip had been completed at Retalhuleu, the airlift of trainees from Florida to Guatemala could begin in earnest. The routine was always the same. A Cuban would make contact with the CIA through the exile groups. If he passed preliminary screening, he would be picked up, brought to a CIA "safe house" at night, and from there, with elaborate hocus-pocus, flown from the mysterious, guarded Opa-locka Airport in Miami to Retalhuleu. Sometimes other airstrips in Florida were used for the clandestine flights, and the CIA had occasional troubles with overzealous local police officers. The Hendry County sheriff's office once investigated a report that unmarked, unlighted planes were picking up groups of men at night from an abandoned airstrip at Clewiston, Florida, near Lake Okeechobee. After the sheriff began poking around, the men disappeared. The CIA had another narrow brush with local guardians of the law shortly before midnight on October 27, 1960, when a plane without lights landed at Opa-locka. Since the place had not been used as an airfield by the Navy for five years, a Miami patrolman radioed

Opa-locka police to investigate. They did, but were waved away by a sentry who explained it was "just a plane low on gas."

Meanwhile, the CIA was not overlooking the propaganda front.

In August, 1960, the *frente* hired Lem Jones, veteran New York public-relations man and former press secretary to Wendell Willkie. Jones had once worked for Twentieth Century-Fox and Spyros P. Skouras, but nothing had prepared him for the production he was about to get into now.

Jones had a friend in the CIA. He decided to call him to make sure that his representation of the Cuban exiles would be in the national interest. He gave him the names of some of the Cubans in the *frente*.

A half-hour later the CIA man called back. He seemed surprised. Do you realize, he asked Jones, what you have gotten into? Then he lowered his voice: A man would call in a half-hour and say he was a mutual friend and would meet Jones alone.

It was the beginning of a series of cloak-and-dagger meetings between Jones and the CIA men. Sometimes the meetings took place in hotel rooms; the CIA also favored Grand Central Terminal. Thus Jones, at the request of the CIA, reported to the agency on his activities for the *frente*, which in turn was being financed by the CIA.

Jones went through a harrowing escapade in September, 1960. That was the month Castro arrived in New York for the United Nations session and staged his famous chicken-plucking episode in the Shelburne Hotel in Manhattan. To counter Castro's appearance in New York, the CIA decided to dispatch two busloads of Cuban mothers from Miami to Manhattan in a "Caravan of Sorrow."

The CIA financed and organized the caravan, which was to end with the mothers praying in Saint Patrick's Cathedral. But when the chartered Greyhound buses left Miami, the CIA did not have a man aboard. Jones had made elaborate preparations for television and newspaper coverage along the way, but somehow the two busloads of mothers got lost for two days. Only one woman on the bus spoke

English, and she had her problems as the caravan inche
northward. Four of the women were pregnant and th
buses had to stop every few miles for them. Finally th
caravan got to Washington, off schedule. The CIA, whic
could not publicly show its hand, hurriedly called Jones i
New York and asked for his help in arranging publicity i
the capital. Jones called a Washington press agent h
knew, who did his best.

The next day the "Caravan of Sorrow" reached Phila
delphia, where Jones had it halted. He had visions of th
buses pulling into New York in the dead of night sar
press coverage. In the morning the Greyhounds limpe
into Manhattan; much to Jones' relief, a picture of th
mothers praying in Saint Patrick's made the New Yor
papers.

In Washington, there were more momentous activitie
at hand. As Richard M. Nixon and John F. Kenned
battled across the autumn landscape for the presidency,
the CIA plan, under Bissell's guidance, was undergoing
gradual metamorphosis. From the original concept of iso
lated guerrilla landings, it moved toward the idea of
larger operation that really amounted to a pocket-size
invasion.

By October it was decided that a force of perhaps fou
hundred men would make a landing in Cuba in the lat
autumn. This group would be a major, well-trained an
well-supplied guerrilla unit within Cuba. It would serve a
a focal point for other guerrillas to rally around. At th
same time, there would be a large-scale program of ai
drops to resupply and strengthen the guerrillas in the Es
cambray, the Sierra Maestra and other areas inside Cuba
Supplies would also be brought in by the CIA in smal
boats.

To fly the clandestine air-drop missions over Cuba, th

* As will be shown in a later chapter, the invasion preparation
played a major part in the secret behind-the-scenes calculations o
both the Nixon and Kennedy camps during the 1960 presidentia
campaign.

CIA needed pilots. The story of Sergio Garcia, one of the men who flew these missions, is fairly typical.

In August, 1960, Garcia managed to smuggle his wife and newborn son out of Havana into Miami. He was screened by Americans, who also gave him a lie-detector test in a motel on Segovia Street in Coral Gables. Two nights later he was flown to Guatemala by the CIA.

For a time Garcia practiced dropping paratroops and cargo near Retalhuleu. In November he began flying a C-46 over Cuba, dropping supplies in the Escambray. The C-46s had no guns and there were Castro air force markings on them. At that time the air operations at Retalhuleu were under the supervision of an American CIA man known as "Colonel Billy Carpenter," a cover name similar to his real one. In all, dozens of overflights of Cuba were carried out by the exile pilots between November, 1960, and March, 1961.

The men flying these missions over Cuban territory were told that if they were captured they were to say they worked for an air transport company owned by the Alejos brothers and had strayed off-course. They were also told to destroy all documents beforehand. The pilots were given the telephone number of a Mr. G. in Miami. If forced down outside of Cuba, they were to call him at once.

When Garcia was briefed at Retalhuleu by the American CIA advisers, he was told to look for lights that would shine at a designated place and time for about ten minutes. As a result, the missions had to be timed to the second.

The flights would come in over the sea at fifty to a hundred feet to avoid Castro's radar. Garcia climbed to 1,000 for the drop, then zoomed back down to sea level and headed for home, chasing the wavetops. Since he frequently encountered anti-aircraft fire in areas supposed to be friendly, Garcia concluded that the CIA's contacts with the underground were not as good as they might be.

He was right. Back in Washington, Bissell and the other CIA operators were dismayed at the lack of success of the air drops. Almost without exception they were flown properly, but the guns and ammunition seldom reached their targets.

Bissell had continual difficulties in organizing the drops. He realized that unless the guerrillas had radios, small beacons and one or two trained people on the spot, the drops would miss their targets. To make an air drop successful, a guerrilla unit has to be able to communicate in code ten to twelve hours before a drop, in order to notify the senders of any change in location. But the guerrillas inside Cuba were communicating by runners back to Havana, a slow, ineffective means.

The CIA was unable to get radios, beacons and trained experts into Cuba, partly because Castro moved much more rapidly than had been anticipated in creating an effective counter-intelligence and counter-guerrilla network.

As Castro had learned when he fought against Batista in the Sierra Maestra, militiamen sent into the mountains in small groups tended to defect to the guerrillas when they made contact. Instead of sending his troops in small groups into the Escambray, Castro deployed them in large numbers around the mountains. He cordoned off the area and prevented the movement of couriers and food into the hills.

The CIA's troubles were compounded by what the Americans considered to be the impossibility of organizing a clandestine operation among "talkative" Cubans. There were leaks, and as a result, agents were being picked up by Castro's intelligence men. Messages went astray and nothing seemed to go right.

In the late fall, bad weather set in and prevented small boats from landing with equipment for the guerrillas. Later, tons of supplies were landed by boat, but the CIA was never sure they were being properly distributed once inside Cuba.

In short, for a variety of reasons, the CIA never succeeded in getting a secure and effective underground operating inside Cuba, equivalent to that inside Europe during World War II.

This was a vitally important factor, because it led di

rectly to the decision by the CIA to abandon the guerrilla concept and to invade Cuba in strength.

On November 13, 1960, a portion of the Guatemalan Army rebelled against President Ydigoras and captured Puerto Barrios, a banana port on the Caribbean. The Cuban exile pilots at Retalhuleu were enlisted to help put down the rebellion. Apparently, the CIA reasoned that if Ydigoras were overthrown, the new government might shut down the training camps.

One Cuban pilot flew a C-46 loaded with troops to Puerto Barrios, as the CIA's B-26s bombarded the rebel stronghold. He actually touched down at the airport in Puerto Barrios, in the mistaken belief that it was in government hands. When his plane drew gunfire, the pilot immediately took off again without unloading any troops. Cuban and American pilots flew the B-26s in this secret sidelight to the Bay of Pigs operation.

The Guatemalan Army rebellion quickly collapsed and the potential threat to the CIA camps was averted. But some Guatemalan politicians later blamed the uprising on the existence of the training camps. And, unknown to the world, CIA aircraft and pilots had been used to put down an internal uprising in Guatemala.

On November 18, 1960, ten days after his victory, President-elect Kennedy summoned Dulles and Bissell to Palm Beach and received a briefing on the state of the Cuban operation.

Already, reports of the training had begun to seep into public print. It started in Guatemala on October 30, when *La Hora*, a Guatemala City daily, carried a front-page article by its editor, Clemente Marroquin Rojas, stating flatly that "in Guatemala an invasion of Cuba is well under way, prepared not by our own country. . . ."

Guatemalans were soon gossiping about the CIA's operation at the Alejos ranch. In November, also, the *Hispanic American Report*, edited by Ronald Hilton of Stanford University, published a story about the Retalhuleu base. The academic journal has limited circulation, but the *Nation* magazine, with a wider audience, picked up the

Hilton disclosures in its November 19 issue, under a headline that asked: "Are We Training Cuban Guerrillas?"

The cocoon of secrecy in which the CIA had, of necessity, wrapped the Cuban operation, was beginning to unwind dangerously.

In January, as the change-over from the Eisenhower to the Kennedy Administration was taking place, things began to happen all at once, on several levels. On January 3, as one of his last diplomatic moves, President Eisenhower broke off diplomatic relations with Castro. In its January 7 issue the *Nation* unveiled a detailed story about the Retalhuleu base by Don Dwiggins, the aviation editor of the *Los Angeles Mirror*. Then, on January 10, real trouble came to the CIA in the form of a front-page story by Paul P. Kennedy in the *New York Times*, datelined Retalhuleu. It didn't mention CIA, but it told of training going on at the base under the instruction of "foreign personnel, mostly from the United States."

Hasty denials were issued in Guatemala and Washington. State Department spokesman Lincoln White said: ". . . As to the report of a specific base, I know absolutely nothing about it."

The exile training posed an extremely knotty problem for those newspapers which *had* learned something about it. The Miami papers, for example, were not unaware of what was going on under their noses. What was their responsibility to a free society, during peacetime? Was it to report the truth to their readers, or to suppress the truth for the government?

Once the *Times* story had run, Miami editors decided there was no further point to playing the game with the CIA. John S. Knight, the president of the Knight newspapers and owner of the *Miami Herald*, had withheld stories about the Guatemala and Florida training camps at the request of the highest level of the United States Government. The day after the *Times* broke the Retalhuleu story, the *Miami Herald* published a story on the Guatemalan camp, and another on the Opa-locka air traffic. A box alongside the story explained:

34

Publication of the accompanying story on the Miami-Guatemala airlift was withheld for more than two months by the *Herald*. Its release was decided upon only after U.S. aid to anti-Castro fighters in Guatemala was first revealed elsewhere.

The lid was off now, but despite the *Times* and *Miami Herald* stories, the fact that the United States was training Cuban exiles for a return to their homeland did not penetrate the mainstream of news. Most Americans remained quite unaware that an invasion was in the making.

January was the month of Kennedy's inauguration. Official Washington ignored the deep snow that blanketed the capital and attended a round of gay parties ushering in the New Frontier. In Cuba the guerrilla movement in the Escambray collapsed. With this collapse, any lingering thoughts of guerrilla infiltration disappeared. There would be a full-scale invasion. Where the landing force had been contemplated at 400 in October, it was now progressively and slowly increased in size. Recruiting was stepped up and more men and material began to flow into Retalhuleu.

Parallel to this development, pressures began to operate on President Kennedy to approve the invasion as soon as possible. The CIA warned him that the rainy season would hamper the landing and make the Guatemala camps unusable if the invasion was postponed much beyond the spring; the CIA also felt that the exiles could not be held together much longer because of morale factors.

The operation was surfacing in the press, and President Ydigoras was urging that a decision of some sort be made. Most important of all, the CIA concluded that between six months and a year from January, 1961, Russian-trained Cuban pilots would be returning to Cuba, and that that alone would make this invasion impossible.

President Kennedy and his advisers were tasting the wine of victory and of power. The young, energetic administration suffered from a bad case of overconfidence; virtually no one at the White House stopped to think about pos-

35

sible failure. And deep inside the secret bureaucracy, the exile operation had acquired something of a life of its own.

In Washington it is not simple to stop a project, overt or covert, once it is under way. Politically, if President Kennedy had halted the invasion plan, he would have risked criticism for abandoning a project started by President Eisenhower, a project designed to overthrow Castro and rid the hemisphere of Communism.

But beyond all that, the President relied on the strong assurances of the CIA and the less enthusiastic assurances of the Joint Chiefs of Staff that the operation could succeed. He was not an expert, so he would have to take the word of the experts.

By the end of January the CIA had selected the invasion site. It was to be the town of Trinidad, in Las Villas Province, on the southern coast of Cuba. Bissell and his advisers had selected Trinidad for tactical reasons. A landing on the south coast was mandatory, since the jumping-off point for the invasion would be Central America. The north coast of Cuba would have been too far away for the invading planes and ships to operate effectively.

But along the south coast of Cuba the charts showed a barrier reef, except at the mouths of rivers. Trinidad was located at such a river mouth, and it also had a small port which could be made usable. The terrain near Trinidad offered a good chance of sealing off and securing the beachhead. In addition, Trinidad was near the Escambray. If something went wrong, it was thought, the invaders could melt into the hills to carry on the fight.

There were some drawbacks, however. The airstrip at Trinidad was not large enough to take B-26s. And there was a detachment of Castro's militia at Trinidad, which could offer immediate resistance. On the other hand, the CIA hoped that shortly after the landing, it could recruit about 1,000 troops from the local population of approximately 5,000.

Under Eisenhower, there had never been any plan to use United States armed forces in the Cuban operation. Kennedy reached the same decision, even though the operation had changed in scope and size.

Because it was later to become a point of confusion and controversy, it should be understood that Kennedy's decision was that the formal, overt armed forces of the United States—the Army, Navy, Air Force and Marine Corps—would not be used in the invasion. His decision, of course, did not apply to covert forces, including the B-26s, guns, ships and Cubans under the control of the CIA. These could and would be used.

Since the operation was secret, or was supposed to be, it remained under Bissell's and the CIA's direction and control. The Joint Chiefs of Staff in the Pentagon, the nation's top military commanders, were consulted as the plans developed, but they did not have primary responsibility.

The Joint Chiefs were briefed on the operation for the first time in January, 1961, although the Office of Naval Intelligence had earlier stumbled on the fact that some kind of CIA operation was under way. The ONI did not know exactly what the CIA was up to, however.

The CIA's proposal for a landing at Trinidad was sent to the Joint Chiefs for their consideration. After studying it, they submitted an opinion signed by General Lyman L. Lemnitzer, the chairman of the Joint Chiefs, saying that the plan for a landing at Trinidad would have an even chance of success.*

Among the Cubans sent to Guatemala after the decision to increase the size of the invasion force was Mario Abril, the private in E Company who on April 15 was to watch the B-26s droning overhead from the deck of the *Houston*.

He and his family had fled Cuba in 1960. A sensitive youth of nineteen, Mario had soft brown eyes and a quiet nature. But he was determined to join the fight against Castro. His experience was typical:

"I met a CIA man named Roger at La Moderne Hotel,

---

* Lemnitzer acted for himself, Admiral Arleigh Burke, Chief of Naval Operations; General Thomas D. White, Chief of Staff of the Air Force; General George H. Decker, Army Chief of Staff; and General David M. Shoup, Commandant of the Marine Corps. Later, some of the chief's papers were signed by Burke, in the absence of Lemnitzer.

37

South West 8th Street on the [Tamiami] Trail. Many of my friends from Cuba were getting training and I heard about it and that's how I got into it. Roger gave us training in explosives and in underground propaganda. Sometimes he did it right in the hotel, and sometimes he took us to the Everglades to shoot with .45-caliber guns. He was about forty years old and he was good, he knew his stuff.

"In January [1961] I heard about the training camps. I went to the recruiting office for those camps at 27th Avenue and 10th Street, South West.

"One night, March 13, they took us to an old house in Coconut Grove and we put on khaki uniforms there with blue baseball caps, boots and duffel bags. It was at night, about 8:00 P.M. We got taken into a truck and we went to Opa-locka. There was about a hundred of us and we waited there for a while. Two Americans joined us. They were dressed just like the rest of us, khaki uniforms and blue baseball caps. So they took us to a DC-4. It had no seats, you know, just seats along the side, and we were packed in on the sides. When there was no more room, they put the rest of them on the floor of the plane.

"When we arrived at Retalhuleu, it was around dawn on March 14. We had a real good breakfast there, bacon, ham, everything we wanted. That felt real good, so I began to like the looks of this place, you know, because we had such a good breakfast.

"About noon we reached camp and we got field mess, dishes and jackets, and I thought, well, we traveled all night, so maybe we rest today. But no, the same day we started shooting with M-1 rifles and they took us up eight, nine thousand feet to practice. There were clouds all around us. So that night I thought we were going to bed, because we started out the whole day before with no rest, but we had lessons in machine guns. So finally they let us go to bed and we slept a long time.

"We were in Trax Base. After about five days they gave us a choice of battalions we could join and I chose the Second Battalion because I had a couple of friends there in E Company. There were about 175 men in the battalion and 40 in E Company. Each battalion had an American instructor. Bob was the second battalion instructor. Another was Jim and another was Juan, who was the only one who spoke Spanish. The chief of the whole place was Colonel Frank.* He was strong, very strong, like a bull. He wore the same uniform we did. But he had a .38-caliber revolver on his hip, like all the American instructors. They all had a revolver. We took hikes and learned to shoot .50-caliber machine guns and mortars and Browning automatic rifles and bazookas.

"When it rained there, you couldn't walk, the roads were covered with water and mud. Every afternoon it rained, and it was some mess, I tell you.

"Every day the American instructors told us that we would have air cover, and that no tanks are going to fight against us. When I was training in bazookas I asked our instructor, Bob, 'What is this for? If we are not going to fight against tanks, what do you need bazookas for?' 'Just in case,' he said. And they told us that the B-26 bombers would give us control of the air."

Almost to a man, members of the brigade say that their CIA advisers promised the invaders would have "control of the air" or "air cover." Few of the Cubans claim that there was any clear promise that U. S. Air Force or Navy planes would provide this control or protection. Rather, this was the conclusion many of the exiles drew. Possibly, some of the CIA advisers wanted to leave this impression.

Under the plan, of course, it was the exile air force, specifically the B-26 bombers, that was to provide "control of the air." It would do so by knocking out Castro's air force on the ground, thus making air cover over the beaches, during the landing operations, unnecessary.

To accomplish this key objective, the CIA created a

---

* An ex-Marine who had fought at Iwo Jima in World War II. Later some CIA analysts concluded it would have been wiser to choose a commander with experience in battalion-strength landings rather than a massive assault like Iwo Jima. The first commander of Trax Base was "Colonel Vallejo," a high ex-Philippine Army officer who had fought the Huks. He was replaced by "Colonel Frank" when the CIA shifted from a guerrilla operation to a larger amphibious landing.

39

sizable air force. It had sixteen B-26s initially. During the invasion eight more were added, making a total of twenty-four. In addition, the rebels had six C-46s and six C-54s. These transports were used in the air drops over Cuba prior to the invasion, and would drop paratroops during the invasion.

To head the Cuban pilots, the CIA selected Manuel Villafana Martinez, an ex-Cuban Air Force pilot who spent three years in jail on a conspiracy charge against Batista. Luis Cosme, the ex-Cuban Air Force fighter pilot who led the April 15 B-26 strike, was named deputy chief.

There were sixty-one Cuban pilots at Retalhuleu, plus navigators, radio operators and maintenance men. Six American instructors stayed with these pilots throughout the months of training and the invasion. Others were rotated in and out.

"Billy Carpenter," the Air Force colonel who was the chief American adviser at first, was replaced by "Lou," who was in turn replaced by "Gar," the top CIA air operations adviser during the actual invasion. Other American advisers included "Billy Belt," a young blond instructor; "Stevens," who told Cubans he had false teeth because the Chinese Communists had pulled out his real ones during the Korean War; and "Seig Simpson," a tall, ruddy-faced man who had a Japanese wife.

None of the CIA advisers used their real names, although several used correct first names. General G. Reid Doster, the chief of staff of the Alabama National Guard, at Birmingham, used the name "Reid" when he was at Retalhuleu as a CIA adviser. Many of the CIA instructors were from the Birmingham area. Several of the Americans were recruited by the CIA through a Miami front from among National Guard pilots who had flown B-26s in World War II.

The B-26s had two-man crews and no tail gunners or guns. These were eliminated to make room for extra fuel to increase the range of the bombers. Each bomber that took off from Happy Valley normally carried ten 260-pound bombs or six 500-pounders. In addition, each was armed with eight five-inch rockets and eight .50-caliber machine guns, each with 360 rounds of ammunition. Although the normal take-off weight for a B-26 is 36,000 pounds, these bombers lumbered off the runways at 40,000 pounds. They were formidable machines of war, but Castro's jets could fly higher and faster. And without tail guns, the bombers were defenseless from the rear.

By now the training camps had become a sensitive political issue in Guatemala. Early in February, President Ydigoras wrote a letter to President Kennedy, saying that morale in the camps was high and the troops ready for action. He urged that the invasion take place immediately. Behind his move was the private alarm of the Guatemalan Government over the unrest in the camps. From their viewpoint, the sooner the invasion, the sooner the camps could be closed and the whole thorny issue removed.

Roberto Alejos flew to Washington with the Ydigoras letter. He called on President Kennedy at the White House and also met with Allen Dulles.

As the pressure mounted, in late February and early March, the CIA and the Joint Chiefs were having trouble behind the scenes in agreeing on a landing site for the invasion. About two weeks after the Joint Chiefs had given a landing at Trinidad a fifty-fifty chance, three alternative sites were submitted to them by the CIA, which had decided it no longer favored Trinidad, partly because the airstrip there was too small for B-26s.

The Joint Chiefs studied the three alternate sites overnight, then held one meeting. They then said the best of the alternate sites would be the Bay of Pigs, but that there would be less chance of ultimate success at the Bay of Pigs than at Trinidad to the east. Nevertheless, they advised that the invasion go ahead in any event.

The Chiefs selected the Bay of Pigs mainly because there were only two access roads leading to the beach. These highways were flanked by swamps. Castro's forces would have to come this way, and the roads could be bombed by the invaders. By the same token, the Chiefs warned that it would be more difficult for the invaders to break out of the beachhead at the Bay of Pigs than at

Trinidad. The CIA's military experts, however, felt the Bay of Pigs was at least as good a site as Trinidad, or better.

While this was going on in Washington, in Guatemala the CIA was having trouble with a group of Cubans who objected to Artime and Captain Jose Perez San Roman, the CIA's hand-picked leaders. The dissidents received rough treatment from the CIA. They were flown to a remote jungle airstrip at Sayaxche, in Peten Province, and then spirited upriver in canoes to a point where the CIA maintained what was euphemistically called a "reindoctrination camp." Actually, it was a CIA prison from which the bitter Cubans were released only after the Bay of Pigs.

From the beginning the CIA had taken political as well as operational control of the exile movement, and it tended to favor the more conservative elements in the community. Now a rival group appeared on the scene.

In May, 1960, Manolo Ray, the Minister of Public Works under Castro, broke with the regime and went underground. In November he escaped to the United States. Ray maintained that he believed in the original social aims of Castro's revolution, but he took the position that Castro had betrayed those aims by leading Cuba down the Communist path. Ray and his followers belonged to the Movimiento Revolucionario del Pueblo, the MRP. It presented a strong competitor on the left to the CIA's *frente* on the right.

With the target date for the invasion fast approaching, something had to be done to prevent a political split in the exile ranks. Under CIA prodding, the *frente* and the MRP were tenuously patched together in a new organization, the Cuban Revolutionary Council. Selected to head the Council was Dr. Jose Miro Cardona, a colorless but dignified fifty-nine-year-old former Havana attorney. The son of a Spanish general who fought for Cuban independence, he was Premier of Cuba for the first six weeks of Castro's regime. He had resigned as Premier but was named Ambassador to the United States by Castro in July, 1960. Instead of taking the job, Cardona went into asylum in the Argentine Embassy. He came to the United States three months later on a safe-conduct pass.

42

The formation of the Council was announced in New York on March 22 at a press conference arranged by Lem Jones. On April 3 the State Department released a White Paper on Cuba. It was not generally realized at the time, but the document was designed to prepare public opinion at home and abroad for the secret invasion now only two weeks away. The White Paper said the Castro regime "offers a clear and present danger" to genuine social, economic and political reform in the Americas. Castro had betrayed the revolution, it said, and Cuba had become "a Soviet satellite." Clearly, it was an attempt to provide a form of philosophical underpinning for the imminent clandestine invasion.

Behind the scenes in Washington, a few voices were raised in opposition to the invasion. Senator J. William Fulbright, the outspoken Arkansas Democrat who headed the Senate Foreign Relations Committee, was invited by the President to ride with him to Palm Beach on March 30. Fulbright, who had heard rumors of the invasion plans, handed a memorandum to the President when he boarded Air Force One, the presidential jet.

It is worth quoting from, because Fulbright displayed an almost uncanny clairvoyance about what was to come:

> Millions of people still think the United States instigated the Castillo-Armas invasion of Guatemala in 1954; but the U.S. hand in that enterprise was far better covered than it is today with regard to the Cuban exiles. Furthermore, as the Cuban exiles intensify their activities aimed at overthrowing Castro, the more difficult it will become to conceal the U.S. hand. . . .
>
> Consideration must also be given to the nature and composition of the government which succeeds Castro. . . . The Front . . . is without the kind of leadership necessary to provide a strong, vigorous liberal government. . . .
>
> The prospect must also be faced that an invasion of Cuba by exiles would encounter formidable resistance which the exiles, by themselves, might not

be able to overcome. The question would then arise of whether the United States would be willing to let the enterprise fail (in the probably futile hope of concealing the U.S. role) or whether the United States would respond with progressive assistance as necessary to insure success. This would include ultimately the use of armed force; and if we came to that, even under the paper cover of legitimacy, we would have undone the work of thirty years in trying to live down earlier interventions. We would also have assumed the responsibility for public order in Cuba, and in the circumstances this would unquestionably be an endless can of worms.[1]

Fulbright also suggested that "even covert support of a Castro overthrow" probably violated the treaty of the Organization of American States as well as United States neutrality laws.

On April 4 the President met with his top advisers at the State Department. He went around the table asking their opinion on the invasion plan. Only Fulbright, who had been invited by the President to attend, spoke up firmly against the operation.

From the start the CIA had established liaison with the State Department to keep the tight circle of officials privy to the plan informed of its progress. Late in 1960, when Christian A. Herter was still Secretary of State, he had named Whiting Willauer, former Ambassador to Honduras, as his special assistant for the Cuban operation.

The CIA assigned Tracy Barnes* to maintain liaison with Willauer. Previously, Barnes had been under cover in the embassy in London. After the Kennedy Administration took over, Willauer was dropped, but Barnes continued to report to the State Department. Principally, he spoke to Adolf A. Berle, a Latin American adviser to the President, and Thomas C. Mann, then Assistant Secretary of State for Inter-American affairs. They were among the few department officials besides Dean Rusk who knew about the invasion.

* The CIA man who briefed Stevenson in April.

44

Late in March, Under Secretary of State Chester Bowles, during a period as Acting Secretary, learned of the invasion plan. On March 31 he wrote a memo to Rusk opposing it. He also asked Rusk to guarantee him half an hour to present his opposition to President Kennedy in the event the plan was approved. However, Bowles came away from his talk with Rusk with the belief that there would be no large-scale invasion. In the remaining two and a half weeks Bowles paid little attention to the matter; he had formed the impression it would be, at most, a small guerrilla landing.

Early in April the Cuban pilots at Retalhuleu were handed sealed envelopes and told to open them only after they were in the air. They obeyed. The orders were to proceed to Puerto Cabezas, Nicaragua, the misnamed Happy Valley that was to be their home for the next few weeks. The entire air operation, including the American advisers, moved from Guatemala to Happy Valley. The exile brigade was airlifted to Puerto Cabezas, their port of embarkation. There, a CIA fleet had been assembled. What amounted to a sizable secret navy had been put together by the CIA chiefly under cover of the Garcia Line Corporation, of 17 Battery Place, New York.

The steamship line was Cuba's biggest. The twenty-five-year-old company, headed by Alfredo Garcia, owned half a dozen vessels. It had main offices in New York and Havana. It also had branch offices in Houston, Texas, and Lake Charles, Louisiana, cities for which two of its ships were named. In the pre-Castro era it plied between East Coast ports, Havana and Central America, carrying rice and sugar.

After Castro, Alfredo Garciá's five sons, Eduardo, Marcos, Alfredo Jr., Lisardo and Francisco, came to the United States. The CIA needed a navy, and the Garcia Line, since it was Cuban-owned and the only Cuban shipping company still operating from Havana, was perfect cover. And the Garcias wanted to help, despite the risks.

The CIA secretly leased the ships. Working chiefly with Eduardo, the agency then mapped out a complex plan to get the vessels to Puerto Cabezas at the last possible moment. The line continued to serve Castro right up to the invasion. Alfredo remained behind in Cuba, which further served to divert suspicion. (He didn't leave there until March 21.)*

As D-Day approached, one by one the *Houston, Lake Charles, Rio Escondido, Caribe* and *Atlantico* sailed for Puerto Cabezas. Their crews were told nothing at first, and believed they were on a normal voyage to Central America. At Puerto Cabezas they were informed about the invasion and given the choice of leaving. A few did—they were held by the CIA at Puerto Cabezas until the invasion was over.

Each of the ships had about twenty-five crewmen, so there were more than a hundred seamen in all who suddenly found themselves in the middle of a shooting war. The ships were 2,400 tons, except for the smaller *Rio Escondido*. The CIA also purchased two World War II LCIs, the *Blagar* and *Barbara J.*, and added them to the invasion fleet.

The Garcia Line provided cover as well as transportation; some of the exiles recruited by the CIA were handed papers to fill out that led them to believe they were signing up, technically at least, as able-bodied hands with the Garcia Line.

While the CIA assembled its secret navy, there were important political moves back in the United States. On April 8 Miro Cardona, in a press conference at the Roosevelt Hotel in New York, issued a call to arms urging Cubans to rise up and overthrow Fidel Castro. The same day Federal Immigration agents in Miami arrested Rolando Masferrer, a notorious Batista henchman who, under the dictator, had run a much-feared and much-hated private army known as "The Tigers."

Masferrer, who had fled Cuba the same day as Batista, was spirited to Jackson Memorial Hospital after his arrest and placed under guard. A "No Visitors" sign was posted

* The day after the invasion Castro seized the company, but of course, Alfredo had already fled. Later, disheartened by the failure of the invasion, he sold the ships that weren't sunk and liquidated the steamship line.

on the door. The hospital listed Masferrer as a "possible coronary," but an attending physician told newsmen: "There seems to be some misrepresentation. No coronary is evident."

Masferrer, it was announced, had been picked up as the result of a letter from Dean Rusk to Attorney General Robert F. Kennedy, which said in part: "The continued presence at large of Rolando Masferrer in the United States and particularly in Florida is prejudicial to our national interest from the point of view of our foreign relations." Two days later a Federal grand jury indicted Masferrer on charges of conspiring to outfit and send a military expedition against Cuba, a violation of the United States neutrality laws.*

Masferrer was charged with breaking the law for mounting an invasion of Cuba—ten days before the government mounted its *own* secret invasion. Masferrer's character and reputation are irrelevant to the cynical manner of his arrest.

Ten days after the Bay of Pigs disaster Federal Judge Emett C. Choate ordered Masferrer released and accused the Federal Government of having shipped him off to a "government concentration camp" in Texas. Assistant United States Attorney Paul Gifford said the Immigration Service acted on direct orders from President Kennedy. "The President," said Judge Choate, "has no authority to direct anyone to disobey the law." Seven months later, on November 9, 1961, the government quietly dropped the case against Masferrer without explanation.

One possible reason for Masferrer's arrest is that the administration believed that charging him with invading Cuba would divert suspicion from the government's own

---

* However, after the Bay of Pigs, Attorney General Robert Kennedy disagreed with a legal brief submitted by 132 lawyers charging that the CIA-backed Bay of Pigs invasion violated United States and international law. "The neutrality laws," said the Attorney General, "are among the oldest laws in our statute books. . . . Clearly they were not designed for the kind of situation which exists in the world today. . . . No activities engaged in by Cuban patriots which have been brought to our attention appear to be violations of our neutrality laws."

invasion plans, then in the final stage of preparation. It was a case of a straight political arrest, something not normally associated with life in the United States.

In addition, the President believed that Masferrer's arrest would demonstrate to the exiles and the world that the United States had no sympathy for Batista supporters. This became clear on April 12, when the President told his news conference: "The Justice Department's recent indictment of Mr. Masferrer, of Florida, on the grounds that he was plotting an invasion of Cuba, from Florida, in order to establish a Batista-like regime, should indicate the feelings of this country towards those who wish to re-establish that kind of an administration inside Cuba."

On April 10, at a White House meeting, the final decision was made to change the landing site from Trinidad to the Bay of Pigs. President Kennedy personally approved the change. The CIA believed that this was a political and foreign-policy decision by the President, prompted by concern over potential world reaction. There would be no shooting of civilians at the Bay of Pigs because hardly anyone lived there, while at Trinidad there was a sizable local population.

It was also thought that the landing at the Bay of Pigs would be virtually unopposed and would have the appearance of an effort to resupply guerrillas, of being a smaller and more spontaneous operation. In short, that it would have better cover.

Despite the fact that the Joint Chiefs predicted the invasion would have less than an even chance at the Bay of Pigs, they went along with the choice.

The Chiefs normally make a distinction between the initial chances of success and ultimate success. In this case, they pointed out that success after the establishment of a beachhead depended upon certain psychological factors inside Cuba, factors which it was not the responsibility of the military to assess. What the Joint Chiefs meant, of course, was that the question of whether the militia and people of Cuba would rise up if sparked by an invasion

48

was an intelligence problem that fell within the purview of the CIA.

The CIA predicted there would be such an uprising if the beachhead could be established and held. The intelligence agency forecast no immediate uprising inside Cuba. Rather, it argued that all would depend on the success of the operation. If the landing was successful, Bissell expected defections among Cubans, although he did not expect them for at least a week after the invasion. The plan was to establish a beachhead; then use the Bay of Pigs airstrip to strike at Castro's communications, and other vital installations. A new Cuban government would be declared at the beachhead by the Council members, and it would then be recognized by the United States. If all this could be done, the CIA argued, Cuba would break wide open.*

The final week before D-Day, the Joint Chiefs were, by and large, an unhappy group. Some of them were irritated by the continual changes in the invasion plan. Accustomed to the strict discipline of an Eisenhower, they were bewildered by what they considered the informality and lack of procedures of the new administration.

Although Admiral Arleigh Burke has declined to comment on the Bay of Pigs, he was disturbed at the way the plan was being constantly modified. At one point Burke was told that the Navy would have to stay outside the three-mile limit off Cuba. Then it became the twelve-mile limit; then the twenty-mile limit. He was first told that the Navy would not make contact with the invasion fleet at all; then that three destroyers could escort the ships, then two destroyers. At one point the Navy was told that submarines could be deployed in the area, then it was told: "No submarines."

---

* After the invasion failed, the CIA was accused of making a faulty prediction that there would be an uprising. Allen Dulles responded in his book, *The Craft of Intelligence*, by stating: "I know of no estimate that a spontaneous uprising of the unarmed population of Cuba would be touched off by the landing." Dulles clearly chose his words with great care. His statement amounted only to a denial that the CIA had forecast a "spontaneous" uprising at the moment of the "landing."

49

The Chiefs were told that the invasion was not a Pentagon operation and that they could give advice only when called upon. Because of the secrecy involved, they were not allowed to take their staffs into their confidence; this, of course, cut down on their overall effectiveness.

It was made crystal-clear to the Pentagon that no United States armed forces were to be used in the actual invasion; however, Burke's destroyers could escort the exile fleet to a point offshore. If the ships were spotted en route to Cuba from Puerto Cabezas, they were to turn around and head back to port. In this event, United States ships and aircraft had the authority to protect the fleet against attack as it returned to Nicaragua.

In April, Burke was acting as the executive agent for the Joint Chiefs. In that role, and in his capacity as Chief of Naval Operations, he ordered elements of the Atlantic Fleet to move into position off Cuba. Moving with the fleet was a battalion of Marines from their base at Vieques Island, off the eastern end of Puerto Rico.

The President had made it clear the Navy was not to take part in the invasion itself. But it was possible that if the landing ran into trouble the President would change his mind and order the Navy and Marines to help. For this reason Burke moved his ships into position off Cuba; he informed both Allen Dulles and the President of his action.

Now the President stated publicly what he had privately decided: On April 12, at his news conference, he served notice that no United States forces would invade Cuba. He was asked how far the United States would go in helping "an anti-Castro uprising or invasion of Cuba." He replied: "First, I want to say that there will not be, under any conditions, an intervention in Cuba by the United States armed forces. This government will do everything it possibly can, and I think it can meet its responsibilities, to make sure that there are no Americans involved in any actions inside Cuba."

The next day Cuban crew members of the eight B-26s that were to fly in the April 15 raid went into security isolation at Happy Valley. If forced down outside of Cuba, the pilots were instructed to say they were defecting

FAR pilots. This was so that their statements would dove-tail with Zuniga's cover story in Miami. They were warned not to land at the United States Naval Base at Guan-tanamo.

Now, four days before D-Day, the CIA's fleet sailed from Puerto Cabezas. The second and fifth battalions were crammed aboard the *Houston*, along with large quantities of ammunition. Their target was Playa Larga, at the upper end of the Bay of Pigs. The third and fourth battalions, both heavy-weapons detachments, and the sixth infantry battalion were aboard the *Rio Escondido* and the other ships. Their objective was Giron Beach, on the eastern edge of the wide bay, which pokes like a finger into the southern coast of Cuba. The first battalion, the para-troopers, would be going in by air behind the beaches.

On Saturday, April 15, as the fleet steamed for Cuba, the B-26 bombers struck. Zuniga landed in Miami, and Roa and Stevenson clashed in the UN. Now, on Sunday, April 16, at Happy Valley, the CIA assembled the Cuban pilots. The American advisers told the Cubans that Castro's planes had been destroyed by the raid the pre-vious day. They displayed a blowup of a U-2 photo to support their contention.

Actually, one of the U-2 photos taken in these final hours before the landing alarmed the CIA. It showed gravel piled on the runways of the airstrip at the Bay of Pigs.

Aboard the *Houston* this Sunday, Private Mario Abril and the other men of E Company attended briefings by their commanders. They were shown aerial photographs to help them memorize landmarks.

"They gave us whiskey in little cans, real bad, yeah, black. I didn't wait, I drank mine right there. I got my ammunition. I got a whole metal can of cartridges, and six hand grenades. My gun, I cleaned up. I tied the ban-doleers around my chest and I got ready. That was 5:00 P.M. At six, we got a speech by the boss. He told us not to smoke, not to light a light or anything, because we were getting near Cuba.

51

"So I couldn't smoke, I thought the best thing to do was rest. I knew we were going to have a hard time, so I lay down on the deck. It was 6:30. The next thing I know, they woke me up. It was dark. My squad leader woke me up, and when I got up, I saw the coast over there. We were really there then. I saw, on my right, some lights, like a storm, you know, and they told me those were the other guys. They were on Giron Beach. They were already fighting.

"I looked at my watch and it was around 1:30 in the morning. The ship started to slow down. We were there. We were in the Bay of Pigs."

4

Invasion

IT WAS MIDNIGHT in Manhattan, Sunday, April 16, when the telephone rang in the fashionable East Side apartment of Lem Jones. Sleepily, Jones answered, then came alert with a jolt. It was the Central Intelligence Agency calling from Washington.

"This is it," Jones's agency contact told him. The invasion had begun. The CIA man dictated the first communiqué, to be issued to the world by Jones in the name of the Cuban Revolutionary Council. Jones took it down in longhand on a pad.

"Before dawn," the CIA man dictated slowly, "Cuban patriots in the cities and in the hills began the battle to liberate our homeland from the despotic rule of Fidel Castro and rid Cuba of international Communism's cruel oppression. . . ."

It had been a peaceful Sunday for Jones, and he had received no advance inkling that midnight would be the start of D-Day. He knew the Council had met during the early afternoon at the Hotel Lexington on 48th Street and Lexington Avenue. (It had named one of its members, Carlos Hevia, to be the minister of foreign affairs when a new government was established in Cuba.) In midafternoon Jones had called the hotel and tried to reach Miro Cardona. He was puzzled when he was told that there was no answer, but thought little about it.

There was a good reason why Jones was unable to reach his clients. At about 3:30 P.M., CIA agents, avoiding the main exit, spirited Cardona, Hevia and the other members of the Council out of the hotel. The Cubans were told only that they were being taken to Miami for something important.

They were driven by the CIA to Philadelphia, where they boarded a plane and were flown to Opa-locka. There, for three days, the men who were to lead a free Cuba were virtually held prisoner in a barracks-like house, all but barren of furniture. They learned about the start of their invasion on a radio.

But Jones knew nothing of this at the time. The call from Washington had instructed him to take the communiqué across town to the Hotel Statler and show it to Antonio Silio, the secretary treasurer of the Council, and Ernesto Aragon, Cardona's right-hand man. Silio was registered at the hotel under an assumed name.

Jones typed the communiqué himself. He grabbed a taxi outside of his apartment at 39th Street and Second Avenue and took it to the Statler, where he showed the announcement to the two Cubans. Then, at 2:00 A.M., he started distributing it, still by taxi, to the wire services. It began:

CUBAN REVOLUTIONARY COUNCIL
Via: Lem Jones Associates, Inc.
    280 Madison Avenue
    New York, New York

FOR IMMEDIATE RELEASE
April 17, 1961

Bulletin No. 1

The following statement was issued this morning by Dr. Jose Miro Cardona, president of the Cuban Revolutionary Council:

"Before dawn Cuban patriots in the cities and in the hills began the battle to liberate our homeland. . . ."

At Puerto Cabezas, Nicaragua, at 1:15 A.M. on Monday, April 17, six B-26 bombers were lined up on the runway, ready to carry out the second strike against Castro's air bases. Their targets were Camaguey, Cienfuegos, San

Antonio de los Banos, Camp Libertad, Santa Clara and also Managua, an Army base where U-2 photos had shown more than forty heavy tanks lined up in the open.

The planes were set to take off from Happy Valley at 1:40 A.M. They would strike just before dawn, finishing the destruction of Castro's air force that had begun with the first strike two days before.

The men in the B-26s had not yet learned of Richard Bissell's message from Washington, canceling the air strike on orders from the President. But when 1:40 A.M. came and went with no clearance to take off, they realized something had gone wrong.

At 1:55 A.M. the Cuban pilots were told their mission had been canceled on orders from Washington. They were not to proceed with the strike against the bases. Instead, they were to fly to the beaches to try to provide air cover for the landing.

Aboard the *Houston*, Mario Abril noticed the ship had come almost to a complete stop.

"They started using the winches to put the boats in the water, with a lot of noise, so much noise that they started shooting from the coast, just a few machine guns. We saw the tracers coming over. My squad was one of the first to get there, Company E. We got in a boat and run for the coast. It was a wood boat, like you might use for water skiing, with an Evinrude outboard motor, with gray paint, the motor I mean. It stopped in the middle of the Bay of Pigs when we were two miles away from shore, so we had to start it up again and they were shooting. We were told not to shoot back because they would see our positions. So we got there, and we had a wreck against the rocks on the beach.* We didn't land at the right place. And then we met the other squads who were around. We got together and start thinking what to do. On both sides we had swamps, water and very marshy. We started walking on the road. . . ."

---

* CIA hydrographic experts believed the beaches were excellent at the Bay of Pigs. An unexpected reef was encountered as the ships moved in, and it slowed down the landing operation.

Hundreds of miles away, on tiny Swan Island off Honduras, the CIA's Radio Swan had begun broadcasting mysterious messages to the underground several hours before:

"Alert, alert—look well at the rainbow. The fish will rise very soon . . . the sky is blue . . . the fish is red. Look well at the rainbow."

Now Radio Swan confidently broadcast the text of "Bulletin No. 1."

At Happy Valley the disappointed B-26 pilots climbed down from their cockpits. New briefings were held in the wooden operations building. New plans had to be drawn up on the spot because of the changed nature of the mission.

It took a B-26 two hours and fifty minutes to fly from Happy Valley to the Bay of Pigs. The bombers had enough fuel to stay over the beaches for two hours if need be and still make it back to base. So it was decided that the bombers would fly over the beaches in pairs, every half-hour. A total of eleven B-26s was sent over the beaches in relays. The first of them took off before daylight.

As exile Brigade 2506 was moving ashore, Castro received word of the invasion. He ordered his T-33 jets and Sea Furies to take off before dawn for the Bay of Pigs.

At 4:00 A.M., as General Cabell was pleading with Secretary Rusk at the Sheraton Park Hotel in Washington, Mario Abril's E Company made contact with the enemy.

"*At 4:00 A.M. we met the first company of those guys, the Castro militia. They were attacking, shouting dirty words and shooting. We lay down and wait for them. We started shouting at each other across the marshes. We gave them the word: 'Surrender.' They said they were going to fight us. They shouted 'Patria o Muerte!' and then we started shooting.*"

The CIA's Radio Swan transmitter crackled again at 5:15 A.M.:

"Forces loyal to the Revolutionary Council have carried out a general uprising on a large scale on the island of Cuba . . . the militia in which Castro placed his confidence appears to be possessed by a state of panic. . . . An army of liberation is in the island of Cuba to fight with you against the Communist tyranny of the unbalanced Fidel Castro . . . attack the Fidelista wherever he may be found. Listen for instructions on the radio, comply with them and communicate your actions by radio.

"To victory, Cubans!"

On the *Houston*, the prow machine-gunner Manuel Perez Salvador had his hands full. Units of the second battalion were still unloading. Perez Salvador, a former catcher for the Fort Lauderdale Braves, a Class C team in the Florida International League, could hardly believe he had been in Miami only twelve days before. He had been recruited for the invasion at the last moment and flown to Happy Valley on April 5 with forty-seven others. He was literally turned into a soldier overnight. After one day's training as a machine-gunner, Perez Salvador was assigned to the *Houston*. Now, at 5:30 A.M., he peered through his gun sights and saw the first T-33s and Sea Furies begin a series of attacks on the ship. In the next five hours Perez Salvador fired 5,000 bullets.

Sergio Garcia had taken off from Happy Valley at 1:16 A.M. at the controls of a C-46 transport loaded with paratroopers. Their target was the strategic Y-shaped crossroads at San Blas, inland behind Giron Beach. His co-pilot was Fausto Gomez. At 6:14 A.M. Garcia began the drop of men and equipment at San Blas. When all the cargo and all but the last paratrooper had been dropped, the cable running the length of the plane snapped. It broke the leg of a parachute drop officer, jammed the tail controls of the plane and left one young paratrooper dangling helplessly from the plane at the end of the cable. Gomez went back to try to help. He and another man managed to pull the paratrooper in and discovered he was only a young boy.

57

A few minutes later the youth, crying, came to the cockpit to plead with Garcia: "Please turn back and drop me. It's the invasion!"

"I can't," Garcia shouted over the noise of the engines. "Your main chute is broken. I can't drop you on a reserve chute. It's against orders."

An hour later, as they were winging back to Happy Valley, Gomez cut open the boy's boot and saw that his leg had been badly gashed when the cable snapped. He was bleeding profusely.

In New York the CIA phoned Jones with Bulletin No. 2 *:

> The Cuban Revolutionary Council announces a successful landing. . . . Because Cuban Revolutionary Council members are now totally occupied with the dramatic events unfolding in Cuba, their views will be made known to the press solely through the Cuban Revolutionary Council's spokesman, Dr. Antonio Silio.

The Council may have been totally occupied, but it was not totally free. Held in their barracks house at Opa-locka, the Cuban leaders were chafing. They were told they had been brought there so they could be flown to the beachhead as soon as it was secured. The United States would then recognize them as the legitimate government of Cuba.†

The Council leaders donned their khaki uniforms, in readiness. They were allowed to take walks along the hard-surface road in front of the house. But when Carlos Hevia,

---

* Although Jones and the Council later came in for some criticism for issuing press releases from a Madison Avenue office, the truth is that he did not write any of them. Each of the six bulletins was dictated directly to Jones by the CIA.

† Castro had realized the danger of this. On June 16, 1961, during a cigar-waving tour of the battlefield for British and American newsmen, he said that because the exiles held forty-three miles of coast at one point "it became an urgent political problem for us to oust them as quickly as possible so that they would not establish a government there."

who was to be the foreign affairs minister of a free Cuba, went to take a stroll, a CIA man warned him not to go very far. The area was rough and wild, the CIA man insisted, and the surrounding shrubbery was full of rattlesnakes.

Mario and the men of E Company had pushed back the militiamen and seized a T-shaped crossroads near Playa Larga.

"*At 6:00 A.M. in the morning we saw the first plane. It had blue stripes on it. The sun wasn't out yet. At first I didn't see the stripes, and I was wondering, Is it going to shoot at us or not? It was ours. At that time we heard a real big noise and saw a couple of lights. It was a truck coming up the road with militia. We shouted the password 'aguila' and the other one answers 'negra.' * But we didn't get any answer. We shouted 'aguila' again but we got no answer. The truck was coming closer, so everybody turned their weapons and started shooting and that thing exploded just like that, Pow! It jumped in the air and came down in flames. Then we saw there were three women and two girls, little ones, that's all, in the truck, and a couple of militiamen. I don't know how that happens but that's what we got out of it, three women and two girls, killed.*"

By dawn Castro's air force was taking a heavy toll of the invasion fleet. About 9:00 A.M., following a direct hit from the air, the *Houston* began to sink. Captain Luis Morse managed to edge the transport onto a reef a mile and a half from shore to keep it from going under completely. Along with most of the 120 men of the fifth battalion, Perez Salvador had to swim to the beach. The one-time professional baseball player stripped to his shorts, kicked off his shoes and jumped into the Bay of Pigs.

At 9:15 A.M. in San Juan, Puerto Rico, CIA Director Allen Dulles mounted the speaker's rostrum in the La Concha Hotel to the applause of the thousand members of the Young Presidents Organization. He launched into

* The two words together mean black eagle.

59

the keynote speech of the convention. For his topic this morning Dulles had chosen "The Communist Businessman Abroad."

Joaquin Varela, a slight, twenty-eight-year-old former Cuban Air Force pilot, led the relays of B-26s over the beaches. With Castro's air force still in action, the bombers were flying straight to disaster. Eight exile pilots died that April morning.

Jose Crespo and Lorenzo Perez, the two fliers who had landed in Key West on Saturday (and who had supposedly gone into asylum), flew over the Bay of Pigs this April 17 under the code name "Puma I." They were just leaving the beach, after firing all their rockets, when their bomber was hit in one engine by a Castro fighter. Crespo feathered the engine, radioed Happy Valley and began limping home at low altitude.

Chirrino Piedra, the twenty-five-year-old pilot so well liked by his comrades, was also turning from the beach when his B-26 was hit in the tail. The plane exploded instantly, killing Piedra and his co-pilot, Jose A. Fernandez.

Matias Farias, only twenty-two, tried to make a forced landing at the little airstrip now in exile hands at Giron Beach. The piles of gravel that had alarmed the CIA when spotted by the U-2 on Sunday had been cleared away. But Farias, coming in for a landing, flipped over and his B-26 lost its tail. Eddy Gonzalez, his co-pilot, was killed. Farias, slightly wounded, survived and was flown out in a C-46 two days later.

Crispin L. Garcia, a short, dark-haired pilot, fought over the beaches but ran short of fuel. He landed at Key West, refueled and took off for Happy Valley with his co-pilot, Juan M. Gonzalez Romero. He nearly made it. About a year later, during a search for a missing P-51, Crispin Garcia's mangled B-26 was found on a hillside eighty miles northwest of Happy Valley.

Antonio Soto, a small (five-foot-four) chestnut-haired ex-Cuban military pilot flew as "Paloma II" and was hit in one engine. He became the second exile pilot to land at Grand Cayman Island. He and his co-pilot, Benito R.

"Campesino" Gonzalez, were flown back to Puerto Cabezas, but their plane remained behind on British territory.

Still the B-26s kept coming. Demetrio Perez, riding the co-pilot seat of one of the bombers, looked at his watch as he crossed the south coast of Cuba en route to the Bay of Pigs. The twenty-five-year-old co-pilot noticed it was 11:56 A.M. He and the pilot, thirty-four-year-old Raul Vianello, were only two minutes behind schedule.

But Perez was worried. The two fliers had been plagued by bad luck since Saturday, when one engine of their bomber burst into flames as they were taking off for the first strike against Castro's bases. They were sidelined. Now, on April 17, they made it off the ground, but ever since take-off they had noticed a persistent smell of gasoline in the cabin.

Remembering their previous embarrassment, the two did not want to return to Happy Valley to face their friends. They decided to keep going. They radioed Soto to come closer for a look, but when he did, he was unable to spot the trouble.

Perez and Vianello met Varela as the squadron leader was returning from the beaches. They radioed him that they had fuel trouble but were going on. As they reached the beach, another pilot warned that a "T-bird" (T-33) was loose in the area. A moment later the Castro jet was diving at them. A burst of machine-gun bullets just missed the B-26.

The bomber turned inland, flew low over the swamps and blew up a Castro machine-gun nest that commanded a highway to the beach. Then the two fliers spotted a large convoy about to enter the sugar-mill town of Australia. They were uncertain whether or not it was a Castro convoy. By the time the bomber received radio confirmation that it was, the convoy was in the town. Rather than shoot at civilians, the fliers waited until the convoy emerged on the other side. As it came out, Perez saw a white ambulance with a red cross on its roof, followed by a jeep, a truck and a tank.

As they swooped low over the convoy for a better look,

they were amazed to see Castro's militia waving their caps and guns at the plane in greeting. Then they realized the militiamen had not noticed the blue stripes under the wings, the only distinguishing marks between the exile bombers and Castro's B-26s.

Some of the militiamen were still waving when the bomber made a second pass, this time with its .50-caliber machine guns blazing. The B-26 also fired two rockets at the convoy. The ambulance blew up. Perez later claimed the attack was justified because the ambulance had armed militiamen in and around it.

At 2:15 P.M., its ammunition gone and fuel running low, the bomber turned for home. Just as Vianello attempted to climb into a bank of clouds for cover, a T-33 caught the bomber with a storm of bullets. The left engine was knocked out and smoke poured into the cockpit.

"Mayday! Mayday!" Perez radioed. Below, the two aviators spotted a destroyer. Assuming it was either American or British, Vianello flew near it. "Bail out!" he ordered the younger man.

Then, before Perez jumped, Vianello, who had a wife and three children, reached over and shook hands. He pointed to the water. "We'll meet down there," he said. "Good luck!"

Perez jumped. As he plummeted through the air he was unable, at first, to find the D-ring on his chute. Finally he did, and yanked with all his strength. The parachute billowed open, and the orange and white silk overhead was a beautiful sight to Perez. He looked up in time to see the bomber burst into flames and nose-dive into the ocean. He never saw Vianello jump.

Perez hit the water, inflated his Mae West and waited to be picked up. Forty-five minutes later, although it seemed hours, he found himself aboard the U.S.S. *Murray*, an American destroyer.*

* It was the start of a weird adventure for Perez, who followed orders and stuck to his cover story that he was a defecting Castro pilot. On April 19 he was flown by helicopter to the aircraft carrier U.S.S. *Randolph* and given an air-conditioned stateroom. From there he was flown to Guantanamo, smuggled across the bay in a launch

Some of the B-26s did make it back to Happy Valley. Mario Zuniga, who had returned secretly from Miami the previous day, flew support over the beaches with Oscar Vega Vera, his co-pilot. They returned safely, as did the B-26s flown by Gonzalo Herrera, Varela, Mario Alvarez Cortina and Rene Garcia.

Crespo, with one propeller feathered and no compass, maintained radio contact as Happy Valley tried to guide him home. Crespo was also in contact with a C-54 pilot who attempted to persuade him to land at Grand Cayman Island. But Crespo did not change course. He radioed a final message to Happy Valley: "Trying to trade air speed for altitude for bail out, only ten minutes fuel left, no ground in sight." He was never seen again.

Eleven B-26s had flown from Happy Valley on this Monday, April 17. They were never told why their mission had been changed at the last moment from an air strike against Castro's bases to air support over the beaches. They obeyed their orders. Eight men died. Six planes were lost. Five planes returned to Happy Valley. Their valiant efforts at such a high cost had not really been very effective over the beaches. "The Monday air cover," as one CIA official later conceded, "was murderous."

With the *Houston* out of action, the men of the second battalion were critically short of the ammunition and supplies the ship carried. In the Zapata swamps Mario Abril, with no food and little ammunition, skirmished with the enemy on Monday afternoon.

"There were only a few militiamen. I got my first one in there. He was in a tree. They were only ten or fifteen guys,

---

to the main Navy base and grilled by Navy Intelligence, whom he exasperated by repeating his CIA cover story. Only after the Navy threatened to send Perez "back" to Havana, did he tell the truth. He was whisked to Washington by jet for further interrogation by the Navy and, finally, by the CIA. He met General Maxwell D. Taylor, the President's military representative, and even made it to the White House. All the while Perez was being kept in a luxurious Alexandria, Virginia, motel. Finally, he was given new clothes and a plane ticket. Still wearing the parachute boots in which he had jumped, Perez returned to Miami.

but they were giving us a hard time because they didn't shoot all the time. They just shoot and keep quiet, shoot and keep quiet. And so this guy in a tree, I shot him down, he kept hanging from there. He was tied up to it and swinging. He just kept swinging."

In the United Nations in New York, Raul Roa was furious. He accused the United States of financing and backing the invasion. Grim-faced and chain-smoking, he charged that the CIA had poured $500,000 a month into the invasion preparations. He said a principal base was the Opa-locka airport. And he said the chief CIA agent in Miami was "Bender." On Monday afternoon, for the second time in forty-eight hours, Adlai Stevenson rose and denied the Cuban's allegations.

Stevenson had not left New York over the weekend and he did not see Kennedy. However, the President had dispatched McGeorge Bundy to New York to co-ordinate with Stevenson. Bundy, following developments on the AP ticker, had hastily briefed Stevenson that morning in the office of the United States mission to the UN. Then he accompanied Stevenson over to the UN, donned his hat and coat and flew back to the White House.

It was a day for denials.

They had begun in Washington, when Joseph W. Reap, a State Department spokesman, declared: "The State Department is unaware of any invasion." The Pentagon said it knew nothing about any invasion, either. The White House was equally uncommunicative. "All we know about Cuba," the Associated Press quoted Pierre Salinger as saying, "is what we read on the wire services."

The strongest assurances came from Secretary of State Rusk, who said of the Cuban situation: '

"There is not and will not be any intervention there by U.S. forces. The President has made this clear, as well as our determination to do all we possibly can to insure that Americans do not participate in these actions in Cuba.

"We do not have full information on what is happening on that island.

"The American people are entitled to know whether we

64

are intervening in Cuba or intend to do so in the future. The answer to that question is no. What happens in Cuba is for the Cuban people themselves to decide."

On the other side of the globe, at his Black Sea villa near Sochi, Nikita S. Khrushchev conferred with his impassive Foreign Minister, Andrei Gromyko. They drafted a note threatening to come to Castro's aid unless Kennedy halted the invasion.

In the Roman era persecuted Christians would draw a fish to indicate a clandestine meeting was to be held. The CIA had selected this as a symbol for the invasion. (Hence the business about fish rising, which Radio Swan had broadcast Sunday night.) In New York, late on Monday, the CIA dictated Bulletin No. 3 to Lem Jones. It contained a reference to a fish standing. When Jones showed it to Silio, the exile official was worried. To Cubans, a phrase about fish rising or standing could have an earthy and much more graphic meaning. Jones argued with Silio, and finally, at 7:15 P.M., the bulletin was issued unchanged, despite the Cuban's apprehensions:

The principal battle of the Cuban revolt against Castro will be fought in the next few hours. Action today was largely of a supply and support effort. . . .

Our partisans in every town and village in Cuba will receive, in a manner known only to them, the message which will spark a tremendous wave of internal conflict against the tyrant . . . before dawn the island of Cuba will rise up en masse in a co-ordinated wave of sabotage and rebellion which will sweep Communism from our country . . . our clandestine radio has been giving instructions to the insurgents throughout the island. In a coded message on this radio yesterday, a statement was made that "the fish will soon stand."

As is well known, the fish is the Christian symbol of the resistance. When the fish is placed in a vertical position it is a sign that internal revolt is in full swing. The fish will stand tonight!

By this hour on Monday night, Dulles was hurrying home from Puerto Rico. In Washington, the full disastrous effect of the cancellation of the second air strike was being felt. It was realized that the invasion was slipping away fast. The exiles had, in the two days since April 15, lost ten of their original force of sixteen B-26s. Ten pilots had been killed in a little over forty-eight hours: Daniel Fernandez Mon, Gaston Perez, Jose A. Crespo, Lorenzo Perez, Chirrino Piedra, Jose A. Fernandez, Crispin L. Garcia, Juan M. Gonzalez Romero, Eddy Gonzalez and Raul Vianello.

Under the circumstances, Washington permitted a second air strike against Castro's bases to be reinstated. But attrition and exhaustion had overtaken the Cuban pilots. And the weather had turned bad. The whole point of that strike had been to catch Castro's air force on the ground before dawn. Now it would take place—eighteen hours late.

Exactly three B-26s took off from Happy Valley at 8:00 P.M. Monday, April 17. Their target was the San Antonio de los Banos airfield. The strike was led by Joaquin Varela, despite the fact that he and his co-pilot, Tomas Afont, had flown that morning. Varela was unable to find San Antonio in the dark. Under orders to hit only military targets, he dropped no bombs and returned to Happy Valley. The second plane, piloted by Ignacio Rojas and Esteban Bovo Caras, developed engine trouble and turned back before reaching the target. So did the third plane, piloted by Miguel A. Carro and Eduardo Barea Guinea.

Two hours later, at 10:00 P.M., two more B-26s took off from Happy Valley. Their crews also had flown earlier that day. Gonzalo Herrera and Angel Lopez were in one bomber. Mario Alvarez Cortina and Salvador Miralles were in the other. They had no more success than the first three planes. Five B-26s had gone out Monday night. All returned, but they inflicted no damage on their targets. The score for the belated second air strike: Zero.

The start of Tuesday, April 18, found the exile brigade strung out along three separate beachheads on Cuba's southern shore. To the east of the Bay of Pigs, the exiles held Giron Beach and had moved inland behind it. At the north end of the wide Bay of Pigs itself, Mario Abril and the entire second battalion of 175 men was positioned in a crater astride a T-shaped crossroads near Playa Larga. The hole had been dug for a traffic circle under construction there. The battalion was alone, because the men of the fifth battalion, swimming ashore from the *Houston*, had been carried by the current to a point about twelve miles farther south of Playa Larga. As a result, the second and fifth battalions never joined up as planned. Shells were bursting all around the crater. The noise was deafening.

"They were shooting at us with mortars and artillery from far away, for three hours. Then at about 12:30, maybe 1:00 A.M., it stopped. It was quiet. And then we start hearing the tanks coming up. I heard 'clank, clank, clank, clank,' real far away. They were coming closer. Our tanks moved into position on both sides of the road. The first Castro tank showed up with its lights on and the hatch closed. One of our tanks shot him and stopped him right in the middle of the road. But they cleared it away. All night long the tanks kept coming. They sent eight, but only one got through to the beach. Then this Stalin tank, real heavy, came up the road. Our tank had no ammunition, so it started pushing him on the side and threw him out of the road. The guys came out of the tank with their hands up and that was real great. We took them prisoners. It was real busy then. It was a real busy night."

At 3:44 A.M., as the second battalion stood off Castro's tanks, Radio Swan broadcast an appeal to the Cuban Army and militia to revolt:

"Now is the precise moment for you to take up strategic positions that control roads and railroads! Make prisoners of or shoot those who refuse to obey your orders! Comrades of the Navy, this is your opportunity to prove your sincerity. . . . Take over and secure your post in the Navy of Free Cuba. Comrades of the Air Force! Listen closely! All planes must stay on the ground. See that no Fidelist plane takes off. Destroy its radios; destroy its tail; break

67

its instruments; and puncture its fuel tanks! Refuse to give service! Inform your friends that freedom and honor await those who join us, as death will overtake the traitors who do not!"

Three hours later, that was followed up with a broadcast urging internal sabotage:

"People of Havana; attention, people of Havana. Help the brave soldiers of the liberation army . . . electrical plants must not supply power today to the few industries that the regime is trying to keep in operation. Today at 7:45 A.M., when we give the signal on this station, all the lights in your house should be turned on; all electrical appliances should be connected. Increase the load on the generators of the electric company! . . . But do not worry, people of Havana, the liberation forces will recover the electrical plants and they can be placed in operation rapidly."

But at Playa Larga, the liberation forces were in trouble. Mario and the second battalion got the bad news; they would have to retreat.

"At 11 A.M. we got the orders to move to Giron Beach to join up with the other battalions. I ask myself, Why? I think we won that battle during the night against tanks with no ammunition, no support, no fifth battalion, which was in another place. So I got on a truck and I was riding to Giron Beach, twenty miles away down the line of the coast. We got there at 12:30, maybe 1:00 P.M. There we got rest and I got a couple of crackers and a bottle of water. We were in a new house Castro built for the workers. In the meantime, Castro's planes were coming and bombing and shooting. We were so tired, it didn't make any difference to us."

The exile air force was still in action, despite the long odds against it. A thunderstorm swelled the little river behind the airstrip at Happy Valley on Tuesday afternoon, and sent the scorpions and snakes near the operations building scuttling for cover. Despite the storm, six B-26s took off at 2:00 P.M. Their target was a large Castro armored column moving toward the shrinking beachhead at Giron.

Mario Zuniga flew in one of the bombers, with the chief of the exile air operations, Manuel Villafana, as his co-pilot. Luis Cosme, Villafana's deputy, took over as the operations officer at Happy Valley.

Rene Garcia, Antonio Soto and Gustavo Ponzoa flew three of the B-26s in the strike force. Despite the presidential pledge that no Americans would participate in the fighting, the other two bombers were flown by American CIA pilots. One was the instructor who used the name "Seig Simpson" and who had told the Cubans he was a U. S. Air Force veteran of the Korean War. His co-pilot was Gustavo Villoldo, a Cuban. Alberto Perez Sordo, a twenty-two-year-old exile, flew as co-pilot with the other American.

It took the six bombers only twenty-five minutes to destroy the Castro convoy on the road to the beach.* All six bombers and crews returned safely to Puerto Cabezas.

The same day, April 18, the exile air force received four P-51 Mustangs from the Nicaraguan Government. The trouble was, the Cuban pilots had not been trained to fly them. The Mustangs went unused.

At 1:20 P.M. on Tuesday in New York, Lem Jones issued Bulletin No. 4 of the Cuban Revolutionary Council. For the first time it took a more pessimistic tone:

> Cuban freedom fighters in the Matanzas area are being attacked by heavy Soviet tanks and Mig aircraft † which have destroyed sizable amounts of medical supplies and equipment.

Meanwhile, the note Khrushchev had drafted at Sochi the day before was transmitted to Washington. The Soviet Premier charged the United States had armed and trained

---

* During his June 16 tour of the battlefield, Castro admitted to newsmen that his forces had made the error of advancing on the open road that cuts through marshes, and as a result were an easy target for the exile air force.

† Castro had no Migs in the air during the invasion. This probably refers to the T-33 jet trainers.

the exiles. He threatened to give Castro "all necessary assistance" unless Washington stopped the invasion. At 7:00 P.M. Soviet Ambassador Mikhail A. Menshikov was handed a note by Rusk at the State Department. In it President Kennedy warned Khrushchev to stay out of the fight. In the event of outside intervention, Kennedy declared, the United States would "immediately" honor its treaty obligations to the hemisphere.

In the UN, Soviet Ambassador Zorin mocked Stevenson's continued denials of United States responsibility for the invaders. "Have these people come from outer space?" asked Zorin.

A few moments earlier Carlos Alejos, Roberto's brother, rose in the UN and said he had just returned from a trip to Guatemala, and wished to state, in answer to Cuba's charges, that the forces which had landed in Cuba had not been trained in Guatemala and had not come from Guatemalan territory. Guatemala, Alejos solemnly assured the UN, had never allowed and would never allow its territory to be used for the organization of acts of aggression against its sister American republics.

At the White House, that Tuesday night, more than a thousand guests had gathered for the President's traditional reception for members of Congress and their wives. Champagne and punch flowed. At exactly 10:15 P.M. the President and Jacqueline Kennedy descended the main stairs. Mrs. Kennedy wore a lovely sleeveless floor-length sheath of pink and white straw lace, with matching pink slippers. A feather-shaped diamond clip glittered in her bouffant hairdo. The Marine Band struck up "Mr. Wonderful." The Kennedys led the first dance. Vice-President Lyndon B. Johnson and his wife Lady Bird, wearing her salmon-pink inaugural gown, joined in. Midway through the first number the Kennedys and the Johnsons switched partners. For the buffet dinner the guests had chicken à la king and pheasant. The President mixed with his guests, smiling and apparently carefree. But at 11:45 P.M. guests noticed he had slipped away.

Still in his formal dress, the President met at midnight

at the White House with his highest military and civilian advisers. The Joint Chiefs and top officials of the CIA were present. The invasion was now near collapse. At the meeting Richard Bissell maintained that the operation could still be saved if the President would authorize the use of Navy jets from a carrier then stationed offshore between Jamaica and Cuba.

But the President had repeatedly stated, both privately and publicly (at his April 12 press conference), that no United States armed forces would be used in Cuba. He was reluctant to change his position now.

Bissell, who had been so deeply engaged in the Cuban operation for more than a year, argued desperately in favor of U.S. airpower to save it now. So did Admiral Burke, who made a series of proposals. Like Bissell he asked that Navy jets be sent over the beaches.

Burke also suggested several alternatives: that a company of Marines be landed; that a destroyer be allowed to give gunfire support to the invaders; that Navy jets be allowed to fly just outside the three-mile limit. General Lemnitzer, the chairman of the Joint Chiefs, supported Burke's plea for Navy jets over the beaches, as did General White, Chief of Staff of the Air Force.

The President declined to accept these various proposals. Then Burke suggested that Navy planes be allowed to fly over the beaches, but that there be no U.S. markings on the planes. As the group talked, the clock ticked past midnight and into Wednesday, April 19. Finally the discussion resulted in a compromise:

The President authorized the unmarked Navy jets from the carrier *Essex* to fly over the Bay of Pigs for one hour just after dawn. Their mission was to be restricted. They were to support an air-to-ground strike that morning by the B-26s from Happy Valley. The Navy jets were to fly "dead cover," which meant they were to interpose themselves between the bombers and any enemy aircraft. In this way they were to try to protect the B-26s against attack by Castro planes. The Navy jets were not to strafe or to initiate any firing. Under the President's authorization, however, they could fire back if fired upon.

There was a subtle and unspoken aspect to this. If the Castro planes fired, the Navy jets would not be able to make the fine distinction of whether the attackers were firing at the bombers or at them. By interposing themselves between the B-26s and Castro's planes, in other words, they would draw fire and be able to fire back.

Burke wrote out the order on a pad. It was telephoned to the Joint Chiefs communication center at the Pentagon, sent immediately to CINCLANT, in Norfolk, Virginia, relayed from there to the Commander, Second Fleet, and thence to the carrier. The markings on the Navy jets were to be painted over.

It was 1:00 A.M. Wednesday when the meeting broke up at the White House.

At Happy Valley a 1:00 A.M. meeting was also in progress, in the building that served as the air operations center. Among those present were General Doster, Riley W. Shamburger, Jr., a CIA pilot who was a close friend of Doster's and on leave as a major in the Alabama Air National Guard, and Luis Cosme, the Cuban operations deputy.

All realized that the situation was grim and that something had to be done. The Cuban pilots were exhausted; ten were dead. The American advisers agreed to fly night missions starting that night, to relieve the weary Cubans. The Americans were not ordered to do so; they volunteered, although it was understood when they signed up with the CIA that they might at some point have to fly combat missions.

Now the pledge that no U.S. armed forces and no Americans would be involved was doubly violated, since American CIA pilots were flying in the invasion and Navy jets were to screen them against attack.

Five B-26s took off during the night. Shamburger and a fellow American, Wade Carroll Gray, flew in one B-26. Two more Americans, Thomas Willard Ray and Leo Francis Baker, flew in another. Three other Americans flew. One was a tall, skinny pilot known simply as "Joe," whose co-pilot was also an American. The other was the pilot known as "Seig Simpson." The fifth B-26 was piloted by a Cuban, Gonzalo Herrera.

Three more Cubans, including Zuniga, were scheduled to fly, but operations were halted before they took off.

Bissell left the White House meeting with the understanding that the Navy jets would appear over the beaches at dawn simultaneously with the B-26s. What happened next has since become clouded in a welter of conflicting interpretations.

Bissell, of course, did not have the responsibility of ordering the Navy jets into the air, but he did have the task of notifying the exile air force. From his secret office he relayed the news that United States air cover would be available for one hour at dawn to support the air-to-ground strike by the CIA B-26s. Bissell did not write the order out himself. He repeated it verbally to the colonel on duty at the CIA office, who in turn transmitted it to Happy Valley.

Bissell's message reached Happy Valley shortly before Shamburger, Gray, Ray and Baker took off. These four Americans, therefore, took off for the Bay of Pigs with the understanding that they would have protection from U. S. Navy jets. They did not.

Somewhere along the line there was a fatal mix-up between the CIA and the Navy. At first the CIA thought that the President's order had reached the carrier so conservatively worded that the jets had been unable to take hostile action against Castro's planes because the jets had not been fired upon. Later the CIA realized the error was one of timing. In the secret post-mortem over the Bay of Pigs, it was officially concluded that the bombers had arrived after the jets had already come and gone, after the clock had run out on the one hour of air support.

How this happened may never be entirely unscrambled (there has been no public explanation), but the evidence pointed directly to the incredible conclusion that the mix-up had occurred because of confusion over time zones. The Bay of Pigs and Washington were both on Eastern Standard Time, but Nicaragua time was an hour earlier.

73

Which means a plane that left Happy Valley, Nicaragua, at 3:30 A.M. local time would have arrived over the Bay of Pigs at 6:30 A.M. Nicaragua time, or just after dawn. But because of the difference in time zones, it was 7:30 A.M. at the Bay of Pigs—an hour too late.

The CIA and the Navy did not co-ordinate their respective orders to the fleet and to Happy Valley. Burke simply sent his order to the fleet and Bissell sent an order to Happy Valley. Neither official saw the order the other had transmitted.

The confusion over time zones may have been compounded by the fact that the Navy always transmits messages in Greenwich Mean Time, but the CIA sometimes uses Standard Time, sometimes GMT.

In any event, the Navy pilots reported they never made contact with CIA bombers. They said they saw no bombers and no Castro planes. After the hour had elasped, they returned to the carrier.

On this morning of April 19 four Americans lost their lives. Riley Shamburger and Wade Gray were shot down and crashed at sea. Ray and Baker were shot down and apparently crashed inland. "Joe," the tall American, never reached the beaches. He heard the cries for help of the four American fliers as they were shot down, and he turned back. Gonzalo Herrera, his plane shot full of holes, also made it back.

At Happy Valley at 8:30 A.M. "Gar," the chief CIA air adviser, asked the Cubans for volunteers to go in again over the beaches. The pilots were called together by Luis Cosme, the Cuban operations deputy. They were willing, but since another trip over the beaches meant almost certain death, they understandably demanded to know why they were being sent out.

"We must hold twenty-four hours more," the CIA chief said. "Don't play the bells loud, but something is going to happen."

It was the sort of vague promise that the Cubans, by this time, were fed up with. Now they rebelled. Cosme addressed the assembled pilots. "I think we've had enough losses," he told them. "I believe this operation is a failure.

I don't see any reason to continue the flights. Either they appoint another operations officer or no airplane takes off from Happy Valley with Cubans aboard."

It was 9:45 A.M. The air operations at Happy Valley were over. In four days of combat the exile air force had flown more than thirty-six missions, against overwhelming odds. It had fought an air battle against faster, more maneuverable planes, jets and conventional fighters that were supposed to have been destroyed on the ground.* Its men were weary from lack of rest and sleep.

It had suffered fifty-percent losses—twelve of its twenty-four B-26s were gone. Fourteen pilots had died—ten Cubans and four Americans.

This final day of the invasion found Mario Abril with his battalion west of Giron Beach fighting against the militia as the perimeter was gradually pushed back.

"We stayed there until 1:00 P.M. At that time Erneido Oliva, the battalion commander, he told us everything was real bad and we were doing pretty bad, no support at all from the Americans. We could see the ships and they don't send nothing. He told us to try to run to the hills. He told us he was going that way, to resist until we can do something. So we started walking that way. At Giron Beach I got water, and with a couple of friends of mine, I started running for the woods. That was 3:30, maybe 4:00 P.M.† I was in real bad condition. I started walking toward Cienfuegos. I got friends there and I believed if I could get there I would be saved."

The invasion was over. By 5:30 P.M. Castro's forces were engaged in mopping-up operations at the Bay of Pigs. At the same hour the indignant members of the Cuban

* The exile pilots received no training in defensive tactics, for example, because it was not anticipated that Castro would be left with any planes.
† Several members of the brigade later claimed they saw U.S. jets flying high over the beaches about this hour. This would have been long after the one hour of air cover at dawn ordered by the President, however.

Revolutionary Council, free at last from their Opa-locka confinement, were meeting secretly with Kennedy at the White House. Arthur M. Schlesinger, Jr., the Harvard historian and assistant to the President, and Adolf Berle had flown to Miami during the night to placate the Cuban leaders, after which the Council was flown to Washington for a meeting that was both emotional and difficult. This meeting was not disclosed by the White House until the next day.

In New York, Lem Jones issued two more bulletins for the CIA. The last one regretted that:

> . . . the recent landings in Cuba have been con-
> stantly though inaccurately described as an invasion.
> It was, in fact, a landing mainly of supplies and
> support for our patriots who have been fighting in
> Cuba for months. . . . Regretfully we admit tragic
> losses in today's action among a small holding force
> which courageously fought Soviet tanks and artillery
> while being attacked by Russian Mig aircraft—a gal-
> lantry which allowed the major portion of our landing
> party to reach the Escambray mountains.
> We did not expect to topple Castro immediately or
> without setbacks. And it is certainly true that we did
> not expect to face, unscathed, Soviet armaments di-
> rected by Communist advisers. We did and survived!
> The struggle for the freedom of six million Cubans
> continues!

Mario Abril, together with hundreds of his fellows, was captured the next day. He spent the next year and a half in prison in Havana. He returned to the United States with the rest of the brigade in the prisoner exchange of Christmas, 1962.

Manuel Perez Salvador, of the Fort Lauderdale Braves, lived for ten days on land crabs and muddy water after he had swum ashore from the *Houston*. Giant flies bit his legs, which became infected and swollen. He still bears round black scars the size and shape of kitchen-faucet washers. He and a companion had just found a tin of

Russian canned meat on the beach and were trying to open it when a militia speedboat rounded the bend with a machine gun trained on them. They surrendered. That was how it went for the majority of the brigade.

A few managed to escape in small boats and were later picked up at sea by American Navy and merchant ships. A very few managed to escape through the Cuban underground. Most were captured.

The exile air force fought no more. Its task was over. And yet not quite. Sergio Garcia, the pilot who had refused to drop the wounded young paratrooper over San Blas, was assigned to a final mission.

On the morning of April 20 he flew far out to sea from Happy Valley, carrying thousands of leaflets that had been printed by the CIA. They were packed in special boxes designed to open after leaving the plane. The leaflets were meant to have been dropped over Cuba ahead of the advancing and victorious invaders. They bore such slogans as "Cubans, you will be free!"

Hundreds of miles off the Nicaraguan coast, out of sight of land, Garcia banked and began the last air drop of the Bay of Pigs. The boxes tumbled from the plane, and opened as they were caught by the wind. Garcia watched as the leaflets fluttered into the sea.

5

The Case of the
Birmingham Widows

FOUR WIDOWS whose husbands had died at the Bay of Pigs were living in Birmingham, Alabama, in 1963. During the long, hot summer of that year, Birmingham was a city of fear and violence. But some of the widows lived in a special atmosphere of fear that had nothing to do with the city's racial troubles.

Partly it was because of an unseen hand that sent them, every two weeks, a check for $245. There was danger that if they said too much the same invisible hand might cut the payments off. For one of the widows, Mrs. Margaret H. Ray, a soft-spoken, attractive brunette, these fears were also compounded by talk of lie-detector tests, suspicion that her telephone was being tapped, that she was under surveillance.

The imaginings of a distraught widow alone in the world with her two young children? Perhaps. And then again, perhaps not. For The Case of the Four Birmingham Widows is, in some respects, a twentieth-century tragedy. It is George Orwell and Franz Kafka come true.

The husbands of these four women were Thomas Willard Ray, Leo Francis Baker, Riley W. Shamburger, Jr., and Wade Carroll Gray, the American CIA airmen who had died on April 19, 1961, while flying in combat at the Bay of Pigs.

One key to the mystery of all that has since happened to the widows could be found in a small two-story building on a quiet palm-lined street in Miami Springs, Florida, not far to the north of Miami International Airport. It was, the sign out front proclaimed, the law office of Alex E. Carlson.

Carlson, a big, blond, heavy-set man, towering well over six feet, saw three years of combat during World War II in New Guinea, the Philippines and Okinawa. After the war he got his bachelor's degree in Spanish at the University of Michigan. By 1952 Carlson, then twenty-seven, was finishing law school at the University of Miami. That year he went to Chile on an exchange scholarship. He then returned to Miami and set up practice in Miami Springs. Most of his clients appeared to be obscure airline and air-cargo firms operating out of Miami International Airport.

But Carlson's most intriguing business activity was the Double-Chek Corporation. According to the records of the Florida Secretary of State at Tallahassee this firm was incorporated on May 14, 1959, and "brokerage is the general nature of business engaged in."

The officers of the Double-Chek Corporation, as of 1963, were listed as "Alex E. Carlson, President, 145 Curtiss Parkway, Miami Springs" (the address of Carlson's law office); "Earl Sanders, Vice-President, same address; Margery Carlson, Secretary-Treasurer, same address." The "resident agent" was listed as "Wesley R. Pillsbury," at the same address.

In 1960 the CIA, having been given the green light by President Eisenhower to organize the Cuban exiles, began looking about for American pilots to serve as PIs—pilot instructors. Because the Cubans would be flying the CIA B-26s, the agency wanted Americans who had flown the plane in wartime.

The CIA decided to do its recruiting through Alex E. Carlson and the Double-Chek Corporation. The agency uses cover of this sort when it recruits pilots for a covert operation. To find the pilots, the CIA naturally turned to the Air National Guard in Alabama, Virginia and Arkansas, the last state units to fly the obsolescent B-26.

From these states, some two dozen pilots were signed up by the CIA, acting through Double-Chek. The majority were from Alabama, and, in turn, the bulk of these were from the Birmingham area. The unit's doctor was from Montgomery.

General Reid Doster, the congenial, bulldog-faced commanding officer of the Alabama Air National Guard, was a key man in the CIA operation at Retalhuleu. (Doster had left the CIA and was back running the Alabama Air Guard and its 117th Reconnaissance Wing as of 1963.)

Because the Alabama Air Guard was under the supervision of the 9th Tactical Air Force at Shaw Air Force Base, South Carolina, Doster went to see Major General David W. Hutchinson, the commanding general there.* He asked for a leave of absence for himself and about a dozen of his men in the Alabama National Guard. Hutchinson approved the leaves of absence; the men, including Doster, joined the CIA as civilians.

Each of the American pilots was sworn to secrecy by the CIA, with the exception of Doster, who gave his word as a general officer. All pledged they would never talk about what happened in the training camps or at the Bay of Pigs.

Thomas Willard Ray, age thirty when he died, was born in Birmingham on March 15, 1931. He began dating Margaret Hayden while he was still in Tarrant High School. He served in the Air Force from 1950 to 1952 and was discharged as a staff sergeant.

In December of that year "Pete" Ray joined the Hayes International Corporation, a large aircraft modification company with its main plant at the Birmingham airport. Ray was a technical inspector at Hayes, but he kept up his pilot's proficiency by flying the B-26s and F-84s at the Alabama National Guard.

He married Margaret and they had two children: Thomas, a crew-cut blond-haired boy of eight when his father died, and Janet Joy, six. Five years before the Bay

* Hutchinson later retired from the Air Force and became an oilman in Oklahoma City. He said, on March 8, 1963, that five, not four, American pilots had died flying in the Cuban operation but implied that the fifth pilot was not lost in combat.

of Pigs, the Rays built a handsome brick home in Center Point, a Birmingham suburb.

Ray did not particularly like flying jets, and, with several buddies, he switched to the Army Reserve. He took leave from Hayes, and for one year before he joined the CIA he was on active duty at Fort Rucker, 170 miles south of Birmingham. In January, 1961, Ray received a telephone call. He told his wife he would be leaving to go to a "combined service school."

On February 5, 1961, Mrs. Ray and the children moved into her mother's home in Birmingham. Her husband left the same day. He did not say where he was going. He told his wife she could write to him at this address:

> c/o Joseph Greenland
> Box 7924
> Main Post Office
> Chicago, Illinois

(There was no Joseph Greenland listed in the Chicago telephone book in 1960, 1961 or 1962. The box was a CIA mail drop; the CIA official who selected "Greenland" apparently was unable to resist choosing a code name suggested by the verdant tropical vegetation of the target island.)

Margaret wrote to her husband c/o Joseph Greenland, and he wrote back, with his letters bearing the return address of different Air Force bases. Pete came home only once, on April 10, for a two-day visit; he had a deep suntan. During that time he did not tell his wife what he was doing, but she had begun to piece it together from newspaper stories and her own suspicions. She gave voice to these suspicions.

"If you've learned anything," he told her, "keep your mouth shut, because they are thinking of giving lie-detector tests to the wives." He indicated that "they" might do this in order to check on whether there had been any security leaks from the wives in Birmingham.

On April 15 Margaret was fixing a girl friend's hair at her mother's house when her friend showed her a newspaper telling of the B-26 strike against Cuba. Margaret's hands began to tremble.

Leo Baker, thirty-four at the time of his death, was a native of Boston. A short, dark-haired, handsome man, he was thought to be Italian by many of his friends because of his appearance and the fact that he owned two pizza shops in Birmingham. Actually, he was the son of a French mother and a father who came from Newfoundland.

He entered the Air Force in 1944, served as a flight engineer and was discharged as a technical sergeant. He married, and was divorced. There was one daughter, Teresa. Baker flew in the Korean War, then, on Lincoln's Birthday, 1957, joined Hayes as a flight engineer. He also started a pizza shop in East Lake. The following year an attractive, blue-eyed brunette walked into Leo's Pizza Shop. He hired her on the spot.

Her name was Catherine Walker. Although born in Kentucky, she was raised in Birmingham and was graduated from Woodlawn High School there. They began dating and were married on August 12, 1959. In December, Baker was laid off by the Hayes Company. But he bought a second pizza shop in Homewood. Cathy managed one; Leo the other. He worked hard—he could not abide lazy people—and his small restaurant business prospered.

They had two children: Beth, born April 22, 1960, and Mary, who never saw her father. She was born September 26, 1961, six months after he died.

In January, 1961, Leo Baker went to Boston for his father's funeral. He told Cathy he was expecting a phone call and it came while he was gone. Soon after, late in January, Baker left home. He did not tell Cathy where he was going. But he told her she could write to him c/o Joseph Greenland at the Chicago address.

His return mail came once from Washington, but usually it was postmarked Fort Lauderdale, Florida. One picture post card from that city showed a motel with a tropical-fish pool. One weekend Leo returned to Birmingham carrying a plastic bag full of tropical fish.

During this period Baker told his wife he was dropping

supplies over Cuba and training pilots. Every two or three weeks he came home briefly. Two weeks before Easter he came home for the last time. He arrived on a Saturday and left on a Sunday, and that was the last time Cathy ever saw him.

"Watch the newspapers early in May," were among the parting words he spoke to her.

Cathy believed he then went to Guatemala. She later learned he had won $300 in a poker game in Central America before the invasion. When someone asked if he planned to send the money home, he had replied: "I'm taking it with me to Cuba. I might be able to buy my way out of trouble."

Cathy did not know how much money Leo was paid. But she received $500 a month while he was away.

Riley W. Shamburger, Jr., the oldest of the four fliers, was born in Birmingham on November 17, 1924. He married Marion Jane Graves, his childhood sweetheart. They had dated for twelve years before their marriage, through grammar school and Woodlawn High. After Pearl Harbor, Shamburger quit high school to join the Air Force. (When the war ended he returned and got his diploma.) A combat pilot in World War II and Korea, Shamburger was a big breezy extrovert who loved to fly.

He was a 209-pounder, six feet tall, with 15,000 hours in the air and eighteen years of flying experience by 1961. A test pilot at Hayes, he was also a major in the Alabama Air National Guard, and was its operations officer at the Birmingham airfield. He was also a good friend of General Doster. Shamburger did well; he owned a substantial home in East Lake.

The Shamburgers were part of a beer-and-barbecue, happy-go-lucky crowd of Air Guardsmen and their wives who frequently socialized together. Aside from flying, Riley liked nothing better than to sit in front of the TV set with a case of beer, eating his favorite food, "parched" (roasted) peanuts. And he liked to barbecue pork chops.

Early in 1961 Riley told his wife: "I'm going to be away at school for three months." He did not say where he was going, but about once a week he returned to Birmingham. He and Doster would fly in together.

Sometimes they would bring news of other Birmingham acquaintances—such as Colonel Joe Shannon—who were part of the mysterious operation. Once, when Riley returned for a visit, he told how the boys had rigged up a beer joint in Central America named after their favorite bar in Birmingham. Over the makeshift saloon a pair of red panties flew in the breeze as a cocktail flag.

Shortly before the invasion, Marion sent Riley a present —a whole cigar box full of parched peanuts.

Wade Carroll Gray, born in Birmingham on March 1, 1928, and thirty-three when he died, had also once been employed at Hayes, as a radio and electronics technician. (But he had been laid off in 1960). He married his pretty wife, Violet, on December 14, 1946. They settled down in Pinson, a suburb where Wade had lived all of his life. They had no children.

Gray left home on February 5, 1961, the same day that Pete Ray said good-bye to Margaret. He told his wife that he was going to Texas to test planes. He said the project was secret and that he could say no more.

He first returned home for a visit in early March, 1961. He, too, told his wife to write c/o Joseph Greenland. Some of the letters Violet Gray wrote were returned to her with her husband's effects after his death. Among these effects were matchbooks indicating he had been in both Guatemala and Nicaragua.

This, then, is the background of the four Americans, and of how they came to be in Happy Valley on Wednesday, April 19, 1961. On that day all four volunteered to fly B-26s over the beaches to relieve the exhausted Cuban pilots.

What happened has already been described: Shortly before they took off, the four CIA fliers were told they would receive air support from the carrier-based Navy jets. (The word had been flashed to Happy Valley by Richard Bissell after the President authorized the unmarked Navy jets to fly for one hour at dawn.) Because of the mix-up over time zones, the B-26s got to the Bay of Pigs after the Navy jets had already gone.

Exactly how the two planes were shot down is a subject of varying accounts, but most versions agree that Shamburger and Gray crashed at sea and that Ray and Baker crashed inland.*

Some evidence that Ray and Baker did crash on Cuban soil was provided by Havana radio on the morning of April 19. At 10:30 A.M. Havana time (9:30 A.M. Nicaragua time), Radio Havana broadcast:

"We give you official government communiqué No. 3. The participation of the United States in the aggression against Cuba was dramatically proved this morning, when our anti-aircraft batteries brought down a U.S. military plane piloted by a U.S. airman, who was bombing the civilian population and our infantry forces in the area of the Australia Central [a sugar mill].

"The attacking U.S. pilot, whose body is in the hands of the revolutionary forces, was named Leo Francis Bell. His documents reveal his flight license number, 08323-LM, which expires 24 December 1962. His social security card is numbered 014-07-6921. His motor vehicle registration was issued to 100 Nassau Street, Boston 14, Massachusetts. The registered address of the Yankee pilot is 48 Beacon Street, Boston. His height is five feet six inches." (This was Baker's height.)

A Havana wire-service dispatch identified the pilot as Leo Francis Berliss. Another story had it as Berle.

In Oklahoma City the Federal Aviation Agency said it had no record at its headquarters there of the pilot's license as reported by Havana. The numbering system, the FAA added, "isn't like that." Reporters in Boston who checked the Beacon Street address found an apartment house. None of the residents had ever heard of Leo Francis

---

* Albert C. Persons, managing editor of the weekly Birmingham *Examiner*, said on March 8, 1963, that the plane carrying Shamburger and Gray was shot down by a T-33 jet. Persons was one of the American pilots at Happy Valley. He had been scheduled to fly in Shamburger's bomber. Doster canceled his mission because Persons had experience flying carrier aircraft rather than the B-26.

85

Berliss. The State Department in Washington said it had no one by that name in either the civilian or military branch of the government.

What Castro had in his hands, of course, was Leo Baker's CIA-prepared credentials, made out with a fake last name. (CIA clandestine officers frequently have bogus papers; some possess three or four United States passports issued under different names.) Presumably, the papers were recovered from Baker's body after the bomber crashed inland.

One week later, on April 26, Margaret Ray received a visit from Thomas F. McDowell, a Birmingham lawyer who was the law partner of Frank M. Dixon, a former governor of Alabama. McDowell was accompanied by another man. They told Mrs. Ray that it was believed her husband had been lost at sea in a C-46 transport plane. They asked her to tell no one. They indicated there was a slim chance he might still be alive.

For the next week Margaret Ray went about her normal life, going to church, to the PTA, to the supermarket. On Wednesday, May 3, she was again visited by McDowell. This time he brought with him a big blond man he introduced as an attorney from Miami. His name was Alex E. Carlson.

They repeated to Mrs. Ray the story about the C-46, but on this visit they said there was no longer any hope that her husband was alive. Carlson said he would tell the same story to the Birmingham newspapers the next day.

Carlson and McDowell visited Margaret for about thirty minutes at her mother's home. Then they left. Margaret hinted to them that she did not believe their story.

On Thursday, May 4, Carlson held a press conference in Birmingham. He announced that the four fliers were missing and presumed dead after their C-46 had left on a cargo mission from an airstrip somewhere in Central America. Carlson said he was an attorney representing the Double-Chek Corporation of Miami. He said Double-Chek had put some anti-Castro Cubans in touch with the fliers early in April. Carlson did not say whether the four had flown in the invasion.

"They were told to use the radio only in case of an emergency," said Carlson. "Then they reported one engine had gone out and they were losing altitude. That was the last they have been heard from."

He said the Double-Chek Corporation had contacted the four on behalf of an organization which requested that its identity remain confidential. "But it is presumed to be an exiled group of Cubans," said Carlson. He said that Double-Chek had hired the four at a monthly salary to fly cargo.

"These men knew what they were getting into," he added. "It was a calculated risk. If they came back, they had a nice nest egg."

To cover its role, the CIA was willing to imply that the four dead Americans were mercenaries. Their reputations were expendable.

The widows were embittered at Carlson's words.

"Riley wasn't a soldier of fortune," Mrs. Shamburger said. "He didn't do this for the money. He was a test pilot at Hayes, and was paid a good salary there. He was an operations officer for the Air National Guard. He held two jobs because he wanted us to have things. I have a maid twice a week. I wear furs. You see the things we have in the house."

Mrs. Gray told a newspaper interviewer her husband was no soldier of fortune either. She said he was paid $1,990 a month during the short period of time he was away. She said she, too, had been visited by Carlson. "He said my husband was dead and to start life anew. He said they had spotted one of the plane's engines floating in the water. I didn't think engines floated."

"They knew what they were getting into, but I didn't," said Cathy Baker.

Three days after he returned to Miami, Carlson told the press he was sure the C-46 had been flying a support mission for the Cuban invasion. But he said the mission was not connected with the main exile organization, the Democratic Revolutionary Front.

"There are many so-called fronts and wealthy individuals, all anxious to do their part," he announced. "This was a small group." Carlson's partner in Double-Chek, Raymond W. Cox, told Miami newsmen that the corporation originally was formed to buy a race horse. He said he knew nothing about any fliers.

Shortly after Carlson's appearance in Birmingham in May, 1961, mysterious checks began arriving for the four widows. At first the checks were issued by the Hialeah-Miami Springs Bank and were signed by Carlson. Soon afterward there was a change, and the checks began coming from the Bankers Trust Company of New York. They came every two weeks. The first fifty-two payments were $225 each. Later they were increased to $245, or a bit more than $6,000 a year for each of the widows. The checks from Bankers Trust were simply signed by an officer of the bank. They were drawn on a trust fund set up at the bank. But there was no indication of where the money came from.

However, it is quite obvious that it came from the CIA. On May 17, 1961, Carlson wrote to Cathy Baker on his law-office letterhead. He enclosed a cashier's check for $1,990 and wrote:

Double Check [sic] Corporation has decided to extend the regular monthly salary through the 4th day of June, 1961, but is regretably [sic] convinced of the finality of your husband's fate. Nevertheless, beginning June 5th, on a monthly basis, you will receive regular benefit allotments, as provided for by your husband's employment contract.

Again let me express my sincere feelings of condolance [sic] in your time of bereavement, and should you have any questions or problems, please feel free to call upon our attorneys in Birmingham for help.
Very truly yours, Alex E. Carlson,
Attorney for Double-Check [sic]

Peculiarly, Carlson seemed unsure both in this letter and in numerous public statements of whether the firm of which he was president was called Double-Check (as he wrote to Mrs. Baker) or Double-Chek, as it was incorporated in the State of Florida.

By "our attorneys in Birmingham," Carlson meant McDowell, who continued to act as a sort of self-appointed overseer of the widows' affairs. McDowell was able to obtain death certificates for the four fliers; he kept them in his safe in Room 533 of the Frank Nelson Building in downtown Birmingham. The widows were under the impression that McDowell had a background in Navy Intelligence, and believed he had something to do with the checks that they receive.

As this surrealistic chain of events unfolded, Riley Shamburger's mother began to try to do something about it. Riley's father was a retired city fireman, a semi-invalid who moved about their Birmingham home in a wheel chair. But Riley's mother, who refused to believe her son was dead, carried on an energetic correspondence with the Federal Government. She did her best to find out what had happened to her son. She even wrote to the Swiss Government, which handled affairs for the United States in Cuba after the break in diplomatic relations between Washington and Havana.

Mrs. Shamburger began by writing to the State Department. She received a reply, dated August 11, 1961, from Denman F. Stanfield, the acting chief of the Protection and Representation Division. It said:

> Reference is made to your letter of July 9, 1961, concerning the welfare and whereabouts of your son.
>
> If you will provide your son's full name, date and place of birth, last known address here or abroad, and any other pertinent information that would assist in locating him, the Department would be pleased to make inquiries.

A few weeks later she received a letter, dated September 14, 1961, from Major Sidney Ormerod, United States Air Force, Division of Administrative Services. This one was briskly efficient:

> (1) Your letters to the Department of State concerning your son have been referred to me for reply.

89

(2) The records in this office do not contain the circumstances surrounding your son's accident. At the time he was not on active duty in his military status.

(3) For more detailed information it is suggested you contact the Hayes Aircraft Corp.,* Birmingham, Alabama, since he was under their jurisdiction at the time in question.

(4) I regret that I was unable to be of assistance to you in this matter.

The letter was deceptive. Hayes Aircraft is a private corporation and has no one under its "jurisdiction." At "the time in question" Riley Shamburger was flying for the CIA. He was certainly not testing aircraft for Hayes over the Bay of Pigs.

A lesser woman might have been discouraged by this, but Mrs. Shamburger was not. The following year she wrote to John McCone. She received a letter in reply, dated July 14, 1962, on CIA stationary and signed by Marshall S. Carter, Lieutenant General, United States Army, Acting Director. It said:

In Mr. McCone's absence, I am replying to your letter of June, 1962, requesting information concerning your son. I am sorry to disappoint you, but this agency is unable to furnish you any such information. Also, we have made inquiries of other government departments, and these, too, have no pertinent information.

We have every sympathy for you in your natural concern for the fate of your son, and I am sorry as I can be that we cannot help. Please be assured that if at any time we are able to furnish information we will contact you promptly.

Still Mrs. Shamburger did not give up. She decided to go

* Hayes was not notably communicative. When one of the authors asked for information about the background of the four men, who had worked for the company for many years, a Hayes public-relations spokesman said he would have to check with "topside." After doing so, he said he could give out no information. "The matter is closed as far as we are concerned," he said.

to the very top. She wrote to the President of the United States. On October 4, 1962, Brigadier General Godfrey T. McHugh, the Air Force aide to the President, wrote back. His letter expressed sympathy and said in part:

If any information is ever obtained on the circumstances surrounding the loss of your son, you will be informed immediately. Unfortunately, at present neither CIA nor any other government agency possesses the slightest pertinent information on your son's disappearance.

Riley Shamburger's mother was determined to keep trying. "I am not going to give up," she said. "They take your boy away and never let you know what happened."

Mrs. Shamburger's correspondence with Washington, of course, was going on behind the scenes. After the brief flurry of publicity right after the Bay of Pigs, the story of the four missing Americans dropped out of the news for almost two years—until it reappeared dramatically on February 25, 1963.

On that date Senator Everett McKinley Dirksen, Illinois Republican and minority leader of the Senate, revealed that four American fliers had been killed at the Bay of Pigs. He said he had learned this in the course of a one-man inquiry into the Cuban invasion.

Dirksen's disclosure was extremely embarrassing for the Kennedy Administration. In the first place, on April 12, 1961, five days before the invasion, President Kennedy had said: "This government will do everything it possibly can, and I think it can meet its responsibilities, to make sure that there are no Americans involved in any actions inside Cuba."

In the second place, on January 21, 1963, Attorney General Robert F. Kennedy, the President's brother, had said in an interview with David Kraslow of the Knight newspapers that no Americans died at the Bay of Pigs.

Robert Kennedy, in this interview and a similar one with *U.S. News & World Report*, said something else of greater, and historical, significance: a ranking official of the government for the first time admitted clearly, and on the record, that the Bay of Pigs was a United States operation, planned by the Joint Chiefs of Staff and the CIA. "The President had to give approval to the plan," [1] Robert Kennedy said. The Joint Chiefs "did approve it, although responsibility for the planning lay primarily with the CIA." *

After Dirksen's statement, newsmen sought out the elder Mrs. Shamburger. "If no Americans were involved," she said, with obvious reference to statements by President Kennedy and Robert Kennedy, "where is my son?"

She said she had written to the President about her son "but he evaded my question."

The White House was alarmed. Andrew T. Hatcher, the assistant presidential press secretary, issued a statement. General McHugh had answered Mrs. Shamburger's letter, Hatcher explained.

"At the direction of the President," he said, "the general extended the President's heartfelt sympathy and explained that the government had, unfortunately, no information to add to that which had been conveyed to Mrs. Shamburger before.

"We are informed that representatives of the organization which employed Mr. Shamburger reported her son's death, and as much as is known of the circumstances, to Mrs. Shamburger in the spring of 1962."

However, the White House carefully did not make public the actual text of its letter to Mrs. Shamburger, in which McHugh had assured her that "at present neither CIA nor any other government agency possesses the slightest pertinent information on your son's disappearance."

Senator Mike Mansfield, the Democratic leader of the Senate, tried to blunt Dirksen's political thrust. He noted that Carlson's announcement in Birmingham on May 4, 1961 (the false cover story about the C-46) had been carried at the time (as a four-paragraph item) in the *New*

---

* Prior to this, the clearest statement by the administration was made by President Kennedy in an interview with the three major TV networks on December 17, 1962. Speaking in general terms of the 1961 Cuban invasion, the President said: "And I was responsible."

York Times. There was nothing new about the story, Mansfield declared. He also said that a few, selected members of Congress had been told at the time that four Americans were killed in the invasion; but Mansfield said he did not know how the fliers met their deaths.

On March 4, 1963, following Dirksen's disclosure, Carlson told newsmen who inquired about the widows' checks that a "Central American group authorized Double-Chek to set up a trust fund for payments in case the men died. Now the widows receive these disbursements."

Then Carlson backed away from his "nest egg" remark of two years earlier. The four men, he said, "never were considered soldiers of fortune. They knew they were going into hazardous duty, involving anti-Castro tasks, but were motivated both by their beliefs and by attractive compensation."

Two days later, on March 6, the administration, under pressure, finally made its first oblique admission about the real role of the four airmen. At a press conference that day, this exchange took place with President Kennedy:

Q. Mr. President, can you say whether the four Americans who died in the Bay of Pigs invasion were employees of the government or the CIA?

A. Well, I would say that there are a good many Americans in the last fifteen years who have served their country in a good many different ways, a good many abroad. Some of them have lost their lives. The United States Government has not felt that it was helpful to our interest, and particularly in the struggle against this armed doctrine with which we are in struggle all around the world, to go into great detail. Let me say just about these four men: They were serving their country. The flight that cost them their lives was a volunteer flight, and that while because of the nature of their work it has not been a matter of public record, as it might be in the case of soldiers or sailors, I can say that they were serving their country. As I say, their work was volunteer.

The administration found itself in an awkward dilemma. It could not admit very much more about the four fliers because to do so would be to admit that it had misled Mrs. Shamburger and had kept the truth from the American public.

And if it opened up the record on the four fliers, this would lead directly to questions about why the carrier-based Navy jets and the B-26s, in which four Americans died, had not arrived over the beaches together.

This, in turn, would raise the question of why the President, having stated on April 12, 1961, that "United States armed forces" would not be used "under any conditions," relented seven days later to the extent of permitting one hour of air support by the unmarked Navy jets.

In March of 1963, the case of the four CIA fliers, in short, held the key to a host of explosively difficult questions for the White House. But these were political questions. Suppression of information about the fliers was justifiable only if national security was involved. And it no longer was.

The need for security *before* the Bay of Pigs operation was understandable, once the President had committed himself to the invasion. It might be argued that in the immediate aftermath of the invasion it was still necessary to protect the position of the United States by fuzzing up the role of the fliers. But once the role of the United States and the CIA was freely and publicly conceded by Robert Kennedy in the two interviews in 1963, it is difficult to see how security could any longer have been a factor in cloaking the story of the four Birmingham fliers.

The administration was locked in with its previous denials to Mrs. Shamburger. It had already informed her, in writing, that it knew nothing about her son. And who could tell how much of this damaging correspondence the elderly lady might choose to reveal?

As for Carlson, he was still sticking to his script. In a private interview in Miami Springs in the summer of 1963, he said that he continued to feel the four men were, basically, flying for money. He pulled out a thick file, and, consulting it, said that Shamburger and Ray had been paid $2,200 a month, Gray $1,500 and Baker $1,700.

"Double-Chek was contacted back in 1960 by a Central

American front," Carlson explained. But a moment later he said the "recruiters," whom he refused to identify, "appeared to be American businessmen." They had been recommended to him, Carlson said, by "someone at the Miami airport," whom he declined to identify.

Carlson said Double-Chek had originally been formed to hold real estate for a client. "I was listed as president to protect the identity of my client." The client, he said, "came from Czechoslovakia and that's where he got the idea for the name." (Carlson allowed as how Cox's story about a race horse was just a bit of "jazz.")

"The recruiters," said Carlson, "came to me and said they wanted pilots for the airline business, and did I have a corporation to use. I checked through my files and found the Double-Chek Corporation. They wanted to use the corporate shell as a broker or a sort of placement agency."

Double-Chek then proceeded to recruit pilots for the "Central American front," he said. Next thing he knew, said Carlson, he got a telephone call from Central America and was told that a C-46 cargo plane had gone down with the four men. Would he please go to Birmingham and notify the widows? Carlson obliged.

Carlson professed to know nothing about the source of the money for the widows' checks. He said that at first "Double-Chek had an account at the Hialeah-Miami Springs bank and I was the authorized signator." After that, he said, the "trust account" was established at Bankers Trust in New York. "I believe there is a lump sum set up there and the interest is what's paying the ladies."

And it was true that the checks continued to come from New York. But that was all the widows had.

Three years after the Bay of Pigs the Birmingham widows had still received no official acknowledgment from the United States Government about their husbands. There had been no written notification to the wives that their husbands died while employed by, and fighting for, the United States. They had nothing official to show their children to explain their fathers' deaths.

6

A History

THE INVISIBLE GOVERNMENT was born December 7, 1941, in the smoke and rubble of Pearl Harbor. It was still a child when the Cold War began after World War II, an adolescent during the 1950s, and it reached its majority a year after President Kennedy took office.

Whatever else the multitude of inquiries into Pearl Harbor proved, they did show that the United States was badly in need of a centralized intelligence apparatus. There were plenty of warning signs before Pearl Harbor of the coming Japanese attack, but they were not pulled together, analyzed and brought forcefully to the attention of the government.

"The CIA," the Hoover Commission said in 1955, "may well attribute its existence to the surprise attack on Pearl Harbor and to the postwar investigation into the part Intelligence or lack of Intelligence played in the failure of our military forces to receive adequate and prompt warning of the impending Japanese attack."

The United States shed its isolationist traditions and emerged from World War II as the leader of the West. Regardless of Pearl Harbor, its new global responsibilities and objectives would have, in any event, led to the creation of a global American intelligence network. Added to this, the early emergence of the Soviet Union as an adversary almost before the V-J celebrations had ended made the growth of an Invisible Government in the United States virtually inevitable.

Even in the absence of a clash between Western democracy and international Communism, the conduct of United States foreign policy in the postwar world would have required intelligence information upon which the policy makers could base their decisions.

This was stated in characteristic style by President Truman in 1952. On November 21, shortly after President Eisenhower's election, Truman stole away from the White House to deliver a talk behind closed doors at a CIA training session.

"It was my privilege a few days ago," Truman said, "to brief the general, who is going to take over the office on the twentieth of January, and he was rather appalled at all that the President needs to know in order to reach decisions —even domestic decisions." The modern presidency, Truman declared, carried power beyond parallel in history, more power than that of Genghis Khan, Caesar, Napoleon or Louis XIV.

No central intelligence organization existed when he became President in 1945, Truman continued. "Whenever it was necessary for the President to have information, he had to send to two or three departments . . . and then he would have to have somebody do a little digging to get it.

"The affairs of the presidential office, so far as information was concerned, were in such shape that it was necessary for me, when I took over the office, to read a stack of documents that high [gesturing], and it took me three months to get caught up."

President Roosevelt had been concerned about the same problem. In 1940 he sent William J. Donovan, then a New York attorney, on an informal intelligence-gathering mission to England, the Mediterranean and the Balkans. "Wild Bill" Donovan returned with the information Roosevelt wanted—and a recommendation that a central intelligence organization be established.

Out of this emerged the Office of Coordinator of Information, with General Donovan as its head. On June 13, 1942, this was split into the Office of Strategic Services, under Donovan, and the Office of War Information. The function of the OSS was to gather intelligence, but it first became famous by dropping parachutists behind enemy lines in France, Norway, Italy, Burma and Thailand, setting a pattern of combining special operations with information-gathering that is still followed by the CIA.

By 1944 Donovan had prepared for Roosevelt a plan to establish a central intelligence agency. It was referred to the Joint Chiefs, and pigeonholed. But after Truman became President (and dug his way out from under the stack of papers he later complained about) he sent for Admiral William D. Leahy and asked him to look into the whole problem.

In the meantime Truman issued an order, on September 20, 1945, disbanding the OSS. Some of the OSS agents went into Army Intelligence. Others were transferred to the State Department. There they formed the nucleus of what became the Bureau of Intelligence and Research, an important branch of the Invisible Government.

Four months after the OSS closed up shop, Truman, on January 22, 1946, issued an executive order setting up a National Intelligence Authority and, under it, a Central Intelligence Group, which became the forerunner of the CIA. The Authority's members were Secretary of State James F. Byrnes, Secretary of War Robert P. Patterson, Secretary of the Navy James V. Forrestal and Admiral Leahy. The Central Intelligence Group was the Authority's operating arm. To head it, Truman selected Rear Admiral Sidney W. Souers, the deputy chief of Navy Intelligence. Souers had been a businessman in St. Louis before the war; the nation's first Director of Central Intelligence once headed the Piggly Wiggly Stores in Memphis.

Souers was anxious to get back to his business interests, and five months later, in June, Truman named Air Force General Hoyt S. Vandenberg to the post. He served until May 1, 1947, when Truman appointed Rear Admiral Roscoe H. Hillenkoetter. An Annapolis graduate who spoke three languages, Hillenkoetter had several years' experience in Navy Intelligence. He had been wounded while aboard the battleship *West Virginia* at Pearl Harbor. Later he set up an intelligence network for Admiral Chester W. Nimitz in the Pacific.

When the CIA was created by the National Security Act of 1947, Hillenkoetter became its first director. The CIA came into being officially on September 18, 1947. The Act is the same as that which established a Department of Defense and unified the armed services. It also created the National Security Council * and, under it, the CIA.

The duties of the CIA were set forth in five short paragraphs:

"(1) to advise the National Security Council in matters concerning such intelligence activities of the government departments and agencies as relate to national security;

"(2) to make recommendations to the National Security Council for the co-ordination of such intelligence activities . . . ;

"(3) to correlate and evaluate intelligence relating to the national security, and provide for the appropriate dissemination of such intelligence within the government. . . . *Provided* that the Agency shall have no police, subpena, law-enforcement powers, or internal-security functions . . . ;

"(4) to perform, for the benefit of the existing intelligence agencies, such additional services of common concern as the National Security Council determines can be more efficiently accomplished centrally;

"(5) to perform such other functions and duties related to intelligence affecting the national security as the National Security Council may from time to time direct."

On the face of it, the law appeared simply to give the CIA the task of correlating, evaluating and co-ordinating the collection of intelligence. How, then, could the CIA mount an invasion of 1,400 men at the Bay of Pigs, complete with its own air force and navy? How could it topple foreign governments, as it has done and was attempting to do at the Bay of Pigs?

* As constituted in 1964 the NSC was composed of the President, the Vice-President, the Secretary of State, the Secretary of Defense and the Director of the Office of Emergency Planning.

The answer lies in the "other functions" which the CIA may perform under the 1947 Act, at the discretion of the National Security Council.

Almost from its inception, the agency has engaged in special operations—clandestine activities, sometimes on a military scale. In 1948, after the Communist take-over in Czechoslovakia, James Forrestal, as the first Secretary of Defense, became alarmed at signs that the Communists might win the Italian elections. In an effort to influence the elections to the advantage of the United States, he started a campaign among his wealthy Wall Street colleagues to raise enough money to run a private clandestine operation. But Allen Dulles felt the problem could not be handled effectively in private hands. He urged strongly that the government establish a covert organization to conduct a variety of special operations.

Because there was no specific provision for covert political operations spelled out in the 1947 Act, the National Security Council—in the wake of the events in Czechoslovakia and Italy—issued a paper in the summer of 1948 authorizing special operations. There were two important guide lines: that the operations be secret and that they be plausibly deniable by the government.

A decision was reached to create an organization within the CIA to conduct secret political operations. Frank G. Wisner, an ex-OSS man, was brought in from the State Department to head it, with a cover title of his own invention. He became Assistant Director of the Office of Policy Coordination.

Under this innocuous title, the United States was now fully in the business of covert political operations. (A separate Office of Special Operations conducted secret actions aimed solely at gathering intelligence.) This machinery was in the CIA but the agency shared control of it with the State Department and the Pentagon. On January 4, 1951, the CIA merged the two offices and created a new Plans Division, which has had sole control over secret operations of all types since that date.

It is doubtful that many of the lawmakers who voted for the 1947 Act could have envisioned the scale on which the

CIA would engage in operational activities all over the world.

President Truman later maintained that he had no idea that this was going to happen. In a syndicated newspaper article, date-lined December 21, 1963, he wrote:

"For some time I have been disturbed by the way CIA has been diverted from its original assignment. It has become an operational and at times a policy-making arm of the government. . . .

"I never had any thought that when I set up the CIA that it would be injected into peacetime cloak-and-dagger operations. Some of the complications and embarrassment that I think we have experienced are in part attributable to the fact that this quiet intelligence arm of the President has been so removed from its intended role that it is being interpreted as a symbol of sinister and mysterious foreign intrigue—and a subject for cold war enemy propaganda." [1]

It was under President Truman, however, that the CIA began conducting special operations.

Although the machinery was not established until 1948, one small hint of what was to come was tucked away in a memorandum which Allen Dulles submitted to Congress back in 1947. It said the CIA should "have exclusive jurisdiction to carry out secret intelligence operations." [2]

Like the Commerce Clause of the Constitution, the "other functions" proviso of the National Security Act has been stretched to encompass activities by the CIA that are not even hinted at in the law. It is not generally realized that the CIA conducts secret political warfare under interpretations of that law. Nor is it widely understood that under the law and subsequent presidential fiat, the Director of the Central Intelligence Agency wears two hats. Not only is he the head of the CIA, but more important, as Director of Central Intelligence he is in charge of the entire intelligence community, of which the CIA is only one, albeit the most powerful, branch.

In 1949 the Central Intelligence Agency Act was passed, exempting the CIA from all Federal laws that required the disclosure of the "functions, names, official titles, salaries, or numbers of personnel employed by the Agency."

And it gave the Director of Central Intelligence the staggering and unprecedented power to spend money "without regard to the provisions of law and regulations relating to the expenditure of government funds." It granted him the unique right to spend the hundreds of millions of dollars in his secret annual budget simply by signing his name. The law allowed "such expenditures to be accounted for solely on the certificate of the director." That and that alone, the law said, "shall be deemed a sufficient voucher." *

Senator Millard E. Tydings, the Maryland Democrat who was chief sponsor of the 1949 Act, explained why he felt it was necessary: "Men in this agency frequently lose their lives. Several have already done so, and under not very pretty circumstances. If we forced the agency to have a record of vouchers, foreign agents could pick up information as to the identity of our agents and what they were doing." [3]

By 1950 the broader outlines of the Invisible Government had begun to take shape, with the CIA at its center. In that year the Intelligence Advisory Committee was created as a board of directors of the covert government. Later its name was changed to the present United States Intelligence Board. Although the names of the men (and of some of the agencies) represented on the board have changed, the main components of the secret government have remained fairly constant. Its overall size, of course, has increased vastly.

Code-breaking and cryptology were consolidated in 1952 in the new National Security Agency, established by presidential directive as part of the Defense Department. And, finally, the military intelligence agencies were brought together under the newly created Defense Intelligence Agency in 1961. But these were essentially administrative reorganizations. What has really changed since 1947 is not the general amorphous shape of the Invisible Government, but its size, technology, scope, power and importance— all of which have increased in geometric progression with

* The 1949 Act also allowed the CIA director to bring in 100 aliens a year secretly and outside of normal immigration laws.

a minimum of Congressional or public examination or understanding.

During the first three years of the CIA's life Admiral Hillenkoetter remained its director. He was replaced at a critical moment in the Korean War by General Walter Bedell Smith, Eisenhower's Chief of Staff during World War II, a former Ambassador to Moscow and the first four-star general in the U. S. Army who was never graduated from West Point or any other military school.

The agency became more aggressive under "Beedle" Smith, who played an important role in the Korean conflict and its intelligence post-mortems. But from the start, the man who placed his personal stamp upon the Invisible Government more than any other was Allen Welsh Dulles.

Dulles was consulted when Congress created the CIA in 1947. The next year Truman named him to head the three-man committee to see how well the new agency was working.*

Dulles submitted the report to Truman after his re-election. In 1950 General Smith summoned Dulles to Washington. He came, expecting, he often said later, to stay six weeks. Instead, he remained eleven years. On August 23, 1951, Dulles was appointed deputy director.

Soon after President Eisenhower was elected, he appointed Smith as Under Secretary of State and on February 10, 1953, named Dulles as Director of Central Intelligence. He took office sixteen days later. Up to that point two admirals and two generals had held the job. Dulles became the first truly civilian director of the CIA.

To the post he brought a brilliant reputation as the wartime OSS chief in Switzerland. Perhaps even more important, his brother was Secretary of State. The emergence of the Invisible Government in the 1950s to a position of unprecedented strength cannot be comprehended unless a word is said about the Dulles brothers and

* The other two members were William H. Jackson, New York investment banker, a wartime intelligence officer and the managing director of J. H. Whitney & Co.; and Mathias F. Correa, a former OSS man and a special assistant to Forrestal. Jackson later became the deputy director of the CIA.

their relationship. Uniquely, they embodied the dualism—and indeed the moral dilemma—of United States foreign policy since World War II.

John Foster Dulles and his younger brother were the sons of Allen Macy Dulles, a Presbyterian clergyman in upstate Watertown, New York. Allen Dulles was born there on April 7, 1893.

Some thought they detected traces of a clergyman's zeal in the sternly moralistic public posture of Foster Dulles as he conducted the nation's foreign policy during the Eisenhower years: the United States would contain the advance of international Communism as it sought to subvert the underdeveloped nations; but America would scrupulously avoid any interference in the internal affairs of other countries. The United States would not, in short, adopt the evil tactics of subversion and secret manipulation practiced by the Communist enemy.

In this, Foster Dulles reflected the American ethic; the world as we would like it to be. While he took this public position, his brother was free to deal with nastier realities, to overturn governments and to engage in backstage political maneuvers all over the globe with the CIA's almost unlimited funds. He was, as Allen Dulles once put it, able to "fight fire with fire" [4] in a less than perfect world. Because he was equally dedicated in his own secret sphere, it was under Allen Dulles' stewardship that the CIA enjoyed its greatest expansion, particularly in the field of government-shaking secret operations overseas.

In pursuing this dual foreign policy, these special operations were largely kept secret from the American people. The exception, of course, was when something went wrong, as at the Bay of Pigs.

This is not to say that the same two-sided foreign policy would never have evolved had the director of the CIA and the Secretary of State not been brothers. It very likely would have. But the natural friction between the objectives and methods of the diplomats and the "spooks," between the State Department and the CIA, was to an extent reduced because of the close working relationship of the

Dulles brothers.* There was consequently less of a check and balance.

In a sense, one might say the Dulles brothers were predestined to take over the levers of power in the conduct of U. S. foreign affairs. Their mother's father, John Watson Foster, was Secretary of State under Benjamin Harrison† in 1892-3. Robert Lansing, an uncle by marriage, was Secretary of State under Woodrow Wilson. Another uncle, John Welsh, was Minister to England under Rutherford B. Hayes.‡ With such a heritage, it is not surprising that Foster and Allen were weaned on a diet of heady discussions of the affairs of state.

Allen Dulles was educated at Auburn, New York, Paris and Princeton. He taught English for a time in an agricultural school in Allahabad, India, and in China and Japan as well. Then he joined the diplomatic service in 1916, serving in Vienna and, during the war, in Berne, chiefly as an intelligence officer. Three years later the two brothers were together in Paris as staff members of the American delegation to the Versailles Peace Conference. Their uncle, Secretary of State Lansing, was a member of the delegation. The following year Allen Dulles married Clover Todd, the daughter of a Columbia University professor. (They had a son, Allen Macy, and two daughters, Clover Todd and Joan.)

In 1926, after service in Berlin, Constantinople and

---

* Some evidence of the closeness of Foster and Allen Dulles was provided even after the Secretary of State had died. President Kennedy had been thinking of changing the name of Washington's new jetport from Dulles, so designated in honor of Foster, to Chantilly, which is the name of the Virginia community where it is located. Under this plan the main building would still have been called the "Dulles Terminal." Allen Dulles and his sister, Eleanor Lansing Dulles, a former official in the German section of the State Department, heard about it and raised hob with the President. Kennedy called it Dulles Airport.
† And later a private adviser to the Empress of China, Tz'u Hsi.
‡ Welsh earned this ministerial plum in an odd way. President Hayes had assured Senator Simon Cameron of Pennsylvania (who had been in Lincoln's Cabinet during the Civil War) that he would appoint anyone Pennsylvania wanted to the London post. Cameron promptly named his father. Hayes, annoyed, appointed Welsh instead.

Washington, Allen Dulles left the world of diplomacy to begin a fifteen-year period of law practice with his brother in the Wall Street firm of Sullivan and Cromwell. As an international lawyer, he knew the political and industrial elite of Europe, and of Germany. This became useful during World War II when General Donovan assigned Dulles as chief of the OSS mission in Switzerland. He had diplomatic cover as an assistant to the minister in the American Legation. But he operated as a master spy from a fifteenth-century house in Berne overlooking the Aar River.

He has been credited with two outstanding feats for the OSS—first, penetrating the German *Abwehr*, Hitler's intelligence service, and second, negotiating the surrender of German troops in Italy.

After the war it was natural enough that Allen Dulles would soon gravitate away from his law practice into the more exciting world of espionage. While it is impossible to make any definite judgment about the talents of a man who operated, for the most part, out of view, the constant and bitter personal attacks upon him by the Communist bloc provide one significant indication of his effectiveness. He certainly bothered them.

The CIA director projected a deceptively grandfatherly image, with his white hair, rimless glasses, his pipe and his sense of humor. There was no official in Washington more charming. Beneath this outward Mr. Chips demeanor was a man fascinated by the world of intelligence, by secret operations and by espionage and all of its ramifications. Although he seemed to fumble a good deal with his pipe and his tobacco, Mr. Dulles perhaps quietly enjoyed the incongruousness of his appearance and his vocation. He was not without a sense of the dramatic.

Dulles was occasionally accused of being too much of a public figure for the head of a secret service. And in 1955 a Hoover Commission task force criticized him for having "taken upon himself too many burdensome duties and responsibilities on the operational side of CIA activities."

"Allen," commented one CIA associate, "couldn't administer himself."

But if the CIA was run in a tweedy, relaxed, pipe-and-slipper manner under Dulles, it was also true that morale was high, and he was well liked within the agency as well as outside of it.

Except for his closest friends, few people knew of the great personal tragedy in Dulles' life. His son, wounded in Korea, suffered brain damage that left him with very little recognition of people or events, and it was finally necessary to place him in an institution in Germany on Lake Constance, just over the Swiss border.

For most of the nine years that Dulles headed the intelligence community, he worked with the same three assistants at the CIA:

Charles Pearre Cabell, a gray-haired but youthful-looking four-star Air Force general and West Point graduate, was his deputy director. A Texan from Dallas (where his brother Earle was the mayor), he was the former head of Air Force Intelligence. He came to the CIA in 1953.

Richard Bissell, the deputy director for plans, who joined the CIA in 1954.

Robert Amory, the brother of the writer Cleveland Amory, and a former Harvard Law School professor. A tall, dark-haired man, he had intelligence and combat experience in World War II. He became the CIA's deputy director for intelligence in 1953.

This was the group which led the CIA during its period of greatest expansion in the 1950s. But even before this, it was evident that the agency was involved in a wide range of activities in many parts of the world.

1948: Bogota

Only six months after the CIA had come into existence, it found itself under fire for what would become a familiar complaint over the years—alleged failure to predict a major international upheaval. In this case, it was the assassination of Jorge Eliecer Gaitan, the popular Liberal Colombian leader, on April 9 on a street in Bogota. The shooting touched off the "Bogotazo," two days of bloody riots that disrupted the Ninth Inter-American Conference and greatly embarrassed Secretary of State George C. Marshall, who headed the American delegation. Marshall blamed the riots on Communist agitators.*

The post-mortem had its strange aspects. In the first place, expecting the CIA to forecast an assassination, is, in most instances, to endow it with supernatural powers. There are limits to what intelligence can predict. In the second place, Admiral Hillenkoetter, hauled before a House Executive Expenditures Subcommittee on April 15, read the text of secret CIA dispatches into the open record for the first and only time in history. This action, which raised hackles at the time, would, if done today, cause pandemonium.

The admiral maintained that although the Communists seized on Gaitan's assassination, the Colombian leader was slain in "a purely private act of revenge" by one Jose Sierra. The CIA chief said Gaitan, as an attorney, had just successfully defended in a murder trial the killer of Sierra's uncle.

Hillenkoetter testified that, furthermore, the CIA had predicted trouble at Bogota as far back as January 2. Then he dropped a bombshell. He charged that a March 23 CIA dispatch from Bogota, warning of Communist agitation, was withheld from Secretary Marshall by Orion J. Libert, a State Department advance man in Bogota, acting with the support of Ambassador Willard L. Beaulac.

The CIA dispatch, dated March 23, said:

Have confirmed information that Communist-inspired agitators will attempt to humiliate the Secretary of State and other members of the United States delegation to the Pan-American conference upon arrival in Bogota by manifestations and possible personal molestation.

Have passed this information on to the Ambassador and other interested embassy personnel with the request that full details on the arrival of delegation be submitted to this office for transmission to local police,

---

* Fidel Castro, then an unknown Cuban student, participated in the Bogota riots with a group of his friends.

who are anxious to give maximum possible protection. . . .

Advanced delegate O. J. Libert, who has been apprised of above, does not consider it advisable to notify the State Department of this situation, since he feels adequate protection will be given by police and does not want to alarm the delegates unduly.[5]

Hillenkoetter then placed a whole sheaf of top-secret dispatches into the record, telling in some detail of Communist plans to disrupt the conference. Possibly Hillenkoetter was egged on by the fact that a few hours before he testified, Truman had told a news conference that he was as surprised as anyone about the riots in Bogota. He had, said Truman, received no advance warning. The government had received information that there might be picketing or demonstrations. But, he added a trifle plaintively, there had been no indication that anyone was going to get shot.

At the State Department, Lincoln White said it was "inconceivable" that the department had suppressed any CIA communications. Besides, he said, Secretary Marshall had known all about the Communist plans and had brushed them aside with what White diplomatically called "salty remarks." That about ended this painful episode. It did not, however, end the recurring question of the adequacy of the CIA's forecasting abilities.

1950: *Korea*

To an extent, the CIA's role in the Korean War became clouded and fuzzed because it was caught up in the emotional storm touched off when Truman finally decided to fire General Douglas MacArthur. What the CIA had or had not predicted, and its freedom or lack of freedom to operate within MacArthur's command, became a subject of dispute between the imperious general and the angry chief executive. Yet the main outline of the CIA's performance and the precise issues in dispute are not difficult to pinpoint from the record.

Harry Truman was sitting in the library of his home in Independence, Missouri, on Saturday, June 24, 1950, when the telephone rang a bit after 10:00 P.M. It was Secretary of State Dean Acheson, calling to say that the North Koreans had invaded South Korea.

Truman hastened back to the capital the next day. On Monday he summoned to the White House the man he assumed should have had the most advance knowledge about what had happened—Admiral Hillenkoetter.

It was something like Bogota all over again, although of course much more serious. The intelligence agency again had to defend itself for not precisely predicting a future event. And once again the CIA had become a subject of domestic political controversy.

After the meeting with Truman, Hillenkoetter told reporters at the White House that his agency had predicted the possibility of such an attack for a year. "The capabilities were there for a year, anyway," he said. He then hurried to Capitol Hill to give the same explanation to the Senate Appropriations Committee. Before testifying, he talked to newsmen about the Communist build-up along the 38th parallel.

"The condition existed for a long time," he said. "It has been expected for a year." Had the attack been anticipated over the weekend? "You can't predict the timing," the admiral replied.

Then the CIA chief appeared in secret before the Senate committee. One of the members said afterward that Hillenkoetter had read a series of reports on troop and tank concentrations in North Korea. The CIA reports covered a period of a year. The last one was dated June 20, four days before the attack. "If I had received those reports," said the senator, who asked that his name not be used, "I certainly would have been alerted to the danger." [6]

Five years later Truman, in his memoirs, supported in part the position Hillenkoetter had taken. He wrote:

"The intelligence reports from Korea in the spring of 1950 indicated that the North Koreans were steadily continuing their build-up of forces and that they were continuing to send guerrilla groups into South Korea.

"There were continuing incidents along the 38th parallel, where armed units faced each other.

"Throughout the spring the Central Intelligence reports said that the North Koreans might at any time decide to change from isolated raids to a full-scale attack. The North Koreans were capable of such an attack at any time, according to the intelligence, but there was no information to give any clue as to whether an attack was certain or when it was likely to come." [7]

As the UN forces regained the initiative in Korea, the next major question faced by the CIA (and MacArthur) was whether Communist China would intervene if UN troops pushed north to the Yalu River. The question became crucial just about the time Truman replaced Hillenkoetter with Walter Bedell Smith.

In his memoirs, Truman, again, has shed some light on this:

"On October 20 * the CIA delivered a memorandum to me which said that they had reports that the Chinese Communists would move in far enough to safeguard the Suiho electric plant and other installations along the Yalu River which provided them with power." [8]

Truman's account was backed up by Allen Dulles eight years later: "I can speak with detachment about the 1950 Yalu estimates, for they were made just before I joined the CIA. The conclusions of the estimators were that it was a toss-up, but they leaned to the side that under certain circumstances the Chinese probably would not intervene. In fact, we just did not know what the Chinese Communists would do, and we did not know how far the Soviet Union would press them or agree to support them if they moved." [9]

It seems reasonably clear, therefore, that the CIA did not, initially, predict the massive Chinese intervention that occurred.

However, some two weeks later, in November, according to Truman, the CIA did warn that Communist China had 200,000 troops in Manchuria and that their entry into

---

* Actually, the Chinese had begun crossing the Yalu four days earlier.

Korea might push the UN forces back. Truman also wrote that MacArthur had launched his ill-fated home-by-Christmas offensive on November 24 despite the CIA summary made available to the general that very day. The summary, Truman went on to say, had warned that the Chinese were strong enough to force the UN armies back into defensive positions.

Truman, who had been gingerly dealing with MacArthur almost as with another chief of state, at last fired the general on April 9, 1951. Testifying at the Senate inquiry into his dismissal, MacArthur cast new confusion over the CIA's role by saying that "in November" the CIA said "there was little chance of any major intervention on the part of the Chinese forces." If the CIA ever made any such optimistic report in November, replied Truman, it was news to him.

Bogota and Korea raised, but did not answer, the fundamental question of how much should be expected of the CIA in its forecasting role. They also set a pattern that has since become familiar—when trouble came, the overt, political officers of the visible government almost invariably would say they had no advance warning. The CIA in turn would say it had provided adequate warning. The public would be left to take its choice, provided it could weave its way through the maze of self-serving semantics from both sides.

1952: *Air-Drops Over Red China*

During the Korean War, another war was waged in secret against Communist China.

On November 23, 1954, a broadcast from Peking announced the capture and sentencing of two Americans, John Thomas Downey and Richard George Fecteau.

At Yale, John Thomas Downey was liked and respected for his strength, moral and physical. He was a quiet, clean-living, athletic lad, an honor student as well as a varsity football player and the captain of the wrestling team. He spent a good deal of time at home, in nearby New Britain, Connecticut, where his mother taught school. He was the type of young man the CIA was looking for.

Richard George Fecteau, of Lynn, Massachusetts, had less of an academic background. He was three years older than Downey. He once enrolled at Boston University with the idea of becoming a football coach, but he decided there was little future or money in it. Instead, he went to work for the government. So did Downey, who was recruited off the Yale campus in 1951, at age twenty-one. Both men later turned up in Japan. That did not seem unusual; with the Korean War on, thousands of young men were being shipped to the Far East.

On November 9, 1952, Jack Downey and Richard Fecteau were captured by the Communist Chinese. This was not revealed by Peking, however, until the announcement more than two years later. The broadcast on that day said that Downey, "alias Jack Donovan," and Fecteau, were "special agents of the Central Intelligence Agency, a United States espionage organization." They were charged with having helped to organize and train two teams of Chinese agents. The men, Peking said, had been air-dropped into Kirin and Liaoning Provinces for "subversive activities," and both Downey and Fecteau were captured when their plane was downed as they attempted to drop supplies and contact agents inside Communist China. It was also claimed that nine Chinese working for the CIA men were taken prisoner with them.

Downey was sentenced to life. Fecteau got twenty years.

That same day, Peking announced it had sentenced eleven American airmen as "spies," charging that the plane carrying these men was shot down January 12, 1953, over Liaoning Province, while on a mission which had as its purpose the "air-drop of special agents into China and the Soviet Union."

Communist China claimed that, all told, it had killed 106 American and Chinese agents parachuted into China between 1951 and 1954 and had captured 124 others. They also said these agents were trained in "secret codes, invisible writing, secret messages, telephone tapping, forging documents, psychological warfare, guerrilla tactics and demolition."

The State Department immediately branded the charges against Downey, Fecteau and the eleven airmen "trumped up." The Defense Department called the accusations against all thirteen men "utterly false."

The American consul general at Geneva was instructed by the State Department to make the "strongest possible protest" to Peking.* The charges against the "two civilians," Downey and Fecteau, were "a most flagrant violation of justice," the State Department said. "These men, John Thomas Downey and Richard George Fecteau, were civilian personnel employed by the Department of the Army in Japan. They were believed to have been lost in a flight from Korea to Japan in November, 1952.

"How they came into the hands of the Chinese Communists is unknown to the United States . . . the continued wrongful detention of these American citizens furnishes further proof of the Chinese Communist regime's disregard for accepted practices of international conduct."

The Pentagon was equally indignant. "Messrs. Downey and Fecteau," the Defense Department declared, "were Department of the Army civilian employees. They were authorized passengers on a routine flight from Seoul to Japan in a plane which was under military contract to the Far East Air Force. A search instituted at the time failed to produce any trace of the plane, and Messrs. Downey and Fecteau were presumed to have been lost. It is now apparent that they were captured. . . ."

In September, 1957, a group of forty-one young Americans on an unauthorized trip to Red China visited Downey and Fecteau in prison. Afterward they reported that during the interview, Fecteau was asked whether he worked "for the Central Intelligence Agency."

"Yes," Fecteau replied, according to a Reuters account of the report issued by the visiting Americans. The same Reuters dispatch reported that Downey, suntanned and

* The protest apparently had some effect. On August 2, 1955, Communist China notified the United States at Geneva that the eleven airmen had been released on July 31.

114

crew-cut, said he had received 680 letters in prison, including some from "lonely hearts." He said he spent a lot of time reading books.

The following month Charles Edmundson, a former USIA official in Korea, who left the government in a dispute over foreign policy, wrote an article for the *Nation*, in which he indicated that Downey and Fecteau were CIA operatives.

At this writing, both men are still in a Chinese prison. The government has never acknowledged them to be CIA agents. As far as Washington is concerned, they are still officially listed as "civilian personnel employed by the Department of the Army."

1950–1954: *Formosa and Western Enterprises, Inc.*

During these years the CIA operated on Formosa as Western Enterprises, Inc. This cover was so thin it became a source of some merriment on the island. The experience of one State Department employee who arrived on Formosa in 1953 is typical.

A fellow employee was showing her the sights as they drove in from the airport. Pointing to one building, her guide said: "And that's Western Enterprises."

"What's that?" she asked innocently.

"Oh, you'll find out," her friend replied.

A few days later, at a party with Chinese government officials, she asked one of them: "By the way, what is Western Enterprises?"

"Oh, that," said the Chinese, with a scrutable oriental smile, "is your CIA."

State Department employees on Formosa did not get along very well with their counterparts in Western Enterprises, Inc. For one thing, the State Department workers felt that the CIA people were being paid far too well and had special privileges.

One of the CIA operatives who turned up on Formosa in 1953 was Campbell "Zup" James, a Yale graduate who affected an English accent, mustache and fancy walking stick. To anyone who asked, he told the outrageously phony story that he was a wealthy Englishman managing a family tea plantation on Formosa. By continuing to maintain this pose, even though almost everyone knew he worked for the CIA, James became a legend throughout Southeast Asia. He turned up later in Laos, still masquerading as a *pukka* Englishman straight out of the pages of Kipling. He was spotted in Bangkok as recently as the summer of 1963, mustache, cane and Mayfair accent intact. Despite his unlikely cover, some observers said he was an effective agent.

By 1954 the CIA's cover on Formosa was so threadbare that the agency changed its name to "Department of the Navy."

There is reason to believe that at least in the past, the CIA trained, equipped and financed Chinese Nationalist commando raids on the mainland, launched from the offshore islands of Quemoy and Matsu.

Early in 1963 a spate of interesting stories appeared from Formosa about renewed Nationalist guerrilla raids on the mainland. The Chiang Kai-shek government announced that the frogmen and commando teams were most active in Kwangtung Province, near Formosa. The chief of the Nationalist Intelligence Bureau estimated that 873 guerrilla agents had infiltrated into the mainland between March and December of 1962.

1953: *Iran*

But guerrilla raids are small actions compared to an operation that changes a government. There is no doubt at all that the CIA organized and directed the 1953 coup that overthrew Premier Mohammed Mossadegh and kept Shah Mohammed Reza Pahlevi on his throne. But few Americans know that the coup that toppled the government of Iran was led by a CIA agent who was the grandson of President Theodore Roosevelt.

Kermit "Kim" Roosevelt, also a seventh cousin of President Franklin D. Roosevelt, is still known as "Mr. Iran" around the CIA for his spectacular operation in Teheran more than a decade ago. He later left the CIA and joined the Gulf Oil Corporation as "government relations" director in its Washington office. Gulf named him a vice-president in 1960.

One legend that grew up inside the CIA had it that Roosevelt, in the grand Rough Rider tradition, led the revolt against the weeping Mossadegh with a gun at the head of an Iranian tank commander as the column rolled into Teheran.

A CIA man familiar with the Iran story characterized this as "a bit romantic" but said: "Kim did run the operation from a basement inTeheran—not from our embassy." He added admiringly: "It was a real James Bond operation."

General Fazollah Zahedi,* the man the CIA chose to replace Mossadegh, was also a character worthy of spy fiction. A six-foot-two, handsome ladies' man, he fought the Bolsheviks, was captured by the Kurds, and, in 1942, was kidnaped by the British, who suspected him of Nazi intrigues. During World War II the British and the Russians jointly occupied Iran. British agents, after snatching Zahedi, claimed they found the following items in his bedroom: a collection of German automatic weapons, silk underwear, some opium, letters from German parachutists operating in the hills, and an illustrated register of Teheran's most exquisite prostitutes.

After the war Zahedi rapidly moved back into public life. He was Minister of Interior when Mossadegh became Premier in 1951. Mossadegh nationalized the British-owned Anglo-Iranian Oil Company in April and seized the huge Abadan refinery on the Persian Gulf.

The refinery was shut down; thousands of workers were idled and Iran faced a financial crisis. The British, with the backing of Western governments, boycotted Iran's oil and the local workers were unable to run the refineries at capacity without British technicians.

Mossadegh connived with the Tudeh, Iran's Communist party, and London and Washington feared that the Russians would end up with Iran's vast oil reserves flowing

* He died September 1, 1963, at age sixty-seven.

117

into the Soviet Union, which shares a common border with Iran. Mossadegh, running the crisis from his bed—he claimed he was a very sick man—had broken with Zahedi, who balked at tolerating the Tudeh party.

It was against this background that the CIA and Kim Roosevelt moved in to oust Mossadegh and install Zahedi. At the time of the coup Roosevelt, then thirty-seven, was already a veteran intelligence man. He was born in Buenos Aires. His father, the President's second son, was also named Kermit. Kim was graduated from Harvard just before World War II, and he taught history there and later at the California Institute of Technology. He had married while still at Harvard. He left the academic life to serve in the OSS, then joined the CIA after the war as a Middle East specialist. His father had died in Alaska during the war; his uncle, Brigadier General Theodore Roosevelt, died on the beaches of Normandy a year later.

The British and American governments had together decided to mount an operation to overthrow Mossadegh. The CIA's estimate was that it would succeed because the conditions were right; in a showdown the people of Iran would be loyal to the Shah. The task of running the operation went to Kim Roosevelt, then the CIA's top operator in the Middle East.

Roosevelt entered Iran legally. He drove across the border, reached Teheran, and then dropped out of sight. He had to, since he had been in Iran before and his face was known. Shifting his headquarters several times to keep one step ahead of Mossadegh's agents, Roosevelt operated outside of the protection of the American Embassy. He did have the help of about five Americans, including some of the CIA men stationed in the embassy.

In addition, there were seven local agents, including two top Iranian intelligence operatives. These two men communicated with Roosevelt through cutouts—intermediaries—and he never saw them during the entire operation.

As the plan for revolt was hatched, Brigadier General H. Norman Schwarzkopf, who used to appear on radio's "Gang Busters," turned up in Teheran. He had reorganized the Shah's police force there in the 1940s. He was best known for his investigation of the Lindbergh baby kidnaping case when he headed the New Jersey State Police in 1932. Schwarzkopf, an old friend of Zahedi's, claimed he was in town "just to see old friends again." But he was part of the operation.

On August 13 the Shah signed a decree dismissing Mossadegh and naming Zahedi as Premier. The uncooperative Mossadegh arrested the unfortunate colonel who brought in his notice of dismissal. Mobs rioted in the streets; the thirty-three-year-old Shah and his queen (at that time the beautiful Soraya) fled to Baghdad by plane from their palace on the Caspian Sea.

For two chaotic days, Roosevelt lost communication with his two chief Iranian agents. Meanwhile, the Shah had made his way to Rome; Allen Dulles flew there to confer with him. Princess Ashraf, the Shah's attractive twin sister, tried to play a part in the international intrigue, but the Shah refused to talk to her.

In Teheran, Communist mobs controlled the streets; they destroyed statues of the Shah to celebrate his departure. Suddenly, the opposition to Mossadegh consolidated. The Army began rounding up demonstrators. Early on August 19 Roosevelt, from his hiding place, gave orders to his Iranian agents to get everyone they could find into the streets.

The agents went into the athletic clubs of Teheran and rounded up a strange assortment of weight-lifters, musclemen and gymnasts. The odd procession made its way through the bazaars shouting pro-Shah slogans. The crowd grew rapidly in size. By mid-morning it was clear the tide had turned against Mossadegh and nothing could stop it.

Zahedi came out of hiding and took over. The Shah returned from exile. Mossadegh went to jail and the leaders of the Tudeh were executed.

In the aftermath, the British lost their monopoly on Iran's oil. In August, 1958, an international consortium of Western oil companies signed a twenty-five-year pact with Iran for its oil. Under it, the former Anglo-Iranian Oil Company got 40 percent, a group of American companies * got 40 percent, Royal Dutch Shell got 14 percent and the Compagnie Française des Petroles 6 percent. Iran got half of the multimillion-dollar income from the oil fields under the deal, and Anglo-Iranian was assured a compensation payment of $70,000,000.

The United States, of course, has never officially admitted the CIA's role. The closest Dulles came to doing so was in a CBS television show in 1962, after his retirement from the CIA.[10] He was asked whether it was true that "the CIA people spent literally millions of dollars hiring people to riot in the streets and do other things, to get rid of Mossadegh. Is there anything you can say about that?"

"Well," Dulles replied, "I can say that the statement that we spent many dollars doing that is utterly false."

The former CIA chief also hinted at the CIA's Iran role in his book *The Craft of Intelligence*. ". . . support from the outside was given . . . to the Shah's supporters," [11] he wrote, without directly saying it came from the CIA.

Although Iran remained pro-West after the 1953 coup, little was done to alleviate the terrible poverty in that ancient land. Somehow, the oil wealth of Iran never trickled down to the people. A total of $1,300,000,000 in United States aid poured in during twelve years since 1951, but much of it appeared to stick to the fingers of the hopelessly corrupt officialdom. In 1957 a report of the House Committee on Government Operations said that American aid to Iran was so badly handled that "it is now impossible—with any accuracy—to tell what became of these funds."

A typical Iranian scandal involved a close friend of Princess Ashraf, Ehsan Davaloo, the "Caviar Queen," who earned the sobriquet by paying officials to get a $450,000-a-year caviar monopoly.

With this stark contrast—caviar and utter poverty side by side—Iran remained a ripe breeding ground for Communism. With the help of a President's swashbuckling

* Gulf Oil, Standard Oil of New Jersey and California, The Texas Company and Socony-Mobil.

grandson, the invisible Government had brought about a political *coup d'état*. It had bought time. But the United States seemed unable to follow this up with badly needed social and economic reforms.

1955: Mr. X Goes to Cairo

Two years after his operation in Iran, Kim Roosevelt turned up across the Red Sea in a mysterious episode in a new setting.

On September 27, 1955, Egyptian Premier Gamal Abdel Nasser announced to the world that he had concluded an arms deal with the Soviet bloc. Washington had been unwilling to sell weapons to Egypt on Nasser's terms, and the Arab leader turned to the East.

The news threw Washington into a turmoil, although the deal had been predicted beforehand by the CIA. It was one case, however, where John Foster Dulles had not been inclined to take too seriously the reports coming from his brother.

The State Department and the CIA had agreed to send Roosevelt to Cairo for a first-hand look. Roosevelt, by now the assistant director of the CIA for the Middle East, did so, and reported back that the negotiations were about to be completed. Foster Dulles sent him a long telegram reiterating his skepticism. Roosevelt fired back a pointed message advising the Secretary of State to read his morning papers, which would carry Nasser's announcement.

Roosevelt was right. On September 28, the day after Nasser's defiant disclosure, George V. Allen, Assistant Secretary of State for Near Eastern Affairs, was summoned to the office of Herbert Hoover, Jr., Under Secretary of State. Hoover was Acting Secretary that day because Dulles was in New York. In George Allen's presence, Hoover telephoned the Secretary of State; it was agreed that George Allen should be sent to see Nasser right away.

It was now 2:00 P.M. By five o'clock Allen was leaving New York on a Paris-bound plane. His hasty departure was announced by the State Department only three minutes before he took off from New York. Secretary

Dulles, who returned to Washington the same day, termed George Allen's trip "only a more or less routine visit." It was far from that. With him, George Allen carried a letter from Secretary Dulles, warning that the arms deal could hand Egypt over to the Communists. Dulles had signed the quickly drafted letter in New York just before Allen departed. While Allen was winging his way to the land of the Sphinx the United States wire services sent out dispatches speculating that he took with him an "ultimatum" to Nasser.

At this point, the CIA's "Mr. Iran" became the central figure in some shadowy backstage maneuvering in the Egyptian capital. British newspaper accounts of the episode later referred to a "Mr. X," a mysterious American official. In reality, he was Kim Roosevelt.

One version of the affair that became widely accepted was given by Nasser himself in a blood-and-thunder speech at Alexandria on July 26, 1956, the same day he seized the Suez Canal.

"After the arms deal was announced," Nasser told a crowd already worked up by his oratory, "Washington sent a representative to Egypt, Mr. George Allen. . . .

"An American official contacted me and sought a special interview. He said that . . . Allen has a strong note from the U.S. Government which might prejudice Egyptian nationality and prestige. I assure you that this note will have no effect because we shall be able to remove its effect. I advise you to accept this message.

"I asked him: 'What is the insult to Egyptian nationality and prestige about?' He said: 'This is a message from Mr. Dulles and is strongly worded. We are astonished how it was sent. We ask you to have cool nerves. You always had cool nerves. Accept this message with cool nerves. . . .'

"He said that no practical outcome would emanate from this message and guaranteed this. I told him: 'Look . . . if your representative comes to my offices and says something unpleasant, I shall throw him out.' [Applause]

"This happened at the beginning of October. Then he came again and told me that he had told this to Mr.

Allen and that Mr. Allen was wondering whether he would be thrown out when he came to convey his message to me, and also whether Mr. Dulles would throw him out if he went back without conveying this message." [Applause]

George Allen did see Nasser, and he was not thrown out. But the disturbing story circulated in Washington that a certain "Mr. X," a high CIA official, had undercut the official foreign policy of the United States by getting in ahead of George Allen and telling Nasser to forget whatever the special envoy told him.*

What had happened, as best it can be pieced together, was this:

When Allen's plane landed in Cairo, he was unaware of the storm kicked up there by reports that he was bringing an ultimatum from the Eisenhower Administration. A mob of Western and Egyptian newsmen were waiting at the airport. Ambassador Henry A. Byroade sprinted aboard the plane to warn George Allen of the situation.

Forearmed, the Assistant Secretary of State was cautiously noncommittal to newsmen who surrounded him when he stepped off the plane. In the crowd, Allen spotted Kim Roosevelt. He nodded to the CIA man, but they kept their distance from each other in public.

Before Allen's arrival, Byroade and Roosevelt had agreed that it would be an intolerable loss of face if the envoy were refused an interview with Nasser. So, in the seclusion of the embassy, Roosevelt, Byroade and Eric H. Johnston, who was there negotiating a water agreement, sat down with Allen and went over the letter from Secretary Dulles. They told Allen it was so patronizing that Nasser would take it as an insult and throw him out of the office. They urged that at the very least, he read the letter instead of handing it to Nasser formally.

As a result of this, George Allen sent a cable to Secretary Dulles recommending that he deliver the tough message

---

* The story was sufficiently upsetting to Senator Paul H. Douglas, the Illinois Democrat, so that he quietly investigated it later during a trip to the Middle East.

orally. That way, Nasser would not have a letter to make public afterward. Dulles cabled back, telling Allen to use his best judgment.

Meanwhile Kim Roosevelt, who knew Nasser well, had gone to see him. Roosevelt's defenders insist he did so to ease the way for Allen. They maintain that he joshed Nasser, told him to act like a grown man and not blow up, and asked him to listen politely when George Allen read his letter. Roosevelt did not, they say, ask Nasser to disregard Allen's message, as Nasser indicated later.

At his own meeting with Nasser on October 1, Allen was accompanied by Byroade. Allen told Nasser that the United States recognized Egypt's right to buy arms where it wanted, but pointed out that the United States had refused to sell jets to Israel and was anxious not to escalate the arms race in the Middle East.

"You wouldn't sell me arms," said Nasser. "I had to buy where I could."

Nasser was vague when Allen pressed to find out whether the arms deal was a prelude to something bigger. Finally, Allen pulled out the letter and formally read its text to Nasser. There was no translation, since the Egyptian Premier's English was entirely adequate. However, Allen did not leave the letter with Nasser.

What is clear, at any rate, is that the assistant director of the CIA saw Nasser ahead of the Assistant Secretary of State.

Eisenhower could not have known of this at the time, because he was under an oxygen tent in Denver, having suffered his heart attack there on September 25. On October 4 Secretary Dulles told a news conference that as a result of the talks between Allen and Nasser there had been achieved a "better understanding."

If by this the Secretary of State meant that through the intervention of "Mr. X," the Assistant Secretary of State for Near Eastern Affairs had not been thrown out of the office of the Premier of Egypt, he was correct.

1956: Suez

With Soviet arms flowing into Egypt, relations between

Nasser and Washington deteriorated rapidly. On July 19, 1956, Secretary of State Dulles pulled the rug out from under the fiery Arab leader. The United States withdrew its offer to help Egypt harness the Nile by constructing a high dam at Aswan (a task which the Russians happily moved in to perform).

Nasser, driven into a rage, seized the Suez Canal a week later. Israel invaded Egypt on October 29 and Britain and France joined in with a Hallowe'en Day attack. The United States condemned the invasion, Moscow threatened to rain missiles on London and Paris, and the assault was called off. All of this happened in the midst of the Hungarian revolt and the windup of the presidential campaign in the United States.

When the sands had settled in the Middle East, Allen Dulles was in a difficult position; the question, once again, was whether the CIA had failed to predict an event—in this case, the Suez invasion. Foster Dulles undercut the CIA's position by telling a Senate committee: "We had no advance information of any kind." [12]

Seven years later Allen Dulles offered an explanation of this. There were many times, said Allen Dulles, when intelligence had guessed correctly, but could not advertise the fact. He added:

"This was true of the Suez invasion of 1956. Here intelligence was well alerted as to both the possibility and later the probability of the actions taken by Israel and then by Britain and France. The public received the impression that there had been an intelligence failure; statements were issued by U.S. officials to the effect that the country had not been given advance warning of the action. Our officials, of course, intended to imply only that the British and French and Israelis had failed to tell us what they were doing. In fact, United States intelligence had kept the government informed without, as usual, advertising its achievement." [13]

The difficulty with this explanation is that it is not what Foster Dulles told the Senate.

On February 1, 1957, Secretary Dulles was being questioned by Senator Mansfield before a joint meeting of the

Senate Foreign Relations and Armed Services committees. He was asked whether Washington had knowledge of the Israeli attack on Egypt or of the British and French participation. "We had no advance information of any kind," he said. ". . . The British-French participation also came as a complete surprise to us."

It is true that this testimony, if taken alone, could be interpreted to mean simply that there had been no advance warning to Washington by the invaders. But two weeks earlier, on January 15, testifying before the same Senate committees, Secretary Dulles was more specific under questioning by Senator Henry M. Jackson, of Washington, who asked whether "the people within the executive branch of the government" knew of the impending Israeli attack on Suez.

"No," Dulles replied, "we had no such knowledge."

"At the appropriate time, Mr. Chairman," said Jackson, "I would like to go into that question when we get into executive session. I will not pursue it any further here now . . . the reason I am not pursuing further questioning along this line is obvious."

What was obvious, of course, was that Jackson was referring to the CIA. (Later questions and answers about whether the CIA had advance knowledge were so heavily censored in the published transcript of the executive session as to be meaningless.)

The questioning took place against a background of continuing domestic and international controversy over Suez. In England, France and the United States, there had been suggestions that the Eisenhower Administration had known in advance of the invasion plans, and had been hypocritical in its outraged reaction and intervention. Democrats felt the pre-election crisis had helped defeat Adlai Stevenson and re-elect Eisenhower. Jackson's questions seemed designed to explore whether the CIA had known all along that the invasion was coming. If this had been the case, Secretary Dulles could ill afford, for political reasons, to say so.

But Jackson's question and the Secretary of State's answer are on the record. Dulles was clearly saying that "the executive branch of the government"—which of course includes the CIA—had "no knowledge" in advance of the Israeli attack which began the Suez invasion.

The truth is always elusive; the truth about a secret agency doubly so. Future historians of the Cold War will have an unenviable task.

1956: Costa Rica

The Invisible Government's activities have not been restricted to chaotic countries, dominated or threatened by Communism. In the mid-1950s CIA agents intruded deeply into the political affairs of Costa Rica, the most stable and democratic republic in Latin America. Knowledgeable Costa Ricans were aware of the CIA's role. The CIA's purpose was to promote the ouster of Jose (Pepe) Figueres, the moderate socialist who became President in a fair and open election in 1953.

In March of 1954, in the course of a Senate speech, Senator Mansfield cited a newspaper report [14] to the effect that "a CIA man was caught red-handed" in the "tapping of the telephone of Jose Figueres. . . . I do not need to point out the tremendous impact which this sort of activity could have in our foreign policy," he said, in calling for tighter Congressional control over the CIA. His warning had no noticeable effect on the CIA's anti-Figueres activities, however.

Figueres had risen to national prominence as the leader of a guerrilla movement organized to install Otilio Ulate as President in 1948. Ulate had won the election, but a right-wing government (with Communist support) and a packed legislature had refused to recognize him. In April of 1948, however, Figueres forced them to back down and the following year Ulate was installed.

Figueres' success vaulted him into the presidency in 1953. But Ulate organized an opposition movement against his former political ally.

Local CIA agents joined in the efforts to unseat Figueres. Their major grievance was that Figueres had scrupulously recognized the right of asylum in Costa Rica —for non-Communists and Communists alike. The large influx of questionable characters complicated the agency's job of surveillance and forced it to increase its staff.

The CIA's strategy was twofold: to stir up embarrassing trouble within the Communist Party in Costa Rica, and to attempt to link Figueres * with the Communists. An effort to produce evidence that Figueres had been in contact with leading Communists during a trip to Mexico was unsuccessful. But CIA agents had better luck with the first part of their strategy—stirring up trouble for the Communists. They succeeded in planting a letter in a Communist newspaper. The letter, purportedly from a leading Costa Rican Communist, put him on record in opposition to the Party line on the Hungarian revolution.

Unaware that the letter was a CIA plant, the leading officials in the American Embassy held an urgent meeting to ponder its meaning. The political officer then dispatched a long classified report to Washington, alerting top policy makers to the possibility of a startling turn in Latin American Communist politics.

No one bothered to tell the embassy or the State Department that the newspaper article was written by the CIA.

1956: The Khrushchev Speech

The CIA's manufacture of bogus Communist material has not always led to a happy result. But the agency has had one noteworthy success in obtaining a real Communist document.

When Khrushchev delivered his historic secret speech attacking Stalin's crimes at the 20th Communist Party Congress in Moscow in February, 1956, Allen Dulles ordered a vast and intensive hunt for the text. He assumed there had to be one, because Khrushchev had spoken for seven hours.

The word went out inside the CIA: whoever could deliver the document would be amply recognized by Dulles

---

* While the CIA was plotting to get rid of Figueres during this period, Ambassador Robert F. Woodward was urging President Eisenhower to lend his prestige to the Costa Rican President by inviting him to Washington. Figueres stepped down in 1958 when his candidate lost the Presidential election.

as an intelligence ace. At whatever price, the CIA was determined to obtain the secret speech.

First, analysts determined what individuals and what Communist nations might have been given a copy—in other words, where to go looking for it. Then agents fanned out all over the Communist world to find it.

One top CIA operator turned up in Belgrade with an intriguing scheme—he would make a direct pitch to the Yugoslav Government to bootleg him a copy. Tito and Stalin, after all, had split in 1948. With the permission of Ambassador James W. Riddleberger, the CIA man called on a certain high Yugoslav official.

For nearly two hours he argued his case, listing the reasons why Washington deserved a copy of the top-secret document. The sales talk must have been convincing, for at one point the Yugoslav seemed ready to hand over a copy. But then he thought better of it, and backed off.

The CIA did finally get its hands on a text—but not in Moscow. Money and other considerations changed hands. The man who made the deal to deliver the speech claimed he needed the money, not for himself, but to make arrangements to protect others who might be involved. At least that is what he told the CIA.

With the speech in Dulles' hands, a new problem had to be faced. Dulles did not want to release the 26,000-word text unless he could be sure it was genuine. For several weeks during May, 1956, the CIA had the text in hand, but said nothing.

CIA analysts pored over the text, examining every word, each phrase in an attempt to authenticate it. The experts finally decided that the document contained information that only Khrushchev could have been in a position to know. Together with other clues buried in the text, this convinced the analysts the document was bona fide. Dulles gave his approval, and on June 4 the State Department released the text.

To this day the CIA does not know precisely what document it obtained: whether it was the speech that Khrushchev prepared for delivery at the Congress, or the verbatim speech he did deliver, or possibly a slightly altered version for distribution to certain satellite nations. The CIA does not know which it is because the text-as-delivered was never published by Khrushchev. On the other hand, Moscow has not flatly denied its authenticity.*

"There is no fatal inevitability of war," Khrushchev said in the speech, in rejecting one of the basic tenets of Lenin. The CIA felt a deserved sense of satisfaction in having run the speech to ground. For it was the first tangible evidence of the historic split between Communist China and the Soviet Union.

1960: The U-2

The U-2 spy plane was developed by Richard Bissell, Trevor Gardner of the Air Force and Clarence L. (Kelly) Johnson of Lockheed, after initially being turned down by the Pentagon on June 7, 1954. The Defense Department finally did approve the ultra-secret espionage project in December of that year. The first model was flying by August, 1955. During the four years, starting in 1956, that the spy plane flew over Russia, it brought back invaluable data on Russian "airfields, aircraft, missiles, missile testing and training, special weapons storage, submarine production, atomic production and aircraft deployments." [15] It flew so high (well over 80,000 feet) that the Russians were unable to shoot it down at first.

The summit conference of Eisenhower, Macmillan, De Gaulle and Khrushchev was scheduled to take place on May 16, 1960. As the date approached, the intelligence technicians who ran the U-2 program decided to get one last U-2 flight in under the wire before the conference. They feared the Paris meeting might result in a detente

* Although Dulles had hinted previously at the CIA's role, he publicly and unequivocally disclosed the CIA's *tour de force* in a speech in Washington in June, 1963, and in a television interview two months later. It was a startling statement, because it was one of the few times that the CIA had openly taken credit for an espionage feat. Dulles said: "You remember . . . Khrushchev's famous speech in 1956, which we got, the CIA got that speech, and I thought it was one of the main coups of the time I was there. . . ." [16]

that would ground the spy plane indefinitely. The feeling within the intelligence community was that a successful conference, followed by Eisenhower's planned trip to Moscow, would make flying the U-2 impossible.

Eisenhower approved each general series of U-2 flights. These groupings allowed considerable flexibility for a set number of missions to be flown within a given time span. Eisenhower did not suspend the program as the summit date approached.

On May 1, 1960, Francis Gary Powers, a CIA pilot from the hill country of Virginia, was downed in his U-2 over Sverdlovsk,* in the Urals. Khrushchev announced on May 5 that a plane had been shot down. This set off an incredible period of confusion in the highest councils of the United States Government.

At first, Washington insisted it was a NASA weather plane that had drifted over the border from Turkey when its pilot had oxygen trouble. After waiting two days for this explanation to sink in, Khrushchev triumphantly revealed he had the pilot and the plane. At that, the State Department admitted the spy flight, but said it had not been authorized in Washington. Two days later Eisenhower reversed this position, took responsibility for the U-2 program and issued a statement widely interpreted to mean that the flights over Soviet territory would continue.

That did it. Khrushchev stormed and demanded an apology at Paris. Eisenhower finally announced at the summit table that no more U-2s would be sent over Russia. But the 1960 summit meeting collapsed.

Why had the CIA and the Eisenhower Administration so confidently issued its original "cover story" about a "weather" plane? One important reason was that Powers had been instructed to blow up his plane in the event of trouble over Russia. This, the CIA expected, would destroy evidence.

The U-2 contained a destructor unit with a three-pound charge of cyclonite—enough to blow it up. U-2 pilots were instructed in the event of trouble to activate a timing

* By a Russian SA-2 missile, the CIA concluded.

device and eject from the plane. It would then explode, so they were told. But Allen Dulles was aware that some of the U-2 pilots were worried about the workings of this intriguing and delicate destructor mechanism. They were not really sure how many seconds they had to get out.

At a Senate hearing[17] after his release by the Russians, Powers testified: "My first reaction was to reach for the destruct switches . . . but I thought that I had better see if I can get out of here before using this. I knew that there was a seventy-second time delay between the time of the actuation of the switches and the time that the explosion would occur." *

Powers testified that he was unable to use the automatic ejection seat because he had been thrown forward in the cockpit. He said he then decided just to climb out. But after he did, he testified, he was unable to reach back into the U-2 "so that I could actuate these destructor switches."

A CIA report issued after Powers had been held for twenty-four days and secretly interrogated by the agency, set forth substantially the same story and stated that "the destruct switches . . . take four separate manipulations to set." The CIA report said Powers lived up to his contract and his "obligations as an American" and would get his back pay.[18]

At the friendly Senate Armed Services Committee hearing, no one asked Powers whether he had been under a mandatory order to destroy his plane. It was obvious that the CIA did not relish any close scrutiny of the fascinating workings of the destructor mechanism.

Some of the weightier political analyses of the confusion in Washington during the U-2 affair have failed to pay enough attention to the vital business of the destructor unit. The cover stories were based on the assumption that

* A few days after his Senate testimony, however, Powers seemed less certain of this. In a radio interview at his home in Pound, Virginia, with James Clarke, then of WGH, Norfolk, he said he *thought* he had seventy seconds on that particular U-2. It was an uncertainty shared by other U-2 pilots. The fact is the pilots did not know precisely how much time they had before the explosion.

Francis Gary Powers had actuated those destructor switches. He had not.

Only the CIA knows what would have happened had he done so.

1963: *Trouble for General Gehlen*

Any casual newspaper reader knows that 1963 was a banner year for spy cases, but one of the most significant received the least attention in the United States, considering that it deeply involved the CIA. On July 11, in a Karlsruhe courtroom, Judge Kurt Weber sentenced three former West German intelligence agents to prison terms for spying for the Soviet Union.

Heinz Felfe, forty-five, drew fourteen years. Hans Clemens, sixty-one, got ten years. Erwin Tiebel, sixty, their courier, got off with three years. The trio had confessed to delivering 15,000 photographs of top-secret West German intelligence files and twenty spools of tape recordings to Soviet agents in East Berlin.

All three had been employed by the West German Federal Intelligence Agency (FIA), better known as the "Gehlen organization" for its founder and chief, the mysterious ex-Nazi general, Reinhard Gehlen. The defendants confessed they had systematically betrayed state secrets from 1950 until their arrest in 1961.

Ironically, their work was so pleasing to both sides, that shortly before their arrest Felfe and Clemens received citations for ten years of meritorious service from both of their employers. From General Gehlen they received a plaque bearing an illustration of St. George slaying the dragon. From Alexander N. Shelepin, then Chairman of the Soviet KGB,* they got a letter of commendation and a cash bonus.

* KGB stands for Komitat Gosudarstvennoi Bezopasnosti (Committee for State Security). It is one arm of the Soviet espionage apparatus, the other being the GRU, or Glavnoye Razvedyvatelnoye Upravlenie, the Soviet Military Intelligence. The KGB is the successor to the Cheka, OGPU, NKVD, MVD and other initials used over the years to designate the often reorganized, purged and renamed Soviet secret police and espionage network.

As Judge Weber summed it up succinctly: "For ten years the Soviet intelligence service had two experienced spies sitting right in the center of the enemy's organization."

Since the Gehlen organization was financed and controlled by the United States Central Intelligence Agency, the Felfe-Clemens-Tiebel case meant nothing less than that the CIA's most vital European subsidiary had been penetrated at the top, virtually from its inception.

The CIA poured millions into the Gehlen apparatus, but the 1963 case raised grave questions about the effectiveness and worth of the whole operation. It also raised moral and political questions in West Germany, where some newspapers were asking why ex-Nazis were running the *Bundesrepublik*'s intelligence service in the first place.

Gehlen, a member of the German General Staff under Hitler, was placed in charge of wartime intelligence for Foreign Armies East. This meant that he ran Germany's espionage against the Soviet Union and Eastern Europe. He is said to have surrendered his organization and files to the United States Army Counter Intelligence Corps when the Nazi empire collapsed in 1945.

With his knowledge of the Soviet Union and Eastern Europe, it was not long before Gehlen was back in business, this time for the United States. When the CIA was casting about for a network in West Germany, it decided to look into the possibility of using Gehlen's talents. And while they were making up their mind about the ex-general, Henry Pleasants, the CIA station chief in Bonn for many years, moved in and lived with Gehlen for several months.

Pleasants, once the chief music critic of the *Philadelphia Evening Bulletin*, and a contributor to the music pages of the *New York Times*, was a highly literate and respected musicologist. His wife Virginia was one of the world's leading harpsichordists. He also probably had the distinction of being the only top U.S. spy to become the center of a literary storm. He had continued to write books after joining the CIA, and in 1955 his *Agony of Modern Music* (Simon & Schuster, New York) caused considerable controversy for its attacks on all contemporary music except jazz.*

Gehlen had named his price and his terms, but it took some months before the CIA said yes. After that Gehlen consolidated an intelligence network that operated in utter secrecy—as far as the West German public was concerned—from a heavily guarded villa in Pullach, outside of Munich. Officially, the Gehlen network was not part of the Bonn Government.

The mystery general reportedly lived in a two-story lakeside villa at Starnberg, Bavaria (fifteen miles southwest of Munich); a sign on the fence surrounding the house said: *Warnung vor dem Hunde* (Beware the Dog). No outsider has ever seen Gehlen. No picture of Gehlen has been taken since 1944—and that one shows him bemedaled in his Wehrmacht uniform.

The evidence indicates that Gehlen staffed his organization with many former SS and Wehrmacht intelligence officers. During the war Felfe ran the Swiss department of the Reich security service, and Clemens and Tiebel were his assistants.

Felfe, while awaiting possible war crimes prosecution, suddenly was given a clean bill of health by a British Zone court and was hired by the Gehlen organization in 1951. He testified he had been approached by a former SS colonel who asked if he was interested in returning to his "old trade."

That trade was also being plied by Dr. Otto John, head of West Germany's Office for the Protection of the Constitution. Dr. John disappeared into East Berlin on July 20, 1954. Since John was the head of West Germany's official counter-intelligence organization, it was as astounding as if J. Edgar Hoover had suddenly turned up in Minsk. Otto John chose the tenth anniversary of the unsuccessful bomb plot against Hitler to do his vanishing act. He had been active in the plot himself and managed

* As recently as April 15, 1962, while he was still the CIA station chief in Bonn, Pleasants had a byline article in the *New York Herald Tribune*, filed from Zurich. It told of the state theater's production of Meyerbeer's *Le Prophète*.

to escape afterwards; his brother Hans was executed. On the day of his disappearance he had attended memorial services at the site of the executions.

Washington, stunned by the news, described John as one of the "two or three best-informed persons in West Germany" on intelligence operations. But the tail end of a *New York Times* dispatch from Berlin gave the most tantalizing reason for John's action:

"Dr. John's organization also was believed to have been in serious competition and difficulties with a more extensive German organization headed by Reinhard Gehlen, a former high-ranking Wehrmacht intelligence officer." [19]

On July 20, 1955, again on the anniversary of the bomb plot, West Germany announced that it was taking over the Gehlen organization, henceforth to be known as the *Bundesnachrichtendienst,** or Federal Intelligence Agency (FIA).

With John's defection and the official recognition of the FIA by Chancellor Konrad Adenauer, Gehlen was the unchallenged spymaster of West Germany.† The Gehlen *Apparat* was now part of the Bonn Government (although it nowhere appears in any official government table of organization). The relationship between the CIA and the FIA remained intimate. That is why the 1963 trial meant, not only trouble for Gehlen, but trouble for the CIA.

During the trial the three defendants admitted that they supplied the Soviet Union with the names of West German agents of the FIA (ninety-five in all) as well as other secret information that was smuggled out in canned baby food, trick suitcases and on special writing paper. Felfe and Clemens testified they were paid about $40,000 each during the ten-year period.

At the time of his arrest, Felfe was the director of the East Division of the Gehlen agency, in charge of spying in Eastern Europe.

In asking for long prison terms for the trio, the West

* Literally, Federal news service.
† John returned to West Berlin on December 13, 1955. He was tried, convicted of treasonable conspiracy and served nineteen months of his four-year sentence.

German prosecutor said it was "without doubt the worst espionage case ever experienced in the Federal Republic." Felfe and Clemens, he said, had done "serious damage to the Federal Republic and to American organizations."

He did not have to spell out the initials CIA to make his meaning clear.

The extraordinary growth of the clandestine activities of the United States in all parts of the world has been pointed up in this brief review of the important operations of the Invisible Government in Germany, as well as in Bogota, Korea, Communist China, Formosa, Iran, Egypt, Costa Rica and the Soviet Union. Other operations, even more fascinating and sometimes disturbing, have been conducted in Burma, Indonesia, Laos, Vietnam and Guatemala.

7

Burma: The Innocent Ambassador

As HE PREPARED to leave Japan in 1952, at the end of a seven-year assignment, William J. Sebald developed misgivings about his new post as Ambassador to Burma.

Sebald's worries centered on a band of 12,000 Nationalist Chinese troops who were squatting on Burmese territory in defiance of the Burmese Government. The Nationalist troops had fled to Burma in 1949 as the Chinese Communists advanced toward victory. The troops made one concerted effort to return by force to Yunnan, their native province in China. But they were easily turned back, and settled down in Burma to a life of banditry and opium-running.

The Burmese Government demanded that they lay down their arms, but the Nationalist troops repulsed the sporadic efforts of the Burmese Army to subdue them. In the more recent fighting they had displayed new equipment and a greater sense of discipline. And they had just acquired a new commander, General Li Mi, an intelligence officer who was spotted commuting between Formosa and Burma by way of a landing strip in Thailand, just across Burma's southeastern border.

To the Burmese Government, burdened by catastrophic World War II destruction and continuous domestic rebellions, the Nationalist troops had long been an intolerable foreign nuisance. Now, revived as a military force, they became a menace to Burmese independence. The troops might easily provide a pretext for an invasion by the Communist Chinese or a coup by the 300,000 Burmese Communists.

Officially, Burma pleaded with the United States to apply pressure on Formosa to withdraw the troops. Unofficially, Burmese officials accused the CIA of supporting the troops as a force that could conduct raids into China or threaten military retaliation if Burma adopted a more conciliatory policy toward Peking.

Ambassador Sebald had spent more than a third of his fifty years as a naval officer and diplomat in the Far East. He knew he would have trouble enough with a touchy new nation of ancient oriental ways without being undermined by another agency of his own government.

On home leave in Washington, Sebald demanded assurances from his superiors that the CIA was not supporting the Nationalist troops. He was told emphatically that the United States was in no way involved.

From the very first days of his two-year assignment in Rangoon, Sebald regularly warned Washington that the troops threatened Burma's very existence as a parliamentary democracy which was friendly to the West. If United States relations were not to turn completely sour, he insisted, the Nationalists would have to be removed. Each time, the State Department responded that the United States was not involved and that Burma should logically complain to Taipeh.

Dutifully, Sebald passed along these assurances to the Burmese Foreign Office. But he never succeeded in convincing the Burmese of American innocence. The most determined of the skeptics was General Ne Win, who as Chief of Staff of the Army was leading the battle against the guerrillas. Fresh from a meeting with his field commanders, Ne Win confronted Sebald at a diplomatic gathering and angrily demanded action on the Nationalist troops. When Sebald started to launch into his standard disclaimer of United States involvement the general cut him short.

"Mr. Ambassador," he asserted firmly in his best colonial English, "I have it cold. If I were you, I'd just keep quiet."

As Sebald was to learn, and as high United States officials

now frankly admit, Ne Win was indeed correct. The CIA was intimately involved with the Nationalist troops, but Sebald's superiors—men just below John Foster Dulles—were officially ignorant of the fact. Knowledge of the project was so closely held within the CIA, that it even escaped the notice of Robert Amory, the deputy director for intelligence. He was not normally informed about the covert side of the agency's operations but he usually received some information about major projects on an unofficial basis. Yet on Burma he could honestly protest to his colleagues in other branches of the government that the CIA was innocent.

Though Sebald was never able to secure an official admission from Washington, he discovered through personal investigation on the scene that the CIA's involvement was an open secret in sophisticated circles in Bangkok, Thailand. There, he learned, the CIA planned and directed the operation under the guise of running Sea Supply, a trading company with the cable address "Hatchet."

In Rangoon public resentment at the CIA's role became so pervasive that the most irrelevant incidents—an isolated shooting, a power failure—were routinely ascribed to American meddling. Sebald persisted in his denials, but by March, 1953, they had turned so threadbare that Burma threw the issue into the United Nations.

In New Delhi, Chester Bowles, finishing his first tour as Ambassador to India, had also been beset by the rumors. To silence the anti-American rumbling, Bowles, like Sebald, sought assurances from Washington. The response was the same: the United States was not involved in any way. Bowles conveyed this message to Prime Minister Jawaharlal Nehru, who stated publicly that, on Bowles' word, he had convinced himself that the United States was not supporting the Nationalist guerrillas.

At the UN, Burma produced captured directives from Taipeh to the Chinese guerrillas, but Nationalist China insisted it had "no control over the Yunnan Anti-Communist and National Salvation Army." At the same time, it conceded paradoxically that Taipeh did have "some in-

140

fluence over General Li Mi" and would exercise its "moral influence" to resolve the problem.

With the UN on the verge of an embarrassing inquest and the Nationalist Chinese in a more conciliatory mood, Sebald's pleas finally began to be heard in Washington. He was instructed to offer the services of the United States in mediating the issue between Burma and Taipeh.

In May the United States suggested that Burma, Nationalist China and Thailand join with it in a four-power conference to discuss the problem. After first balking at sitting down with Nationalist China, Burma finally agreed. A four-nation joint military commission convened in Bangkok on May 22. Full accord on an evacuation plan was reached on June 22. The procedure called for the Nationalist guerrillas to cross over into Thailand for removal to Formosa within three or four weeks.

But the guerrillas refused to leave unless ordered to do so by Li Mi. When the commission demanded his presence in Bangkok, the general pleaded illness, then announced he would under no condition order his troops out.

Negotiations and fighting continued inconclusively throughout the summer of 1953, and Burma again brought the issue before the UN in September.

"Without meaning to be ungrateful," said the chief Burma delegate, U Myint Thein, "I venture to state that in dealing with authorities on Formosa, moral pressure is not enough. If something more than that, such as the threat of an ouster from their seat in the United Nations, were conveyed to the authorities on Formosa, or if the United States would go a step further and threaten to suspend aid, I assure you the Kuomintang army would disappear overnight."

Nevertheless, Burma agreed reluctantly to a cease-fire when Nationalist China pledged to disavow the guerrillas and cut off all aid to them after those willing to be evacuated had started out by way of Thailand. The withdrawal, which began on November 5, was disturbing to the Burmese from the start. The Thai police were under the control of General Pao, the Interior Minister, who was involved with the guerrillas in the opium trade. And he refused to allow Burmese representatives to accompany other members of the joint military commission to the staging areas.

The suspicions of the Burmese were stirred anew when "Wild Bill" Donovan, the wartime boss of the OSS and then Ambassador to Thailand, arrived on the scene, flags waving, to lead out the Nationalist troops.

The evacuation dragged on through the winter of 1953-1954. It was largely bungled, in the view of U.S. officials in Rangoon, mainly because Washington failed to exert enough pressure on Taipeh. About 7,000 persons were flown to Formosa, but a high percentage of them were women, children and crippled noncombatants.

On May 30, 1954, Li Mi announced from Taipeh the dissolution of the Yunnan Anti-Communist and National Salvation Army, but by July fighting had resumed between the guerrillas and the Burmese Army.

Burma returned to the UN but soon realized that the evacuation of the previous winter "represented the limit of what could be accomplished by international action." On October 15 the issue was discussed in the UN for the last time.

Sebald resigned as ambassador on November 1, citing the ill health of his wife, and returned to Washington as Deputy Assistant Secretary of State for Far Eastern Affairs. He was to spend the next three years struggling to open lines of communication between the State Department and the CIA so that the left hand of the United States might know what the right hand was up to in its international dealings.

But the repercussions of the CIA's operation remained to complicate United States relations in Burma. Despite the long and painful negotiations, half of the Nationalist guerrillas, and the best of them, were still deployed in Burma. They joined with other rebel factions and skirmished repeatedly with the Burmese Army. It was not until January of 1961 that they were driven into Thailand and Laos.

They left behind them, however, a new source of embarrassment to the incoming administration of President

Kennedy. As the Burmese advanced, they discovered a cache of U.S.-made equipment, and the following month they shot down a U.S. World War II Liberator bomber en route from Formosa with supplies for the guerrillas.

The captured arms included five tons of ammunition packed in crates which bore the handclasp label of the United States aid program. The discovery sent 10,000 demonstrators into the streets outside the American Embassy in Rangoon. Three persons were killed and sixty seriously injured before troops brought the situation under control. Premier U Nu called a press conference and blamed the United States for the continued support of the guerrillas.

Three U.S. military attachés were quickly dispatched to inspect the captured equipment. They reported that the ammunition crates bore coded markings, which were forwarded to Washington for scrutiny.

"If we can trace these weapons back," said an embassy official, "and show that they were given to Taiwan, the United States will have a strong case against Chiang Kaishek for violating our aid agreement."

Taipeh refused to accept responsibility. It insisted the weapons had been supplied by the "Free China Relief Association" and flown to the guerrillas in private planes. The United States filed no formal charges against Nationalist China.

Behind the scenes, however, W. Averell Harriman, the new Assistant Secretary of State for Far Eastern Affairs, moved quickly and forcefully. He was a bitter opponent of the United States policy in Asia during the Eisenhower years, particularly John Foster Dulles' decision to "unleash Chiang."

Harriman considered the Dulles decision a form of theatrics. Harriman felt that there was no hope of returning Chiang to the mainland but that Dulles was forced, nonetheless, to commit the United States to a policy of rolling back the Bamboo Curtain in order to redeem his pledges to Nationalist China and the domestic right wing. In Harriman's view, Dulles' decision led inevitably to the transfer of responsibility for Southeast Asian affairs from the traditional diplomatists in the State Department to the more militant operatives in the Pentagon and the CIA.

With the full backing of President Kennedy, Harriman set out to reverse the situation without delay. When informed of the new guerrilla incident in Burma, he directed that Taipeh be firmly impressed with the fact that such ventures were no longer to be tolerated by the United States.

The Nationalist Chinese quickly announced on March 5 that they would do their utmost to evacuate the remaining guerrillas.

But Harriman's forceful action had little effect in dispelling Burma's suspicions about United States policy. And conditions took a turn for the worse on March 2, 1962, when General Ne Win seized the government in a bloodless army coup. Ne Win had intervened briefly in 1958 to restore order and assure a fair election (the government was returned to civilian control early in 1960). In 1962, however, the general came to power with a determination to move the nation to the Left and to reduce its traditional ties of friendship with the West.

Burma's economy was rapidly becoming more socialistic: the rice industry, source of 70 percent of the nation's foreign exchange earnings, was nationalized; private banks, domestic and foreign, were turned into "peoples' banks"; and most Western aid projects were rejected. Communist China was invited in with 300 economic experts, an $84,000,000 development loan and technical assistance for twenty-five projects.

Burma, which had been created in the image of the Western democracies in 1948, was, a decade and a half later, turning toward Peking. In 1952, when Ne Win rebuked Sebald for the CIA's role in support of the guerrillas, Burma was struggling to maintain its neutrality despite the ominous closeness of a powerful and aggressive Communist neighbor. Now, with Ne Win in control, Burma found its independence increasingly threatened.

The leftward turn of Burma's policy might have baffled the American people, but it should not have puzzled the American Government.

8

Indonesia: "Soldiers of Fortune"

THE INDONESIAN anti-aircraft fire hit the rebel B-26 and the two-engine bomber plunged toward the sea, its right wing aflame. The pilot, an American named Allen Lawrence Pope, jumped clear and his parachute opened cleanly. But as he drifted down onto a small coral reef, the chute caught a coconut tree and Pope's right leg was broken.

It was May 18, 1958, and the twenty-nine-year-old pilot had just completed a bombing and strafing run on the Ambon Island airstrip in the Moluccas, 1,500 miles from Indonesia's capital at Jakarta. It was a dangerous mission and Pope had carried it off successfully. But when the Indonesians announced his capture, Ambassador Howard P. Jones promptly dismissed him as "a private American citizen involved as a paid soldier of fortune."

The ambassador was echoing the words of the President of the United States. Three weeks before Pope was shot down, Dwight D. Eisenhower had emphatically denied charges that the United States was supporting the rebellion against President Sukarno.

"Our policy," he said, at a press conference on April 30, "is one of careful neutrality and proper deportment all the way through so as not to be taking sides where it is none of our business.

"Now on the other hand, every rebellion that I have ever heard of has its soldiers of fortune. You can start even back to reading your Richard Harding Davis. People were going out looking for a good fight and getting into it, sometimes in the hope of pay, and sometimes just for the heck of the thing. That is probably going to happen every time you have a rebellion."

But Pope was no freebooting soldier of fortune. He was flying for the CIA, which was secretly supporting the rebels who were trying to overthrow Sukarno.

Neither Pope nor the United States was ever to admit any of this—even after his release from an Indonesian jail in the summer of 1962. But Sukarno and the Indonesian Government were fully aware of what had happened. And that awareness fundamentally influenced their official and private attitude toward the United States. Many high-ranking American officials—including President Kennedy —admitted it within the inner circles of the government, but it is not something that they were ever likely to give public voice to.

Allen Pope, a six-foot-one, 195-pound Korean War ace, was the son of a moderately prosperous fruit grower in Perrine, just south of Miami. From boyhood he was active and aggressive, much attracted by the challenge of physical danger. He attended the University of Florida for two years but left to bust broncos in Texas. He volunteered early for the Korean War, flew fifty-five night missions over Communist lines as a first lieutenant in the Air Force, and was awarded the Distinguished Flying Cross.

After the war Pope returned to Texas, got married, had a daughter, and was divorced. He worked for a local airline but found it dull stuff compared with the excitement he had experienced as a combat pilot in the Far East. And so in March of 1954 Pope signed on with Civil Air Transport, an avowedly civilian airline based on Formosa. He spent two months flying through Communist flak to drop supplies to the French at Dienbienphu. CAT grew out of the Flying Tigers and inherited much of its technique and swagger.

Pope found the outfit congenial. After Dienbienphu he renewed his contract, rising in three years to the rank of captain with a salary of $1,000 a month. He met his second wife, Yvonne, a Pan American stewardess, in Hong

Kong. They settled down in a small French villa outside Saigon and had two boys.

Big-game hunting in the jungles of South Vietnam was their most daring diversion. Pope was ready for an even more dangerous challenge when the CIA approached him in December, 1957. The proposition was that he would fly a B-26 for the Indonesian rebels, who were seeking to topple Sukarno. A half-dozen planes were to be ferried in and out of the rebel airstrip at Menado in the North Celebes from the U.S. Air Force Base at Clark Field near Manila. In the Philippines the planes would be safe from counterattack by Sukarno's air force.

The idea of returning to combat intrigued Pope, and he signed up. His first mission, a ferrying hop from the Philippines to the North Celebes, took place on April 28, 1958. That was two days before President Eisenhower offered his comments about "soldiers of fortune" and promised "careful neutrality. . . . We will unquestionably assure [the Indonesian Government] through the State Department," he declared, "that our deportment will continue to be correct."

But Sukarno was not to be easily convinced. A shrewd, fifty-six-year-old politician, he was a revolutionary socialist who led his predominantly Moslem people to independence after 350 years of Dutch rule. Sukarno knew he was deeply distrusted by the conservative, businesslike administration in Washington. A mercurial leader, he was spellbinding on the stump but erratic in the affairs of state. He was also a ladies' man (official Indonesian publications spoke openly of his "partiality for feminine charm" and quoted movie-magazine gossip linking him with such film stars as Gina Lollobrigida and Joan Crawford) and has had four wives.

In particular, Sukarno was aware of Washington's understandable annoyance with his sudden turn toward the Left: he had just expropriated most of the private holdings of the Dutch and had vowed to drive them out of West Irian (New Guinea); he had requested Russian arms; and he had brought the Communists into his new coalition government.

From the start of its independence in 1949 until 1957 Indonesia was a parliamentary democracy. The power of the central government was balanced and diffused by the local powers of Indonesia's six major and 3,000 minor islands stretching in a 3,000-mile arc from the Malayan peninsula. But in February, 1957, on his return from a tour of Russia and the satellites, Sukarno declared parliamentary democracy to be a failure in Indonesia. He said it did not suit a sharply divided nation of close to 100,000,-000 people. Besides, the government could not successfully exclude a Communist Party with over 1,000,000 members.

"I can't and won't ride a three-legged horse," Sukarno declared. His solution was to decree the creation of a "Guided Democracy." It gave him semi-dictatorial powers while granting major concessions to the Communists and the Army.

The Eisenhower Administration feared that Sukarno would fall completely under Communist domination. And that, of course, would be a genuine disaster for the United States. Although its per capita income of $60 was one of the lowest in the world, Indonesia's bountiful supply of rubber, oil and tin made it potentially the third richest nation in the world. And located between the Indian Ocean, the Pacific Ocean, Asia and Australia, it commanded one of the world's principal lines of communication.

Many of Indonesia's political leaders, particularly those outside of Java, shared Washington's apprehensions about Sukarno's compromises with the Communists. And many in the CIA and the State Department saw merit in supporting these dissident elements. Even if Sukarno were not overthrown, they argued, it might be possible for Sumatra, Indonesia's big oil producer, to secede, thereby protecting private American and Dutch holdings. At the very least, the pressures of rebellion might loosen Sukarno's ties with the Communists and force him to move to the Right. At best, the Army, headed by General Abdul Haris Nasution, an anti-Communist, might come over to the rebels and force wholesale changes to the liking of the United States.

On February 15, 1958, a Revolutionary Council at Padang, Sumatra, proclaimed a new government under the leadership of Dr. Sjafruddin Prawiranegara, a forty-seven-year-old Moslem party leader and former governor of the Bank of Indonesia. A multi-party cabinet was established, with representation from Java, Sumatra and Celebes.

Sukarno declared: "There is no cause for alarm or anxiety. Like other countries, Indonesia has its ups and downs."

General Nasution promptly asserted his allegiance by dishonorably discharging six high-ranking officers who had sided with the rebels. A week later Indonesian Air Force planes bombed and strafed two radio broadcasting stations in Padang and another in Bukittinggi, the revolutionary capital forty-five miles inland. The attack, carried out by four old U.S. planes, succeeded in silencing the rebel radios.

In testimony to Congress early in March, John Foster Dulles reiterated the United States pledge of strict neutrality. "We are pursuing what I trust is a correct course from the point of international law," he said. "And we are not intervening in the internal affairs of this country. . . ."

On March 12 Jakarta announced that it had launched a paratroop invasion of Sumatra, and the next week the rebels formally appealed for American arms. They also asked the United States and the Southeast Asia Treaty Organization to recognize the revolutionary government.

On April 1 Dulles declared: "The United States views this trouble in Sumatra as an internal matter. We try to be absolutely correct in our international proceedings and attitude toward it. And I would not want to say anything which might be looked upon as a departure from that high standard."

A week later, commenting on Indonesia's announcement that it was purchasing a hundred planes and other weapons from Communist Poland, Yugoslavia and Czechoslovakia, State Department spokesman Lincoln White declared: "We regret that Indonesia turned to the Communist bloc to buy arms for possible use in killing Indonesians who openly opposed the growing influence of Communism in Indonesia."

Jakarta responded angrily that it had turned to the Communists only after the United States had refused to allow Indonesia to buy $120,000,000 worth of American weapons. Dulles confirmed the fact the same day but claimed the Indonesians were rebuffed because they apparently intended to use the weapons to oust the Dutch from West Irian.

"Later, when the Sumatra revolt broke out," Dulles added, "it did not seem wise to the United States to be in the position of supplying arms to either side of that revolution. . . .

"It is still our view that the situation there is primarily an internal one and we intend to conform scrupulously to the principles of international law that apply to such a situation."

During the night of April 11, some 2,000 Indonesian Army troops launched an offensive against the rebels in northwest Sumatra, and at sunrise on April 18 a paratroop and amphibious attack was hurled against Padang. Twelve hours later, after modest resistance, the rebel city fell. Turning his troops inland toward Bukittinggi, Nasution declared he was "in the final stage of crushing the armed rebellious movement."

Throughout that month Jakarta reported a series of rebel air attacks against the central government, but it was not until April 30 that the United States was implicated. Premier Djuanda Kartawidjaja then asserted that he had proof of "overt foreign assistance" to the rebels in the form of planes and automatic weapons.

"As a consequence of the actions taken by the United States and Taiwan adventurers," Djuanda commented, "there has emerged a strong feeling of indignation amongst the armed forces and the people of Indonesia against the United States and Taiwan. And if this is permitted to develop it will only have a disastrous effect in the relationships between Indonesia and the United States."

Sukarno accused the United States of direct intervention and warned Washington "not to play with fire in

Indonesia . . . let not a lack of understanding by America lead to a third war. . . .

"We could easily have asked for volunteers from outside," he declared in a slightly veiled allusion to a secret offer of pilots by Peking. "We could wink an eye and they would come. We could have thousands of volunteers, but we will meet the rebels with our own strength."

On May 7, three days after the fall of Bukittinggi,* the Indonesian military command charged that the rebels had been supplied weapons and ammunition with the knowledge and direction of the United States. The military command cited an April 3 telegram to the Revolutionary Government from the "American Sales Company" of San Francisco. Robert Hirsch, head of the company, confirmed that he had offered to sell the arms to the rebels but said he had done so without clearing it with the State Department. In any case, he said, the arms were of Italian make and none had been delivered.

The State Department flatly denied the accusation, and the *New York Times* editorialized indignantly on May 9:

"It is unfortunate that high officials of the Indonesian Government have given further circulation to the false report that the United States Government was sanctioning aid to Indonesia's rebels. The position of the United States Government has been made plain, again and again. Our Secretary of State was emphatic in his declaration that this country would not deviate from a correct neutrality. The President himself, in a news conference, reiterated this position but reminded his auditors, and presumably the Indonesians, that this government has no control over soldiers of fortune. . . .

"It is always convenient for a self-consciously nationalistic government to cry out against 'outside interference' when anything goes wrong. Jakarta . . . may have an unusually sensitive conscience. But its cause is not promoted by charges that are manifestly false. . . .

"It is no secret that most Americans have little sympathy for President Sukarno's 'guided democracy' and his en-

* The rebels then moved their capital to Menado, which fell late in June.

151

thusiasm to have Communist participation in his government. . . .

"But the United States is not ready . . . to step in to help overthrow a constituted government. Those are the hard facts. Jakarta does not help its case, here, by ignoring them."

The following week, one day after the United States officially proposed a cease-fire, Allen Pope was shot down while flying for the rebels and the CIA. However, the Indonesian Government withheld for nine days the fact that an American pilot had been captured. On May 18 it announced only that a rebel B-26 had been shot down.

Nevertheless, with Pope in Indonesian hands things began to move rapidly in Washington. Within five days: (1) the State Department approved the sale to Indonesia for local currency of 37,000 tons of sorely needed rice; (2) the United States lifted an embargo on $1,000,000 in small arms, aircraft parts and radio equipment—destined for Indonesia but frozen since the start of the rebellion; and (3) Dulles called in the Indonesian ambassador, Dr. Mukarto Notowidigdo, for a twenty-minute meeting.

"I am definitely convinced," said the ambassador with a big smile as he emerged, "that relations are improving."

But the Indonesian Army was not prepared to remain permanently-silent about Pope. On May 27 a news conference was called in Jakarta by Lieutenant Colonel Herman Pieters, Commander of the Moluccas and West Irian Military Command at Ambon. He announced that Pope had been shot down on May 18 while flying a bombing mission for the rebels under a $10,000 contract.

Pieters displayed documents and identification papers showing Pope had served in the U.S. Air Force and as a pilot for CAT. He said Philippine pesos, 28,000 Indonesian rupiahs, and U.S. scrip for use at American military installations were also found on the American pilot. Pieters said 300 to 400 Americans, Filipinos and Nationalist Chinese were aiding the rebels, but he did not mention the CIA.

Many Indonesian officials were outraged by Pope's activities, and accused him of bombing the market place in Ambon on May 15. A large number of civilians, church-bound on Ascension Thursday, were killed in the raid on the predominantly Christian community. But the government did its best to suppress public demonstrations.

Pope was given good medical treatment, and he could be seen sunning himself on the porch of a private, blue bungalow in the mountains of Central Java. Although the Communists were urging a speedy trial, Sukarno also saw advantages in sunning himself—in the growing warmth of United States policy. Pope's trial was delayed for nineteen months while Sukarno kept him a hostage to continued American friendliness.

Late the next year, however, Sukarno found himself in a quarrel with Peking over his decision to bar Chinese aliens from doing business outside of the main cities of Indonesia. The powerful Indonesian Communist Party was aroused over the issue and Sukarno may have felt the need to placate them.

Pope was brought to trial before a military court on December 28, 1959. He was accused of flying six bombing raids for the rebels and killing twenty-three Indonesians, seventeen of them members of the armed forces. The maximum penalty was death.

During the trial, which dragged on for four months, Pope pleaded not guilty. He admitted to flying only one combat mission, that of May 18, 1958. The other flights, he testified, were of a reconnaissance or non-combat nature. Contrary to the assertion that he had signed a $10,000 contract, Pope insisted he got only $200 a flight.

The court introduced a diary taken from Pope after his capture. It contained detailed entries of various bombing missions. Pope contended it listed the activities of all the rebel pilots, not just his. He replied to the same effect when confronted with a pre-trial confession, noting that he had refused to sign it.

Asked what his "real motive" had been in joining the rebels, Pope replied: "Your honor, I have been fighting the Communists since I was twenty-two years old—first in Korea and later Dienbienphu. . . .

"I am not responsible for the death of one Indonesian—armed or unarmed," he asserted in his closing plea. "I have served long enough as a target of the Communist press, which has been demanding the death sentence for me."

On April 29, 1960, the court handed down the death sentence, but it seemed unlikely that the penalty would be imposed. It had not once been invoked since Indonesia gained its independence eleven years before.

Pope appealed the sentence the following November, and when it was upheld by the Appeals Court, he took the case to the Military Supreme Court. Mrs. Pope made a personal appeal to Sukarno on December 28 during the first of two trips to Indonesia, but she was offered no great encouragement despite the prospect of improved relations between Sukarno and President-elect Kennedy.

Sukarno received an invitation to visit Washington a month after Kennedy took office. The Indonesian leader had been feted by President Eisenhower during a state visit to the United States in 1956; and he had more or less forced a second meeting with Eisenhower at the United Nations in the fall of 1960. But on most of his trips to the United States, Sukarno felt snubbed. Kennedy's invitation clearly flattered and pleased him.

The two men sat down together at the White House the week after the Bay of Pigs. The meeting went well enough, but Kennedy was preoccupied with the CIA's latest failure at attempted revolution.

During the visit Kennedy commented to one of his aides: No wonder Sukarno doesn't like us very much. He has to sit down with people who tried to overthrow him.

Still Sukarno seemed favorably disposed toward the new Kennedy Administration. The following February, during a good-will tour of Indonesia, Robert Kennedy asked Sukarno to release Pope. (Secret negotiations were then far advanced for the exchange the next week of U-2 pilot Francis Gary Powers and Soviet spy Rudolph I. Abel. And the White House was favorably impressed with the tight-lipped Mr. Pope as contrasted with Powers, a CIA pilot who talked freely about his employer.)

Sukarno's first reaction to Robert Kennedy's request was to reject it out of hand, but when the Attorney General persisted, he agreed to take it under consideration. Six months later, on July 2, 1962, Pope was freed from prison without prior notice and taken to the American Embassy for interrogation by Ambassador Jones and other officials. Then he was put aboard a Military Air Transport Service plane and flown back to the United States.

Pope was hidden away for seven weeks and the State Department did not reveal his release until August 22. Pope insisted there had been no secret questioning (such as that to which Powers was subjected by the CIA on his return from Russia). The State Department's explanation of the long silence was that Pope had asked that the release be kept secret so he could have a quiet rendezvous with his family.

Back in Miami, Pope settled down to what outwardly seemed to be a happy relationship with his family; but in December, Mrs. Pope filed for divorce, charging him with "extreme cruelty" and "habitual indulgence in a violent and ungovernable temper."

At the divorce hearing on July 2, 1963, Mrs. Pope testified that on his return from Indonesia, her husband insisted upon keeping a loaded .38-caliber pistol by their bedside, despite the potential danger to their two young boys. She also asserted that Pope had sent her only $450 since he had left her seven months before.

Mrs. Pope made no mention in the proceedings of her husband's work for the CIA. A security agent of the government had warned her that it would be detrimental to her case if she talked about her husband's missions. She did not, and Pope did not contest the divorce.

"There's an awful lot of cloak-and-dagger mixed up in this," said her Miami lawyer, Louis M. Jepeway, who otherwise refused to talk about the case. "I can understand it, but I don't have to like it."

Mrs. Pope won the divorce and custody of the children on grounds of cruelty. But she received no financial settlement because Pope was declared outside the jurisdiction of the court.

On December 4, 1962, Pope had put his things in storage—some personal items, ten stuffed birds, four animal heads, one stuffed animal, antelope antlers and water-buffalo horns. Then he left the country to go to work for Southern Air Transport. The Pentagon described this airline as a civilian operation holding a $3,718,433 Air Force contract to move "mixed cargo and passenger loads on Far East inter-island routes." Its home address was listed as PO Box 48-1260, Miami International Airport. Its overseas address was PO Box 12124, Taipeh, Formosa.

However, when asked what sort of work Southern Air Transport did, the company's Miami attorney explained that it was a small cargo line which simply "flies chickens from the Virgin Islands."

The attorney was Alex E. Carlson, the lawyer for the Double-Chek Corporation that had hired the American pilots who flew at the Bay of Pigs.

9

Laos: The Pacifist Warriors

WINTHROP G. BROWN had been Ambassador to Laos for less than three weeks when the right-wing military government, created by the CIA and the Pentagon at a cost of $300,000,000, was overthrown without a shot by a twenty-six-year-old Army captain named Kong Le.

Brown, a tall, thin, gray-haired Yankee, had been transferred from New Delhi on short notice with only a superficial knowledge of the long, tortured and expensive history of the United States experiment in Laos. Yet even a quick look convinced him that the CIA and its Pentagon allies were wrong in their assessment of the captain.

The young paratrooper and his battalion of 300 men had taken over the capital city of Vientiane in a pre-dawn coup on August 9, 1960. They had not been paid in three months and were tired of being the only fighting unit in the quasi-pacifist army of 25,000. Kong Le was personally outraged by the high-living, CIA-backed regime of General Phoumi Nosavan. He decided to strike while Phoumi and his cabinet were out of town inspecting a sandalwood tree that was to be turned into a burial urn for the late king.

The CIA and the American military mission viewed the coup with horror. They considered Kong Le to be Communist-inspired, despite his many battles against the pro-Communist Pathet Lao. But Ambassador Brown, a fifty-three-year-old former Wall Street lawyer who tried to see things with detachment and a fresh eye, was inclined to accept the American-trained paratrooper for what he purported to be: a fine troop commander who lived with his men and shared their rations; a patriot weary of civil war.

"I have fought for many years," Kong Le said. "I have killed many men. I have never seen a foreigner die."

Laos is a pastoral land, blessed with magnificent scenery —soaring mountains, swift rivers, verdant valleys—and populated by a strange mixture of isolated tribes alike only in their distaste for physical labor. It is the "Land of the Million Elephants," whose only cash crop is opium, and whose people are 85 percent illiterate.

Almost all Laotians are Buddhists, peace-loving by instinct and precept. In battle, to the dismay of their American advisers, they were accustomed to aiming high in the expectation that the enemy would respond in kind.

In 1960 the principal attraction of Phoumi's royal army to a recruit was the pay—$130 a year, twice the average national income. Although United States aid had amounted to about $25 a head for the two million Laotians, military pay was about all that filtered down to the average citizen. More than three fourths of the money went to equip a modern, motorized army in a nation all but devoid of paved roads. All of this, as formulated by John Foster Dulles, was meant to convert Laos from a neutral nation, vulnerable to left-wing pressures, into a military bastion against Communism.

When the French withdrew in 1954, after a futile eight-year war with the Vietnamese Communists, a neutralist government had been organized under Prince Souvanna Phouma, a cheerful, pipe-smoking, French-educated engineer. He held power for four years, unsuccessfully struggling to integrate the two Communist Pathet Lao provinces into the central government. Then, in 1958, after Communist election gains and signs of military infiltration by the North Vietnamese, he resigned.

Souvanna was followed by a series of right-wing governments in which General Phoumi emerged as the strongman. Finally, Phoumi succeeded in easing out Premier Phoui Sananikone, an able man with advanced ideas about grass-roots aid and village development; he was also firmly non-Communist but he had too many independent notions for the CIA. He was replaced by Tiao Somsanith, a thoroughly pliable politician.

Phoumi then rigged the 1960 elections—not one Pathet Lao was elected—and settled in for a long, U.S.-financed tenure. Even Kong Le's coup failed to dim his vision of permanent affluence. He still had his army intact with him at Savannakhet in the south. And he was unshakably convinced that the United States would put him back in power. As tangible support for that conviction, Phoumi could point to the personal contact man the CIA kept by his side.

He was Jack Hazey, an ex-OSS man and former French Legionnaire whose face was half shot away during World War II. Occasionally, Hazey would be challenged for being out of step with public statements of U.S. policy. Clearly implying that he was under higher, secret orders, Hazey would retort: "I don't give a damn what they say."

The conflict between the public and secret definitions of United States policy on Laos was particularly pronounced in the summer of 1960. Shortly after Phoumi and his puppet Premier were ousted, Kong Le called back Souvanna Phouma to form a coalition government. To reduce the chances of discord, Souvanna then asked Phoumi to join the government as Vice-Premier and Minister of Defense.

Ambassador Brown dashed off a cable to Washington urging unqualified support for Souvanna's new government.* But the CIA and the State Department decided to hedge: they announced formal recognition of Souvanna but continued substantive support for Phoumi. The decision served to reinforce Phoumi's conviction that the CIA and the American military mission would in the end put him back in power.

Brown persuaded himself that he had the complete

---

* Later, Brown's only regret was that, restrained by a newcomer's caution, he did not make the recommendation even more strong. A key diplomat agreed: "Now we'd gladly pay $100,000,000 for that government."

backing of the CIA station chief, Gordon L. Jorgensen, and the leaders of the military mission; but Washington's ambivalent policy put the ambassador in an embarrassing predicament. He tried to make the best of it by seeking out Souvanna and asking him if he had any objections to the continued support of Phoumi by the United States. No, the princely Premier replied, provided the equipment was not used against him; he would need Phoumi's army to fend off the Pathet Lao.

Brown then sent emissaries to Phoumi, assuring him that Souvanna was not scheming to deprive him of his U.S. aid and pleading with him at least to return to Vientiane and negotiate. But this man who had been highly regarded by the CIA and the Pentagon for his fighting qualities was afraid of venturing beyond his closely guarded stronghold. He had a broken line in the palm of his hand and a fortuneteller had once warned him that he would die violently. Even under maximum security he wore a bullet-proof vest during all his diplomatic dealings.

Confronted by Phoumi's intransigence, Souvanna began to despair of his ability to carry on. He called in the Western ambassadors in mid-September and warned them that he urgently needed the support of the royal army. "I am at the end of my capacity to lead," he told them.

Souvanna's government was also in dire need of rice and oil, which had been cut off by a blockade imposed by Thailand's military strongman, Prime Minister Sarit Thanarat, a close friend of Phoumi. Washington said it was entreating Sarit to lift the blockade, but the vise continued to tighten around Souvanna.

Early in October, J. Graham Parsons, former Ambassador to Laos and then Assistant Secretary of State for Far Eastern Affairs, flew to Vientiane and demanded that Souvanna sever his relations with the Pathet Lao. This amounted to a demand that the neutralist government abandon its neutrality. Souvanna refused.

Then a high-level mission from the Pentagon, including John N. Irwin, Assistant Secretary of Defense for International Affairs, arrived for secret talks with Phoumi.

Souvanna concluded that the United States was in the

process of withdrawing all support from the neutralist government and again throwing its full power behind Phoumi. Early in December he made a final and unsuccessful appeal to Brown for rice and oil. In desperation, Souvanna turned to the Russians, who saw an irresistible opportunity: to achieve political dominance in Laos at a cut rate and, at the same time, to replace the Chinese as the principal Communist influence in Southeast Asia. Without delay the Soviets started an airlift from Hanoi on December 11, 1960.*

Two days earlier Phoumi had ordered his troops northward; and on December 18 the royal army recaptured Vientiane. Souvanna fled to Cambodia and Kong Le retreated to the north, distributing close to 10,000 American rifles to the Pathet Lao along the way.

Phoumi quickly established a government, naming Prince Boun Oum, a middle-aged playboy, as Premier. But despite his recent military success, Phoumi failed to pursue Kong Le. Instead, he settled back into his old ways. He had never been within fifty miles of the front lines and he saw no need to break with this tradition.

The Russians, meantime, were moving in substantial amounts of weapons by air and truck. And the North Vietnamese began to infiltrate crack guerrilla troops in support of the Pathet Lao. Kong Le joined forces with them, and by early 1961 he had captured the strategic Plain of Jars with its key airstrip fifty miles from North Vietnam.

By the time President Kennedy was inaugurated, on January 20, it seemed as if only the introduction of U.S. troops could keep the Pathet Lao from overrunning Vientiane and the Mekong River Valley separating Laos from Thailand. Kennedy was so informed by President Eisenhower and Defense Secretary Thomas S. Gates, Jr., in his first Laos briefing on January 19. Eisenhower apologized for leaving such a "mess."

One of Kennedy's first official acts was to ask his military

---

* Deputy Foreign Minister Georgi M. Pushkin told Harriman at the Laotian talks in Geneva in 1961 that the airlift had been organized and executed on the highest priority of any peacetime operation since the Russian Revolution.

advisers to draw up a plan for saving Laos. They recommended that an Allied force, including U.S. troops, take over the defense of Vientiane under the sanction of the Southeast Asia Treaty Organization. The idea was to free Phoumi's army for a full-fledged campaign in the Plain of Jars.

While weighing the advice, Kennedy ordered the Seventh Fleet within striking distance of Laos and promised Phoumi substantial new support if his troops would show some determination to fight.

Early in March, however, a royal army detachment was easily routed from a key position commanding the principal highway in northern Laos. The new administration became skeptical of Phoumi at the outset.

The Allied occupation plan was further undermined when the British, French and other SEATO powers (with the exception of Thailand) balked at providing troops. In addition, the President could not obtain assurances from the Joint Chiefs of Staff that U.S. forces would be able to save Laos without resort to tactical nuclear weapons.

In a nationally televised news conference on March 23 Kennedy warned that the Western powers would "have to consider their response" if the Communist attack continued in Laos. The clear implication was that the United States was prepared to intervene with military force. But, privately, the President told Harriman that he decidedly did not want to be faced with the prospect of using troops, that he wanted a political settlement.

On April 1 the Russians, apparently wary of a direct confrontation with the United States, agreed in principle to a British proposal for a cease-fire. The next month a fourteen-nation conference on Laos was convened in Geneva. And in the only meeting of minds at their talk in Vienna in June, Kennedy and Khrushchev promised to work for a neutral and independent Laos.

By November the outlines of an agreement had been reached at Geneva: Souvanna Phouma was to be recalled to create a neutralist government including the three Laotian factions, the pro-Western royalists, the neutrals and the pro-Communist Pathet Lao.

But once again Phoumi balked. He refused to relinquish the Defense and Interior Ministries, as was decreed at Geneva. If he held out long enough, he reasoned, the CIA and the Pentagon would again come to his rescue.

President Kennedy rebuked him in private messages, but Phoumi steadfastly refused to submit. Had he not been told in 1960 that the United States was determined to have him join Souvanna's coalition? And in the end had not the CIA and the Pentagon supported him in his return to power? And, as in 1960, were not the CIA representatives still with him?

Washington was reluctant to yank out the CIA men abruptly. Precipitate action could only diminish the agency's prestige and usefulness. But Phoumi was proving so intractable that McCone, acting on Harriman's recommendation, ordered Hazey out of the country early in 1962.*

Nevertheless, Phoumi's reliance on the CIA had become so firmly ingrained that he could not be budged, even after the United States cut off its $3,000,000-a-month budgetary assistance to his government in February of 1962.

That spring Phoumi began a large-scale reinforcement of Nam Tha, an outpost deep in Pathet Lao territory, twenty miles from the Chinese border. Ambassador Brown warned him personally that the reinforcement was provocative and that the royal troops were so badly deployed that they would be an easy mark for the Pathet Lao. In May, Brown's admonition proved accurate. The Communists retaliated against the build-up, smashed into Nam Tha and sent Phoumi's troops in wild retreat. Two of his front-line generals commandeered the only two jeeps in the area and fled into Thailand.

The Nam Tha rout finally convinced Phoumi that he could not go it alone; and the Pathet Lao, verging on a complete take-over, halted when President Kennedy ordered 5,000 U.S. troops to take up positions in Thailand near the Laos border on May 15.

* Hazey was then stationed in Bangkok, where he could be called upon quickly in a crisis.

The three Laotian factions finally agreed to the coalition government on June 11 and the Geneva Accords were signed on July 23. In October the United States withdrew the 666 military advisers assigned to Phoumi's army.

But Communist North Vietnam failed to comply with the Geneva agreement. It refused to withdraw about 5,000 troops stationed in Laos in support of the Pathet Lao. On March 30, 1963, the Communists launched a new offensive which brought much of the Plain of Jars under their control.

The United States responded predictably: the Seventh Fleet took up position in the South China Sea off Vietnam; some 3,000 troops were sent to Thailand for much-publicized war games; and Harriman flew to Moscow to confer with Khrushchev. The Russian leader reaffirmed his support for a neutral and independent Laos. He also seemed to agree with Harriman that the Pathet Lao was responsible for the renewed fighting. It was clear that Moscow had lost control of the situation in Laos to Peking and Hanoi.

At the same time, United States policy makers were becoming increasingly convinced that Laos was not the right place to take a stand in Southeast Asia. The assessment of the Kennedy Administration was that most of the country, particularly the northern regions, would never be of much use to anyone. Administration officials were fond of debunking the Dulles policy with the quip: "Laos will never be a bastion of anything." The administration felt, nonetheless, that certain areas would have to be retained at all cost: Vientiane and the Mekong Valley. But it opposed the use of U.S. troops on any large scale.

In the event the neutralist government was about to be completely overwhelmed, the official plan, as it was outlined at a briefing of Pentagon officials by Dean Rusk, called for the movement of a modest American force into Vientiane. This would be designed to provoke a diplomatic test of the Geneva Accords. Failing in that, the United States was prepared to strike against North Vietnam as dramatic evidence that the Communist forces in Laos could advance farther only at the risk of a major war.

So it was that by the start of 1964, after a decade of humiliating reverses and the expenditure of close to half a billion dollars, United States policy had come full circle: during the 1950s Souvanna Phouma and his plan for a neutral Laos had been opposed with all the power of the Invisible Government; now the United States was ready to settle for even less than it could have had five years earlier at a fraction of the cost.

10

Vietnam: The Secret War

When Ngo Dinh Diem was deposed and assassinated in an Army coup on November 1, 1963, a bloody, frustrating decade came to a close for the Invisible Government.

For nearly ten years the intelligence and espionage operatives of the Pentagon, the CIA and the State Department had been intimately involved with Diem, attempting at every turn to shore him up as a buffer against Communism in Vietnam. But in his last months the Buddhist majority rose against the repressive policies of Diem, a Roman Catholic, and the Invisible Government was forced to reconsider its single-minded support. Now, with Diem dead, those very American agencies which had helped him stay in power for so long were accused by his supporters of having directed his downfall.

At the beginning, the Invisible Government had high hopes for Diem. In 1954, at the age of fifty-three, the pudgy five-foot, five-inch aristocrat returned to Vietnam from a self-imposed exile to become Emperor Bao Dai's Premier. He had served under Bao Dai in the early 1930s, but quit as Minister of the Interior when he discovered the government was a puppet for the French. The Japanese twice offered Diem the premiership during World War II, but he refused.

When the French returned after the war, he resumed his anti-colonial activities. He left the country in 1950, eventually taking up residence at the Maryknoll Seminary in Lakewood, New Jersey (he had studied briefly for the priesthood as a boy). He lobbied against United States aid to the French in Indochina and warned against Ho Chi Minh, the North Vietnamese Communist guerrilla leader.

Shortly after Diem's return to Vietnam, the French Army was routed at Dienbienphu and the Communists seemed on the verge of total victory in Indochina. President Eisenhower, aware of Ho Chi Minh's popularity,* was looking for an anti-Communist who might stem the tide.

Eisenhower and John Foster Dulles were impressed by Ramon Magsaysay's successful campaign against the Communist Huk guerrillas in the Philippines. They thought the same tactics might work in Vietnam and requested a briefing by Edward Lansdale, an Air Force colonel who had been a key figure in the CIA-directed operation in support of Magsaysay.

Lansdale was called back from the Philippines to appear before a special panel of intelligence and foreign-policy officials, including Foster Dulles. He emerged from the meeting with a mandate from Dulles to find a popular leader in Vietnam and throw the support of the Invisible Government behind him.

Lansdale arrived in Saigon just after the fall of Dienbienphu and found political and military chaos. He canvassed the various factions in the city and the countryside and concluded that Diem alone had enough backing to salvage the situation. He met with Diem almost daily, working out elaborate plans for bolstering the regime. He operated more or less independently of the American mission assigned to Saigon, although he communicated with Washington through CIA channels (the agency maintained a separate operation with a station chief and a large staff).

Lansdale's free-wheeling activities in Vietnam provoked a mixed reaction. To some, he seemed the best type of

* In his book, *Mandate for Change*, Eisenhower wrote: "I have never talked or corresponded with a person knowledgeable in Indochinese affairs who did not agree that had elections been held as of the time of the fighting, possibly 8o percent of the population would have voted for Ho Chi Minh."

167

American abroad, a man who understood the problems of the people and worked diligently to help them. He was so represented under a pseudonym in the book *The Ugly American*. To others, he was the naïve American who, failing to appreciate the subtleties of a foreign culture, precipitated bloodshed and chaos. Graham Greene patterned the protagonist in *The Quiet American* after him.

Lansdale thrust himself into the middle of Vietnam's many intrigues. In the fall of 1954 he got wind of a plan by several high-ranking Vietnamese Army officers to stage a coup against Diem. He alerted Washington, and General J. Lawton Collins, former Army Chief of Staff, was rushed to Saigon as Eisenhower's personal envoy to help Diem put down the uprising.

The coup failed, but Collins became skeptical of the stability of the Diem regime. He favored a proposal to create a coalition government, which would represent all the power elements and factions in the country. The proposal was sponsored by the French, who were maneuvering to salvage their waning influence in the affairs of Indochina.

In the spring of 1955 Diem moved against the Binh Xuyen, a quasi-criminal sect which controlled the Saigon police. He ordered his troops to take over the gambling, opium and prostitution quarter run by the Binh Xuyen. But elements of the French Army which had not yet been evacuated from the country intervened for the avowed purpose of preserving order and preventing bloodshed. Collins sided with the French and a truce was declared.

Lansdale fired off a message to Washington through the CIA channel, taking strong exception to Collins' decision. Lansdale argued that Diem's move against the Binh Xuyen had broad popular support. He also discounted the fears of Collins and U.S. Army Intelligence that Diem's troops would turn against the regime.

Collins returned to Washington for consultation, then flew back to Saigon with the impression that his views would be sustained. But in his absence Lansdale had obtained a reaffirmation of the policy of support for Diem. Furious, Collins accused Lansdale of "mutiny." But the die was cast. Assured of the complete backing of the United States Government, Diem crushed the Binh Xuyen and the other warlike sects.

Then, at Lansdale's urging, Diem agreed to hold a referendum designed to give the regime a popular legitimacy. The ballot presented a choice between Diem and Emperor Bao Dai, who had been discredited as a tool of the French. Diem polled 98 percent of the vote on October 23, 1955, and was declared President of Vietnam. His brother, Ngo Dinh Nhu, was established as his official political strategist.

Some measure of stability had now been achieved in South Vietnam. But Diem and Nhu refused to grant political freedom to the opposition parties, despite Lansdale's warning that the country would be plagued by conspiracy if legitimate parties were not permitted to operate openly.

Lansdale made a special trip to Washington in an effort to induce the Dulles brothers to apply pressure on Diem to institute political reforms in South Vietnam. But Lansdale failed. He was told that it had been decided that Diem provided the only practical alternative to a Communist take-over and that he was to be supported without qualification.

Overruled, Lansdale lost his influence as the unofficial emissary of the Invisible Government in Vietnam. Thereafter, the CIA took his place as the secret link with the Diem regime. A CIA man was ordered to establish liaison with Nhu. It was the start of an intimate relationship which was to last until 1963.

During the next few years the United States committed itself increasingly to the support of the regime. More than a billion dollars in military and economic aid was provided between 1955 and 1960. But it was not until 1961 that the commitment became complete.

In the early years of Diem's rule the Communist Vietcong conducted only a hit-and-run guerrilla campaign against him. In 1959, however, the Vietcong operations were greatly expanded. Two theories have been advanced in explanation. The official theory of the State Department was that Diem was bringing off a political and economic

169

"miracle" and the Communists could not bear the contrast to their bad showing in North Vietnam.

Diem's critics offered a conflicting theory. They claimed the populace had become so disaffected by Diem's repression that the Communists decided the time was ripe for action. In 1960 a group of young, discontented Army officers felt the same way. They attempted a coup but Diem put them down without serious difficulty.*

In any event, conditions had so disintegrated by 1961 that Diem's government was master of only a third of the territory of South Vietnam. In May of that year President Kennedy sent Vice-President Johnson to Saigon.

On May 13 Johnson and Diem issued a joint communiqué stating that aid would be provided for Vietnam on an expanded and accelerated basis. The United States agreed to underwrite the cost of an increase in the Vietnamese Army from 150,000 to 170,000 men, and to equip and support the entire 68,000-man Civil Guard (armed police) and the 70,000-man Self-Defense Corps.

But the Vietcong continued to advance, and in October, 1961, Kennedy sent General Maxwell D. Taylor to make "an educated military guess" as to what would be needed to salvage the situation.

Taylor recommended a greatly increased program of military aid. He also saw an imperative need for reform within the Army. He cited the political activities of the top military, failure to delegate enough authority to field commanders, and discrimination against younger officers on political and religious grounds.

Diem balked at Taylor's reforms and implied he might turn elsewhere for aid. However, on December 7 he applied for assistance, and the United States again came to his support.

No limit was placed on the aid either in terms of money or of men. In effect, the United States committed itself to

* In April, 1963, at the start of the CIA's reassessment of its links with the regime, Nhu accused the agency of being involved in the 1960 uprising. But the commander of the rebels, Colonel Nguyen Chanh Thi, who fled to Cambodia, said U.S. intelligence men tried to discourage the coup and persuaded the rebels not to kill Diem.

a massive build-up for an undeclared war. At the same time, the administration took great precautions to keep the build-up a secret, perhaps because it violated the letter of the Geneva Accords,* perhaps because of the domestic political danger if Americans were sent into another Asian war.

When the new U.S. Military Assistance Command was created on February 8, 1962, about 4,000 American military men were already serving secretly in Vietnam. However, the Pentagon refused to comment on the troop level and attempted to imply that the 685-man Geneva ceiling was still in effect.

Additional thousands of troops poured into Vietnam, but the Defense Department continued the deception until June. Then Rear Admiral Luther C. (Pickles) Heinz, who was co-ordinating the operation for Defense Secretary McNamara at the Pentagon, permitted press spokesmen to say that "several thousand" U.S. military men were in Vietnam on "temporary duty."

In January, 1963, McNamara provided the first official figure. In testimony before Congress he confirmed that 11,000 troops were in Vietnam. But the Pentagon quickly reverted to generalities; asked in July to comment on reports from Saigon that the troop level had reached 14,000, it said that was "about the right order of magnitude."

The Pentagon also went to great lengths to obscure the fact that U.S. military men were involved in combat—leading troops, and flying helicopters and planes. The official view was that the Americans were in Vietnam purely in "an advisory and training capacity." Despite eyewitness reports to the contrary, the Pentagon insisted that American troops were firing only in self-defense.

Military information officers were forced to ludicrous extremes in denying the obvious. When an aircraft carrier

---

* The United States did not formally subscribe to the Geneva Accords, which divided Indochina into Laos, Cambodia and Vietnam after Dienbienphu. But Bedell Smith, the delegate to the negotiations, declared the United States would abide by them. The Accords set a limit of 685 on the number of U.S. military men permitted in Indochina.

sailed up the Saigon River jammed with helicopters, a public information officer was compelled to say: "I don't see any aircraft carrier."

There was a great deal more that was not seen. In 1961 a campaign had been quietly started to put 90 percent of South Vietnam's 15,000,000 people into 11,000 strategic hamlets or fortified villages. The program, patterned after the successful "new villages" of the British anti-guerrilla campaign in Malaya, was designed to protect the peasants against Vietcong terror.

Many claimed credit for introducing the strategic-hamlet idea to Vietnam, including Nhu, who said he launched it with the blessing of the CIA (a former CIA man ran the program for the Agency for International Development). By 1964 more than three fourths of the Vietnamese were listed as being protected by the hamlets. But many of the peasants were forced into the program against their will and many of the forts were easily penetrated by the Communists.

The Communists had also been successful in keeping open a supply route from North Vietnam. Although the Vietcong's best weapons were captured U.S. equipment, they received some additional supplies by infiltration through Communist-held Laos, which borders on both halves of Vietnam.

To cut the supply routes, the CIA decided to train the Montagnards, primitive mountain tribesmen, as scouts and border guards. They were induced to exchange their spears and bows and arrows for modern weapons, including Swedish Schneisers (light machine guns).

Between 1961 and the start of 1963 the cost of the Montagnard program rose from $150,000 to $4,500,000. The CIA achieved considerable success in sealing the border, but in the process perhaps created a Trojan horse: ten percent of the trained Montagnards were judged to be Vietcong sympathizers, and the Vietnamese, who regarded the tribesmen as subhumans, were fearful that the weapons eventually would be used against them.

The Montagnard training was carried out by the Vietnamese Special Forces, an elite corps created by the CIA along the lines of the U.S. Army Special Forces. The CIA organized the Special Forces for the regime well before the 1961 build-up and supported them at the rate of $3,000,000 a year. They were chosen for their toughness and rugged appearance. They were trained in airborne and ranger tactics and were originally designed to be used in raids into Laos and North Vietnam. But inevitably they fell under the control of Nhu, who held the bulk of them in Saigon as storm troopers for the defense of the regime.

By 1963 more than 16,000 American military men were in Vietnam. United States aid had reached $3,000,000,000, and was running at an average of $1,500,000 a day. The government declared itself confident that victory was in sight despite the popular discontent with Diem's rule.

Two Vietnamese Air Force pilots had bombed Diem's palace in February, 1962. But the State Department discounted the significance of the attack: "The question of how much popular support Diem enjoys should be considered in terms of how much popular support his opponents command. Neither of the recent non-Communist attempts [1960 and 1962] to overthrow him appeared to have any significant degree of popular support." [1]

Admiral Harry D. Felt, the commander of the U.S. forces in the Pacific, predicted the South Vietnamese would triumph over the Communists by 1966. And only a month before Diem was toppled, President Kennedy and the National Security Council stated that "the United States military task can be completed by the end of 1965." [2]

But there were skeptics. In 1963 Senator Mike Mansfield returned from a tour of Vietnam and declared: "What is most disturbing is that Vietnam now appears to be, as it was [in 1955], only at the beginning of a beginning in coping with its grave inner problems. All of the current difficulties existed in 1955 along with hope and energy to meet them . . . yet, substantially the same difficulties remain if indeed they have not been compounded." [3] The GIs in the rice paddies summed it up in a slogan: "We can't win, but it's not absolutely essential to pick today to lose."

This slogan reflected the awareness of many Americans in Vietnam that Diem's popular support, always tenuous, was rapidly disintegrating. The discontent broke into the open on May 8, 1963, in Hue, Diem's ancestral home, when the Buddhists staged a demonstration against the regime's ban on the flying of their flag.

Diem's troops opened fire, killing nine marchers. And in an effort to arouse world opinion, Buddhist monks responded by burning themselves to death in the streets in a series of spectacular public protests. Madame Nhu, Diem's sister-in-law, ridiculed the suicides as politically inspired "monk barbecue shows."

Diem was warned privately that the United States would condemn his treatment of the Buddhists unless he redressed their grievances. But to all outward appearances it seemed as if the United States might be supporting the Buddhist repressions. For on August 2 Nhu sent the Special Forces in a raid on the Buddhist pagodas. Hundreds of Buddhists were jailed and scores were killed and wounded in a brutal attack by forces which many Vietnamese knew were supported by CIA money.

Immediately after the raids, Henry Cabot Lodge, the Republican vice-presidential candidate in 1960, arrived in Saigon to be the new ambassador, replacing Frederick E. Nolting, Jr., who had been closely identified with the regime. Lodge quickly made it clear to Diem that the United States wanted his brother and Madame Nhu removed from power. After nearly a decade of support for the regime, the United States was reassessing its position.

Even though the CIA decided to continue its $250,000-a-month subsidy to the Special Forces during September, the funds were cut off in October. And on October 4 the CIA station chief in Saigon, John H. Richardson, was recalled to Washington at Lodge's request.

Richardson, a dapper, bald man with heavy horn-rimmed glasses, had served as the CIA's personal link with Nhu. He was also close to most of the regime's top officials, including those in the secret police. From his small second-floor office in the American Embassy, Richardson directed the agency's multifarious activities in Vietnam. A hardliner, he had little use for Diem's opponents, and was the very symbol of the Invisible Government's commitment to the regime. As long as he remained in Vietnam, it was all but impossible to convince either Diem or his enemies of any change in United States policy.

When Richardson was recalled, many took it as evidence that the CIA had been operating on its own in Vietnam in defiance of orders from Washington. But President Kennedy assured a news conference on October 9 that the "CIA has not carried out independent activities but has operated under close control." The implication was clear that Richardson's recall reflected a shift in policy, not displeasure with insubordination.

The implication was not lost on Nhu. He charged on October 17 that the CIA was plotting with the Buddhists to overthrow the regime. "Day and night," he declared, "these people came and urged the Buddhists to stage a coup. It is incomprehensible to me why the CIA, which had backed a winning program, should reverse itself."

The coup against the regime came on November 1, but it was by the Army, not the Buddhists. Diem and Nhu were assassinated. The United States denied any complicity in the coup or the deaths. But Madame Nhu, who had been in the United States bitterly attacking the Kennedy Administration, indicated her belief that her husband and brother-in-law had been "treacherously killed with either the official or unofficial blessing of the American Government. . . . No one," she said, "can seriously believe in the disclaimer that the Americans have nothing to do with the present situation in Vietnam."

The United States repeated its denial. But at least one distinguished American remained uneasy. President Eisenhower sought assurances on the assassinations before floating a trial balloon for Ambassador Lodge as the Republican nominee for President in 1964:

"General Eisenhower wanted to be assured on one paramount question," said Felix Belair in the *New York Times* on December 7, 1963. "He wanted to know of the ambassador whether anyone would ever be able to charge, with any hope of making it stick, that he had had any responsibility, even indirectly, in the assassination of President Ngo Dinh Diem of South Vietnam and of his brother Ngo Dinh Nhu.

"Mr. Lodge was emphatic on the point. He said he had feared for the personal safety of the two men if the military coup was successful in that country. He said there was irrefutable proof that he had twice offered them asylum in the United States Embassy and that President Diem had refused the offer for them both."

What was intriguing about this account was the statement that President Eisenhower found it necessary to make an inquiry of this nature. But the former President, after all, had an intimate understanding of the tactics and workings of the Invisible Government.

11

Guatemala: CIA's Banana Revolt

"WELL, BOYS," Ambassador John E. Peurifoy told his assembled staff, "tomorrow at this time we'll have ourselves a big party."

The scene was the American Embassy on Octava Avenida in Guatemala City, and the unlikely ambassadorial quote was clearly recalled by one of the participants in the meeting. The date was June 18, 1954. The CIA's coup against the Communist-dominated regime of President Jacobo Arbenz Guzman had begun. That afternoon, Colonel Carlos Castillo-Armas, a U.S.-trained Guatemalan exile, had crossed the border from Honduras with about 150 men. Now the invasion was on. It had the full advance approval of President Eisenhower.

Peurifoy, a tough but soft-spoken South Carolinian, was overly optimistic. His party to celebrate Arbenz's downfall had to be postponed for two weeks. What the CIA had planned as an overnight coup dragged on for twelve difficult days. Before it had ended, Peurifoy was deeply involved in political cloak-and-dagger maneuvering. And the President of the United States, over the objections of the State Department, found it necessary, clandestinely, to send in three more fighter planes to bail out the CIA's banana revolt.

Unlike the Bay of Pigs, the 1954 Guatemalan operation succeeded. Like Iran the year before, Guatemala was one of the CIA's early triumphs in the field of overthrowing governments. Some of those who participated have begun to say so openly.

On June 10, 1963, in Washington, Dwight D. Eisenhower made a little-reported but extraordinary speech. The former President for the first time conceded, for all practical purposes, that the United States had overthrown the government of Guatemala in 1954. "There was one time," he said, "when we had a very desperate situation, or we thought it was at least, in Central America, and we had to get rid of a Communist government which had taken over, and our early efforts were defeated by a bad accident and we had to help, send some help right away." [1]

Eisenhower did not mention Guatemala by name, but his meaning was perfectly clear, particularly since he shared the speaker's platform with Allen Dulles, his Director of Central Intelligence.

What the ex-President was referring to was this: Four days after Peurifoy's ebullient prediction to the embassy staff in Guatemala City, Eisenhower was told that disaster had overtaken the CIA's modest air force, which consisted of a few World War II P-47 Thunderbolts. One had been shot up in action, and another had crashed. The Thunderbolts had been bombing Guatemala City to encourage Arbenz to vacate the Presidential Palace.

Allen Dulles wanted the planes replaced immediately. Henry F. Holland, Assistant Secretary of State for Inter-American Affairs, was aghast. Providing the CIA with planes for Castillo-Armas was one thing *before* the invasion had actually started. But doing so now, Holland felt, would expose the United States to the hated charge of intervention in Latin American affairs. News of the President's action might leak out, Holland reasoned.

Allen Dulles, however, felt there could be no stopping now. Many months of careful preparation had gone into the Castillo-Armas invasion. Jerry Fred DeLarm, a World War II American fighter pilot who was flying one of the P-47s for the CIA, had enjoyed astonishing success in his raids on Guatemala so far.

A White House meeting was scheduled in the afternoon to discuss the question of the planes.

"Now different people, including Mr. Dulles and a member of the State Department and so on, came into my office to give their differing views," Eisenhower recalled in his 1963 speech.

"And the man* who opposed going any further was very vehement in his representation and he wanted no part. He thought we should stop right there, wash our hands of the thing and let it stand right there. Well, Mr. Dulles was on the other side. And when all of the views were presented, I decided we would go ahead and the orders went out [to send more planes].

". . . I said to Mr. Dulles . . . before I made this decision I said 'What are the chances that this will succeed?' Well, he said he thought about twenty percent. I told him later, 'If you'd have said ninety percent, I'd have said no, but you seemed to be honest.'

"He told me later, 'Well, you know, I knew that my opponent had lost the argument because he came in your office with three law books under his arm.'"

While campaigning in the 1960 and 1962 elections, Senator Thruston B. Morton, the Kentucky Republican, had spoken just as freely about Eisenhower's role in the Guatemala coup. Morton's remarks in Kentucky did not gain national attention, however, until he repeated them at a party dinner in Baltimore in February, 1963, and on a television program.

Whiting Willauer, Ambassador to Honduras during the Guatemala coup, had openly discussed the CIA's role as far back as 1961. In little-noticed testimony before a Senate Committee [2] Willauer said that after the Guatemala coup, "I received a telegram from Allen Dulles in which he stated in effect that the revolution could not have succeeded but for what I did. I am very proud of that telegram."

Then the questioning went as follows:

Q. Mr. Ambassador, was there something of a team in working to overthrow the Arbenz government in Guatemala, or were you alone in that operation?

* Henry Holland, the State Department's representative at the meeting.

A. There was a team.

Q. Jack Peurifoy was down there?

A. Yes, Jack was on the team over in Guatemala; that is the principal man, and we had Bob Hill, Ambassador Robert Hill, in Costa Rica . . . and we had Ambassador Tom Whelan in Nicaragua, where a lot of the activities were going. And, of course, there were a number of CIA operatives in the picture.

Q. What was Mr. Dulles' involvement in that area?

A. Mr. Allen Dulles?

Q. Yes.

A. Well, the CIA was helping to equip and train the anti-Communist revolutionary forces.

Q. Would you say you were the man in charge in the field in this general area of all these operations?

A. I certainly was called upon to perform very important duties, particularly to keep the Honduran Government—which was scared to death about the possibilities of themselves being overthrown—keep them in line so they would allow this revolutionary activity to continue, based in Honduras.

The former ambassador was amazingly explicit in his testimony about the coup in Guatemala, a land best known to the outside world for coffee, bananas and the quetzal, which is both its national bird and the name of its monetary unit.

About 60 percent of Guatemala's population of 3,800,000 is Indian. The Indians are Mayas, descendants of the highly sophisticated culture that flourished a thousand years before the Spanish conquistadors came and ruled all of Central America from the Guatemalan city of Antigua. The rest of the population is of mixed Spanish and Indian descent. These are the *ladinos*. The Indians are largely illiterate; they provide a cheap labor force and have little communication with the *ladinos*.

Guatemala is a truly feudal state. About 2 percent of the population owns more than 70 percent of the land. For decades the most important two words in Guatemala have been *la Frutera*, the United Fruit Company. The American banana company owned and ran as a fiefdom hundreds of square miles of land in Bananera and Tiqui-sate. It was also a major stockholder in the country's rail-road—and a ready-made gringo political target.

When Arbenz took office in March, 1951, one of the first demands he faced came from coffee workers, who insisted that their minimum wages be doubled. This might seem unreasonable except for the fact that their pay was forty cents a *day*. The labor unions also demanded more for United Fruit's banana workers, who were paid $1.36 a day.

A bold student revolt had ousted Dictator Jorge Ubico in 1944. After that, President Juan José Arevalo, a socialist who turned violently anti-American, paved the way for Arbenz and the Communists.

Jacobo Arbenz Guzman, a professional Army officer, was the son of a Swiss father who migrated to Guatemala and became a druggist. (It was later rather widely whis-pered that Arbenz himself took drugs.) As President, Arbenz in 1952 tried to do something about the country's lopsided land ownership. He pushed through a land-reform program, but, predictably, it ended with small farmers, large *finca* owners and the United Fruit Company up in arms.

With his high-pitched voice and bad temper, Arbenz was no crowd-pleaser. And the students, always a powerful factor in Latin America, ridiculed him. The students had an annual lampooning parade, the *Huelga de Dolores* (grievance strike), of which Guatemalan officials lived in horror. Not long before Arbenz's fall from power, the students paraded by with a float that showed Uncle Sam poking a Guatemalan Indian lady with a banana; Arbenz and his hypodermic needle lurked behind a Russian bear, prodding the Guatemalan lady from the other direction. It about summed up the political situation.

For the bear was loose in the banana groves, all right. To maintain his power, Arbenz turned more and more to the Communists. Just as there is debate over whether Castro started out a Communist or became one later, there has been some dispute over the political evolution of Arbenz. But there is little dispute that by 1954 the Communists were running Guatemala. They had gained a foothold and a base in the hemisphere.

Arbenz made one fatal mistake, however. He trusted the Guatemalan Army, an essentially peace-loving organization little inclined to unnecessary strife and combat. Unlike Castro, Arbenz did not penetrate the Army politically, and when he needed it most, it turned on him. Late in the game he had placed spies, popularly known as *orejas* (the Ears), in various Army posts, but it was too late.

He made one other big mistake—he expropriated 225,000 acres of United Fruit's best Pacific-slope holdings. Later the Arbenz regime charged that the United States had supported the Castillo-Armas invasion to protect *la Frutera's* $40,000,000 investment in Guatemala.

In the era of the Cold War, keeping Soviet power and influence out of the hemisphere, and particularly out of the Panama Canal area, was far more important to Washington than old-style banana diplomacy. But certainly the seizure of United Fruit's holdings without adequate compensation forced Eisenhower to take action. And it was one more indication of the direction things were taking in Guatemala.

Although a shipment of Czech arms to Guatemala in May, 1954, was later widely cited as the reason for the CIA-organized coup, the fact is that the machinery to topple Arbenz had been set in motion long before that.

Late in 1953 John Emil Peurifoy arrived on the scene. Peurifoy, known as "Smiling Jack" around the embassy in Guatemala (although not to his face), was a small-town boy from Walterboro, South Carolina, who had enjoyed a phenomenal rise in the State Department. This may not have been unrelated to the fact that his father was once an associate of the powerful James F. Byrnes, who was a senator at the time Peurifoy landed his first job with the State Department in 1938.

Peurifoy was proud of the fact that he once ran the Capitol elevator and equally proud of his small-town background. "Why, that town was so small," he was fond of saying, "you could drive right through it and not know you had been theah."

Beneath his courtly Old South exterior, Peurifoy was tough. He had been through hard times in the depression years. He quit West Point, knocked about the country for a while, became assistant manager and cashier of the Childs restaurant chain in New York, ran the elevator in Congress, watered plants at Washington's Botanical gardens and held a variety of other odd jobs before becoming a diplomat.

He never bothered to learn foreign languages, although in Guatemala he would occasionally wave to the crowd, smile and say "*Amigos!*" Fresh from Greece, where he had helped shore up that country after its war with the Communists, Peurifoy was just the man to have on the scene if there was to be trouble in the land of the quetzal bird.

And there was to be trouble. It was already brewing. Miguel Ydigoras Fuentes, who later became Guatemala's President, was in exile in El Salvador early in 1954. In his recent book, Ydigoras wrote:

"A former executive of the United Fruit Company, now retired, Mr. Walter Turnbull, came to see me with two gentlemen whom he introduced as agents of the CIA. They said that I was a popular figure in Guatemala and that they wanted to lend their assistance to overthrow Arbenz. When I asked their conditions for the assistance I found them unacceptable. Among other things, I was to promise to favor the United Fruit Company and the International Railways of Central America; to destroy the railroad workers labor union; . . . to establish a strong-arm government, on the style of Ubico. Further, I was to pay back every cent that was invested in the undertaking." [3]

By late 1953 Eisenhower had reached his decision: Arbenz must go. To implement this decision, he turned to the CIA and Allen Dulles. A plan was evolved.

Peurifoy's assignment to Guatemala was part of it. Eisenhower's election had left Peurifoy without any political backing. His diplomatic career seemed over. The

CIA went to Peurifoy and persuaded him to join the operation as Ambassador to Guatemala. At first, Peurifoy was leery of the idea, but a persuasive CIA official convinced him that the operation offered him his big chance to revitalize his career. Peurifoy said yes; the CIA arranged his ambassadorial appointment. In February, 1954, Eisenhower called in a former high United States diplomat to serve as a secret civilian adviser to the operation. The President had also asked his brother, Dr. Milton Eisenhower, to join the clandestine operation, but Milton, pleading his wife's serious illness at the time, did not participate.

Henry Holland, as the State Department Latin Chief, was privy to the operation. So were the Joint Chiefs of Staff. So was Senator Thruston B. Morton, then Assistant Secretary of State for Congressional Relations.

Although Dulles and his deputy, General Cabell, were in charge of the CIA's participation, the major immediate responsibility for carrying out the Guatemalan operation was placed in the hands of Frank G. Wisner, the Mississippi-born CIA deputy director for plans. (He was Bissell's predecessor.)

Wisner, a dedicated and hard-driving "black" operator, was an old hand in the intelligence business. In World War II he had been the OSS mission chief in Istanbul and Bucharest. He also worked for the OSS in Germany. After the war, commuting from his home in the suburbs to his Manhattan law firm, Carter, Ledyard & Milburn, seemed dull compared to the days of wartime intrigue along the Bosporus. On November 12, 1947, it was announced that Frank Wisner had been named Deputy Assistant Secretary of State.

Now, in Guatemala in 1954, what Wisner and the CIA needed was someone to serve as a leader of the coup and a focal point around which anti-Arbenz Guatemalans could rally. The man chosen was Colonel Carlos Castillo-Armas, a dapper, dedicated and ascetic-looking career officer who had tunneled his way out of prison to freedom after leading an unsuccessful revolt against Arbenz in 1950.

Castillo-Armas set up headquarters in Tegucigalpa, Honduras, and with the CIA's help, began plotting to return to his homeland. A onetime classmate of Arbenz at the Escuela Politecnica, Guatemala's military school, Castillo-Armas had spent two years just after World War II at the U. S. Army Command and General Staff School at Fort Leavenworth, Kansas.

The first evidence that the plot was afoot came on January 29, 1954, when Guatemala released intercepted correspondence between Castillo-Armas and Ydigoras.

The Guatemalan charges had a basis in fact, because the two exile leaders had been in touch and had signed a *Pacto de Caballeros* (gentlemen's agreement) at the border between El Salvador and Honduras. The pact provided that there would be a coup, and then free elections.

Guatemala charged that the plot was centered in Managua, the capital of Nicaragua, and enjoyed the support of President Anastasio Somoza and of General Rafael L. Trujillo, the dictator of the Dominican Republic. The Arbenz government also surmised that the "government of the North" had endorsed the plan.

It charged that the operation was known by the code name *El Diablo* (the Devil) and that training of rebels was going forward at El Tamarindo, President Somoza's plantation, at Puerto Cabezas (which became the air base for the Bay of Pigs operation seven years later) and on the island of Momotombito in Lake Managua.

The Guatemalan Government also charged that a "Colonel Carl T. Struder" who "was retired" from the U.S. Army, was training the sabotage teams. It said that arms were coming from H. F. Cordes & Company, in Hamburg, West Germany. State Department officials in Washington said they would not comment because that would "give the story a dignity it doesn't deserve."

But the training of Castillo-Armas' forces was in fact taking place on Momotombito, a volcanic island (actually the top of a volcano) which had earned its sonorous name from the sound the Indians thought it made when it rumbled. And "Tacho" Somoza, Nicaragua's President, was indeed heavily involved in the plans to overthrow Arbenz. In Nicaragua the training was directed by a CIA officer who went under the name of "Colonel Rutherford."

The most powerful military element in the coup was the CIA's air force. The handful of P-47 Thunderbolts and C-47 transports operated out of Managua International Airport. The pilots were Americans. The most daredevil of these, as events later proved, was Jerry Fred DeLarm, a slim, short, hawk-featured man who liked to lay a .45 down on the table in front of him when talking to a stranger.

DeLarm, a native of San Francisco, was a barnstorming, adventurous flier well known in Central America. He had been flying in the area since he was nine, with his father, a pioneer pilot named Eddie DeLarm. Jerry DeLarm spoke Spanish fluently. When World War II broke out, he was flying in Panama City. During the war he shot down two Japanese Zeros over Saipan. He was discharged as a captain and shortly thereafter set up an airline in Costa Rica.

DeLarm's wife was related to Dr. Rafael Calderon-Guardia, the former President of Costa Rica. In 1948, when Otilio Ulate was elected President of that highly democratic nation, Calderon-Guardia tried to block him from taking office. In the revolt that followed, Jose Figueres battled Calderon-Guardia, and emerged as head of a victorious junta.

DeLarm fought on the losing side, for Calderon-Guardia. He flew a DC-3 rigged up with a machine gun in the co-pilot seat and another poking through the floor of the rear bathroom, for ground strafing.

After Costa Rica, DeLarm moved on to Guatemala. During the election of 1950 he took a job doing skywriting and aerial broadcasts for Arbenz. He was promised $20,000 by the man he later helped to overthrow, and was understandably disturbed when the money did not come through after Arbenz won. That, DeLarm reflected later, was when he first began to suspect Arbenz was a Communist.

By 1954 DeLarm was flying for Castillo-Armas and the CIA. Until shortly before the invasion, he remained behind in Guatemala City, giving flying lessons and using this and an automobile dealership as cover. He had the code name "Rosebinda."

Meanwhile, events were moving in the public arena as well. John Foster Dulles and Henry Holland led the American delegation to the tenth Inter-American conference at Caracas in March. Dulles pushed for an anti-Communist resolution aimed squarely at Guatemala. Arbenz's foreign minister, Guillermo Toriello, angrily accused Foster Dulles of trying to create a "banana curtain." But the American resolution passed, seventeen to one, with Guatemala in opposition.

In May matters began moving to a climax. The CIA learned that a shipload of Czech arms, delivered through Poland, was on its way to Guatemala. The estimated 2,000 tons of rifles, machine guns and other armaments were aboard the Swedish freighter M/S *Alfhem*, en route from the Polish port of Stettin on the Baltic Sea.

The *Alfhem* operated out of Uddevalla, Sweden, and her owner was Angbats, Bohuslanska & Kusten, Inc. But Czech funds paid for a "straw charter" of the *Alfhem*, through the British firm of E. E. Dean in London. And the ship was taking a route to Guatemala as roundabout as its intricate charter arrangements. It sailed first to Dakar, then to Curaçao, then to Honduras and finally to Puerto Barrios, on the east coast of Guatemala, where it docked on May 15.

The CIA had a difficult time tracking the arms ship across the vast Atlantic. At the time, it knew everything about the ship except its name: *Alfhem*. That made tracking difficult, since the freighter was playing hide-and-seek. Although the CIA had the help of the Navy, the agency lost the ship as it was going south along the African coast. It didn't catch up with the *Alfhem* until it turned up at dockside in Guatemala.

The State Department revealed the arms shipment on May 17. A week later the United States announced that as a countermeasure, it had begun shipping arms to Nicaragua in giant Globemaster planes. At least fifty tons of small arms and machine guns were flown in to "Tacho" Somoza.

But Eisenhower's efforts to get the Western Allies to join a quarantine on arms shipments to Guatemala met with less than a rousing success. The United States drew a protest from the Dutch when it searched the freighter *Wulfbrook* at San Juan, Puerto Rico. Britain refused to allow its ships to be searched.

On June 7, with the invasion date approaching rapidly, a strange event took place in Guatemala. It was disclosed that Ferdinand F. Schupp, identified as a "former deputy chief of the United States Air Force Mission" in Guatemala, had fled the country along with Colonel Rodolfo Mendoza Azurdia, the ex-chief of the Guatemalan Air Force.

The United States Embassy announced that Schupp had "resigned" his embassy post in 1952 to go into a "farming project" in southern Guatemala. Later, Schupp turned up in Guatemala City, like Jerry DeLarm, giving flying lessons. It is believed that Mendoza took off in a private plane on a seemingly routine flight and stopped off in a pasture to pick up Schupp. The two landed in El Salvador and asked for "asylum."

The CIA's air operation was drawing closer to readiness. Mendoza and Schupp had escaped to join it. A few days before Castillo-Armas crossed the border, DeLarm also slipped out of Guatemala, aboard a regular Pan American flight.

On June 8 Foster Dulles branded "totally false" Guatemalan charges that the United Fruit Company was at the heart of the dispute between Guatemala and Washington. Dulles said the Communist problem would remain even "if they gave a gold piece for every banana."

A couple of days before the invasion commenced the Secretary of State invited Thruston Morton to a White House meeting. As Assistant Secretary for Congressional Relations, Morton was aware of the CIA operation, since it had been his task to brief a few key senators about its true nature.

"You'd better come along," Secretary Dulles told Morton, "because if this thing blows up and goes wrong, you're going to have to straighten things out for us on the Hill."

Morton went along. The breakfast meeting with Eisenhower took place in the second-floor dining room of the White House. Eisenhower, the Dulles brothers, representatives of the Joint Chiefs of Staff and other aides were present, as Morton later recalled it. He said Eisenhower had asked the men around the table: "Are you sure this is going to succeed?" Told that it would, Eisenhower responded: "I'm prepared to take any steps that are necessary to see that it succeeds. For if it succeeds, it's the people of Guatemala throwing off the yoke of Communism. If it fails, the flag of the United States has failed."

It is generally agreed by the participants, however, that at no point in the invasion planning did Eisenhower ever discuss sending in United States armed forces should the CIA operation fail.

On June 18 Castillo-Armas and his small "Army of Liberation" crossed the border into Guatemala from Honduras. He drove in a battered station wagon, leading his men down the road to Esquipulas. Before dawn the P-47s had bombed San Jose, Guatemala's major port on the Pacific coast.

In Guatemala City the government announced the invasion had begun. In Washington the State Department said it had been in touch with Peurifoy. It added blandly: "The department has no evidence . . . that this is anything other than a revolt of Guatemalans against the government."

Newsmen from all over the world converged on Guatemala and Honduras—only to discover that there was no war to cover. Castillo-Armas and his Liberation Army settled down six miles over the border in Esquipulas, the site of the Church of the Black Christ, the country's major religious shrine. The strategy was to wait for the Arbenz regime to collapse. Then the invaders would march triumphantly into Guatemala City.

With the Army of Liberation bogged down just inside the Guatemalan border, "Tacho" Somoza decided to invite Ydigoras to lunch with him at the Presidential Palace in Managua to discuss the situation. "Tacho" introduced

Ydigoras to "Colonel Rutherford," and added: "He is just back from Korea."

"Tacho" was standing in front of a map with pins in it showing the disposition of the Castillo-Armas columns. Four of the pins were in the shape of airplanes. The Nicaraguan President was bitterly complaining about how slowly the freedom forces were advancing.

"What kind of a crummy military school did Castillo-Armas go to?" Somoza asked.

"The same one I did," Ydigoras replied mildly.

The most active of the planes represented by the pins on "Tacho's" map was that of DeLarm. On the first day of the invasion he dropped propaganda leaflets on Guatemala City, but had orders not to fire or drop any bombs. On subsequent raids on the capital, however, he bombed and strafed several targets, effectively demoralizing the government leaders.

The CIA's planes became known among the Guatemalan populace as *Sulfatos*—the Guatemalan word for laxative—because of the alleged effect their appearance had upon the Arbenz officials.

Then disaster struck the CIA's force of P-47s, when one was shot full of holes and another cracked up. On June 20 the Guatemalan Government charged in the UN that two American fliers had crash-landed in Tapachula, Mexico, after having bombed the Guatemalan city of Coban.*

On the same day the Guatemalan Government was voicing its charge in the UN about American fliers, Henry Cabot Lodge, the United States Ambassador to the world organization, denied categorically that his government was behind the invasion. "The situation does not involve aggression but is a revolt of Guatemalans against Guatemalans," he stated.

---

* That same day William A. Beall, a thirty-year-old American flier from Tyler, Texas, showed up in Mexico City saying he had crash-landed his plane in the Pacific Ocean off Guatemala two days before. He had flown to Mexico City from Tapachula. Beall said two other American fliers had crashed off Guatemala a few days earlier, but had been rescued "by the United States Navy."

It was about this time that Allen Dulles made an urgent appeal for more airplanes. This led to the meeting of Eisenhower, Allen Dulles and Henry Holland, whose legalistic objections were overruled.

What Eisenhower did not say in his speech relating to this incident, is that the planes had to be "sold" by the U.S. Air Force to the government of Nicaragua in order to mask United States participation, which was surfacing at the UN. As cover for the transaction, Nicaragua had to put down $150,000 in cash to purchase the planes. After some interesting financial legerdemain, Nicaraguan Ambassador to Washington Guillermo Sevilla-Sacasa managed to come up with cover payment, and the new planes were dispatched to Nicaragua. Ultimately, it was CIA money that paid for them. The planes were flown down unarmed, to be armed upon arrival.

At one point during the trouble over the airplanes, General Cabell, the CIA deputy director, learned that one of the P-47s had been shipped to Nicaragua minus a landing-gear wheel. The plane could not operate without it. The U.S. Air Force rushed the part down and the Thunderbolt flew in the invasion.

On June 24, two days after the secret White House meeting, a P-47 swooped over Guatemala City, strafed gasoline stores and knocked out a radio station. It was not, as luck would have it, the Communist station, but a Protestant missionary station operated by Harold Von Broekhoven, an evangelist from Passaic, New Jersey.

In New York, a spokesman for the United Fruit Company said that banana harvesting was at a standstill because of the war. He said they were keeping in close touch with the company manager in Guatemala City, Mr. Almyr Bump. The spokesman added confidently: "It is classical in these revolutionary movements down there that they confine themselves to national versus national, and Americans who stand on the sidelines and keep out of the way should be in no great danger."

American newsmen were certainly in no great danger. Castillo-Armas, as *New York Herald Tribune* correspondent Homer Bigart reported, clearly did not want them hanging around Esquipulas. Bigart had to retreat across the frontier to Nueva Ocotepeque, Honduras, which the newsmen referred to more conveniently as "New Octopus."

Defying the Army of Liberation ban, Evelyn Irons, a correspondent for the *London Evening Standard*, rented a mule and loped down the road to Esquipulas. There, Castillo-Armas stopped her. He would not allow her to proceed to the front, which had by now moved to Chiquimula. Nevertheless, Miss Irons had scooped her competitors, and mule prices in Nueva Ocotepeque soared.

But under the air attack, Arbenz was losing his nerve. The defection of Mendoza, the Air Force chief, was proving to be a key factor, because it demoralized the Guatemalan Air Force. It became so unreliable that Arbenz grounded his own planes.

At the front, Arbenz' reluctant Army commanders sent back messages saying that their forces were being overwhelmed by the invaders. It wasn't true, but it had a psychological effect on Arbenz. The CIA was reading the traffic from the front, and it knew what messages Arbenz was receiving. CIA clandestine radio operators intercepted the military communications and fed back false messages on the same wave length to further confuse the situation.

On June 25 a P-47 raided Guatemala City again. On June 27 Arbenz capitulated, following a long day of maneuvering by Peurifoy. The American ambassador first met at the palace with Foreign Minister Toriello. Then he conferred with Colonel Carlos Enrique Diaz, the chief of the Guatemalan armed forces, and a group of ranking colonels. By nightfall Arbenz was on the air broadcasting his resignation. Colonel Diaz became head of the junta that took over. He made an immediate tactical error.

Diaz, whose nickname was *Pollo Triste* (Sad Chicken), went on the air and announced: "The struggle against the mercenary invaders of Guatemala will not abate. Colonel Arbenz had done what he thought was his duty. I shall carry on."

This would never do. Diaz was operating on the radical

assumption that it was his duty to fight when his country was invaded.

Peurifoy instantly recognized that this would be a disaster. If the junta, to which the State Department's ambassador had given at least his tacit blessing, went out to fight the CIA's Army of Liberation, it would be a fine spectacle. What would Henry Holland and Frank Wisner say?

Peurifoy put on a "siren" suit, strapped a .45 to his belt, and began maneuvering to topple Diaz. The CIA, which of course wanted Diaz out, nevertheless felt that Peurifoy was making himself entirely too conspicuous for the good of the operation.

The next day Jerry DeLarm bombed Guatemala City in earnest. He knocked out the radio station (the right one) and then dropped two bombs right in the middle of Fort Matamoros, the major installation of the Guatemalan Army.

That did it. Diaz, President for one day, was ousted at the point of machine guns (according to one account) by Colonel Elfego Monzon. With two other colonels, Monzon took over as head of a new, less bellicose junta, acceptable to Peurifoy.

The war was over.

But the CIA and the State Department were worried that it might break out again at any moment. Peace talks between Monzon and Castillo-Armas were scheduled to take place in El Salvador. Washington gave Peurifoy *carte blanche* to bring the junta and the CIA's Castillo-Armas together.

"They want me to go over there to El Salvador," Peurifoy confided to an aide, "and knock heads together."

With the Papal Nuncio, Monsignor Gennaro Verolino, the American ambassador flew off to El Salvador for the talks. On July 2, with tearful if cautious embraces, Monzon and Castillo-Armas signed a peace pact. It left Monzon top man, but only until the junta voted formally on a chief. The deal was signed in the Hall of Honor in the Presidential Palace. Castillo-Armas then flew back to

Chiquimula to convince his followers that it was not a sellout to Monzon.

The next day Castillo-Armas came home to a huge welcome in Guatemala City. He arrived not at the head of his conquering troops, however, but in Peurifoy's embassy plane.

Meanwhile John Foster Dulles addressed the United States on radio and television. He said the struggle in Guatemala exposed the "evil purpose of the Kremlin" to find "nesting places" in the Americas and added: "Led by Colonel Castillo-Armas, patriots arose in Guatemala to challenge the Communist leadership—and to change it. Thus the situation is being cured by the Guatemalans themselves." [4]

If the CIA's coup had routed Communism in Guatemala, democracy is not what followed in its wake. As its first act, the ruling junta canceled the right of illiterates to vote, thereby disenfranchising in one stroke about 70 percent of Guatemala's population—almost all the Indians.

The junta elected Castillo-Armas as its President on July 8. In August the liberator suspended all constitutional guarantees. The ideological basis of the coup was further undercut when the chief CIA man in Guatemala quit the agency and went into the cement business there. The free election Castillo-Armas had promised when Arbenz fell turned out to be "*sí*" or "*no*" vote on whether to continue Castillo-Armas as President. Castillo-Armas won.

In rapid succession, the new regime set up a Robespierre-like Committee for Defense Against Communism with sweeping police-state powers. The government took back 800,000 acres of land from the peasants, returned to United Fruit the land Arbenz had seized, and repealed amendments to a 1947 law that had guaranteed rights to workers and labor unions.

Within a week of Castillo-Armas' election as head of the junta, the new government announced it had arrested 4,000 persons on suspicion of Communist activity. By August it had passed the Preventive Penal Law Against Communism. This set up the Defense Committee, which met in secret and could declare anyone a Communist—with no right of appeal.

Those registered by the committee could be arbitrarily arrested for periods up to six months; they could not own radios or hold public office. Within four months the new government had registered 72,000 persons as Communists or sympathizers. A committee official said it was aiming for 200,000.

Castillo-Armas was generally regarded as an honest, proud and rather simple man who genuinely loved his country. But he had a covey of advisers, and some of them were less dedicated than their chief. After the 1954 coup American gambler types began drifting into Guatemala, and certain of the liberator's lieutenants were cut in. Castillo-Armas could not bring himself to realize that some of his followers were treacherous. A gambling casino was built in which various Army officers shared a heavy financial interest with the Americans.

Castillo-Armas closed down the casino, and shortly afterward, on July 26, 1957, he was assassinated by a member of the palace guard. The crime was first blamed on Communists, then on Castillo-Armas' enemies within the government. It has never been solved.

The following year, Ydigoras was elected President and settled down for a term that was at least never dull. At one point, when rumors of official corruption were rife, he went on television with his ministers. Like a schoolteacher, Ydigoras went down the line, saying, "Now, Mr. Minister, you wouldn't steal from the treasury, would you?" One by one, the ministers said no, they certainly would not.

Another time, a newspaperman accused Ydigoras of being a *viejo enclenque*, or enfeebled old man. Ydigoras went on television again, repeated the charge and said: "I will show him." Then he proceeded to skip rope and juggle Indian clubs before the amazed Guatemalan audience.

Still, Ydigoras was nobody's fool. When the CIA came to him in 1960 asking for Guatemalan bases for the Bay of Pigs training, he said yes—although fully aware that he was risking his political neck. In fact, the November, 1960, uprising (which CIA pilots helped to put down) was partly blamed on the issue of the Cuban training bases in Guatemala.

On March 31, 1963, Ydigoras was ousted by Colonel Enrique Peralta in one of the first of a series of military coups in Latin America that threatened to make a mockery of the political reforms at the base of the Alliance for Progress. Colonel Peralta's regime was recognized by Washington in less than three weeks.

If any efforts were made by Washington to save the legally elected Ydigoras government—which had risked its future to provide bases for the CIA for the Cuban invasion—they were certainly not effective. There is, in fact, no available evidence that any such efforts were made.

And so, a decade after the CIA's liberation of Guatemala from Communism in 1954, the lot of Guatemalans was about the same. The *finca* owners prospered. The 2,000,000 Indians, still largely illiterate, toiled on for wages still ridiculously low. (Eighty cents a day is considered generous in many areas of the country.) And another military junta was in the saddle.

As is so often the case, the Invisible Government had moved in, accomplished its task, and moved on. The yoke of Communism had been thrown off but in its place there remained the yoke of poverty and an indifferent oligarchy. The abysmal conditions that led to Arbenz in the first place were as apparent as ever.

12

The Kennedy Shake-Up

THE CIA emerged from the coup in Guatemala with a reputation in the Invisible Government as a clever and efficient operator in Latin American affairs. And despite the agency's subsequent difficulties in other areas of the world, that reputation was essentially untarnished when President Kennedy took office in January of 1961.

When the invasion failed, however, a sharp reaction set in. A few days after the Bay of Pigs, President Kennedy called in Clark M. Clifford, a Washington lawyer and close confidant who later became the chairman of the President's Foreign Intelligence Advisory Board. Kennedy complained that he had been given bad information and bad advice by his intelligence and military advisers. "I was in the Pacific," said the ex-PT boat skipper. "I know something about these things. How could they have put all the ammunition in one ship or two ships?"

Referring to the Joint Chiefs of Staff, the President told another visitor: "They don't know any more about it than anyone else." He vowed to shake the intelligence community from top to bottom. He was determined that the Bay of Pigs would not happen again. "One more," he stated ruefully, "will sink me."

The President then set out to gain control of the intelligence establishment and to make it genuinely submissive to his ideas and purposes. As a first order of business, he decided to conduct an extensive investigation of the Cuban debacle.

"We intend to profit from this lesson," he told the American Society of Newspaper Editors on April 20, the day after the invasion collapsed. "We intend to re-examine and reorient our forces of all kinds—our tactics and our institutions here in this community. We intend to intensify our efforts for a struggle in many ways more difficult than war."

At his news conference the next day, the President declined to get into details about the Bay of Pigs on the grounds that it would not "aid the interest of the United States." But he denied any desire to "conceal responsibility. . . . I'm the responsible officer of the government," Kennedy declared, "and that is quite obvious."

But in this moment of extreme political vulnerability, high administration officials began to point out in private post-mortems with reporters that Kennedy had inherited the Bay of Pigs idea from President Eisenhower.

On April 23, Interior Secretary Stewart L. Udall made the mistake of giving public voice to the administration line, and the Republicans, predictably, pounced upon him.

"Here was a plan conceived by one administration," Udall declared. "This from all I can find out began over a year ago and President Eisenhower directed it."

"Cheap and vicious partisanship," retorted Richard M. Nixon.

Kennedy stepped in quickly the next day to prevent all-out political war. He told Pierre Salinger to issue a public statement.

"President Kennedy has stated from the beginning," Salinger declared, "that as President he bears sole responsibility for the events of the past days. He has stated on all occasions, and he restates it now, so it will be understood by all. The President is strongly opposed to anyone within or without the administration attempting to shift the responsibility."

Kennedy's full public acceptance of the blame seemed to be the Republicans' price for laying off the Cuban issue, at least temporarily. In the week after the invasion, the President discussed the operation at length with Eisenhower, Nixon, Senator Barry M. Goldwater of Arizona and

Governor Nelson A. Rockefeller of New York. Eisenhower set the Republican line on emerging from an eighty-five-minute conversation with Kennedy at Camp David on April 22.

"I am all in favor," Eisenhower declared, "of the United States supporting the man who has to carry the responsibility for our foreign affairs."

Kennedy used the momentary truce to set in motion a sweeping reorganization of the Invisible Government. Even before the Bay of Pigs, he had planned a major shake-up in the hierarchy of the CIA. He had indicated to several high-ranking officials that he would put Richard Bissell in charge of the agency when Dulles stepped down.

Now, in the shadow of the Cuban fiasco, it was clear that Bissell would have to go and that the shake-up would have to be deferred for a decent interval. Dulles' resignation was not accepted until September 27, 1961. He was succeeded on November 29, 1961 by John McCone. General Cabell retired as the deputy director on January 31, 1962. He was replaced by Army Major General Marshall Sylvester Carter, fifty-two. Bissell resigned as the deputy director for plans on February 17, 1962. He was succeeded by his assistant, Richard M. Helms, forty-eight. Robert Amory, the deputy director for intelligence, was shifted to the Budget Bureau to become the director of its International Division. He was replaced on May 16, 1962 by Ray S. Cline, forty-four.

The top-level shake-up at the CIA was not completed until a full year had passed. But two days after the invasion Kennedy ordered General Maxwell Taylor to head an investigation and to make recommendations for the reform of the intelligence community.

Taylor was a World War II paratroop commander who quit as Army Chief of Staff in 1959 in protest against the refusal of the Eisenhower Administration to adopt his views on conventional warfare. After the Bay of Pigs investigation, he became Kennedy's personal military adviser and, finally, the chairman of the Joint Chiefs of Staff.

Joining Taylor in the investigation were Robert Kennedy, Allen Dulles and Arleigh Burke. It was clear that the Attorney General was to become the untitled overseer of the intelligence apparatus in the Kennedy Administration. The appointment of Dulles and Burke, holdovers from the Eisenhower Administration, was designed to gather broad political support for the shake-up and to forestall suggestions that a whitewash operation was afoot.

Kennedy moved to take an even tighter grip on the Invisible Government on May 4, when he revived the President's Board of Consultants on Foreign Intelligence Activities under a new title, the President's Foreign Intelligence Advisory Board. The original group had been set up by President Eisenhower on January 13, 1956, on a recommendation by the Hoover Commission. It was headed by James R. Killian, Jr., the president of the Massachusetts Institute of Technology. Joseph P. Kennedy, the President's father, served on it for the first six months.

The board had disbanded on January 7, 1961, when the entire membership resigned in anticipation of the new administration. But now Kennedy called it back into existence, again under the chairmanship of Killian.*

The President's instructions to the new board were to investigate the entire intelligence community, to recommend detailed changes and to make sure that the changes were carried out. The original board had met just twice a year and had been only marginally informed about intelligence activities. Kennedy ordered the new board to meet six to eight times a year and, between times, to carry out specific assignments for him at home and abroad.

The Killian and Taylor groups had scarcely begun their secret inquiries before the tenuous political truce on the

* The new members were Frank Pace, Jr., former Secretary of the Army; Dr. Edwin H. Land, president of the Polaroid Corporation; Dr. William O. Baker, vice-president for research of the Bell Telephone Laboratories; Lieutenant General James H. Doolittle, retired, board chairman of Space Technology Laboratories, Inc.; Dr. William L. Langer, professor of history, Harvard University; Robert D. Murphy, former Under Secretary of State and president of Corning Glass International; Gordon Gray, former head of the Office of Defense Mobilization; and Clark Clifford, who had been a leading adviser to President Truman. Clifford succeeded Killian as chairman on April 23, 1963.

Bay of Pigs began to be breached. On June 11, 1961, William E. Miller, the New York congressman and the chairman of the Republican National Committee, charged that the invasion had failed because Kennedy "rescinded and revoked the Eisenhower plan to have the Cuban freedom fighters protected by American air power."

Miller said his accusation was based on comments by Eisenhower to a group of Republican leaders. But the former President corrected him the very next day. Eisenhower denied that American air power had been approved during his time in office. He had merely stated, the general explained, that an amphibious operation could not succeed without air support of some kind.

This was the first of many confusing exchanges during the following weeks and months on the issue of air cover. Republican and Cuban exile leaders charged repeatedly that the Bay of Pigs invasion failed because President Kennedy withdrew American air cover.

The Kennedy Administration held its tongue for close to two years. But finally, in January of 1963, Robert Kennedy denied the accusation in interviews with the *Miami Herald* and *U.S. News & World Report*.

"I can say unequivocally," he declared, "that President Kennedy never withdrew U.S. air cover. . . . There never were any plans made for U.S. air cover, so there was nothing to withdraw. . . ." [1]

And again: "There never was any promise. Not even under Mr. Eisenhower was American air cover in the picture." [2]

The air-cover controversy had grown out of a massive confusion over what was included in the original air plan for the Bay of Pigs. As we have seen in earlier chapters, the original plan envisioned no need for the direct intervention of U. S. Navy or Air Force planes. Castro's air force was to have been destroyed on the ground by the CIA's Cuban exile bombers. In that event, the Cuban invaders logically would not have required aerial protection against nonexistent planes. But the President canceled the second strike against Castro's air bases. Accordingly, Castro's planes were in the air to harass the invaders on the beach and to sink the ships carrying their equipment, ammunition, fuel and communications.

The real question in the controversy is whether the invasion could have succeeded if Kennedy had not canceled the second strike. The Taylor group grappled with this question but failed to reach agreement.

Taylor and Robert Kennedy concluded that the invasion plan had been thoroughly faulty and stood no chance of success in any event. "It simply cannot be said," the Attorney General later commented, "that the invasion failed because of any single factor. There were several major mistakes. It was just a bad plan. Victory was never close." [3]

Burke, on the other hand, took the position that the invasion very nearly succeeded, and probably would have if the President had not canceled the second air strike. The invasion might have worked without air support of any kind, the admiral argued, if the first air strike had not been scheduled two days in advance of the landing eliminating the element of surprise.

Dulles took a position somewhere in between. He thought success could have been achieved if all had gone according to plan (he had left Washington for San Juan at the time of the invasion with no idea that the plan would be changed). But Dulles felt the CIA and the Joint Chiefs made a mistake in not arranging for alternatives in case the second strike failed or did not come off. He thought there should have been a contingency plan to make sure the invaders got ashore with their equipment.

The Taylor committee presented its views, secretly and orally, to President Kennedy in the summer of 1961.* The committee had worked for about four months, meeting secretly at the Pentagon in an office close to the Joint Chiefs' area. The group interviewed virtually everyone of significance in the Bay of Pigs invasion, including the CIA

---

* Late in 1962 the administration's findings were drawn up in a White Paper, prepared mainly by Roger Hilsman, then the State Department's director of intelligence and research. At the White House, Bundy and Salinger recommended that it be released to the public in January, 1963. But Robert Kennedy urged that it remain secret, and the White Paper was not released.

man who directed the air operations and Mario Zuniga, the Cuban pilot who told the cover story about defecting from Castro's air force.

The committee reached more than thirty conclusions, including findings that communications were very bad and that there was an overcentralization of the operation in Washington. They also reached a meeting of minds on another crucial point. After the Bay of Pigs, there was considerable pressure within and without the government to limit the CIA to intelligence-gathering alone. It was argued that the agency was inevitably tempted to warp its intelligence estimates to justify its pet projects; and that it would be better to transfer responsibility for all clandestine operations to some other agency, possibly the Pentagon.

This argument was strenuously opposed by Dulles and Cabell. They contended that a separation of intelligence-gathering from operations would result in expensive duplication of personnel and facilities, particularly at overseas posts. They also warned that foreign agents would tend to play off one branch of the spy apparatus against the other, bidding up the price of information and confusing the evidence.

Dulles pleaded that, contrary to popular belief, no intelligence agency in the world is split into separate information-gathering and operational units. When the British set up a Special Operations Executive in World War II, he maintained, they ran into serious difficulties and had to revert to a CIA-type system.

These pleadings proved persuasive to the Taylor committee, which declined to recommend that all clandestine operations be divorced from the CIA's responsibilities. The President agreed and the CIA continued to function essentially in its old ways.

However, the Taylor group did come to the conclusion that the Bay of Pigs operation was too large and too unwieldly to have been conducted by the CIA. In the future, the CIA was to be limited to operations requiring military equipment no larger or more complex than side arms— weapons which could be carried by individuals. In other words, the CIA was never again to direct operations involving aircraft, tanks or amphibious ships. Operations of that size were to be conducted by the Pentagon.

Put another way, the CIA was henceforth to be restricted to paramilitary operations which would be "plausibly deniable." The Bay of Pigs invasion was not plausibly deniable because it was too large and pervasive to escape the notice of alert officials, newspapermen and private citizens in a free society.

It is clear from all this that the leaders of the government had finally come to the realization that certain types of clandestine operations are incompatible with the democratic system. In a totalitarian society, where the organs of communication are tightly controlled, secret ventures can be mounted on a large scale with minimum risk of disclosure. But this is extremely difficult in an open society in which freedom of speech and the press is constitutionally guaranteed.

As Robert Kennedy emphasized, President Kennedy canceled the second air strike because "U.S. participation in the matter was coming to the surface . . . contrary to the pre-invasion plan." [4]

It had been expected that Mario Zuniga would get away with the tale of defection he told in Miami on the Saturday before the invasion. But a few influential newspapers and UN delegates began to express skepticism and the President felt compelled to change the military plan in an effort to conceal the fact that the United States was behind the invasion.

Immediately after the invasion failed, the President revealed his concern about the limitations imposed upon the government by the institutions of free speech and a free press. He went before the American Newspaper Publishers Association on April 27, 1961, with a plea for voluntary censorship.

"If the press is awaiting a declaration of war before it imposes the self-discipline of combat conditions," Kennedy remarked, "then I can only say that no war has ever posed a greater threat to our security."

But despite his chagrin and his momentary impatience with the workings of a democracy, the President had not lost perspective on the dangers of toying with fundamental freedoms.

"The very word 'secrecy' is repugnant in a free and open republic," he declared, "and we are as a people inherently and historically opposed to secret societies, to secret oaths and to secret proceedings. We decided long ago that the dangers of excessive and unwarranted concealment of pertinent facts far outweighed the dangers which are cited to justify it. Even today, there is little value in opposing the threat of a closed society by imitating its arbitrary restrictions. Even today, there is little value in insuring the survival of our nation if our traditions do not survive with it."

13

The Secret Elite

THE MOST controversial of President Kennedy's moves to reorganize the Invisible Government was his appointment of John McCone as Director of Central Intelligence. The strong-willed, stern-looking multimillionaire was not of the stuff to inspire love among the bureaucrats.

"When he smiles," a CIA man cautioned, "look out."

McCone had aroused much fear and antagonism in his rise to the top in the world of business and government. Influential scientists were outraged by what they believed was an effort by McCone to have ten of their brethren fired from the California Institute of Technology in 1956.

The Caltech scientists had come out in support of Adlai Stevenson's proposal for a nuclear test ban during the presidential campaign that year. And McCone, a trustee of the Institute, retorted by accusing the scientists of being "taken in" by Soviet propaganda and of attempting to "create fear in the minds of the uninformed that radio-active fallout from H-bomb tests endangers life."

McCone denied that he had attempted to have the scientists dismissed.[1] But some remained unconvinced and still more were embittered by the blunt language of McCone's denunciation.

Outside the scientific community, many were disturbed by McCone's big wartime profits in the ship-building business. Ralph E. Casey of the General Accounting Office, a watchdog arm of the Congress, testified in 1946 that Mc-

Cone and his associates in the California Shipbuilding Company made $44,000,000 on an investment of $100,000.

"I daresay," Casey remarked, "that at no time in the history of American business, whether in wartime or in peacetime, have so few men made so much money with so little risk and all at the expense of the taxpayers, not only of this generation but of generations to come." [2]

Again, McCone denied the accusation. He insisted that the investment of California Shipbuilding—including loans, bank credits and stock, in addition to the cash—amounted to over $7,000,000. He also disputed Casey's profit figures as inflated.* In any event, he testified, the government got back 95 percent of the profits in taxes.[3]

Another of McCone's business activities which provoked opposition was his long relationship with the international oil industry. During the Senate Armed Services Committee hearings on his nomination in January, 1962, McCone told of his former directorship of the Panama Pacific Tankers Company, a large oil-carrying fleet, and of the $1,000,000 in stock he held in Standard Oil of California, which operates extensively in the Middle East, Indonesia and Latin America.

"Every well-informed American knows," commented Senator Joseph Clark, the Pennsylvania Democrat, "that the American oil companies are deep in the politics of the Middle East . . . [and] the CIA is deep in the politics of the Middle East." [4]

Clark opposed McCone's appointment on the ground that his ownership of the oil stock amounted to "a legal violation and a very unwise holding." McCone offered to dispose of the stock but the committee refused to consider it. From the tenor of the questioning it was clear that the great majority of senators was not at all disturbed by McCone's record. They were, in fact, abundantly impressed.

"I have not had the opportunity of knowing Mr. McCone well, only through reputation," said Senator Strom Thurmond, the South Carolina Democrat, "but in

* Senator Stuart Symington, the Missouri Democrat, also saw nothing amiss. He observed: "It is still legal in America, if not to make a profit, at least to try to make a profit."

looking over this biography, to me it epitomizes what has made America great."

The biography showed that McCone was born into a prosperous San Francisco family on January 4, 1902. He was graduated *magna cum laude* from the University of California with an engineering degree in 1922. That year he joined the Llewellyn Iron Works in California and, before moving into the executive suite, served briefly as a riveter, a surveyor, a foreman and a construction manager. When Llewellyn merged into the Consolidated Steel Corporation in 1929, McCone assumed a series of executive positions, including vice-president in charge of sales. In 1933 he became an executive vice-president and director.

McCone left the steel business in 1937 to form a new engineering concern, the Bechtel-McCone-Parsons Corporation of Los Angeles. This firm specialized in the design and construction of petroleum refineries, processing plants and power plants for installation in the United States, South America and the Middle East.

In 1939, when war broke out in Europe, McCone joined the Six Companies Group in the formation of the Seattle-Tacoma Corporation which built merchant ships for the U. S. Maritime Commission and the British Government. During the war McCone and his enterprises were also active in the modification of Air Force bombers for combat.

After the war McCone took over the Joshua Hendy Iron Works at Sunnyvale, California, and broadened his business interests in a dozen major corporations, including the Curtiss-Wright Corporation, Standard Oil of California and Trans World Airlines. He entered government service in 1947 as a member of President Truman's Air Policy Commission. In 1948 he became special deputy to James Forrestal, the Secretary of Defense. He prepared the first two budgets of the newly unified Defense Department and worked closely with Forrestal in his efforts to create the CIA.

McCone was named Under Secretary of the Air Force in 1950. He returned to private life the next year, but was back in the government in 1958 as the chairman of the

Atomic Energy Commission. He served in that post until the end of the Eisenhower Administration.

During his government service, McCone gained a reputation as an uncompromising supporter of John Foster Dulles' doctrine of massive retaliation, the Air Force's atomic warfare theories, and the hard-line strategy against the Soviet Union.

A member of the Roman Catholic Church, McCone was designated by Pope Pius XII as a Knight of St. Gregory and awarded the Grand Cross of the Order of St. Sylvester. He and Clare Booth Luce served as Eisenhower's official representatives at Pope Pius' funeral in 1958.

These credentials—particularly McCone's reputation as a hard-nosed executive who could get things done quickly and efficiently—impressed Robert Kennedy, who had been looking around for a successor to Allen Dulles.

There had been some thought that the Attorney General might take the job himself, but this inevitably would have provoked Republican charges that the Kennedys were creating a dynasty. And it probably would have stirred up new demands for tighter Congressional control of the CIA —a prospect which the President did not relish.

Serious consideration was given to the possibility of offering the job to Clark Clifford, who had impressed Kennedy mightily when he directed the change-over in the White House staff between administrations. But the handsome and prosperous Washington lawyer was not interested.

The President then turned to Fowler Hamilton, a Wall Street lawyer and close friend of Senator Symington. The White House was on the verge of announcing Hamilton's appointment when Kennedy encountered a series of difficulties in finding a director for the Agency for International Development (AID).

The foreign-aid job had been scheduled to go to George D. Woods, the board chairman of the First Boston Company. But Woods felt compelled to withdraw his name because of renewed talk about First Boston's implication in the Dixon-Yates scandal. Kennedy then tried to fill the

AID opening with Thomas J. Watson, Jr., the president of the International Business Machines Corporation. But Watson said no and the President named Hamilton as the AID director.

It was then that Kennedy decided upon McCone as Director of Central Intelligence. The decision, announced on September 27, 1961, shocked official Washington. The members of the President's Foreign Intelligence Advisory Board were stunned that Kennedy had not asked their advice in advance of the appointment; and there were further grumblings over the Caltech incident and McCone's close ties with the Republican Party. "I think," a board member was heard to comment, "that the President should have got a Kennedy man."

But that, of course, was precisely what the President did not want. After the Bay of Pigs, both Kennedy and the CIA were extremely vulnerable to political attack from the Republicans, particularly from the right wing of the party. With a conservative Republican at the head of the Invisible Government, the President, clearly, thought the political fire would be somewhat diverted.

"You are now living on the bull's eye," Kennedy said as McCone was sworn into office on November 29, 1961, "and I welcome you to that spot."

A week later, on December 6, McCone's wife died unexpectedly of a heart attack. They had been married for twenty-three years and were unusually close. McCone was grief-stricken. Allen Dulles volunteered to take care of the arrangements for flying the body back to the West Coast. On the way to the airport, McCone poured out his anguish.

"I can't go on," he told his predecessor. "I'm going to have to tell the President that I can't take the job."

"You must," Dulles replied firmly. "You owe it to the country."

McCone followed Dulles' advice and set out almost immediately on extensive tours of agency installations in Europe and Asia. His nomination came to a vote in the Senate on January 31, 1962, after a brief, bitter debate, and he was confirmed seventy-one to twelve.* Two weeks earlier, on January 16, the President had outlined the new responsibilities of the Director of Central Intelligence in a letter to McCone:

> It is my wish that you serve as the government's principal foreign intelligence officer and that you undertake as an integral part of your responsibility, the co-ordination and effective guidance of the total U.S. intelligence effort. . . .
>
> As head of the Central Intelligence Agency, while you will continue to have overall responsibility for the agency, I shall expect you to delegate to your principal deputy, as you may deem necessary, so much of the direction of the detailed operation of the agency as may be required to permit you to carry out your primary task as director of Central Intelligence.

The President noted "with approval" that McCone had designated his deputy, General Carter, to sit on the United States Intelligence Board (USIB) as the CIA's representative.

"Pat" Carter had risen in the Army as a staff man. A graduate of West Point and the Massachusetts Institute of Technology, he became a close aide to General George C. Marshall in World War II. He gained experience in international affairs as an important military figure at several wartime and postwar conferences, including the World War II summit meeting in Cairo in 1943.

Despite the broadened powers implied in the President's

---

* One of the nay votes was cast by Senator J. William Fulbright, the Arkansas Democrat and chairman of the Foreign Relations Committee. Fulbright said he could not vote for McCone because his committee had not been consulted about the appointment nor given an opportunity to question McCone about his views on foreign policy.

Ten days later, at three o'clock in the morning, Fulbright was roused from bed by a phone call from McCone, who wanted to inform him of the exchange of U-2 pilot Francis Gary Powers and Soviet spy Rudolf I. Abel. Annoyed, Fulbright made it clear this was not the type of consultation he had in mind.

letter, Carter had no illusions about his position in the CIA. Kennedy had wanted to put a civilian in the deputy's job and settled upon Carter only under strong Congressional pressure for the appointment of another military man. When some of Carter's old military friends would arrive at the CIA from the Pentagon for an intelligence briefing, the general left no doubt as to who was the real boss of the agency. "Welcome," he would say, "to McConey Island."

As Director of Central Intelligence, McCone was responsible not only for the CIA but also for all of the other government agencies involved in intelligence work. McCone directed the intelligence community formally through USIB, a committee of intelligence agency representatives, which was called into session each week in a room adjacent to his top-floor office in the CIA's new building in Langley, Virginia. McCone also maintained informal supervisory contact with the principal members of the intelligence community: Army Intelligence, the Office of Naval Intelligence, Air Force Intelligence, the Atomic Energy Commission, the Federal Bureau of Investigation, the State Department's Bureau of Intelligence and Research, the National Security Agency, the Defense Intelligence Agency, as well as the CIA.

Army Intelligence

The Army G-2 is the oldest of the nation's intelligence services, with a tradition dating back to World War I. In World War II it carried off several coups: the capture intact of a high-level Nazi planning group in North Africa; the advance seizure of a map of all enemy mines in Sicily; and the capture of the entire Japanese secret-police force on Okinawa. On a bureaucratic level, it did battle with the OSS and the ambitious intelligence men of the Army Air Corps. After the war the G-2 absorbed many of the OSS operatives under a directive by President Truman. But it lost air intelligence when the Air Force was created as a separate service. The Army yielded further ground after the formation of the DIA, but retained four vital functions: (1) technical intelligence on the types, quantity

212

and quality of army weapons of foreign powers; (2) the attaché system, which tries to estimate the size, organization and deployment of foreign armies through the efforts —mainly overt—of Army representatives in the major United States embassies; (3) the Counter Intelligence Corps, which is charged with detecting and preventing treason, espionage, sabotage, gambling, prostitution and black marketeering; (4) the Army Map Service, which is responsible for meeting most of the government's mapping needs.

Office of Naval Intelligence

The ONI is the smallest of the intelligence branches of the three services. Its total complement amounted to 2,600 men in 1961,* and the number has undoubtedly declined as the DIA has absorbed more and more of the service intelligence functions. The Navy maintains no separate counter-intelligence unit such as the Army's CIC. But it makes use of an attaché system, and it deploys intelligence men at all of its installations, ashore and afloat. The principal mission of the ONI is to collect information on foreign naval forces. It keeps a special weather eye on the Soviet submarine fleet and compiles elaborate dossiers on the world's major beaches, harbors and ports.

Air Force Intelligence

The A-2 is the most mechanically sophisticated of the service intelligence operations. It employs the latest electronic gear to determine the missile, bomber, satellite and radar potential of the Soviet Union. The Electronics Division, through its Reconnaissance, Equipment and Control Branches, gathers the electronic intelligence (a separate chapter will deal with the startling advances that have been made in this field). Under a Pentagon directive in 1961, the Air Force controls all reconnaissance satellites orbiting the Soviet Union. A Target Division is responsible

---

* All figures on the number of persons involved in intelligence work are highly classified. But the ONI's figure slipped out through the oversight of a Pentagon censor in testimony released in 1961 by the House Defense Appropriations Subcommittee.

for sorting out the intelligence intake and maintaining a current list of potential enemy targets. It also compiles and publishes the *Bombing Encyclopedia*, a compendium of target information. The A-2 conducts a world-wide attaché system through its International Liaison Division. It also maintains a Military Capabilities Branch and a Wargame Branch in the Threat Assessments Division of its Directorate of Warning and Threat Assessments.

Atomic Energy Commission

The AEC is responsible for making estimates of the atomic-weapons capabilities of the Soviet Union and other nuclear powers. Since 1948 the United States has maintained round-the-clock monitoring of the atmosphere to detect radioactive particles from atomic tests. Samples are collected by the U-2 and other high-flying aircraft. From an analysis of the samples, the AEC can determine not only the fact that atomic explosions have taken place but also the type and power of the weapons detonated. The AEC also plays an important role in assessing test-ban proposals. It carries out intensive experimentation in ways to shield atomic explosions from detection and ways to pierce the shielding devised by other nations.

Because of the law which set it up and its close relationship to the Joint Committee on Atomic Energy in the Congress, the AEC is one of the most independent branches of the Invisible Government. One of Eisenhower's parting admonitions to Kennedy was: "You may be able to run lots of things around here. But one of them you can't run is the AEC."

Federal Bureau of Investigation

As the investigative arm of the Department of Justice, the FBI is responsible, among its other duties, for catching spies. In this phase of its work—as opposed to its conventional criminal investigations—the FBI is an intelligence agency, and as such, part of the Invisible Government. The assistant to J. Edgar Hoover, the FBI director, sits on USIB, and the FBI has a liaison man who reports to work at the CIA headquarters in Langley every day.

Actual counter-espionage work is conducted by the FBI's hush-hush division Number 5. This is the Domestic Intelligence Division, headed by William C. Sullivan. It is in charge of espionage, sabotage and subversion cases.

In Miami, New York and Washington, there are FBI agents permanently assigned to counter-espionage. A squad supervisor is assigned to intelligence in each of the FBI's fifty-five field offices in the United States. Agents who normally conduct ordinary criminal investigations are assigned to espionage cases when necessary.

About 20 percent of the 650,000 cases investigated by the FBI in 1963 were espionage-internal security cases, although the exact figure is classified.

"Over the years," Hoover told a House committee in 1962, "no phase of American activity has been immune to Soviet-bloc intelligence attempts. The Soviets have attempted to obtain every conceivable type of information. The targets have been all-encompassing and have included aerial photographs, maps and charts of our major cities and vital areas, data regarding the organization of our military services and their training programs, technical classified and unclassified information concerning nuclear weapons, planes, ships and submarines. Of prime interest to the Soviets is information concerning U.S. military bases, including missile sites and radar installations.

"They have probed to penetrate our most critical intelligence and counter-intelligence organizations." [5]

Although Hoover did not say so, some of these penetration attempts are controlled by "Department Nine" of the KGB. This is the division of the Soviet secret police that keeps dossiers on Russian émigrés.

The FBI exposed one "Department Nine" operation in Washington in 1963. It began on April 6 of that year, when a Soviet citizen arrived in the United States with papers identifying him as "Vladimir Gridnev," forty-nine, a temporary employee of the Soviet Embassy.

It was a false name. "Gridnev" was actually brought here by the KGB to try to recruit his brother, a Soviet defector employed by the CIA.

The first move in the game was made at 9:00 P.M. on

April 28, when the defector returned from work to his home in an apartment house in a Virginia suburb of the capital. As he reached for his key, a voice behind him whispered his name. He turned to find his brother, Volodya, whom he had not seen for twenty-three years, and who had entered the country as "Gridnev."

They embraced and went inside to a third-floor apartment. A few moments later, there was a knock on the door. A Russian whom Volodya introduced as "Ivan Ivanovich," his embassy "driver," entered the room. He was actually Gennadiy Sevastyanov, a thirty-three-year-old Russian agent working under diplomatic cover as an attaché in the cultural division of the Soviet Embassy.

Two days later Volodya met his brother again at a bus stop in Arlington, Virginia. Sevastyanov joined them. The entire scene was filmed by the FBI with a sixteen-millimeter movie camera. The three men drove to a restaurant, where Volodya tried to persuade his brother to stay at the CIA but to work for the Russians.

Sevastyanov made the same proposal, and promised that later on he could return to his homeland and be well taken care of. On May 2 the three met once more. Sevastyanov gave the CIA man a password and other instructions for clandestine meetings. Volodya was allowed to return to the Soviet Union on May 4—since he was regarded by the FBI as a helpless pawn in the Soviet operation. Sevastyanov and Volodya's brother met once more on June 13.

On July 1 the State Department ordered Sevastyanov expelled from the country for trying to recruit a United States Government employee. The CIA man had cooperated with the FBI throughout.

Since 1950 a total of thirty-four Soviet and seventeen Communist-bloc diplomats have been expelled from the United States for a variety of reasons. Like Sevastyanov's activities, many of the espionage efforts of Soviet agents operating as diplomats seem bumbling and almost amateurish. There is a long record of such cases.

By contrast, Soviet "illegals"—spies operating under deep cover—are skilled experts and therefore much harder for the FBI to detect. They slip into the country with false documents, pass for ordinary Americans, and enjoy no embass protection.

The FBI s counter-espionage work is concentrated within the continental United States. Although the bureau operated in the Western Hemisphere and cracked Nazi espionage rings in South America during World War II, espionage and counter-espionage abroad became the province of the CIA and the military intelligence organizations after the war. Contrary to popular belief, however, the FBI does have some agents overseas. They are assigned to American embassies, usually under the cover of "legal attachés."

The FBI had 14,239 employees in 1964 (of whom 6,014 were agents), but its budget of $146,900,000 ranked it as one of the smaller units of the Invisible Government, even though its counter-espionage work is vital to national security.

Bureau of Intelligence and Research

INR, the State Department's intelligence agency, is really misnamed, in the view of one of its former directors, Roger Hilsman.

"To be frank with you," he told a House Appropriations Subcommittee in 1961, "I am uneasy about this word 'intelligence' in the title of the bureau. It is, in a real sense, not really an intelligence agency as you think of the word and it does not collect as such.

"It is analysis—research and analysis is its function as an agency. [But] it has functions relating to the intelligence community. Normally, quick data comes from the other collection agencies, and from the diplomatic reporting which is not part of our bureau, but the embassies overseas."

As Hilsman indicated, INR relies upon the information of others—the diplomatic service, the CIA, the military attachés and the published documents and maps of foreign nations. INR analyzes this information for the use of the Secretary of State and the other branches of the intelligence community.

Its main function on USIB is to make sure that the final intelligence estimates reflect the political, social and economic facts of life, as seen from the State Department's viewpoint.

The absence of cloak-and-dagger in INR is reflected in the fact that it is the only member of USIB whose intelligence budget is part of the public record. It employs about 350 persons and spends approximately $2,800,000 annually (the figures vary slightly from year to year). It produces over 16,000 pages of social, political, economic and biographic analyses each year. By its own estimate, 40 to 60 percent of the raw data for these analyses come from the diplomatic reports of United States embassies abroad. INR also makes use of the scholarly output of the universities and periodically commissions a study by the academic community. It briefs the Secretary of State every day.

INR, the FBI, the AEC and the intelligence branches of the military services represent the lesser agencies of the Invisible Government. The big ones, in terms of men, money and influence, are the National Security Agency, the Defense Intelligence Agency and the CIA.

14

The National Security Agency

PROBABLY the most secretive branch of the Invisible Government is the National Security Agency. Even more than the CIA, the NSA has sought to conceal the nature of its activities.

The CIA's functions were revealed in general outline by Congress in the National Security Act of 1947. But the NSA's duties were kept secret in the classified presidential directive which established the agency in 1952.

The only official description of its activities is contained in the *U.S. Government Organization Manual,* which states vaguely: "The National Security Agency performs highly specialized technical and co-ordinating functions relating to the national security."

Nevertheless, it is no secret that the NSA is the nation's code-making and code-breaking agency. It is impossible, however, to receive official confirmation of that obvious fact. Unlike Allen Dulles and other high-ranking CIA men who have occasionally talked to the press and on television, NSA officials have refused to grant interviews under any circumstances.

As a sub-agency of the Defense Department, the NSA is watched over by the deputy director of defense research and engineering. But the various men who have held this post have been similarly uncommunicative.

During the Eisenhower years, the job of overseeing the NSA was held by military men. The Kennedy and Johnson

Administrations turned to civilians with broader scientific expertise. In 1963 the assignment was taken on by Dr. Eugene G. Fubini, a fifty-year-old Italian-born physicist.

Fubini was confirmed by the Senate without difficulty despite a challenge from Senator Thurmond, the South Carolina Democrat. During the Armed Services Committee hearings on June 27, 1963, Thurmond questioned Fubini closely on his political affiliations in Italy prior to his emigration to the United States in 1939.

Fubini admitted that he had been a dues-paying member of the GUF, the Fascist student organization in the universities. But he explained that membership was "almost a compulsory thing" in Mussolini's Italy, and that he finally left his homeland in political protest.

Fubini made it clear, to Thurmond's evident relief, that he had never been associated with Communist or Socialist movements. His biographical data also underscored the fact that he had served ably as a scientific consultant and technical observer with the U.S. Army and Navy in Europe during World War II.

After the war Fubini joined the Airborne Instruments Laboratory of Long Island, New York. He worked on several classified electronic projects and rose to become the vice-president of the company. By the time he joined the Pentagon in 1961 he was thoroughly impressed with the need for tight security. He became convinced that a mass of vital national secrets was being given to the Russians through careless public disclosure.

Fubini and his staff maintained a long list of security violations which appeared in the press and elsewhere. Prominent on the list were public statements by Defense Secretary McNamara and his deputy, Roswell Gilpatric. In their zeal to defend administration policy, notably in McNamara's television extravaganza after the Cuban missile crisis, Fubini felt his bosses were sometimes imprudent about national security.

Fubini's dedication to security was matched by the agency he inherited. The NSA's U-shaped, three-story steel-and-concrete building at Fort Meade, Maryland, is surrounded by a double barbed-wire fence ten feet high.

The fences are patrolled night and day, and guards with ready machine guns are posted at the four gatehouses.

The interior, including the longest unobstructed corridor in the world (980 feet long and 560 feet wide), is similarly patrolled. The building is 1,400,000 square feet, smaller than the Pentagon but larger than the CIA's Langley headquarters. It houses high-speed computers and complicated radio and electronic gear. It is said to have more electric wiring than any other building in the world.

Special security conveyor belts carry documents at the rate of a hundred feet a minute and a German-made pneumatic tube system shoots messages at the rate of twenty-five feet a second.

The NSA headquarters was built at a cost of $30,000,000 and was opened in 1957. It contains a complete hospital, with operating rooms and dental offices. It also houses eight snack bars, a cafeteria, an auditorium and a bank. All of the building's windows are sealed and none can be opened.

Comparable precautions have been taken with NSA employees. They are subject to lie-detector tests on application and intensive security indoctrination on acceptance. Periodically, the indoctrination briefing is repeated and employees are required to sign statements that they have reread pertinent secrecy regulations.

Even so, the NSA has had more than its share of trouble with security violations. In 1960 two young mathematicians, William H. Martin and Bernon F. Mitchell, defected to Russia. They held a news conference in Moscow, describing in detail the inner workings of the NSA. They were soon discovered to be homosexuals, a fact which led indirectly to the resignation of the NSA's personnel director, and the firing of twenty-six other employees for sexual deviation.

It also led on May 9, 1963 to a vote by the House, 340 to 40, to give the Secretary of Defense the same absolute power over NSA employees as the Director of Central Intelligence had over his employees. Under the legislation, which was introduced by the Un-American Activities Committee, the Secretary of Defense was authorized to fire

NSA employees without explanation and without appeal if he decided they were security risks. The bill also required a full field investigation of all persons before they were hired.

The legislation was attacked by several congressmen.

Thomas P. Gill, the Hawaii Democrat, warned that the bill opened the way to "arbitrary and capricious action on the part of government administrators. . . . There has been much said about danger to the national security. Democracy itself is a dangerous form of government and in its very danger lies its strength. The protection of individual rights by the requirement of due process of law, which has long endured in this nation of ours, is a radical and dangerous idea in most of the world today.

"This dangerous concept is outlawed in the Soviet Union, in Red China, in Castro's Cuba, indeed, in all of the Communist bloc and many of those countries aligned with it. I think we might well ask: How does one destroy his enemy by becoming like him?"

Edwin E. Willis, the Louisiana Democrat and a member of the Un-American Activities Committee, defended the bill on grounds that the NSA "carries out the most delicate type intelligence operations of our government. . . . The National Security Agency plays so highly specialized a role in the defense and security of the United States that no outsider can actually describe its activities. They are guarded not only from the public but from other government agencies as well. The Civil Service Commission, which audits all government positions, is not allowed to know what NSA employees do."

If the bill was so important for the NSA, Willis was asked, why shouldn't it be applied to all other sensitive agencies?

"As to the other agencies," Willis replied, "we will have to take them one at a time."

Although the Martin and Mitchell case stirred the House to action, it was only one of several sensational security scandals to hit the NSA.

In 1954 Joseph Sydney Petersen was tried and convicted on charges of misusing classified NSA documents. He was accused of taking and copying documents to aid another nation. In the court papers the government said Petersen "copied and made notes from classified documents indicating the United States' success in breaking codes utilized by The Netherlands." The Dutch Embassy in Washington admitted it had exchanged "secret intelligence" with Petersen on the assumption that he had acted with the knowledge of his superiors.

In 1959, during his visit to the United States, Khrushchev bragged that he had obtained top-secret American codes and had intercepted messages from President Eisenhower to Prime Minister Nehru. "You're wasting your money," Khrushchev remarked to Allen Dulles. "You might as well send it direct to us instead of the middleman, because we get most of it anyway. Your agents give us the code books and then we send false information back to you through your code. Then we send cables asking for money and you send it to us."

On July 22, 1963, *Izvestia* published a letter from Victor Norris Hamilton, a naturalized American of Arab descent who had sought asylum in the Soviet Union. Hamilton said he had worked for a division of the NSA which intercepted and decoded secret instructions from Arab countries to their delegations at the United Nations. Hamilton claimed UN Ambassador Henry Cabot Lodge had sent a letter to the division thanking them for the information. The Pentagon admitted Hamilton had been an employee of the NSA and said he had been discharged in 1959 because he was "approaching a paranoid-schizophrenic break." (The NSA has an unusually high rate of mental illness and suicide.)

An even graver security breach at the NSA was also disclosed in July of 1963. Army Sergeant First Class Jack E. Dunlap committed suicide when he realized he had been discovered selling top-secret NSA documents to Soviet officials. Dunlap reportedly received $60,000 during a two-year period for disclosing United States intelligence on Russian weapons advances, the deployment of their missiles and troops, as well as similar information about the NATO countries.

The playboy sergeant, who had a wife and five children, spent the money on several girl friends, two Cadillacs and frequent trips to the race track. A Pentagon official described the case as "thirty to forty times as serious as the Mitchell and Martin defections."·

These security violations revealed a mass of information about the NSA. And most of it was indirectly confirmed by the Pentagon in its contradictory statements on the case, and by the House Un-American Activities Committee in issuing a public report stressing the seriousness of the Martin and Mitchell defection. Out of it all a painstaking enemy analyst could have derived the following picture of the National Security Agency:

NSA was divided into four main offices. The Office of Production (PROD) attempted to break the codes and ciphers * and read the messages of the Soviet Union, Communist China, other Communist countries, United States Allies and neutral nations.

The Office of Research and Development (R/D) carried out research in cryptanalysis, digital computing and radio propagation. It also developed new communications equipment.

The Office of Communications Security (COMSEC) produced U.S. codes and tried to protect them. And the Office of Security (SEC) investigated NSA personnel, conducted lie-detector tests and passed on the loyalty and integrity of employees.

While the NSA was reading the secret communications of over forty nations, including the most friendly, it shared some of its secrets through a relationship between its United Kingdom Liaison Office (UKLO) and its British counterpart, the GCHQ. The NSA, at least according to Martin and Mitchell, also provided code machines to other nations and then intercepted their messages on the basis of its knowledge of the construction and wiring of the machines.

The NSA gathered its raw information through more than 2,000 intercept stations around the world. They were

* Codes use symbols or letter groups for whole words or thoughts. Ciphers use letters or numbers for other letters or numbers.

designed to pick up every electronic emanation and communication in the Communist bloc: countdowns at missile sites, tell-tale sounds of industrial construction, military orders for troop movements, and air defense instructions to radar installations and fighter-plane squadrons.

In addition, the NSA sent its eavesdropping equipment along on flights by the U-2 and other aircraft over the Soviet Union (until 1960) and over Communist China. Separate flights, called ELINT (for electronic intelligence) missions, skirted Communist borders, picking up the location and characteristics of enemy radar stations. Occasionally, the planes would play "foxes and hounds," feinting toward or into Soviet defenses so as to analyze the nature of the response on nearby U.S. radar screens and listening gear.

The NSA also practiced what is known in the trade as "audio surveillance" and in layman's terms as "bugging," or "telephone tapping."

It was clear that the United States had come a long way from that day in 1929 when Secretary of State Henry L. Stimson closed the "black chamber," the State Department's primitive code-breaking section, with the explanation:

"Gentlemen do not read each other's mail."

15

The Defense Intelligence Agency

THE DIA, the newest member of the Invisible Government and the most powerful competitor of the CIA, owes its existence to the post-Sputnik "missile gap" controversy of the late 1950s.

As the Soviets demonstrated the range and accuracy of their missiles in a series of spectacular space shots, the Air Force demanded that the United States embark on a massive ICBM program of its own. Almost weekly in the period between 1957 and 1960 the Air Force went before the United States Intelligence Board to argue that the Russians were deploying hundreds of ICBMs and were tipping the military balance of power in their favor.

To substantiate the claim, Air Force photo-interpreters introduced scores of pictures taken by the U-2 spy plane, which started to fly over the Soviet Union in 1956.

"To the Air Force every flyspeck on film was a missile," a CIA man remarked scornfully. Allen Dulles, relying on the independent interpretation of the photos by the CIA's Research Division, challenged two thirds of the Air Force estimates.

USIB's meetings were dominated by long and bitter arguments over the conflicting missile estimates. The situation reflected the perennial problem of interservice rivalry. Each service tended to adopt a self-serving party line and pursue it relentlessly. At budget time each year the Air Force would see endless numbers of Soviet missiles and bombers; the Navy would detect the latest enemy submarines just off the East Coast; and the Army would mechanize a few dozen more Russian divisions.

Overwhelmed by the constant bickering, USIB and the civilian leaders of the Pentagon were anxious to find some mechanism for resolving the conflict. They turned the problem over to a Joint Study Group which was set up in 1959 to conduct a sweeping investigation of the intelligence community.

The group was composed of military men, active and retired, and career intelligence officials in the State Department, the Defense Department and the White House. It was headed by Lyman Kirkpatrick, then the inspector general of the CIA. A polio victim who was confined to a wheel chair, Kirkpatrick was often spotted overseas, pursuing his many investigations.

The Joint Study Group submitted a comprehensive list of recommendations late in 1960. One of the most important called for the creation of the DIA and for the removal of the service intelligence agencies from USIB. The DIA was to serve as the arbiter of the conflicting service estimates and to present its findings to USIB as the final judgment of the Pentagon.

The idea appealed strongly to Thomas S. Gates, Jr., the last Secretary of Defense in the Eisenhower Administration. When the Kennedy Administration took office in January, 1961, Gates forcefully urged McNamara to put the recommendation into effect without delay.

McNamara was quickly persuaded of the wisdom of Gates' advice. After a thorough study of the missile-gap claims, McNamara concluded that there was no foundation in the argument that the United States was lagging behind the Soviet Union in the production or deployment of ICBMs. The study convinced him of the dangers inherent in the fragmented intelligence operation at the Pentagon. He saw great value in subordinating the service intelligence branches to a centralized agency directly under his supervision.

Accordingly, McNamara recommended the speedy creation of the DIA. But Dulles balked at the idea. Despite his many wrangles with the services, Dulles felt it was imperative that they continue to have a voice in the deliberations of the intelligence community. He feared that the creation of the DIA would lead to the elimination of the service intelligence branches from USIB.

Then the CIA would be cut off from direct access to the facts and opinions developed by the military men and would be forced to rely on whatever information the DIA saw fit to give it. Dulles was impressed with the service argument, which ran something like this:

Yes, the services have been guilty at times of analyzing intelligence from a parochial point of view. But other agencies of the government are no less susceptible to self-serving judgments. The function of USIB is to serve as a forum for all viewpoints—even extreme viewpoints. Only then can the Director of Central Intelligence, and through him the President, arrive at comprehensive and objective assessments. Dissent should be aired at the highest possible level and not suppressed outside the orbit of presidential observation.

If the service intelligence branches were removed from USIB, the DIA would become the sole representative of the government's biggest producer and biggest consumer of intelligence. And the DIA as an agency subordinate to a political appointee—the Secretary of Defense—would be more vulnerable to political influences than are the services which have a semi-autonomous status by law.

Dulles was particularly worried about the possibility that the DIA would gain a monopoly over aerial reconnaissance. The Defense Department controlled the reconnaissance equipment and Dulles feared that the DIA would be tempted to hoard the photographs produced by the equipment. He was determined to prevent any such thing.

During the U-2 era, the CIA had built up a skilled corps of civilian photo-interpreters and they would surely quit if the Pentagon monopolized aerial photographs. Without interpreters, the CIA would have no way to verify Defense Department estimates. At a time when electronic espionage was bulking ever larger, Pentagon control of aerial reconnaissance could result in Pentagon dominance of the entire intelligence community.

Dulles expressed his misgivings to McNamara, who responded with assurances that the DIA would be only a co-ordinating body and that it would not supplant the intelligence branches of the Army, Navy and Air Force. Some of Dulles' advisers suspected that the Pentagon had covert ambitions for the DIA which were being suppressed temporarily for tactical reasons. But Dulles felt McNamara's pledge left no ground for him to oppose the DIA. He went along with the proposal. So did John McCone, then head of the AEC.

The DIA was created officially on October 1, 1961. Named as director was Lieutenant General Joseph F. Carroll, who had been the inspector general of the Air Force. Carroll started his career with the FBI and was a leading assistant of J. Edgar Hoover at the time he moved to the Air Force in 1947 to set up its first investigation and counter-intelligence section.

CIA men delighted in pointing out that all of Carroll's experience had been as an investigator and that he had no credentials as a foreign or military intelligence analyst. More to the CIA's liking were Carroll's two subordinates, both of whom had served with the CIA: Major General William W. (Buffalo Bill) Quinn, a former West Point football star, who was named deputy director; and Rear Admiral Samuel B. Frankel, a Chinese- and Russian-speaking expert on the Communist world, who became the DIA's chief of staff.

Both of these men had worked closely with Allen Dulles. Frankel served under him on USIB. Quinn, the G-2 for the Seventh Army in Europe during World War II, acted as personal courier for the information Dulles gathered in Switzerland on Nazi troop movements. (Quinn left the DIA to become the commander of the Seventh Army in November, 1963.)

The original charter for the DIA provided that the new agency was to: (1) draw up a consolidated budget for all the intelligence units within the Pentagon; (2) produce all Defense Department estimates for USIB and other elements of the intelligence community; (3) provide representation on USIB in the person of its director; and

(4) develop plans for integrating the intelligence schools run by the various services.

Although the original list of functions seemed relatively modest, an expansion of the DIA's responsibilities was clearly implied in its authorization by McNamara to provide "overall guidance for the conduct and management" of all duties retained by the individual services.

And with the inevitability of Parkinson's Law, the DIA quickly added to its domain. By 1964, when the DIA became fully operational, it had more than 2,500 employees. It had acquired 38,000 feet of Pentagon office space and had submitted a request for a separate $17,000,-000 building.

It had succeeded in eliminating the separate service intelligence publications and supplanting them with two of its own; and it had launched a *Daily Digest*, which was viewed by the CIA as duplicatory and competitive to its own *Central Intelligence Bulletin*.

The DIA had also supplanted the J-2, the intelligence staff of the Joint Chiefs of Staff, both on USIB and in supplying information to the Chiefs themselves. It had replaced the services in the production of "order of battle" intelligence—estimates of the size and deployment of enemy forces. And it was occasionally providing information directly to the President without funneling it through USIB. The DIA did so on request in 1963 when Kennedy wanted quick intelligence on whether the Guatemalan Army would be able to handle expected Communist riots.

By 1964 the DIA's control over military intelligence had expanded to such a degree that the services were reduced to the role of providing technical information on enemy weapons, running the attaché system and collecting—but not analyzing—raw intelligence.

Most significantly, the leaders of the Invisible Government had decided to remove the service intelligence agencies from USIB. Only a veto by President Johnson could prevent the DIA from becoming the sole military voice on the board. Allen Dulles' apprehensions were being realized.

"There is, of course, always the possibility," Dulles had

observed with monumental understatement, "that two such powerful and well-financed agencies as CIA and DIA will become rivals and competitors." [1]

16

CIA: *"It's Well Hidden"*

THROUGH the large picture window of his immaculate private dining room atop the CIA's $46,000,000 hideaway in Langley, Virginia, the Director of Central Intelligence can watch deer and other wild life gambol in the woodland below.

When John McCone took over as CIA director in November, 1961, he must have found a glimpse of an occasional passing fawn a pleasant relief from the cares of office. He could dine, if he chose, in utter isolation and complete quiet, twenty minutes and eight miles from downtown Washington and the lunchtime hustle and bustle that is the lot of less powerful, and less secluded, bureaucrats.

As far as the eye can see, the lovely rolling hills of Virginia's Fairfax County surround the CIA building on all four sides. The Pentagon is bigger; but that colossus is easily visible from almost anywhere in the capital.

Appropriately, the CIA's concrete headquarters is invisible, an architectural diadem set in bucolic splendor in the middle of nowhere and modestly veiled by a thick screen of trees. In the State Department, which does not always love its brothers in the intelligence world, the CIA is often referred to as "those people out in the woods." And it is literally true.

Part of the reason for this is that it makes guarding the building much easier. The advantages of a rustic retreat were extolled by Allen Dulles when he went before a

House Appropriations Subcommittee in June, 1956, to seek funds for the CIA headquarters. He submitted a report which said:

"Located on a 125-acre tract forming an inconspicuous part of a larger 750-acre government reservation, the Langley site was chosen as the one location, among many sites inspected in detail, most adequate for safeguarding the security of CIA's operations. . . . This site, with its isolation, topography and heavy forestation, permits both economical construction and an added measure of security safeguards. . . ."

Three years later guests, in response to engraved invitations from Dulles, attended the cornerstone-laying ceremony. Colonel Stanley Grogan, the CIA's public information man at that time, handed out a press release.

"The entire perimeter of the main part of the site is bounded by trees," it noted, "and very little of the building will be visible from the public highways."

One CIA official summed it up. "It's well hidden," he said with a note of pride.

The fact that the CIA could send out public invitations to lay the cornerstone of its hidden headquarters reflects a basic split personality that plagues the agency and occasionally makes it the butt of unkind jokes. This dichotomy pervades much of what the CIA does. On the one hand it is supersecret; on the other hand it isn't.

When Allen Dulles became the CIA director in February, 1953, the agency was housed in a ragged complex of buildings at 2430 E Street in the Foggy Bottom section of the capital. A sign out front proclaimed: "U.S. Government Printing Office."

Once President Eisenhower and his brother Milton set out to visit Dulles. They were unable to find the place. Dulles investigated the secrecy policy. When he discovered that even guides on sightseeing buses were pointing out the buildings as "the CIA," he had the printing-office sign taken down and one that said "Central Intelligence Agency" put up.

When the CIA moved across the Potomac to its Langley home in 1961, the matter of secrecy still proved bothersome. Large green and white signs pointed the way to the CIA from the George Washington Memorial Parkway, which had been extended to the new headquarters at a cost of $8,500,000. Originally, the signs were erected to guide workmen to the site during construction. After the CIA moved into the building, some of its officials felt there was no need to leave them up. As one put it: "We knew where it was."

But the signs stayed up—for a while. As he drove to and from work each day, Robert Kennedy, who lived in nearby McLean, Virginia, would pass the signs that trumpeted the way to the CIA. One day they abruptly disappeared. In their place, there was only a small green and white marker reading "Parkway," with an arrow pointing along the highway, and "B.P.R.," with an arrow pointing to the CIA turn-off.*

The lack of signs causes scant inconvenience. No outsiders venture into the CIA anyhow unless they are on official business. No social visiting is allowed. A CIA employee cannot tell his wife or mother-in-law to drop in on him.

Another example of the now-you-see-it-now-you-don't atmosphere surrounding the building is the way the CIA answers the telephone. Other government-agency switchboards answer with the name of their department. Although the CIA is listed in two places in the Washington telephone book,† a call to the number, 351-1100, is answered by a switchboard girl who says simply, "Three five one, one one hundred." Only a few officials can be reached by name; for most, the caller must ask for the extension he wants.

Despite the atmosphere of secrecy which surrounds the building, a KGB agent trying to find the CIA head-

---

* The "B.P.R." stands for Bureau of Public Roads, which really does have two buildings at Langley. One is a research laboratory for testing road materials; the lab also has a wind tunnel to measure the effect of breezes on suspension bridges.
† Under Central Intelligence Agency and under United States Government. The 1964 Washington phone book had something new—it listed a downtown "Employment Office" for the CIA.

quarters would have no difficulty. He could drive to the nearest Amoco station and ask for a map of Washington, which (like most other maps) clearly identifies the CIA site at Langley. On the other hand, the Russian spy would not have to drive; he could get to the CIA from downtown Washington by taxi for $4.50. Or he could make the trip for forty-four cents on a public-transit bus, as do hundreds of the CIA's regular employees. (An enterprising few have commuted across the Potomac by canoe.)

A caller who asked the transit company for the schedule to Langley received this reply:

"Going to CIA? Buses leave at 7:12 A.M., 7:46 A.M. and 8:16 A.M., and arrive at CIA thirty-four minutes later. Returning in the evening at 4:38 P.M., 5:08 P.M. and 5:40 P.M. Have a nice trip."

If the Soviet spy were a top "illegal," as the Russians call their agents who have no embassy cover, he could check the *Washington Post* for a suitable location. In March, 1963, for instance, the paper carried a large advertisement for the Broadfalls Apartments in Falls Church, Virginia. Not only did the building advertise a Kelvinator refrigerator and tiled baths in every apartment, but it also headlined: "Convenient to CIA–Dulles Airport–Pentagon." And below the inviting headline, leaving nothing to chance, there appeared a map showing exactly how to get from the apartment house to the CIA.

There is such a thing as an apartment house becoming *too* convenient to the CIA. Early in 1963, an enterprising realtor, who owned thirteen acres adjacent to the CIA, applied to the local zoning board for permission to build apartment houses on his land. It was with a sense of growing horror that the CIA learned that from the fourth or fifth floor, residents would be able, with a spyglass, to look right into McCone's picture window and read his classified documents. Secretly, the CIA ordered the government's General Services Administration to buy up the land in the area forthwith.

What happened next is best told in the words of Dr. H. Hatch Sterrett, a physician who lived on Saddle Lane near the CIA: "The first I heard of it was when the GSA called my office and asked when they could have an appointment to arrange to take over my property. They kept saying they didn't know who wanted it or why it was wanted and that the only reason for taking it was that there was an established need for it. They said there was just no recourse, that there wasn't anything I could do about it."

The distraught physician consulted with his attorney, Samuel E. Neel, who was advised that the entire subject had been "classified." Neel persevered, and finally diagnosed it as a severe case of CIA.

The agency killed off the apartment-house project by buying up most of the land, but it finally permitted the doctor to keep his home. Under the agreement, however, the CIA can screen and reject anyone to whom he wishes to rent or sell. The reason? In the summer the CIA is invisible behind the trees. But in winter, when the leaves are gone, the CIA can be glimpsed through the branches from the Sterrett home.

The headquarters building has been a subject of some difficulty for the CIA from the outset. When Bedell Smith was head of the CIA, he requested $30,000,000 for a new building. To preserve security, the request was concealed in the budget the agency sent to Capitol Hill. When economy-minded congressmen discovered $30,000,000 with no apparent purpose, they cut it out of the budget.

Not until after Dulles had become the director did Congress, in July, 1955, finally vote the funds to begin planning and construction. Although the CIA's main headquarters at that time was the E Street complex, which had been used by the OSS in World War II, the agency was scattered about in thirty-four buildings all over Washington. An elaborate system of couriers and safeguards was needed to shuffle papers back and forth with security.

L. K. White, a CIA deputy director, told the House Appropriations Committee hearing in 1956 that by moving the agency into one building, "we will save about 228 people who are guards, receptionists, couriers, bus drivers and so forth." The CIA estimated it would save $600,000 a year by eliminating time lost shuttling between buildings.

Dulles had asked for a $50,800,000 building. The Budget Bureau slashed this to $50,000,000 and Congress finally authorized $46,000,000.* Noting that construction costs had risen, Dulles testified that for $46,000,000 "we could have a very austere building" which would house only "87 percent of the people for which we had originally planned."

Dulles, of course, carefully omitted saying how many people that was. And he foiled anyone who might try to compute precisely how many people worked at Langley. Someone could attempt to do so by dividing the standard amount of office space needed by a Washington worker into the CIA building's net floor space of 1,228,100 square feet.

"Our plans," Dulles told the House Committee, "are based on an average net office space utilization per person which is considerably below the government-wide average of net office space per employee in Metropolitan Washington." †

In the fall of 1961, the CIA moved in.

A visitor to the new headquarters turns off at the "B.P.R." sign at Langley and comes shortly to a ten-foot-high wire-mesh fence, which surrounds the entire CIA site. On the fence are various signs—none saying CIA. One reads: "U. S. Government Property for Official Business Only." Another says: "Cameras Prohibited." In case anyone failed to get the message, a third sign says: "No Trespassing."

Beyond the gate is a guardhouse, but a visitor who appears to know where he is going is waved through

---

* The exact final construction cost is classified, according to a spokesman for the General Services Administration.
† Each worker in a government building takes up an average of about 150 square feet of office space, according to figures compiled nation-wide by the GSA since 1960. On this basis, the CIA building would hold 8,187 people. However, as Dulles indicated, the space-per-worker figure can be much lower. Washington's new Civil Service Commission building has 135 square feet per worker, for example. At that figure, the CIA would house 9,097 people. Based on these space-utilization figures, some 8,000 to 10,000 people would work at the CIA headquarters at Langley.

without having to stop and show credentials. A sharp left, and the building, still half-hidden by the trees, comes into view. Finally, several hundred feet farther along, near the main entrance, the building emerges from the trees for the first time.

It is massive, grayish-white concrete, several stories high and cold in appearance. The windows are recessed and those on the lower floors are barred with a heavy mesh. Off to the right of the main entrance a separate domed structure housing a 500-seat auditorium gives an almost Martian atmosphere to the grounds.

But what strikes the visitor most of all is the complete silence outside the building. In the summertime, only the hum of the building's air conditioners and the sound of crickets and birds can be heard. In the winter, not even that. The effect is eerie. The building might be a hospital or a huge private sanitarium in the woods.

On this same site, half a century ago, Joseph Leiter, the son of a millionaire Chicago businessman, built a beautiful home and called it the Glass Palace. He and his wife entertained lavishly and enjoyed the view of the Potomac. After Leiter died in 1932, the government bought up the land. The Glass Palace burned down in 1945.

There is still glass in the CIA's concrete palace, but it is mainly on the second and seventh floors, where the outside walls are formed by continuous windows. On the grounds, there are twenty-one acres of parking space for 3,000 cars. (Dulles had asked Congress for space for 4,000.) The cafeteria seats 1,400 persons at a time.

On the roof, there are $50,000 worth of special radio antennas, a vital part of the CIA's own world-wide communication system. Deep inside the CIA headquarters is a central control room to which alarm systems throughout the building are wired. Three security incinerators, built at a cost of $105,000, gobble up classified wastepaper.

The domed auditorium outside is used mostly for training courses for junior CIA executives, and as Colonel Grogan's press release noted, it has, fittingly, "a small stage with a disappearing curved screen. . . ."

Inside the vast headquarters, a visitor can get about as

238

far as the inscription in marble on the left wall—"And ye shall know the truth and the truth shall make you free. John VIII–XXXII"—before he is stopped by a guard. He is then directed to a reception room, where he signs in. A security escort takes him where he is going, waits until he is through and escorts him back to the front door. There, just inside the airy lobby, a mammoth official seal with the words "Central Intelligence Agency" is set in the marble floor, with an eagle's head in the center. As he walked through the corridors, the visitor might have noticed that most of the doors to offices were closed and unmarked, giving the false impression of a virtually deserted building.

Like a battleship, the CIA headquarters is built in compartments. An employee in one office would not necessarily know what was happening a few feet away on the other side of the wall.

The CIA report to the House Appropriations Committee explained that this was a major consideration in the plans drawn up by Harrison & Abramovitz, the New York architects: "The new building will consist of block-type wings, readily compartmented from one another, so that specially restricted areas can be established and special security controls maintained in each section."

Among the building's special facilities is a $200,000 scientific laboratory, where the CIA perfects some of its miniaturized weapons, invisible inks, special explosives and other devices.

One of the really spooky instruments at Langley is the CIA's electronic "brain," which stores and retrieves the mountains of information that flow into the building. The CIA's library is split into four parts: a regular library of books and documents, special libraries known as "registers" which store biographic and industrial intelligence, a document center—and the electronic brain.

The brain is called WALNUT and it was developed just for the CIA by IBM. A desired document is flashed in front of the CIA viewer by means of a photo tape robot called Intellofax.

WALNUT and Intellofax, unlike humans, are infallible.

Aside from the vast amounts of classified data that come into the CIA, the agency collects 200,000 newspapers, books and other "open" material each month. The information is stored on 40,000,000 punch cards.

When a CIA man wants a particular item, be it a Castro speech or a top-secret report on Khrushchev's health, he feeds into WALNUT a list of key words—perhaps twenty-five—about the subject. The brain finds the right microfilmed document and photographs it with ultraviolet light. The tiny photo is then projected on the viewing machine. The whole thing takes five seconds. The CIA has also been experimenting with another brain called Minicard, developed by Eastman Kodak for the Air Force.

The CIA also has a special spy-fiction library, which it does not advertise. This library contains thousands of past and current mystery and spy stories. It should please fans of Ian Fleming, Helen MacInnes and Eric Ambler to know that the CIA makes a point of keeping up with the latest tricks of fictional spy heroes. Before Langley, the spy fiction was housed in the old Christian Heurich Brewery near the State Department.

CIA men and women lead a cloistered life. By and large they stick to themselves. Intermarriage is not unusual, the most notable recent example being the U-2 pilot Francis Gary Powers. After his release by the Russians, Powers continued to work for the CIA at Langley.* He divorced his wife Barbara, and on October 26, 1963, in a quiet ceremony at Catlett, Fauquier County, Virginia, he married Claudia Edwards Downey, a twenty-eight-year-old divorcée and a CIA psychologist. Mrs. Downey, the

---

* Lockheed Aircraft Corporation, which built the U-2 and along with NASA served as a front for the CIA, announced on November 3, 1962, that Powers had taken "a routine test pilot job" with Lockheed at Burbank, California. "It involves checking out the U-2s that are modified, maintained and overhauled," said a Lockheed public-relations spokesman. A CIA source said the same day that Powers had left the agency because "his work was finished." After the U-2 was shot down in May, 1960, both NASA and Lockheed announced that Powers was a civilian pilot employed by Lockheed. Actually, he was flying for the CIA under a $30,000-a-year contract he had signed with the intelligence agency in 1956.

mother of a seven-year-old girl, was said to have resigned from the CIA to become Mrs. Powers.

In Washington, a highly social city given to much partying and mixing of many diverse circles, it is remarkable how few CIA men are casually encountered on the cocktail circuit. The reason is that CIA couples give parties mostly for each other.

In bygone years, CIA employees were barred from admitting where they worked. In social situations they usually managed to hint at it anyhow. Nowadays, overt employees are permitted to say where they work—although not to a foreign national. Those in the Clandestine Services are not, however, normally allowed to say they work for the CIA.

And cover names are used even inside the CIA. "I don't know the names of everyone I deal with at the agency," one high official confided. "We often use pseudonyms in-house, in case a wire is tapped or a piece of paper gets into the wrong hands. And we never use real names in communications."

The CIA is constantly facing little problems that no other agency faces. For example, suppose an agent in the Clandestine Services breaks his arm in the line of duty. Blue Cross? Ah, but then Group Hospitalization would find out his name when he filled out the inevitable form. And for the first few years after the agency's creation, that is exactly what happened, much to the CIA's irritation. When agents were hospitalized, Group Hospitalization had to know who they were. So in 1956 the CIA canceled its contract with Blue Cross. It took its business to Mutual of Omaha, which benevolently agreed to waive the paperwork on ailing spies.

Although CIA employees are not technically under Civil Service, they qualify for the government's normal retirement provisions and their pay is equivalent to those in Civil Service. Secretaries start at GS-3, which is $3,820 a year. The director's salary is $21,000. The deputy director gets $500 a year less.

In 1963 McCone asked Congress to set up a better retirement system for his top people, similar to that of the

State Department's Foreign Service. A House Armed Services Subcommittee heard McCone's plea *in camera*. Later, in 1964, Congress passed a law allowing high-ranking agents with twenty years of service to retire at age fifty. The CIAR, as the pension plan was called, would cost an estimated $4,000,000 by 1969, or $900,000 a year.

The Armed Services Committee, in approving the measure, said that "many CIA employees serve under conditions which are at least as difficult and frequently more onerous and dangerous" than those faced by the FBI and other agencies.

In a report to the House Committee, the CIA said the pension system would help it to weed out older men in the ranks. "The Central Intelligence Agency," it said, "needs to attract and retain a force of highly motivated careerists . . . agency requirements demand that this group of careerists be composed of younger and more vigorous officers than are generally required in government service."

Many of the CIA's younger people are recruited off college campuses. The agency tries to select students standing near the top of their class. CIA stays quietly in touch with college deans and hires most of its research analysts this way. On every large campus there is usually someone who serves secretly as the CIA's talent scout.

At Yale, for example, during the early 1950s, it was Skip Walz, the crew coach. John Downey, who was imprisoned by Communist China in 1952, was recruited off the Yale campus in 1951. The college recruits are enrolled as CIA JOTs—junior officer trainees. Recently, in the manner of large business corporations, the CIA quietly published a booklet, *The Central Intelligence Agency*, extolling the virtues of a career in the agency. The booklet's cover, in yellow, red, brown, violet and white, portrays a handsome young man with jaw on hand, pondering his future.

From every 1,000 persons considered, the CIA selects 200 for security investigation. Of this 20 percent, about 11 percent are screened out because "they drink too much, talk too much, have relatives behind the iron curtain, which may make the applicants subject to foreign pressures; for serious security reasons 4 percent of this 11 percent are screened out. These latter are individuals who have contacts that render them undesirable for service in this highly sensitive agency." * What this boils down to is that 178 out of 1,000 applicants are accepted.

From the start, the CIA has employed lie detectors. The polygraph is standard equipment at the agency and all new employees take the test.

The most revealing information on this delicate subject came in a televised interview with Allen Dulles, carried by the American Broadcasting Company: [1]

Q: In that connection, sir, of how great a value is the lie detector to an agency like CIA in detecting potential spies, agents and/or homosexuals?

A: In my experience in the CIA we found it of great indicative value. No one is ever convicted or cleared just on a polygraph test, a lie-detector test. . . .

Q: What kind of cases do you turn up most easily by using lie detectors?

A: Well, we turn up homosexual cases particularly, but not only that. There can be other weaknesses. . . .

Q: Almost every CIA employee had to undergo a lie-detector test as a condition of employment?

A: Well, I won't say no, it is not a condition of employment. I know of people who have said they didn't for various reasons want to take the lie-detector test, and they have not been dismissed or terminated for that reason.

Q: But were they hired?

A: But generally when people come on board, the general rule is that they take the test. But it is not any formalized rule, as far as I know.

Should an applicant pass all these hurdles and be accepted by the CIA, he must sign a security agreement in which he swears never to divulge classified information or intelligence (except in the performance of his official duties) unless he is specifically authorized, in writing, by the director of the CIA. Employees are thus barred from talking about their work even after they leave the agency:

* From a twenty-page limited-circulation booklet the CIA published about itself in 1961.

they certainly cannot go out and write their memoirs about their CIA experiences.

Criticism that the CIA is an "Ivy League" institution is only partially accurate. Although the top twenty executives have always been largely from Ivy League colleges, this is not true of the agency generally. Nevertheless, a good education is highly prized. About 60 percent of the senior 600 employees at the CIA have advanced degrees, many of them Ph.D.s. This is not surprising in an agency that devotes a major portion of its efforts to research and analysis.

To satisfy the interests of its scholarly employees, the CIA publishes its own digest-sized magazine, the most exclusive magazine in the world. It can't be purchased. It is not available at outside libraries. It is called *Intelligence Articles*.

The magazine was begun because the CIA has so many former professors who, for the most part, cannot publish on the outside. *Intelligence Articles* provides an anonymous outlet for their scholarship. Like any specialized periodical, it has studies of current interest in the field, in this case, intelligence. But there is one difference: most of the articles and book reviews have no bylines.

The literary style leans toward a rather heavy prose. There is an attempt to treat on a high academic level such subjects as how to keep a double agent from being tortured and shot by the enemy. Other forms of mayhem are dealt with in a similar scholarly vein.

One issue not long ago featured an article explaining the difference between a "write-in" and a "walk-in." (Both are volunteer spies: the terms apply to the way in which they offer their services.) The article, entitled "A Classic Write-In Case," was a study of Captain Stephan Kalman, a Czech Army officer who in 1936 betrayed secrets to the German High Command until he was caught and hanged.

"The agent of an adversary service," the article begins, "or a person high in an adversary bureaucracy, if he wishes to make contact with another intelligence or security service, can choose from a number of different means. He can present himself physically as a walk-in. He can use an intermediary in order to retain some control, especially with respect to his own identity. He can send a messenger, make a phone call, or establish a radio contact. Or he can simply write a letter, anonymous or signed."

After detailing the story of Kalman's treachery, the CIA publication, under the headline "Moral of the Story," asks: "What conclusions can be drawn from the Kalman case? . . . One conclusion derives from positive and negative aspects of the Czech performance with respect to security. Security applies on every echelon of command. There is no place for laxness, even if it may seem overbureaucratic and ridiculous. The application of security measures has to be executed precisely in every detail. There is no place for overconfidence in friends and old acquaintances. That Kalman, with his alien loyalties, came to be trusted with sensitive materials is evidence of such overconfidence."

A discerning CIA reader might come to suspect that, all in all, *Intelligence Articles*' academic objectivity leaves something to be desired. Another excerpt worth quoting in this respect is from the magazine's review of a book * that presented ideas about foreign policy not at all to the liking of the CIA reviewer. For one thing, the book suggested that the CIA is ineffective.

After noting that the book was written under the pseudonym "John Forth Amory," the equally anonymous CIA reviewer concludes: "If his identity is worth a search, one might look for a fervent Jeffersonian and F. D. Rooseveltian who has some bookish knowledge of the United States Government and of big business and who entertains a particular sympathy for Indonesians, having had opportunities to discuss with them their philosophy of social change—a neoacademic sort, probably juvenile or with development arrested at the simplistic stage, possibly an instructor in some local college course for fledgling foreign service officers."

If the CIA has its cloistered advantages for the scholar at Langley, there are hazards for agents in the field. Espionage is a dangerous business and some of the CIA's

* *Around the Edge of War*, Clarkson N. Potter, Inc., New York, 1961.

clandestine employees crack under the pressure. (Even at Langley, there are strains. One deputy director drove himself so hard, he had to be transferred to a less demanding post overseas.)

Many CIA employees, working irregular hours in odd corners of the globe, suffer from what the agency itself calls "motivational exhaustion." A CIA report to the House Armed Services Committee in 1963 explained: "This term is used to describe a gradual lessening of interest and enthusiasm of an officer as a result of impingements on his personal and family life. These stem from the transient nature of his assignments, the complications and restrictions of security requirements and intrusions on his family life."

The agency has a fairly high rate of suicides, which usually get little attention outside of the Washington newspapers. In October, 1959, for example, a thirty-two-year-old CIA employee and his wife, just back from a two-year tour of duty in Germany, jumped into the Potomac River rapids in a suicide pact.

The CIA man, James A. Woodbury, drowned, but his blond wife was pulled out. Police quoted her as saying her husband had a lot on his mind. "They wanted to put him in a psycho ward," she said, "and we figured it best to do away with ourselves." The police said Mrs. Woodbury would not elaborate on her reference to "they."

Despite the risks, CIA employees have no job security. Under the 1947 law they can be fired by the director "in his discretion" with no appeal. In at least one instance, this led to a series of embarrassing disclosures about the agency's operations and personnel.

On January 30, 1961, Dulles fired a veteran CIA intelligence officer and contact specialist named John Torpats, who then went into Federal Court seeking reinstatement. Dulles filed an answer urging the case be thrown out. In the course of it, Dulles stated that "George B. Carey," an assistant director of the CIA, had notified "Emmet Echols," the director of personnel, that Torpats was allowed to discuss his case with "Ralph Poole" and "Fred Lott," both assistants to Echols.

Torpats decided if Dulles could name names, so could he. In an affidavit filed June 30, 1961, in answer to the CIA director, Torpats said:

"In early 1956 a situation had developed in a European mission of CIA which my then area superiors, Frank G. Wisner, Richard Helms, John M. Maury, Jr., and N. M. Anikeeff, felt had been mishandled by the personnel of the mission. The mission reports were considered to be unsatisfactory in our component. My superiors felt that I could handle the problem more effectively and expeditiously and decided to send me to do it. The principal figures in this particular mission were Mr. Tracy Barnes, Mr. Thomas Parrott and Mr. Paul Losher. At the time of my separation, Mr. Barnes and Mr. Parrott were employed by the Agency in the Washington, D. C., office.

"Notice was given to the mission in April of 1956 that I was being sent over. I was given no special instructions before I left; I was to be on my own. The mission had sent a report on the problem which I later proved was incorrect. Had the mission report been followed, it would have done incalculable harm to the United States.

"When I finished my assignment, for which I received several commendations from headquarters, but before I could file my report, Mr. Barnes, on a complaint by Mr. Parrott, put me under house arrest; ordered an investigation, shipped me home; cabled charges against me to headquarters with a demand that I be fired."

The ousted CIA man then detailed a long history of his case as it dragged on through the agency bureaucracy for several years. He said one charge against him was that he had disobeyed a high CIA official in the office of the DDP "and visited a station contrary to his orders."

In addition, Torpats said, a CIA fitness report claimed he had an "inability to handle agents" and "total lack of objectivity where Estonian émigré matters are concerned." He said he was transferred out of the Clandestine Services and eventually fired.

Dulles angrily filed an answer to Torpats on July 2, citing an old Civil War case to support his contention that employees of secret services cannot air their grievances in court. Torpats, Dulles said, "understood that the nature of his work was secret, and that the disclosure of his duties and the names of fellow employees would not be in the best interest of his government. Moreover, he swore, as a condition of his employment that he would never reveal such information."

If CIA employees can go into court every time they feel they are treated unfairly, said Dulles, it would be no way to run an espionage apparatus. "Operation of the Central Intelligence Agency, with liability to publicity in this way," he said, "would be impossible." *

Even CIA employees who make it to the top can look forward to little overt recognition after their long years of service. President Kennedy, speaking to CIA employees at Langley on November 28, 1961, told them: "Your successes are unheralded—your failures are trumpeted."

President Eisenhower voiced a similar sentiment when he spoke at the cornerstone-laying at Langley on November 3, 1959. "Success cannot be advertised: failure cannot be explained," he said. "In the work of intelligence, heroes are undecorated and unsung, often even among their own fraternity."

This is not completely correct. The truth is that some CIA men *are* decorated. Despite the fact that he was eased out after the Bay of Pigs, for example, Richard M. Bissell received a secret intelligence medal honoring him for his years as deputy director for plans.

There was no public announcement of the award, and Bissell was not allowed to talk about his medal, to show it to anyone or to wear it. As far as the CIA was concerned, officially the medal did not exist.

The Invisible Government had awarded him an invisible medal.

* Torpats lost his case. Both the U. S. District Court and the Court of Appeals upheld Dulles.

17

CIA: The Inner Workings

ON A WARM DAY in June of 1963, Senator Frank Church, the Idaho Democrat, dispatched a Senate page across the river to Langley with an envelope stamped: "Personal for the Director."

Church had stumbled on some information which he thought John McCone ought to have immediately. Three and a half hours later a bedraggled and distraught page returned to Church's office. He reported that he had fallen into the hands of CIA security police, who had questioned him at length about what he was up to. They released him after a few hours but would not accept the letter. Senator Church finally mailed it.

Although the Senate messenger, like most Americans, thus never got a peek inside CIA headquarters, the agency's operations are not a total mystery. It is possible to piece together a fair idea of its internal workings, and organization, as well as the techniques and methods it uses both at home and abroad.

The CIA is, of course, the biggest, most important and most influential branch of the Invisible Government. The agency is organized into four divisions: Intelligence, Plans, Research, Support, each headed by a deputy director.

The Support Division is the administrative arm of the CIA. It is in charge of equipment, logistics, security and communications. It devises the CIA's special codes, which cannot be read by other branches of the government.

The Research Division is in charge of technical intelligence. It provides expert assessments of foreign advances in science, technology and atomic weapons. It was responsible for analyzing the U-2 photographs brought back from the Soviet Union between 1956 and 1960. And it has continued to analyze subsequent U-2 and spy-satellite pictures. In this it works with the DIA in running the National Photo Intelligence Center.

Herbert "Pete" Scoville, who headed the Research Division for eight years, left in August of 1963 to become an assistant director of the Arms Control and Disarmament Agency. He was replaced as the CIA's deputy director for research by Dr. Albert D. Wheelon.

The Plans Division is in charge of the CIA's cloak-and-dagger activities. It controls all foreign special operations, such as Guatemala and the Bay of Pigs, and it collects all of the agency's covert intelligence through spies and informers overseas.

Allen Dulles was the first deputy director for plans. He was succeeded as DDP by Frank Wisner, who was replaced in 1958 by Bissell, who, in turn, was succeeded in 1962 by his deputy, Richard Helms.

A native of St. David's, Pennsylvania, Helms studied in Switzerland and Germany and was graduated from Williams College in 1935. He worked for the United Press and the *Indianapolis Times,* and then, during World War II, he served as a lieutenant commander in the Navy attached to the OSS. When the war ended and some OSS men were transferred to the CIA, he stayed on and rose through the ranks.

Helms' counterpart as the deputy director for intelligence in the CIA hierarchy after the Bay of Pigs was also an ex-OSS man. Ray Cline got into the intelligence business as a cryptanalyst in 1942, moving on to the OSS and the CIA. He was born in Anderson Township, Illinois, and was graduated from Harvard, where he was elected to Phi Beta Kappa. He also received his Ph.D. at Harvard and studied later at Oxford.

With the CIA, Cline served for a period as liaison man with British intelligence, the most important of the sixty-odd foreign intelligence organizations with which the CIA is linked. Before he was named the DDI, Cline ran the CIA operation on Formosa under the cover title of Director, United States Naval Auxiliary Communications Center, Taiwan.

The job of the Intelligence Division is essentially a highly specialized form of scholarship. And 80 percent of its information comes from "open sources": technical magazines, foreign broadcast monitoring, scholarly studies, propaganda journals, and data produced by such visible branches of the government as the U.S. Information Agency,* the Agriculture, Treasury, and Commerce † Departments, and the Agency for International Development.

The Intelligence Division's function is to take the mass of information available to it and "produce" intelligence, that is, to draw up reports on the economic, political, social and governmental situation in any country in the world. The division is subdivided into three major groups: one makes long-range projections of what can be expected in crisis areas; a second produces a daily review of the current situation; and a third, established by Cline shortly after he took over, is supposed to detect the gaps in what the CIA is doing and collecting.

Cline and his subordinates pride themselves on their independence and detachment from operational problems. They maintain that they evaluate information flowing in from the CIA Plans Division on an equal basis with intelligence coming in from elsewhere in the government. They contend that they do not have any ax to grind or any vested interest or operation to protect and, therefore, that

* Donald M. Wilson, the deputy director of USIA, was asked by the House Foreign Affairs Subcommittee on February 21, 1963, to explain what type of contact USIA had with the State Department, the CIA and other intelligence agencies. "Very close," Wilson replied. "We have daily contact with them on a number of levels."
† The flow of information is sometimes both ways. In 1959, when the CIA wanted to get translations of Soviet scientific and technical journals into the hands of American scientists and technicians, the Commerce Department's Office of Technical Services agreed to serve as the channel. The procedure provided a conventional veneer for an unusual practice.

they produce the most objective reports of any branch of the government.

The most important of these reports are prepared, sometimes on a crash basis, by the Office of National Estimates (ONE), which acts as the staff of the twelve-man Board of National Estimates (BNE), long headed by Sherman Kent, a sixty-year-old former Yale history professor. A burly, tough-talking, tobacco-chewing man, Kent directed the European-African Division of the OSS during World War II. Kent and his board turn out National Intelligence Estimates (NIE) and, in times of crisis, quick reports known as Special National Intelligence Estimates.

"National Intelligence Estimates," Lyman Kirkpatrick, the executive director of the CIA has said, "are perhaps the most important documents created in the intelligence mechanisms of our government. . . . A national estimate is a statement of what is going to happen in any country, in any area, in any given situation, and as far as possible into the future. . . .

"Each of the responsible departments prepares the original draft on that section which comes under its purview. Thus the Department of State would draft the section on the political, economic or sociological development in a country or an area or a situation, while the Army would deal with ground forces, the Air Force with the air forces, and the Navy with the naval forces, and the Department of Defense under the Joint Chiefs of Staff with the guided-missile threat.

"The Board of Estimates would then go over the individual contributions very carefully—sometimes very heatedly—and arrive at a common view. Any one of the intelligence services has the right of dissent from the view which will be expressed as that of the Director of Intelligence." [1] (This is known as "taking a footnote.")

These National Intelligence Estimates go to the United States Intelligence Board for review. Under Dulles, Sherman Kent's board generated its own studies and was under the jurisdiction of the deputy director for intelligence. One of the changes made by McCone was to bring the Board of National Estimates directly under his personal command. McCone then controlled the frequency and subject matter of NIE reports. USIB functioned as an advisory group to McCone and estimates were frequently rewritten at his direction.

The NIE was then transmitted to the President as the estimate of the Director of Central Intelligence. Ultimately, therefore, despite all this vast intelligence machinery, the end product goes to the President as the personal responsibility and personal estimate of one man.

It is in this area that the structure of the Invisible Government is the most complex. The Director of Central Intelligence is the ultimate arbiter of the vital security information, predictions and evaluations that are placed on the desk of the President. He presides over the branches of the intelligence community represented on USIB; but, as has been seen, he also heads the CIA, which is one of these branches. He controls not only the intelligence product of CIA but also the product of the entire Invisible Government. He is therefore both umpire and player, the chairman of the board and a member of it.

In addition to producing the raw material for the national estimates, the CIA also provides the President with a daily top-secret checklist of the major world crises. Copies go to the Director of Central Intelligence and to the Secretaries of State and Defense. Top-ranking men in the CIA's Intelligence Division get to work at 3:00 A.M., to read the overnight cables and compile the checklist.

During the Kennedy Administration, the checklist was presented to the President the first thing each morning by Major General Chester V. (Ted) Clifton, the chief White House military aide. Under President Johnson, McGeorge Bundy initially assumed the responsibility for the morning intelligence briefing.

Special procedures have been established to assure that the President and the three other recipients of the checklist can be reached instantly in an emergency. An Indications Center is manned twenty-four hours a day by representatives of the CIA, the Pentagon and the State Department. It works under the guidance of a Watch Committee, which meets once a week to survey crisis situations and, if necessary, to recommend an immediate convening of the Board of Estimates.

Although that board no longer operates directly under the authority of the CIA deputy director for intelligence, the power of his office has been enlarged in another direction. Ray Cline was the first DDI to be informed about the secret operations of the Plans Division. Prior to McCone's rule, this was not the practice.

The CIA had been rigorously compartmented in the interests of maximum security. The agency's left hand was purposely prevented from knowing what the right hand was doing. The Intelligence Division would receive all of the covert information collected by CIA agents abroad, but it was kept in ignorance about all clandestine operations. In the parlance of the trade, all cloak-and-dagger schemes were "vest pocketed" by the Plans Division.

For example, as already described, Cline's predecessor as DDI, Robert Amory, was never told in advance about the Bay of Pigs. And there was a feeling that President Kennedy might have abandoned the operation if all of his intelligence advisers had not been sponsors and, therefore, devout advocates of the plan.

Soon after McCone took office, he decided to change the system. He set up a three-man study group composed of Lyman Kirkpatrick, General Cortlandt Van Rensselaer Schuyler, executive assistant to Governor Rockefeller, and J. Patrick Coyne, former FBI agent and executive director of the President's Foreign Intelligence Advisory Board.

Perhaps the most important change decided upon by McCone was his instruction to the Plans Division to keep the Intelligence Division continuously posted on all its activities. Thereafter, the Intelligence Division received "sanitized" reports (names of agents removed) on all current operations. The intelligence analysts were thus in a position for the first time to contest the special pleading of the men who were running the operations. On the basis of the large pool of information available to them from all branches of the Invisible Government, they could recommend changes in or complete cancellation of doubtful schemes.

Although there is some interchange of personnel, a natural suspicion exists between the Plans Division, which tends to attract activists and risk-takers, and the Intelligence Division, which tends to attract academic and contemplative types.

In its political complexion, too, the CIA splits roughly along the lines of its major functional responsibilities.

"The DDI side," one veteran CIA official explained, "tends to be liberal: they're at home with people like Schlesinger and Bundy. They tend to be liberal Democrats and liberal Republicans. The other side of the house has many ex-FBI types. It tends to get more conservative people, Bissell excepted. Helms has no politics, he's just a good professional intelligence man. But there are all kinds in CIA, as you'd expect."

A frequent charge against the CIA, justified in part, is that it tends to support right-wing, military governments that it regards as "safe," ignoring more liberal elements that might, in the long run, provide a more effective hedge against Communism.

Viewed in this context, it is significant that officials in the Plans Division are considered by their colleagues to be by instinct and background more conservative than the pure intelligence analysts. It is the agents serving in foreign stations under the DDP, after all, who are most directly concerned in the field with the question of where to throw CIA support in a complex political situation.

While the work of all of these divisions is centered at Langley, the CIA also operates inside the United States in many locations and in many guises. Although few Americans are aware of it, the CIA has offices in twenty cities throughout the country. The National Security Act of 1947, establishing the CIA, stated that "the agency shall have no police, subpena, law-enforcement or internal-security functions." Since the CIA was created to deal exclusively with foreign intelligence, the question might be raised as to why it has field offices across the nation.

The answer CIA officials give is that the offices are needed to collect foreign intelligence domestically, principally from travelers returning from abroad.

The CIA operates under a number of classified directives issued by the National Security Council since 1947. NSC directive No. 7 permits the CIA to question people within the United States.

The CIA's use of tourists and travelers to gather intelligence was clearly forecast in a memorandum which Allen Dulles submitted to the Senate Armed Services Committee in 1947, when it was considering the Act establishing the CIA. The memorandum is a public document.[2] It concludes:

> Because of its glamour and mystery overemphasis is generally placed on what is called secret intelligence . . . but in time of peace the bulk of intelligence can be obtained through overt channels. . . . It can also be obtained . . . through the many Americans, business and professional men and American residents of foreign countries, who are naturally and normally brought in touch with what is going on in those countries.

It is not unusual for the CIA to contact Americans about to go behind the Iron Curtain as tourists. Not every tourist is approached, of course, and many decline to get involved in high-risk amateur spying.

Recently, a New York publishing executive and his wife were about to leave for Russia as tourists when a telephone call came from the CIA. Would the editor be willing to report any interesting conversations? Would he turn over any interesting pictures he might take? The couple politely declined.

In addition to approaching legitimate tourists, the agency also plants its own tourists behind the Iron Curtain, occasionally with disastrous results. On August 25, 1960, two Air Force veterans, Mark I. Kaminsky and Harvey C. Bennett, of Bath, Maine, were arrested while touring the Soviet Union.

Both men were proficient in Russian. Kaminsky, twenty-eight, taught Russian at Ann Arbor, Michigan, High School; and Bennett, twenty-six, had just graduated in Slavic studies from the University of California at Berkeley.

Kaminsky was sentenced to seven years in prison by a court in Kiev. Then the Russians changed their minds and expelled the pair.

They returned to the United States on October 20. At a press conference at Idlewild International Airport, Kaminsky denied any spying, and said he had planned to write a book called *The Soviet Union Talks Peace While Preparing for War*. The two said they had traveled to Russia on grants of $2,000 each from the "Northcraft Educational Fund of Philadelphia." However, they were not able to describe the operations of the fund, which was not listed then or later in the Philadelphia telephone book, the National Education Association's file of foundations, *The Foundation Directory*, or any other standard reference list.

In a similar case in 1961, another American, Marvin William Makinen, of Ashburnham, Massachusetts, was arrested while touring Russia. Makinen, only twenty-two, had studied chemistry at the University of Pennsylvania and had just completed a year as an exchange student at the Free University of West Berlin. He spoke fluent German and Finnish. He was arrested and sentenced to eight years after the Russians charged he took pictures of military installations in Kiev. The Russians said he had confessed to spying.

In February, 1962, James Donovan came within an ace of freeing Makinen in the Powers-Abel exchange. But Makinen remained in Vladimir Prison (where Powers had been held) until October 12, 1963, when he was returned to the United States in a four-way trade.* Makinen had little to say to reporters when he stepped off a BOAC airliner at Idlewild International Airport just after dawn. When asked about his arrest, he replied in a low voice: "I guess it was mainly because of my confession."

Aside from tourist-contact work, there are many other types of activities operating from the CIA's twenty regional offices within the United States. In Miami and New

---

* Two accused Soviet spies, Ivan D. Egorov, a UN personnel officer, and his wife, Aleksandra, were traded for Makinen and the Reverend Walter Ciszek, a Jesuit priest held by the Russians for twenty-three years.

York, the agency financed and directed Cuban refugee activities. In New York and Chicago, it may be assumed that it conducts similar activities with Eastern European anti-Communist émigré groups.

At least a few whiskers of this particular cat were peeping out of the bag when McCone testified before the Senate Armed Services Committee during hearings on his nomination on January 18, 1962.

Senator Margaret Chase Smith, the independent-minded lady from Maine, was questioning McCone:

SENATOR SMITH: It has been alleged to me, Mr. McCone, that the CIA has been or is supporting the political activities of certain ethnic groups in this country, such as the Polish and Hungarian groups; is this true, and if so, what comment do you have to make?

MR. MCCONE: I can make no comment on it.

SENATOR SMITH: Pardon?

MR. MCCONE: I could make no comment on that.

SENATOR SMITH: Is it true?

MR. MCCONE: I couldn't comment on it.

Later, Senator Richard B. Russell, the Democratic chairman, and Senator Leverett Saltonstall, the Massachusetts Republican, both powerful Congressional protectors of the CIA, attempted to smooth over the delicate and unpleasant question asked by Mrs. Smith—but only succeeded in getting into deeper water.

CHAIRMAN RUSSELL: As a matter of national policy, and speaking as a citizen and not as a nominee for this position, Mr. McCone, do you see anything immoral or wrong about any agency of this government undertaking to encourage ethnic groups in this country that have brethren behind the Iron Curtain . . . ?

MR. MCCONE: No sir; I do not . . .

CHAIRMAN RUSSELL: Our enemies are certainly trying to seek to destroy us in every possible way, appealing to all ethnic groups in any way they can get their hands on them. I do not see any reason why we should have our hands tied.

SENATOR SALTONSTALL: Will the Senator yield? I would

just like to supplement what the chairman has said. Is it not true, Mr. McCone, in your understanding of the CIA, that any work on the ethnic groups in this country would not be within the province of the CIA, in any event; am I correct in that?

MR. MCCONE: I cannot answer that, Senator.

SENATOR SALTONSTALL: Perhaps that should not be answered.

Actually, for a decade, a $100,000,000 fund was available for this type of activity. A 1951 amendment to the Foreign Aid Act had provided the money for persons "residing in or escapees from" the Soviet Union, the satellite nations or any other Communist area of the world, either to form them into military units "or for other purposes." It drew wrathful attacks from the Soviet Union in the United Nations. In 1961 Congress repealed the amendment at the request of the Agency for International Development. Asked whether the $100,000,000 fund had ever been used for clandestine work, an AID official said: "It was never used for anything other than refugee aid after they had escaped."

The CIA's domestic field offices are also useful in obtaining intelligence from business firms that have extensive foreign operations. In addition, the offices serve as contact points with universities. The relationship between the CIA and the universities is two-way—the CIA secretly finances research programs at some universities; in turn the universities help recruit personnel. Perhaps even more important, the universities provide a pool of expert knowledge about foreign countries upon which the intelligence agency can, and does, draw.

Despite the possible loss of academic freedom, most universities and professors have shown little reluctance to work for the CIA. The agency has been able to obtain the services of almost all of the academic institutions and individuals it has approached.

Harvard has refused to accept money for classified projects, but some of its faculty members have done research for the CIA by the simple expedient of funneling their work through the Center for International Studies at the nearby Massachusetts Institute of Technology.

The MIT Center, which was set up with CIA money in 1950, has adopted many of the practices in effect at the CIA headquarters in Virginia. An armed guard watches over the door and the participating academicians must show badges on entering and leaving.

The Center was founded by Walt Whitman Rostow, an economics professor who served in the OSS in World War II and later as the chief of the State Department's Policy Planning Staff in the Kennedy and Johnson Administrations. In 1952 Max F. Millikan, another economist, became the director of the Center after a two-year tour of duty as an assistant director of the CIA in Washington.

In a practice which has subsequently become standard procedure at MIT and elsewhere, Rostow and his colleagues produced a CIA-financed book, *The Dynamics of Soviet Society*, in 1953. It was published in two versions, one classified for circulation within the intelligence community, the other "sanitized" for public consumption.

One of Rostow's subordinates at the Center was Andreas F. Lowenfeld, who became a legal adviser in the State Department under Kennedy and Johnson. Lowenfeld was questioned about his work at MIT in testimony before the Senate Internal Security Subcommittee on June 12, 1962:

SOURWINE (Subcommittee counsel): Were you ever, Mr. Lowenfeld, connected in any way with the CIA?

LOWENFELD: Not in any direct way. The reason that I hesitate in my answer is that I was connected with the Center for International Studies at MIT.

SOURWINE: That was during what period of time?

LOWENFELD: That was 1951-1952. And they had some kind of contract with the CIA. So that it is conceivable that I was cleared by them.

SOURWINE: Yes.

LOWENFELD: But I never formally worked for them.

SOURWINE: Did you know that the Center for International Studies was a CIA operation?

LOWENFELD: I was never formally told, but it became apparent.

One of the dangers inherent in the liaison between the universities and the CIA is the opportunity it provides for Communist propagandists to question the intellectual objectivity and detachment of American scholars.

On December 21, 1963, Cyril Black, the head of the Slavic Department at Princeton, was accused by Communist Bulgaria of having acted as the CIA's contact man with Ivan-Assen Khristov Georgiev, a Bulgarian diplomat who was shot the next month as an alleged spy for the United States.

At his trial, Georgiev testified that he met repeatedly with Black, the son of the former head of the American College in Sophia, during his five-year assignment at the UN. Georgiev said he had been paid $200,000 for his services but spent it all on a series of mistresses, three of whom supposedly were flown to New York for him at CIA expense.

Professor Black denounced the accusations as a "complete fabrication." "It is so preposterous," he said, "that it should not be dignified by a detailed rebuttal." Although Black's denial was not questioned by his colleagues, the incident, nonetheless, sent a shiver of discomfort through the academic community.

The question which troubled the professors was whether the Bulgarian accusations presaged a concerted Communist campaign to discredit the growing number of their colleagues who were working for the CIA.

In addition to its links with the academic community, there is evidence that the CIA subsidizes some foundations, cultural groups and a publishing house as well.

Most Americans are totally unaware of the CIA's domestic activities. In most cases, in a particular city, there is a telephone number for the Central Intelligence Agency under the "United States Government" listings. But there is no address given for the CIA office. As at Langley, the switchboard girl at a field office doesn't answer "CIA." She simply repeats the number.

Here is a sample of CIA listings in 1963 city telephone directories around the nation:

> New York—Mu 6 5517
> Chicago—De 7 4926
> Los Angeles—Ma 2 6875
> *Boston—Li 2 8812
> Detroit—To 8 5759
> Philadelphia—Lo 7 6764
> San Francisco—Yu 6 0145
> Miami—Hi 5 3658
> Pittsburgh—(simply listed as "Central
>   Intelligence") 471 8518
> Houston—CA 8 1324
> St. Louis—MA 1 6902
> New Orleans—JA 2 8874
> Seattle—MA 4 3288
> Denver—388 4757
> Minneapolis—FE 5 0811

But the listed offices are only the beginning of the story. The CIA has other offices in some United States cities in addition to its listed ones. In Miami, for example, in 1963, besides its listed number in Coral Gables, the CIA was operating as Zenith Technical Enterprises, Inc.

The CIA cover firm was listed this way in the 1963-64 telephone book:

> Zenith Technical Enterprises, Inc.
> Univ of Miami South Campus Perrine 238-3311

In true Ian Fleming fashion, the CIA cover office listed no precise address—the university south campus is a big place. It can be revealed, however, without imperiling national security, that the CIA has been operating from

---

* The CIA got into a dispute with its Boston landlord early in 1963 after the government ruled that field offices of Federal agencies could not rent in segregated buildings. The CIA, the major tenant in the Boston building, which also housed two restaurants, insisted that the landlord insert a nondiscrimination clause into leases with all of his tenants.

Building 25. (Perrine, incidentally, is the home town of Allen Lawrence Pope, the pilot who flew for the CIA in Indonesia.)

The CIA has operated under at least three other commercial cover umbrellas in Miami—the Double-Chek Corporation, previously mentioned, the Gibraltar Steamship Corporation and the Vanguard Service Corporation, which will be dealt with separately in another chapter.

The point of all this is that the CIA is not simply an agency that gathers foreign intelligence for the United States in far-off corners of the globe.* It is deeply involved in many diverse, clandestine activities right here in the United States in at least twenty metropolitan areas. It can and does appear in many guises and under many names—Zenith, Double-Chek, Gibraltar Steamship and Vanguard in one city alone.

On university campuses and in the great urban centers of America, the foundation, the cultural committee, the émigré group, the Cuban exile organization, the foreign-affairs research center, the distinguished publishing house specializing in books about Russia, the steamship company, the freedom radio soliciting public contributions, the innocent-looking consulting firm—all may in reality be arms of the Invisible Government. And these examples are not idly chosen.

Whether this state of affairs was intended by Congress when it passed the National Security Act of 1947, or, indeed, whether the Congress is even aware of those facts, is another matter entirely.

The CIA's internal, domestic activities have only rarely surfaced to cause it embarrassment. One noteworthy episode took place in Seattle in 1952. A Federal grand jury indicted a travel agent on charges that he had willfully given false information to the government to the effect that Owen Lattimore, the Johns Hopkins University Far Eastern expert, was planning a trip behind the Iron Curtain. At the time, Lattimore was under attack by Senator Joseph R. McCarthy of Wisconsin.

* More than 70 percent of CIA's employees are in the United States; the rest are overseas.

The Finnish-born defendant in the case, Harry A. Jarvinen, worked for the Where-to-Go Travel Agency in Seattle. Jarvinen's attorney, Gerald Shucklin, explained that his client "did make some statement at a social gathering when he was a bit tipsy and a Central Intelligence agent was there."

Jarvinen's tip to the CIA reached the State Department on May 26, 1952, and on June 11 the department issued a "stop order" barring Lattimore from leaving the country. After Jarvinen was indicted, the State Department apologized profusely to Lattimore.

But three months later the two CIA agents involved, Wayne Richardson and Miller Holland, refused on security grounds to testify in Federal Court at Jarvinen's trial. Jarvinen was acquitted.

Federal Judge William J. Lindberg sentenced the two CIA men to fifteen days in prison for contempt of court. The government, the judge noted tartly, had initiated a prosecution against a citizen with one hand and thwarted it with the other.

The two CIA agents appealed their conviction. President Truman stepped in and ended the farce by issuing full pardons to Richardson and Holland, thereby saving the country the spectacle of two CIA men doing a stretch in a Federal jail.

In March, 1954, Senator Mike Mansfield asked: "Does this incident mean that the CIA is getting into the internal security field in competition with the FBI? Does it mean that officials of this government agency can defy the courts?" Mansfield got no answers to his questions.

Overseas, the CIA operates principally under embassy cover and commercial cover. In several corners of the world the CIA operates what appear to be small business concerns but which are really covers. No subject is touchier to the agency than the question of cover, for cover is the "cloak" in cloak and dagger, the professional intelligence man's *sine qua non*.

On February 1, 1963, J. Edgar Hoover, testifying before a House Appropriations Subcommittee, stated that "historically, the official personnel of the Soviet bloc countries assigned to this nation, including those at the United Nations, have been used extensively for espionage purposes. . . .

"At the same time," the FBI director added, "the Soviet bloc intelligence services make full use of their commercial representatives, exchange groups and tourists visiting this country in their efforts to reach their intelligence objectives.

"As of January 1, 1963, there were 761 Soviet bloc official personnel in this country. They were accompanied by 1,066 dependents, some of whom are also trained as intelligence agents."

Essentially, the CIA operates the same way. In United States embassies across the globe, there is a restricted floor, or a section of the embassy, that houses the CIA mission. Each mission is headed by a station chief with several intelligence officers reporting to him. These officers in turn recruit local "agents" to collect intelligence information.

The CIA personnel are listed as State Department or Foreign Service officers. This is their "cover." In many cases, the identity of the CIA station chief is quickly known to diplomats and newspapermen—and, of course, to their Soviet opposite numbers in the KGB and the GRU. This is in sharp contrast to the British and Soviet secret service mission chiefs, whose identities are very seldom known. In the case of the CIA, agents below the level of station chief are usually less well known outside of the embassy. Within the embassy, State Department employees usually come to know in fairly short order who the CIA people are.

The fact that the CIA operates under embassy cover is not something that the government discusses or would be expected to confirm. Very occasionally, references to it pop up in unexpected places, however.

On April 12, 1962, Navy Captain Charles R. Clark, Jr., the naval attaché in the American Embassy in Havana from 1957 to 1960, was being questioned at a hearing of the Senate Internal Security Subcommittee by J. G. Sourwine, the chief counsel.

MR. SOURWINE: Were there CIA people in the embassy?

CAPTAIN CLARK: Yes, sir. A considerable number.

MR. SOURWINE: Was their cover good?

CAPTAIN CLARK: I thought it was terrible. Everybody in town who had any interest in it knew who they were . . . their cover was so shallow that it was very easily seen through.

MR. SOURWINE: Now, do you have knowledge of an occasion when all of the CIA people at the embassy were at a single party?

CAPTAIN CLARK: One time down there I was invited to a party . . . this Cuban doctor who had operated on one of my kids was giving it. . . . He had almost the entire CIA staff at his home for a party one night, and I was about the only non-CIA man there and he knew that they were all CIA and worked with them as such.

Two years earlier, on August 30, 1960, the former Ambassador to Cuba, Earl E. T. Smith, testified before the same committee that "the chief of the CIA section" in the American Embassy in Havana was pro-Castro and that "the Number 2 CIA man in the embassy" had encouraged a revolt of Cuban naval officers in Cienfuegos in September, 1957.

"In the trial of the naval officers," Smith testified, "it came out that the Number 2 man had said that if the revolution was successful, that the United States would recognize the revolutionaries. I do not believe that the Number 2 man in the CIA intended to convey that thought. His story to me was that he had been called over to interview some men believed to be doctors, because they were dressed in white coats, and when they advised him of the revolt that was to take place, they wanted to know what the position of the United States would be.

"And he inadvertently intimated something to the effect of which I am not quite sure, that the United States might give recognition."

Smith testified he repeated all this to Batista. The American ambassador's efforts to explain to the Cuban dictator that the Number 2 CIA man in the embassy could not tell the difference between a Navy uniform and a medical white coat must have made fascinating listening.

Normally, the CIA men in the embassies are listed in the State Department *Biographic Register* as "attachés," "Foreign Service officers," or, frequently, as "Foreign Service reserve officers."

For example, Henry Pleasants, widely known as the CIA mission chief in Bonn, West Germany, was listed in the 1963 *Biographic Register* as an "attaché," with "S-1" rank, meaning the highest category of Foreign Service staff officer.

Frank Wisner, the former CIA deputy director for plans, who ran the Guatemalan operation in 1954, was listed as an "attaché" and an "R-1" (Foreign Service reserve officer) after he was sent to London as station chief on August 6, 1959. The 1963 *Biographic Register* lists "govt. ser. 48-59" for Wisner, to account for the period prior to his London assignment.

Similarly, Robert Kendall Davis, the Guatemala mission chief who set up the Bay of Pigs training camps, was listed as an "attaché" and later as "first secretary" of the embassy. He, too, was carried on the State Department's rolls as a Foreign Service reserve officer.

William Egan Colby, the former CIA station chief in Vietnam, was listed as a "political officer" in 1959, and later as "first secretary" of the embassy. By 1963 he had shed his diplomatic cover and was back in Washington as the head of the CIA's Far East division.

John H. "Jocko" Richardson who became the new CIA station chief in Saigon, was listed as "first secretary" of the embassy when he arrived there after serving in Athens and Manila.

In 1961 the Russians published a 160-page propaganda book called *Caught in the Act* (initials: CIA), which detailed alleged attempts by the CIA to infiltrate spies into the Soviet Union. The book also grumbled bitterly about "spy diplomats" on the staff of the United States Embassy in Moscow.

Two years later the Russians ousted five Americans from the embassy in the sensational Penkovsky spy case. Oleg

V. Penkovsky was the deputy chief of the Soviet State Committee for the Coordination of Scientific Research, and very likely was also a colonel in Soviet military intelligence. At his show trial in May, 1963, he confessed passing 5,000 frames of exposed miniature-camera film, containing classified information about Soviet rockets and other secrets, to American and British agents.

The Russians charged that Penkovsky, a "money-hungry traitor who loved to dance the Charleston and the twist," would hide his information in a matchbox behind the radiator in the hallway of a Moscow apartment house at No. 5-6 Pushkin Street. He would mark a circle with charcoal on lamppost No. 35 near a bus stop on Kutusovsky Prospekt.

The Soviets said he would then telephone either Captain Alexis H. Davison, an assistant air attaché at the American Embassy (who was also the embassy doctor) or Hugh Montgomery, the internal security officer.

Davison would go to the lamppost, the Russians claimed. If he found the charcoal circle it meant there was something ready to be picked up at the Pushkin Street drop. According to the Moscow version, Richard C. Jacob, the twenty-six-year-old embassy "archivist" from Egg Harbor, New Jersey, would go to the radiator and retrieve the little package. When the information was picked up, the Americans would make a black smudge on the door of the fish department of a Moscow food store (presumably after a casual purchase of a pound or two of sturgeon as cover). Then Penkovsky would know the transfer had been accomplished.

The Russians also sought to link Penkovsky to Rodney W. Carlson, the thirty-one-year-old assistant agricultural attaché at the embassy, and to William C. Jones III,* the second secretary.

* All five Americans were declared *persona non grata* on May 13, 1963. The Russians claimed two other American Embassy personnel were involved in the case—Robert K. German, second secretary, and William Horbaly, agricultural attaché. They also ousted two embassy aides in October, 1962, just before the Penkovsky case surfaced publicly. They were Commander Raymond D. Smith, of Brooklyn,

Penkovsky, it was alleged, also passed information in a box of chocolates to Greville M. Wynne, a London businessman who was actually working for British Intelligence. Wynne supposedly got the chocolates out of Moscow by giving them to the children of a British diplomat.

The Russians convicted Penkovsky and later announced he had been executed. Wynne drew an eight-year prison sentence.

Considering the fact that no fewer than twelve Americans and British diplomats were linked, one way or another, to a serious charge of espionage, London and Washington were exceedingly quiet about it all.

But there are likely to be more spy cases involving diplomats. The Kennedy Administration, while Dulles was still the CIA director, made some efforts to reduce the number of agents operating under diplomatic cover in American embassies. But embassy cover is still central to the agency's operations.

There is a great danger in relying heavily on diplomatic cover. If relations are severed between countries, or war breaks out, then the CIA tends to be cut off from its sources of information. In January, 1961, for example, when Washington broke off relations with Havana, the CIA lost its embassy base in Cuba. Ironically, the Cubans retained two legations in the United States—their delegation to the Organization of American States in Washington* and their UN mission in New York.

CIA agents operating abroad under commercial cover pose, as the term implies, as legitimate businessmen, rather than as diplomats. Not long ago a CIA man in Washington told all his friends he was quitting the agency

assistant military attaché, and Kermit S. Midthun, of San Francisco, first secretary. Smith was arrested in Leningrad on October 2, carrying a tiny tape recorder, a Minox camera and high-powered binoculars. The Russians said he was photographing naval installations. The American Embassy said he was taking a walk in the park. Midthun, forty-one, was accused on October 11 of having tried to get secret data from a Soviet official. The Russians also expelled five British diplomats in the Penkovsky case.

* Until Cuba was expelled from the OAS in January, 1962.

to go to Switzerland for Praeger books. Very possibly he was telling the truth and was really leaving the agency, but not all of his friends believed him.

A CIA officer operating overseas under embassy or commercial cover recruits "agents" locally to feed him information. The most valuable information often comes not from a trusted agent, but from the occasional highly placed defector from the opposition camp.

The most useful defector is a Communist official who can be persuaded to stay at his job, at least for a while, and transmit intelligence to the West. This is known as a defector "in place." The most prized defector of all is one who works, or who has worked, in the Soviet intelligence apparatus.

A delicate aspect of the CIA's work is the care and protection of its colony of important defectors who have fled the Communist world. On a CBS television interview [3] Dulles called defectors "one of the two or three most important sources of intelligence." He added: "When you get a man—and we have got several—who have worked inside the KGB, their secret service, or the GRU, their military service, it's just almost as though you had somebody inside there for a time."

Dulles estimated that the number of high-level valuable defectors who had come over to the West was "in the range of a hundred."

Not all of these Russians are "surfaced" by the CIA. Those who remain underground are protected by the agency. Some go to work for the CIA. Others are given a new identity that, hopefully, will protect them in the United States from the long arm of KGB assassins.

Recently, a resident of McLean, Virginia, near the CIA headquarters, was intrigued when an obviously Russian family moved in across the street; two huge dogs guarded the premises, and a chauffeur-driven car came to take the children to school every day. But the Russian hardly budged from his house, except to go to a neighbor's occasional cocktail party, where he would identify himself as an "historian." The "historian" was very likely a defector being kept on ice by the CIA.

Not all stories of Soviet defectors under CIA protection come to such happy endings, however. On October 21, 1952, a lieutenant in the KGB, Reino Hayhanen, entered the United States under the name of Eugene Maki and became an assistant to Rudolf Abel, the Russian master spy who posed as a mousy photographer-artist in Brooklyn under the alias of Emil R. Goldfus.

Hayhanen drank and talked too much; he was not a very good spy. Exasperated, Abel finally shipped his assistant home. Hayhanen decided his reception might be unpleasant; so on May 6, 1957, while en route to Moscow, he walked into the American Embassy in Paris and defected to the CIA.

He was rushed back to New York, where he identified Abel, which led to the arrest of the top Russian spy who had been his boss. After Abel's trial and conviction that October, Hayhanen dropped out of sight. The CIA gave him a new identity and kept him in a house in New England, guarded by a dog. Two "lawyers" who lived next door were actually CIA bodyguards almost constantly at Hayhanen's side.

But Hayhanen the defector was no drier than Hayhanen the secret agent. He continued to imbibe heavily, which made the task of the CIA bodyguards an unenviable one.

After the Bay of Pigs invasion, Attorney General Robert Kennedy wondered if there might not be some way to improve the CIA's then sagging public image. When the National Broadcasting Company suggested a television program, the Attorney General liked the idea and ordered Hayhanen temporarily released to appear on the show.*

The Hayhanen interview was filmed about July, 1961, but was not shown until the following November. In the interim, word spread around the intelligence community that Reino Hayhanen was dead; the CIA's prize defector had been killed in a mysterious "accident" on the New

---

* The Attorney General also took the extraordinary step of allowing NBC to film shots of Abel in Atlanta Prison, which were shown on the same program. At the time, the Powers-Abel swap was secretly in the making; the films may perhaps have been shown to reassure the Russians that Abel was alive and well.

Jersey or the Pennsylvania Turnpike. Nevertheless, the filmed NBC program was telecast, as scheduled, on November 8. Hayhanen's face was "kept dark for his own protection," David Brinkley, the narrator, said.

At the close of the program, Brinkley explained that after Abel went to prison, by contrast Hayhanen "was set up in a comfortable house in the northeastern United States under the care and protection of the CIA. He came out of the security briefly for this interview and went back. . . . That's the end of this spy story, but we are authorized to say, indeed asked to say, that if any others like Eugene Maki [Hayhanen] care to step forward any time they will be guaranteed security, physical and financial."

The CIA definitely did not ask NBC, however, to tell its millions of viewers that they had just watched an interview with a dead man.

Like any intelligence agency, the CIA employs methods and techniques that are not normally the subject of polite drawing-room chit-chat. These techniques include sex, money, wiretapping and the use of hidden microphones.

Allen Dulles may be cited as an authority on the subject of sex-and-spying. When he appeared on ABC's *Issues and Answers* in June, 1963, the scandal over Britain's Secretary of State for War John D. Profumo and call-girl Christine Keeler was at its height. It had also been disclosed that Profumo and the Soviet naval attaché, Captain Yevgeni Ivanov, shared Miss Keeler's favors.

Dulles offered one professional observation about the use of Miss Keeler: "I must say the question they apparently gave the young lady to ask as to when the Germans were going to get the atomic bomb was not a very penetrating intelligence question to ask."

Then this exchange took place on the television panel:

Q. Whether or not it is involved in the Profumo case, the Soviets have been known to use sex as a lure in espionage. How widespread is this? Is this something we meet repeatedly in counter-espionage work around the world?

A. I think it is world-wide. As long as there is sex, it is going to be used.

Q. Does American intelligence ever use sex as a bait to get information?

A. I don't discuss those matters very much.

Q. We at least don't use it as widely as the Soviets do?

A. No, we certainly do not. We recognize the existence of sex and the attraction of sex, though.

Four years earlier, the Russians had accused Dulles of using voluptuous women CIA agents to seduce the Soviet Olympic team at Melbourne, Australia, in 1956. The racy claim was made by the newspaper *Literary Gazette*.

"The American intelligence service," the paper said indignantly on April 2, 1957, "did its utmost to force upon Soviet athletes an acquaintance with young women. Its agents more than insistently importuned them to 'have a good time.'" The paper implied that the Soviet athletes scorned the temptresses and stuck to their hammer-throwing and pole-vaulting.

Another tool of the trade—money—is used by the CIA, as it is by other intelligence services, to pay agents, and double agents, and to buy information, where necessary. Money was no object when Dulles was hunting for Khrushchev's secret speech in 1956.

The CIA is a major purchaser of electronic listening devices and wire-tap equipment. The most famous case involving such equipment was the CIA's "Berlin tunnel," a secret wire-tap installation in a tunnel that led from a mock United States "experimental radar station" across the border into East Germany. The tap hooked into the cables of the Soviet military headquarters.

The Russians discovered the tunnel on April 22, 1956, and decided to try at least to recover some propaganda value from the CIA's coup. They invited Western correspondents to tour the underground wire tap and turned it into a tourist attraction. Three photographs and a diagram of the tunnel appear in *Caught in the Act*.

Sometimes there are simpler ways to intercept Soviet communications. In Montevideo, a few years ago, the Tass man was filing 1,000 words a day, attacking Washington's policies in Latin America. A CIA man had instant access to the file through the commercial cable company the Tass correspondent used. The CIA also persuaded the Montevideo chief of police to put taps on the telephones at the Soviet and Czech Embassies. For a time, the CIA monitored all their conversations. Later the police chief quit; his successor was less friendly to the CIA and the game ended.

A fascinating case of CIA wire-tapping that received far less public attention than the "Berlin tunnel" began unfolding at 1:00 A.M. on September 15, 1960, when a key turned in the door of a twenty-third-floor apartment in the Seguro del Medico Building, in Havana's fashionable Vedado Beach section.

Mrs. Majorie Lennox, a lovely twenty-six-year-old divorcée with shoulder-length blond hair, was alone in her apartment. She was listed as a secretary in the United States Embassy in Havana. The men who entered her apartment were Castro intelligence agents. They arrested her; she was accused of being a spy and ordered out of Cuba two days later. She told newsmen who met her at Miami International Airport: "It's all so silly. I was all by my little self, practically asleep in bed, when the lights went on about one A.M. Thursday. I thought it was my maid, but these men had pistols. When I demanded an explanation they told me: 'You are a spy. We found your apartment key in a raid on a spy ring.' "

Mrs. Lennox wore a softly tailored gray suit as she chatted with reporters. Now her mobile face broke into a sweet smile. "Me a spy!" she said. "What a laugh."

When a newsman asked if she had ever given her key to anyone in the United States Embassy, she replied: "I can't answer that."

The same day that Mrs. Lennox was expelled from Cuba, Havana arrested six other Americans and accused them, along with her, of being members of a spy ring that had tapped the telephone wires of the Havana office of Hsinhua, the Communist Chinese news agency. The Castro regime identified three of the Americans as Daniel

L. Carswell, a forty-two-year-old "electrical engineer"; Eustace H. Danbrunt, thirty-four, a "mechanical engineer"; and Edmund K. Taransky, thirty, an "electrical engineer."

Also arrested were Robert L. Neet, who the Cubans said was an employee of the American Embassy, and Mr. and Mrs. Mario Nordio. Havana said Nordio was a dance instructor and an Italian-born, naturalized American citizen who had lived in New York City. It was also announced that Nordio had leased his apartment to Mrs. Lennox.

On December 17, 1960, a military court in Havana held a one-day trial for the three "engineers" and Mario Nordio. They were accused of setting wire taps in the Hsinhua office to learn about a trade treaty between Cuba and Communist China and about the establishment of diplomatic relations between the two countries.

The prosecutor, Lieutenant Fernando Flores, asked for thirty-year prison terms for the four Americans. The defendants, dressed in blue prison uniforms, denied the charges. The "engineers" said they had been hired to repair some electronic equipment in Neet's apartment, which was located in the same building as the Communist Chinese news agency.

On January 10, 1961, the three "engineers" were sentenced to ten years in prison. Nordio was deported.

United States Ambassador Philip W. Bonsal had filed an angry formal protest over the arrest of Mrs. Lennox. He was silent about the three "engineers" and the dancing instructor, however.

There were good reasons for this. The three "engineers" were in reality on an electronic eavesdropping assignment for the CIA. Washington was particularly concerned lest the high-ranking Carswell, who knew about similar electronic operations in other parts of the world, be turned over to the Russians for questioning.

Quietly, behind the scenes, the CIA and the State Department began making efforts to free twenty-seven Americans held in Castro jails, including the three "engineers." The release was finally arranged in April, 1963, by James Donovan, who had successfully "exchanged" the Bay of Pigs prisoners for drugs and food four months earlier.

The citizenship of some of the prisoners was in doubt. The primary reason for Washington's efforts was to get the three CIA men out, and Robert A. Hurwitch, the State Department official who handled the matter, was perfectly well aware of this. It was also made clear to Donovan.

Late in April, strange things began to happen. On the night of April 22, Governor Nelson A. Rockefeller of New York commuted the twenty-years-to-life prison term of Francisco (The Hook) Molina, a pro-Castro Cuban who shot up a New York restaurant during Castro's visit to the UN in September, 1960. During the shooting brawl, Molina killed a nine-year-old Venezuelan girl, Magdalena Urdaneto, who was an innocent bystander. Rockefeller, on the assurance of the Federal Government that he was acting "in the national interest," released The Hook from the state prison at Stormville.

Simultaneously, Attorney General Robert Kennedy announced that charges had been dropped by the Justice Department against three Cubans, including an attaché at Castro's UN mission, who had been arrested for plotting to blow up defense installations around New York City. The three plus The Hook were hustled out of the country by plane. They were flown from Florida to Havana as Donovan brought back the Americans from Cuba in what amounted, in effect, to a straight swap of three saboteurs and a killer for three CIA men.

When they landed in Miami, Carswell, Danbrunt and Taransky vanished. They declined to talk to reporters. And for some reason, unlike the other returnees, they would not tell the American Red Cross their destination.

18

The Search for Control

To MAINTAIN THE CIA and the other branches of the intelligence establishment, the government spends about $4,000,000,000 a year. The exact figure is one of the most tightly held secrets of the government and it appears in none of the Federal budget documents, public or private. It is unknown, in fact, even to many of the key officials in the Invisible Government. Because the intelligence community is carefully fragmented, those in one branch find it difficult to estimate the budgets of the others.

All of the budgets are pulled together by the director of the International Division of the Budget Bureau. He is assisted by four experts, each of whom handles about $1,000,000,000 of the Invisible Government's money. One assistant checks on the National Security Agency, the second on the CIA, the third on the DIA and military intelligence, and the fourth on overhead reconnaissance.

All of the Invisible Government's hidden money is buried in the Defense Department budget, mainly in the multibillion-dollar weapons contracts, such as those for the Minuteman and Polaris missiles. The Comptroller of the Pentagon knows where the money is hidden, but so carefully is it camouflaged, even his closest assistants are unable to guess at the amount.

It is not startling, then, that even those at the very center of the Invisible Government vary in their estimates of what is being spent. In a private briefing for high-ranking military men in the summer of 1963 McCone offered a figure of $2,000,000,000 * and estimated that 100,000 persons were involved in intelligence work.

However, McCone appeared to be limiting his estimate to the money spent by the CIA and the other agencies on the more conventional forms of intelligence work. In addition, $2,000,000,000 is spent each year on electronic intelligence (the NSA and aerial spying). When the two forms of intelligence are included, the total budget reaches $4,000,000,000 and the personnel figure amounts to about 200,000.

It is often assumed that the National Security Council controls this vast intelligence establishment. But in practice much of the activity of the Invisible Government is never examined at NSC meetings. Nor is it disclosed to the United States Intelligence Board (which, for example, was not informed in advance of the Bay of Pigs).

The important decisions about the Invisible Government are made by the committee known as the Special Group. Although the composition of the committee has varied slightly, its membership has generally included the Director of Central Intelligence, the Under Secretary of State for Political Affairs (or his deputy), and the Secretary and Deputy Secretary of Defense. In the Kennedy and early Johnson Administrations, the presidential representative—and key man—on the Special Group was McGeorge Bundy. The others members were McCone, McNamara, Roswell Gilpatric, Deputy Secretary of Defense, and U. Alexis Johnson, Deputy Under Secretary of State for Political Affairs.

The Special Group was created early in the Eisenhower years under the secret Order 54/12. It was known in the innermost circle of the Eisenhower Administration as the "54/12 Group" and is still so called by a few insiders. The Special Group grew out of the "OCB luncheon

---

* Significantly, many CIA officials estimate that the Soviet Union spends $2,000,000,000 a year on its spy apparatus. On the other hand, Soviet Secret Police Chief Alexander N. Shelepin estimated in 1959 that the CIA spent $1,500,000,000 a year and employed 20,000 persons.

group." * It has operated for a decade as the hidden power center of the Invisible Government. Its existence is virtually unknown outside the intelligence community and, even there, only a handful of men are aware of it.

The Special Group meets about once a week to make the crucial decisions—those which are too sensitive or too divisive to be entrusted to USIB. The more grandiose of the Invisible Government's operations have been launched in this exclusive arena. It is here in this hidden corner of the massive governmental apparatus that the United States is regularly committed to policies which walk the tightrope between peace and war.

CIA men generally have the Special Group in mind when they insist that the agency has never set policy, but has only acted on higher authority.

"The facts are," Allen Dulles has declared, "that the CIA has never carried out any action of a political nature, given any support of any nature to any persons, potentates or movements, political or otherwise, without appropriate approval at a high political level in our government *outside the CIA.*" [1]

To the average citizen, Dulles' statement might logically conjure up a picture of the Cabinet, the National Security Council or some special presidential commission meeting in solemn session to debate the wisdom of a dangerous clandestine operation.

But, in fact, some decisions of this type have been made by the Special Group in an informal way without the elaborate records and procedures of other high government committees. And these fateful decisions have been made without benefit of outside analysis. Little detached criticism has been brought to bear on the natural human tendency of the leaders of the Invisible Government to

---

* The OCB, the Operations Coordinating Board, was composed of the Under Secretary of State, the Deputy Secretary of Defense, the President's Special Assistant (National Security Affairs), and the directors of CIA, USIA, and the old International Cooperation Administration. They were supposed to make sure the President's decisions were carried out in their departments. The OCB was abolished by President Kennedy in his first month in office.

embark upon ventures which might prove their toughness, demonstrate their vision or expand their power.

The "euphoria of secrecy goes to the head," as C. P. Snow, the English scientist-novelist, has observed, and the Special Group has operated in an atmosphere of secrecy exceeding that of any other branch of the United States Government.

It is apparent, then, that the two presidential watchdog committees, the Board of Consultants on Foreign Intelligence Activities of the Eisenhower Administration and the Foreign Intelligence Advisory Board of the Kennedy and Johnson Administrations, have had great difficulty getting to the bottom of things. Both committees were composed of part-time consultants who met only occasionally during the year.

The original committee had, in fact, been established by Eisenhower in 1956 at least partly to head off closer scrutiny of the Invisible Government. In 1955 the full Hoover Commission had recommended that such a presidential committee be established. But it had also proposed the creation of a Joint Congressional Committee on Foreign Intelligence.

The Eisenhower Administration compromised. It complied with the first and more innocuous of the recommendations, but opposed the Joint Congressional Committee, which was anathema to the CIA.

The Hoover Commission's Intelligence Task Force, headed by General Mark W. Clark, had submitted a much stronger recommendation. It had proposed a single watchdog commission composed of senators, congressmen, and presidential appointees.

"The Task Force . . . is concerned," its report stated, "over the absence of satisfactory machinery for surveillance of the stewardship of the Central Intelligence Agency. It is making recommendations which it believes will provide the proper type of 'watchdog' commission as a means of re-establishing that relationship between the CIA and the Congress so essential to and characteristic of our democratic form of government."

The Task Force was critical in tone: "There is still

much to be done by our intelligence community to bring its achievements up to an acceptable level.

"The glamour and excitement of some angles of our intelligence effort must not be permitted to overshadow other vital phases of the work or to cause neglect of primary functions. A majority of the Task Force is convinced that an internal reorganization of the CIA is necessary to give assurance that each of these functions gets adequate attention without diversionary interest." [2]

Earlier studies of the CIA had been less critical. The 1949 Hoover Task Force, headed by Ferdinand Eberstadt, a Wall Street broker, found the CIA "sound in principle," although it recommended that "vigorous efforts be made to improve the internal structure . . . and the quality of its product." [3]

In 1954 a special presidential study group, led by General James H. Doolittle, said the CIA was doing a "creditable job." But it detected "important areas in which the CIA organization, administration and operations can and should be improved." [4]

In between, Allen Dulles surveyed the CIA for President Truman prior to joining the agency. But his report was kept secret.

By 1954 substantial pressure had built up in Congress for a closer scrutiny of the intelligence community. Mike Mansfield, then a freshman senator from Montana, submitted a resolution that would have carried out the Hoover Commission recommendation by creating a Joint Committee on the Central Intelligence Agency. In its final form, the resolution called for a twelve-man committee, six from the Senate and six from the House, and for the appropriation of $250,000 for staff expenditures during the first year.

Thirty-four senators joined Mansfield in sponsoring the resolution. But by the time the proposal came to a vote on April 11, 1956, fourteen of these sponsors had reversed themselves, and the resolution was defeated, fifty-nine to twenty-seven. Thirteen of those who had changed their minds were Republicans evidently reflecting White House pressure. Many of the Democrats who voted against the resolution clearly were worried about disturbing Senator Richard B. Russell, the chairman of the Armed Services Committee, and other Democratic titans who opposed the idea.

Mansfield's language in introducing the resolution was not calculated to please the conservative inner club of the Senate, which enjoyed special relations with the Invisible Government.

"An urgent need exists," Mansfield said, "for regular and responsible Congressional scrutiny of the Central Intelligence Agency. Such scrutiny is essential to the success of our foreign policy, to the preservation of our democratic processes and to the security of the intelligence agency itself. . . .

"If we fail to establish some sort of permanent, continuing link between Congress and the CIA, the only result will be growing suspicion. . . . In the first place, the whole concept of peacetime foreign intelligence operations has been alien to the American tradition. . . .

"Our form of government . . . is based on a system of checks and balances. If this system gets seriously out of balance at any point the whole system is jeopardized and the way is opened for the growth of tyranny. . . .

"CIA is freed from practically every ordinary form of Congressional check. Control of its expenditures is exempted from the provisions of the law which prevent financial abuses in other government agencies. Its appropriations are hidden in allotments to other agencies. . . .

"I agree that an intelligence agency must maintain complete secrecy to be effective. However, there is a profound difference between an essential degree of secrecy to achieve a specific purpose and secrecy for the mere sake of secrecy. Once secrecy becomes sacrosanct, it invites abuse.

"If we accept this idea of secrecy for secrecy's sake, we will have no way of knowing whether we have a fine intelligence service or a very poor one. Secrecy now beclouds everything about the CIA—its cost, its efficiency, its successes and its failures." [5]

As the Mansfield resolution approached a vote in April of 1956, the powers-that-be in the Senate massed their forces in a counter-attack.

"It would be more desirable," Russell declared, "to abolish the CIA and close it up, lock, stock and barrel, than to adopt any such theory as that all the members of the Congress of the United States are entitled to know the details of all the activities of this far-flung organization." [6]

Senator Alben W. Barkley of Kentucky, the former Democratic Vice-President, declared: "The information I received as a member of the National Security Council, in my capacity as Vice-President, was so confidential that I would lose my right arm before I would divulge it to anyone, even to members of my own family. . . .

"Some of the information gathered by the Central Intelligence Agency and laid before the National Security Council itself was so confidential and secret that the very portfolios in which it was contained were under lock and key. The members of the National Security Council were not even permitted to take those folders and portfolios to their homes. They had to be unlocked in the presence of the other members. . . .

"To say that now we should establish a Joint Committee to pry into and look into secret documents, to submit them before the Joint Committee, and to make them public seems to me incredible." [7]

Russell also raised the specter of critical national secrets leaking out of the Joint Committee. He contended that the very creation of the committee would increase "the hazards to the lives of those who work for the CIA, and dry up sources of information, which are vital to the national security." He insisted that the CIA was already subjected to adequate scrutiny by members of the Senate Armed Services and Appropriations Committees.*

---

* In the 88th Congress the CIA subcommittee in the Senate was composed of Russell, Harry Flood Byrd, Virginia Democrat, John Stennis, Mississippi Democrat, and Leverett Saltonstall, Massachusetts Republican, all members of the Armed Services Committee; and Carl Hayden, Arizona Democrat and chairman of the Appropriations

"Although Mr. Allen W. Dulles has been before us," Russell said, "and although we have asked him very searching questions about some activities which it almost chills the marrow of a man to hear about, he has never failed to answer us forthrightly and frankly in response to any question we have asked of him." [8]

Republican Senator Leverett Saltonstall of Massachusetts said the CIA subcommittee met with CIA officials "at least twice a year" * and that the witnesses stated their willingness to answer all questions.

"The difficulty in connection with asking questions and obtaining information," Saltonstall remarked, "is that we might obtain information which I personally would rather not have, unless it was essential for me as a member of Congress to have it." [9]

Nevertheless, Saltonstall would call his close friend, Allen Dulles, from time to time to get a personal explanation of some CIA operation.

The CIA's view on whether there should be more Congressional scrutiny was stated officially in a letter to Mansfield from General Cabell on September 4, 1953. "It is our opinion," he wrote, "that, from our point of view, the present ties with Congress are adequate."

Allen Dulles agreed: "Any public impression that the Congress exerts no power over CIA is quite mistaken. Control of funds gives a control over the scope of operations—how many people CIA can employ, how much it can do and to some extent what it can do. . . .

"The chairman of the House [Appropriations] Subcommittee [on the CIA] is Clarence Cannon, and a more careful watchdog of the public treasury can hardly be found." [10]

Committee, and Milton R. Young, North Dakota Republican and Appropriations Committee member. A. Willis Robertson, Virginia Democrat and Appropriations Committee member, joined the CIA subcommittee on occasion.

* In a debate on August 14, 1963, Representative Walter Norblad, the Oregon Republican, said the House Armed Services Subcommittee on the CIA (of which he was a former member) "met annually one time a year for a period of two hours in which we accomplished virtually nothing."

Whether or not Dulles' judgment held true for other budgetary matters, the eighty-three-year-old Cannon had no great reputation on his subcommittee as a "careful watchdog" of the CIA. In fact, he was such a good friend and great admirer of Dulles that much of the secret CIA hearings during Dulles' tenure were taken up with mutual congratulations. CIA officials came armed with thick black volumes, but the other members of the House Subcommittee * never had time to probe deeply into the agency's activities. Some of the members displayed annoyance but could do little about it in view of Cannon's absolute control over the committee.

Nevertheless, Cannon once sought to have the CIA checked by the General Accounting Office. The request threw the CIA into consternation: should it turn him down and lose a good friend or co-operate and risk the disclosure of operational secrets? The decision was to go along with Cannon but to steer the GAO into a non-sensitive area. The auditors were taken to the facilities of the CIA's broadcast information service which monitors the radio programs of foreign countries, particularly the Communist bloc. The GAO spent a year at the foreign broadcast service, but to the satisfaction of the CIA, turned in a harmless set of recommendations.

"They can't find the side of a barn," said one contented CIA man.

GAO men were not inclined to dispute the assessment. They despaired of the practicality of auditing covert opera-

---

* In the 88th Congress they were Democrats George Mahon of Texas and Harry R. Sheppard of California, and Republicans Gerald Ford of Michigan and Harold C. Ostertag of New York.

In the House there was also a CIA subcommittee of the Armed Services Committee. It was composed of Carl Vinson, Georgia Democrat and chairman of the Armed Services Committee; L. Mendel Rivers, South Carolina Democrat; F. Edward Hebert, Louisiana Democrat; Melvin Price, Illinois Democrat; Charles E. Bennett, Florida Democrat; George Huddleston, Jr., Alabama Democrat; Leslie C. Arends, Illinois Republican; William G. Bray, Indiana Republican; Bob Wilson, California Republican; and Frank C. Osmers, Jr., New Jersey Republican.

tions where, as a GAO official put it, "they pay off some guy under a rock in the desert."

Prior to 1954 the GAO kept two of its men on permanent assignment with the CIA as consultants. When a problem arose in a non-sensitive area, the CIA accountants would ask the GAO men to judge whether they were acting properly. Taking the facts as presented to them, the GAO men would then refer the problem to the Comptroller General's office for approval.

Since the procedure amounted to a certification of CIA practices without the authority to investigate them, Joseph Campbell withdrew the GAO men from the CIA when he took over as Comptroller General in 1954.

Still, the GAO continued to bump into an occasional CIA project while investigating large defense contracts. But under the 1949 law, which removed Congress' power to audit the CIA, the GAO was prohibited from looking further, even if it had suspicions that the contractor might be juggling non-CIA funds.

Congress' difficulties with the intelligence community have been matched by those of American ambassadors in foreign countries. In 1959 the Senate Foreign Relations Committee compiled a booklet of anonymous quotations from retired Foreign Service officers. One of them noted:

"Every senior officer of the Department of State and every senior officer of the Foreign Service has heard something of CIA's subversive efforts in foreign countries and probably most of them have some authentic information about CIA operations of this nature in some particular case. Unfortunately, most of these activities seem to have been blundering affairs, and most, if not all of them, seem to have resulted to the disadvantage of the United States and sometimes in terrible failure. . . . The situation is exacerbated by the fact that in most diplomatic and consular establishments abroad espionage agents of the CIA are stationed masquerading as diplomatic and consular officers." [11]

Several ambassadors complained about being used as fronts for espionage activities. But the CIA insisted that embassy cover was essential to its work. Without the immunity accorded to diplomatic property, the CIA's codes, files and communications would not be secure. The CIA maintains its own codes and an independent communications system (as does the Pentagon through the Defense Communications Agency), and unless CIA agents choose to tell an ambassador what they are up to and what they are reporting to Washington, he has no independent means for finding out.

Friction between Foreign Service men and CIA operatives became so pronounced by the end of the Eisenhower Administration, that President Eisenhower issued an executive order in November of 1960, stating: "The several chiefs of the United States diplomatic missions in foreign countries, as the representatives of the President and acting on his behalf, shall have and exercise, to the extent permitted by law and in accordance with instructions as the President may from time to time promulgate, affirmative responsibility for co-ordination and supervision over the carrying out by agencies of their functions in the respective countries."

The Eisenhower order seemed, on the surface, to reestablish the ambassador's supremacy over all United States agencies operating overseas. But many were troubled by the possibility of secret "instructions" to the CIA circumventing the ambassador's authority.

When President Kennedy entered office, he took prompt action to reaffirm the powers of the State Department and the ambassadors. On May 29, 1961, Kennedy sent a letter to all ambassadors:

You are in charge of the entire United States diplomatic mission, and I shall expect you to supervise all of its operations. The mission includes not only the personnel of the Department of State and the Foreign Service, but also the representatives of all other United States agencies which have programs or activities in [name of country]. I shall give you full support and backing in carrying out your assignment.

Needless to say, the representatives of other agencies are expected to communicate directly with their offices here in Washington, and in the event of a decision by you in which they do not concur, they may ask to have the decision reviewed by a higher authority in Washington.

However, it is their responsibility to keep you fully informed of their views and activities and to abide by your decisions unless in some particular instance you and they are notified to the contrary.

The moving force behind Kennedy's letter was Chester Bowles, then Under Secretary of State for Political Affairs. In the summer of 1961 Bowles set out on a round-the-world trip to explain the new arrangement. A fifteen-man team, including leading representatives of the State Department, the CIA and the AID, accompanied Bowles to seven regional meetings with ambassadors and their staffs.

Bowles told the meetings that the ambassadors were to be kept fully informed on all CIA operations and were to receive copies of all CIA messages to Washington. At each meeting the CIA men would express skepticism: What, they asked, about situations in which ambassadors do not understand the CIA's special problems?

Let us know, Bowles replied, and we'll get new ones.

Do we tell the ambassador the sources of our information? the CIA men asked incredulously. Yes, Bowles answered, the ambassador should be in a position to cross-check information if he runs across one of the informants at a diplomatic function.

The CIA appealed for permission to circumvent the ambassador in "overriding circumstances." But Bowles said no, and a year later, when he made a check of each United States embassy, he received not a single complaint or comment from the CIA. The new system, Bowles concluded, was working well.

But a different impression was gained by a staff of experts sent on a world-wide inspection late in 1962 by the Subcommittee on National Security Staffing and Operations of the Senate Government Operations Committee. The experts concluded that the Kennedy letter was a "shadow" and had not been interpreted as covering the

CIA. Ambassadors were still unable to give orders to the CIA or to stop an agency operation. The only evident change was that the ambassador now appeared to be in a better position to protest about a CIA program and delay it until a decision came back from Washington.

These conclusions were watered down in the staff report published by the subcommittee in January, 1963. But the report did point out that the military services and the CIA tend to "take a restricted view of the ambassador's right to interpose himself" between them and their superiors in Washington.

And in a cautious observation that might equally have applied to the Invisible Government's relationship with the government as a whole, the report said:

"To a degree the primacy of the ambassador is a polite fiction."

19

Purity in the Peace Corps

THE CONFLICT in the field between the ambassador and the intelligence operator is reflected on a larger scale in the frequent clashes in Washington between the State Department and the CIA. The uneasiness felt in other government agencies over the role of the CIA runs deeper than that, however.

This uneasiness is little known outside of the government, and it is almost never talked about. But the Peace Corps provides the best example.

During the 1960 campaign, John F. Kennedy had promised, if elected, to establish a Peace Corps. He kept his word, created the new agency by an executive order in March, 1961, and asked his brother-in-law, Sargent Shriver, Jr., to head it.

Shriver accepted, but he very quickly concluded that the Peace Corps, with its thousands of young volunteers dispersed over the globe, could well look like an all but irresistible "cover" to an intelligence agency always on the alert for new ways to disguise its people. At the same time, Shriver knew that the Peace Corps, because it would offer genuine help to the emerging nations of the world, would be an equally tempting target for Communist propaganda, which would seek at all costs to discredit it.

Therefore, Shriver privately proclaimed his determination to take every possible step to divorce the Peace Corps from even the faintest smell of intelligence work. He was well aware that even one "spy" incident involving a volunteer might destroy the Corps.

An anecdote that went the rounds of the executive suite of the Peace Corps at the time of its birth is revealing. It had the then Vice-President, Lyndon Johnson, advising Shriver to "beware the three C's—Communism, Cuties, and the CIA."

In the spring of 1961 Shriver made a trip seeking to persuade neutral nations to accept Peace Corpsmen. He discovered that the leaders of those countries were blunt in asking whether he would let the Corps be used as a cover for intelligence agents. Shriver replied just as bluntly that he was doing everything he could within the government to make sure that the CIA stayed out of his agency. He also promised to assist individual countries in any security checks they might care to make.

As early as March 16, 1961, Radio Moscow was attacking the Peace Corps as a plan for "the collection of espionage information for Allen Dulles' agency." On May 11 Tass, the Soviet news agency, sent out a dispatch in English to Europe, headlined "Peace Corps Head Shriver CIA Agent."

As a first step in his campaign to prevent the Peace Corps from becoming tarred as an instrument of Cold War intelligence-gathering, Shriver went directly to President Kennedy. "Jack Kennedy gave me his promise," Shriver later told a friend, "that there would be no CIA agents in the Peace Corps."

President Kennedy followed up this verbal assurance to Shriver by issuing orders to Allen Dulles and later to his successor, John McCone, which continued in effect after President Johnson took office. In addition, Shriver met with Dulles and later with McCone and obtained their guarantee that the CIA would stay away from the Peace Corps.

But the problem was more subtle than that. Shriver's dilemma was a peculiar one, bred of the Cold War and inconceivable in the America of even twenty years before. Could he be certain that the White House attitude would be reflected all along the line? Could he be sure, for example, that a lower-echelon CIA official might not quietly attempt, despite everything, to plant agents in the Peace Corps, in the honest belief that he was acting in some higher national interest?

Shriver must have decided he could not be sure of the answers to these delicate questions, for he did not rely on presidential assurances alone. A careful screening process was set up. It was designed, of course, to catch any Communist or security risk who might try to get into the Peace Corps. But it was also designed—hopefully—to spot any CIA "volunteer" before he could unpack his cloak and dagger.

It might come as a jolt to most Americans to know that one agency of the United States Government feels it must protect itself against infiltration in its ranks—by another agency of the United States Government. But the Peace Corps has taken elaborate steps to prevent just that.

Shriver designated William Delano, the Peace Corps' young general counsel, to ride herd on the problem and make sure no intelligence men slipped through the net. As insurance, Shriver laid down a firm rule. No one with any intelligence background, even years ago, would be accepted.

As Peace Corps officials soon discovered, there was a hitch. Openly acknowledged "overt" employees of the CIA are allowed to say so when they seek a new job. But covert employees of the CIA are not permitted to reveal it, even years later on a government job application form. They might put down the name of a commercial cover company or perhaps some other branch of the government for which they had ostensibly worked.

And a routine Civil Service check, Peace Corps officials realized, would not reveal whether applicants had been or were still covert CIA agents. Some applicants, unaware of Shriver's policy, innocently listed such past jobs as "CIA secretary, summer of 1951." They were immediately eliminated.

Others, more sophisticated, sought to fuzz their past employment by listing "U. S. Government" to cover a period of a year or two. But the would-be volunteers, in these cases, were questioned by Civil Service investigators, who naturally demanded to know more details.

One high Peace Corps official estimated that ten to twenty ex-CIA employees who had listed "U. S. Government" on their applications have been turned down since the Peace Corps began.

Screening out persons with a background in intelligence was only part of the problem. The Peace Corps also decided that it had to guard against the possibility of the CIA approaching a volunteer after he had been accepted into the Corps.

During orientation courses for volunteers, it became standard practice for a Peace Corps instructor to get up and pose the following question:

"Suppose a man asks you to have a cup of coffee with him and he identifies himself as a CIA agent. He says he doesn't want you to spy, but that he'd like you to get together with him and just chat every couple of weeks, and perhaps tell him a couple of things you've learned. What would be your reaction?"

Most of the volunteers replied they would have no part of any free-lance spying of this sort.

"Just so that no one will have any doubts about it," the instructor would then add, "if such a solicitation is made, you are to report it to the Peace Corps country representative within ten minutes, if you can get to him that quickly, because the CIA man would be defying the President's order to Dulles and McCone. Furthermore, the CIA man will be kicked out of the country faster than you can see, if you report it."

Because of this orientation, Peace Corps officials felt it was unlikely that their volunteers would be solicited to do any intelligence work. Still, one official admitted, the real problem would be "covert people trying to infiltrate. I don't see any way we can spot them. It would be a fluke. The more deliberate the attempt, the harder it would be to find."

Shriver's concern over keeping his agency "clean" was

reinforced in September, 1961, when Secretary of the Army Elvis J. Stahr made a speech suggesting that an Army Peace Corps be established.

"We must plan so that we can use our tools in cold war as well as hot war and employ them anywhere in the world," said Stahr. General Barksdale Hamlett, Army Deputy Chief of Staff, gave added details of the plan, which seemed to envision use of the Army in worthy social projects in underdeveloped countries—but linked to paramilitary activities.

To Shriver, it smacked of precisely the sort of military and intelligence overtones he was trying so hard to avoid. Shriver objected strenuously. A high-level meeting was held at the Pentagon, attended by Stahr, Shriver, General Hamlett and a platoon of beribboned Army brass.

The generals at the meeting insisted that the Army Peace Corps would have no relation to any intelligence work. At that, Lee St. Lawrence, a Peace Corps official, spoke up. St. Lawrence had served with the Agency for International Development in Southeast Asia and was familiar with CIA operations in that part of the world.

He asked the generals to name the officers who would be in charge of the proposed "Army Peace Corps" in Southeast Asia. When they did, St. Lawrence singled out some as CIA men. He offered to reel off the names of others, but there was no need. The project was dropped.

But Communist attacks on Shriver and the Peace Corps continued. United States intelligence obtained, from Eastern Europe, what appeared to be a guide for satellite nations on how to phrase propaganda against the Peace Corps. The document stressed the general line that the Corps was a CIA operation and that volunteers were selected by the CIA. Peace Corps officials believed that it served as a primer for subsequent propaganda emanating from various points in the Communist world.

Certainly the Russian and Communist Chinese attacks followed a familiar pattern. In March, 1962, for example, Radio Moscow broadcast in Hindi to India: "U.S. agents are sent to Afro-Asian countries under the U.S. Peace Corps label. The plan to organize the corps was jointly prepared by the U. S. State Department, Pentagon and CIA. Director of the Corps, Shriver, is an old employee of the CIA."

Radio Peking joined in, and so did Fidel Castro. Radio Havana broadcast attacks on the Peace Corps that paralleled the Moscow barrage.

Also in Havana, the newspaper *Hoy* warned Venezuela to "watch out" for the Peace Corps. "These Corps are land U-2s. Their mission consists in poking their noses into all places where meek rulers open the door for them."

On March 27, 1963, a Polish paper published an article attacking the Peace Corps by charging that girl volunteers were Mata Haris. It ran photographs of girls training, with the caption: "The Americans consider all means acceptable. Where other methods do not succeed, sex * may be very useful. Girl members of the Corps on the exercise field."

About the same time, Tass picked up the sex theme and charged that a wicked Peace Corps woman teacher in Somalia tried to teach pupils the "indecent movements" of the twist.

By the spring of 1963, United States analysts concluded that the Soviet Union, having had little success with this loud, public campaign against the Peace Corps, had embarked on a simultaneous behind-the-scenes campaign against the Corps. In Ghana, for example, the Soviet ambassador succeeded in persuading the government of President Kwame Nkrumah to impose some restrictions on the Peace Corps. And in May, 1963, the *Ghanaian Times*, regarded as the unofficial spokesman for Nkrumah, openly attacked the Corps as an alleged CIA tool.

There seemed no likelihood that the public attacks would stop, but their very intensity logically dictated that

* Actually, the Peace Corps has rather strict rules about sex. "In-service marriages of single volunteers must have the prior approval of the Peace Corps representative in charge of the project," a Peace Corps booklet warns sternly. "Approval will not be granted when the future spouse has come from the U.S. or from some other country for the purpose of marrying a volunteer . . . married couples who find they are to become parents must notify their Peace Corps representative as quickly as possible."

Shriver, more than ever, would want to keep the Peace Corps pristine. A spy incident involving a volunteer would give the Russians a propaganda field day and could possibly wreck the Peace Corps, and Shriver's political career as well.

The Peace Corps, it should be noted in fairness to the CIA, maintains it does not know of a single case in which it could be sure of an attempted infiltration by an intelligence agent seeking to use the Corps as cover.

But the fact that Shriver felt he had to take the astonishing precautions he did, speaks volumes. It reflects the atmosphere of mistrust that is felt, rightly or wrongly, by many overt officials of the United States Government toward their less visible colleagues. The distrust is not universal, however. Some unlikely departments of the government have become vehicles for secret operations of various shadings. The story of one of these begins in a house in Cuba.

20

A Gray Operation

OUTSIDE the high garden wall of the decaying villa in Miramar, on the outskirts of Havana, guards armed with Tommy guns patrolled back and forth.

Inside, James Donovan, the remarkable, soft-spoken New York attorney, picked up the telephone and asked the Cuban operator to put him through to a number in the United States.

He took out a black wallet, of the type that was large enough for foreign bills, and reached into an apparently empty pouch. From a concealed pocket in the wallet he pulled out a typewritten sheet of onionskin paper.

On it, down the left-hand side, were key words like "negotiations." On the right side were various phrases such as "I am meeting with" and then a list of various people, including the name "Fidel." The sheet also contained what appeared to be a list of stocks.

By ordering his "broker" to "sell Quaker City" and by using other innocuous key words, Donovan, through his code sheet, was able to convey to the CIA men on the line in the United States the real progress of his negotiations to ransom the lives of more than 1,000 prisoners.

James Donovan was on his most important mission. He was playing for high stakes—the freedom of the 1,113 survivors of the Bay of Pigs invasion. The men were captives in the jails of Fidel Castro.

Donovan was a silver-haired, forty-six-year-old former

OSS man, short but powerfully built. In February, 1962, on the bridge in Berlin, he had traded the Soviet master spy Rudolf Abel (whom he defended five years earlier in Federal Court) for the U-2 pilot Francis Gary Powers and Yale student Frederic L. Pryor, held on a charge of espionage by the East Germans. It was the most spectacular spy swap in the history of the Cold War.

Donovan's Cuban adventure began a few months later, early in June, 1962, when Attorney General Robert Kennedy sent to him a delegation of Cubans made up of survivors of the Bay of Pigs brigade and their families.

Up to that time, sixty prisoners had been ransomed for a pledge of cash, but efforts to free the rest had failed in June, 1961, when negotiations between Castro and a Tractors for Freedom Committee collapsed. The committee, sponsored by the Kennedy Administration, had been unable to reach agreement with Castro on the dictator's continually shifting offers to trade the prisoners for 500 tractors or bulldozers.

Donovan, after listening to the pleas of his visitors, agreed to become the general counsel to the group. It was called the Cuban Families Committee for Liberation of Prisoners of War, Inc., a charitable corporation that had been granted tax-exempt status by the Internal Revenue Service.

On August 29, 1962, Donovan went to Cuba for his first talks with Castro. He stayed at the crumbling villa in Miramar and conferred with Castro at the Presidential Palace in Havana. He made it clear he would offer drugs and baby foods for the men, but no cash or tractors. Castro agreed to negotiate on this basis, provided the Cuban Families Committee came up with the $2,900,000 it had pledged in return for the sixty prisoners released the previous April.

Donovan returned to New York and visited John E. McKeen, the president of Charles Pfizer Company, who lived in the penthouse of Donovan's apartment building near Prospect Park in Brooklyn. They called in John T. Connor, head of Merck, Sharp & Dohme, another friend of Donovan. The executives of the two drug companies offered to donate medicines to help Donovan get the men out.

The CIA separately approached the drug industry trade association, to explore the chances of large-scale donations by manufacturers.

In the meantime, Donovan had entered the political arena. On September 18, shortly after his return from Cuba, Donovan won the Democratic nomination for United States Senate. His opponent was the Republican incumbent, Senator Jacob K. Javits.

On October 2 the drug-company pledges in his pocket, Donovan returned to Havana, confident he could reach agreement with Castro. The Pfizer Company quietly began moving $2,000,000 worth of drugs in refrigerator cars to Idlewild International Airport. The United States Government began making preparations to receive the influx of prisoners in Miami.

It was on this second trip that Castro agreed to trade the men for baby foods and medicines. All was going well except for a painful attack of bursitis in Donovan's right shoulder that forced him to fly to Miami briefly for treatment.

He returned to Havana to continue his talks with Castro, but back in the United States there were charges that Donovan was seeking to make political capital out of his role as Cuban negotiator. And some members of Congress said that the United States ought not to be dickering with Castro at a time when it was asking other countries to cut off trade.

The White House refused to say whether any government funds would be used to ransom the men. It insisted Donovan was acting as a private attorney but said he was keeping President Kennedy advised of his activities. Donovan returned from Cuba on October 11.

Three days later a U-2 plane flying secretly over western Cuba took a photograph of a Soviet mobile medium-range missile site.

The Cuban missile crisis was on. The world moved close to nuclear war during the latter half of October. Against this background of tension it looked as though Donovan's chances of reaching an agreement to free the men had been shattered. He suffered a personal, although not unexpected, blow when he lost the election on November 6 to Senator Javits.

By late November the situation was this:

Donovan still had Castro's general agreement to a swap. But now in the wake of the missile crisis, the drug industry was unwilling to take the risk of donating medicines to Castro unless the Kennedy Administration made it publicly clear that the deal was in the national interest. The drug firms, already hit hard by the Senate investigation of their high prices, had no desire to bring a new wave of public disapproval down upon themselves.

On November 30 a meeting was held at the Justice Department of top aides to Robert Kennedy and officials of the Internal Revenue Service, the State Department and the CIA (including Lawrence R. Houston, the general counsel of the CIA, Donovan's CIA contact in the Powers-Abel trade). Deputy Attorney General Nicholas Katzenbach and Assistant Attorney General Louis F. Oberdorfer represented the Justice Department. Robert Hurwitch spoke for the State Department.

The high-level meeting concluded that Castro's demand of $53,000,000 in drugs would cost only $17,000,000 at wholesale U.S. prices. It was also decided to study the tax angle involved in possible contributions of drugs by the companies. It was agreed that a memorandum would be prepared over the weekend to be ready for Robert Kennedy on Monday December 3.* In the meantime, a drug-industry representative was contacted informally.

On Monday morning the *New York Herald Tribune* published a front-page story by Warren Rogers, Jr., stating

* The memorandum noted that some drug companies might gain a tax "windfall" by making charitable contributions to the prisoner exchange deal. An accompanying letter by Oberdorfer to Robert Kennedy pointed out that the drug companies would nevertheless insist on approval of the deal by someone at least as high as a Cabinet officer as well as "maximum protection from legislative and public criticism in two particular directions: (a) charges of pro-Communism and (b) criticism for inferences drawn from any price mark-up exposed in the transaction."

that the President felt a "moral obligation" to free the men. It was the kind of reassurance the drug companies had been looking for. Donovan's phone began to ring in Brooklyn with additional pledges of drugs from the industry.

In Washington, Robert Kennedy called on the President at the White House, and at noon the Attorney General phoned Oberdorfer to give him the green light to go ahead with the operation. The American Red Cross then agreed to accept the drugs as contributions to charity and to deliver them to Havana.

The next day Donovan slipped into Washington to confer with Robert Kennedy. On December 7 the Attorney General met with officials of the Pharmaceutical Manufacturers Association. He told the drug manufacturers that the Bay of Pigs invasion had been launched by the United States, that the plan had been started by the Eisenhower Administration and continued by the Kennedy Administration, and that both the nation and the government had a moral obligation to get the men out.

Robert Kennedy talked about the courage of forty members of the brigade who had escaped and crossed the Caribbean in an open boat. He went on to say that the United States could not directly conduct negotiations with Cuba because it would be "misunderstood" by the world and would be a diplomatic disaster if the deal failed. He said that all departments had received a list of the drugs Castro wanted and that none were considered strategic.

Finally, the Attorney General assured the companies that the sight of the returning prisoners would still any criticism of the drug companies for contributing to Castro. He made it clear that contributions were voluntary.

He then ordered Oberdorfer to devote his full time to the project. And on December 9, Robert Kennedy gave the same talk to a group of baby-food manufacturers.

Oberdorfer's office in the Justice Department became the command post for "Project X." Additional telephones were installed. A group of private attorneys, including John E. Nolan, Jr., and E. Barrett Prettyman, Jr., were brought in to help. (Both later joined the administration.)

From Oberdorfer's office, the private attorneys (and two Justice Department lawyers) now began telephone solicitation of the drug companies. The Justice Department attorneys did not identify themselves as government employees, but said they were calling as representatives of the Cuban Families Committee.

The Justice Department team obtained clearances from the Civil Aeronautics Board and the Interstate Commerce Commission to permit charitable contribution of air and surface transportation to haul the drugs to Miami. The CIA, the Air Force, the Immigration and Naturalization Service and the Department of Health, Education and Welfare began making arrangements to receive and process the prisoners in Florida. The Commerce Department granted export licenses for the food and drugs.

During this time Donovan told the Justice Department that Castro was demanding a guarantee of full payment of the ransom; otherwise he would hold back the brigade officers until the last payment was made. Katzenbach flew to Montreal on December 14, but the Royal Bank of Canada balked at issuing a letter of credit without some formal guarantees by American banks. The Justice Department official flew back to New York. The Morgan Guaranty Trust Company of New York and the Bank of America agreed to participate; special meetings of their boards of directors were hastily convened to approve the plan.

To complete the financial arrangements, the Continental Insurance Company wrote out a $53,000,000 performance bond without charge, guaranteeing that the Red Cross would meet its obligations to deliver the drugs to Cuba.

Meanwhile, the drugs contributed to "Project X" by the manufacturers were flooding into Miami and creating a monster job of cataloging and bookkeeping at Opa-locka (ironically, the same CIA air base used as a jumping-off point for the Bay of Pigs trainees). The CIA provided a pharmacist, Stephen Aldrich, who helped log the drugs as they arrived in Florida.

On December 16 Donovan began his final mission. He

stopped off in Washington to confer with officials and then went on to Miami, where he disappeared. The press could not find him, and with good reason.

Donovan stayed in a CIA house in Miami on December 16 and 17, telephoning to Havana. About 9:00 P.M. December 17, Donovan called Washington to say that he had arranged to go to Havana in the morning. He also reported that one of Castro's negotiators had a sick child who needed a certain medicine immediately.

Katzenbach called Walter Reed Hospital and got ten vials of the medicine. Shortly after midnight Oberdorfer, his assistant Frank Michelman, John Nolan and a CIA attorney flew to Miami from Washington, taking the medicine along.

They did not arrive at the CIA "safe house" until 5:00 A.M. on December 18. There, Donovan received a final pre-dawn briefing. Then he flew into Havana. Nolan stayed at the house, helping to man the CIA telephones. The rest of the team flew back to Washington.

Two days later Donovan returned briefly to Miami. Then he flew back to Havana, taking with him Dr. Leonard Scheele, the former Surgeon General of the United States. On December 21 Donovan and Castro signed a Memorandum of Agreement. But Castro was wary of Donovan's representations. Donovan suggested that Castro's aides inspect some of the drugs.

Shortly after midnight three Cuban Red Cross officials in olive drab flew secretly into Miami. They were met by Dr. Scheele and Barrett Prettyman, shown the supplies at Opa-locka and then taken to Port Everglades to inspect the drugs being loaded on the *African Pilot*, a ship donated by the Committee of the American Steamship Lines.

The Cubans then adjourned to a Howard Johnson's motel and said to Prettyman they wanted to remain for the day. It was now 5:00 A.M., December 22. Nolan and Prettyman were alarmed at what would happen if the press learned that Castro emissaries were holed up in a Florida motel. One of the Cuban Red Cross men smoked big cigars and, in his olive uniform, did not project the image of a man of mercy. Nolan and Prettyman finally prevailed on the Cubans to fly back to Havana, which they did at 9:00 A.M.

That same day the *African Pilot* sailed for Havana with the first shipload of drugs. Early on Sunday, December 23, Nolan and Prettyman joined Donovan in Havana. The *African Pilot* docked that afternoon. Castro met the ship.

The prisoner exchange seemed to be proceeding smoothly. At 5:00 P.M. the first plane left the San Antonio de los Banos airport for Homestead Air Force Base south of Miami. It landed in Florida an hour and five minutes later. All told, four planeloads and a total of 426 prisoners left Cuba by nightfall.

But, in Havana, it had become obvious to Donovan that the airlift would be halted by Castro unless the Cuban Families Committee came up with the $2,900,000 that had been pledged as ransom for the sixty wounded prisoners released in April before Donovan entered the picture.

At 2:00 A.M. on Monday, December 24, Nolan flew to Miami. He placed a 5:00 A.M. phone call to Robert Kennedy in Washington. Nolan made it clear that unless the money was raised by three o'clock that afternoon, the deal would collapse.

"What are you going to tell Jim Donovan?" Robert Kennedy asked.

"I'm going to tell him you're going to get the money," Nolan replied.

There was a pause. Then Robert Kennedy said: "Have a nice trip back."

Nolan flew back to Havana. The Attorney General called Richard Cardinal Cushing, the Roman Catholic Archbishop of Boston, who pledged $1,000,000. Robert Kennedy also called General Lucius Clay, who was a sponsor of the Cuban Families Committee.

Clay borrowed the remaining $1,900,000 on his own signature, then solicited contributions from American business firms to cover that amount. Texaco, Standard Oil of New Jersey and the Ford Motor Company Fund each contributed $100,000.

In Cuba, that Monday, two more planeloads of prisoners were permitted to take off. Then Castro stalled.

First he staged a military air show at San Antonio de los Banos to tie up the airport. Then, about 1:00 P.M., Castro halted all flights until he received word about the money. Late in the afternoon Castro was assured the Royal Bank of Canada had deposited it in Montreal. Donovan and Castro then met at the Canadian consul's office to accept the financial guarantees.

At 9:35 P.M. the last of the planes carrying the returning prisoners touched down at Homestead Air Force Base. Aboard was James Donovan, a quiet American—his mission accomplished.

For each of the returning prisoners, the routine was the same. Clean clothes, a meal and then a bus trip to Dinner Key Auditorium, where their families and friends were waiting. There, they marched between double lines of fellow members of Brigade 2056 as a band played the march from *The Bridge Over the River Kwai*.

It was Christmas Eve, 1962.

There were some people who were not content to accept the prisoner exchange as a humanitarian act arranged by a private citizen. Months later, in June, 1963, all thirteen Republican members of the House Foreign Affairs Committee called for a Congressional inquiry into Donovan's role. They charged that many aspects of the exchange "remain baffling."

Donovan replied: "I was a private citizen acting on behalf of the Cuban Families Committee."

It was not, of course, quite as simple as that, as has been shown. Although both Donovan and the White House took this position (for reasons Robert Kennedy had explained privately to the drug industry on December 7, 1962), the fact is that no fewer than fourteen branches of the government participated in the complex deal: the CIA, the Air Force, the Departments of Health, Education and Welfare, Justice, Defense, Commerce, Agriculture, Treasury, the Internal Revenue Service, the White House, Immigration, the CAB, the ICC and the State Department.

In January, 1963, the Agriculture Department gave 5,000,000 pounds of dried milk to the Red Cross for shipment to Cuba and pledged more as needed. In all, the Agriculture Department contributed a total of 35,000,000 pounds of surplus food to the prisoner exchange—15,000,000 pounds of dried milk and 20,000,000 pounds of shortening.

But the administration was fearful that it would come under political attack for helping Castro. The milk-and-shortening deal was played down.

Furthermore, the Agriculture Department announced on January 8, 1963, that "the Red Cross had indicated that the Cuban Families Committee expects to raise funds to reimburse the department." In other words, the government was saying that it would be paid back in cash for the surplus food.

What happened was somewhat different.

The dried milk cost the government $2,505,000 when it was bought from producers as part of the farm price-support program. The shortening cost the government $3,150,000. Consequently, the government gave away commodities for which it had paid $5,655,000.

However, in calculating the value of the milk and shortening given to the Red Cross, the government figured its contribution as worth just under $2,000,000—the lower price the milk and repackaged shortening might have brought had it been sold by the government on the world market. Normally, the government uses the higher price that it paid to producers when it figures the value of a contribution of surplus food to charity. In this instance, it obviously sought to minimize the size of the donation because of the domestic political implications of giving anything away to Castro.

Nor was the government paid back any amount in cash for its donation of milk and shortening. Instead, in a bit of complex bookkeeping that leaves the onlooker breathless, the government accepted as "reimbursement" 4,000,000 pounds of an insecticide called Sevin. The Union Carbide Company had contributed $2,000,000 worth of the bug-killer to the Red Cross for the prisoner exchange. The Commerce Department ruled that the insecticides would be of strategic economic value to Castro by helping his sugar-cane crops.

So the following took place: The Red Cross accepted the insecticides, then immediately turned them over to the Agency for International Development, which dispatched them to India, Pakistan and Algeria. The government accepted this as repayment for the milk and shortening. This was not quite the same as the "funds" which the Agriculture announcement had indicated would be raised "to reimburse the department."

A conservative estimate of what it cost the government to extricate itself *after* the Bay of Pigs would be $29,793,-000. This consists of a $20,000,000 tax loss * to the government as a result of the drug companies' charitable deductions; $5,655,000 in skim milk and shortening; $4,000,000 in secret CIA payments to families of the Bay of Pigs prisoners over a twenty-month period; and $138,000 in costs to the Department of Health, Education and Welfare when the prisoners returned. (Each man got a $100 check; the other costs were clothing, housing and food.)

Because of the political risks at home of dealing with Castro, the government felt it necessary to mask its participation in the prisoner exchange both by acting through Donovan and by a certain amount of fiscal hocus-pocus. It decided that the realities of the situation were such that even an act of humanity had to be approached with the utmost political caution.

Nevertheless, Donovan succeeded and the prisoners' lives were saved. As an unexpected part of the deal, Donovan persuaded Castro not to let the Red Cross ships sail away empty. Castro began releasing thousands of refugees previously unable to leave Cuba, including over 5,000 members of the families of the prisoners.

Then in March and April of 1963 Donovan won the release of more than thirty Americans held in Cuban jails, including three CIA men. On July 3, when the last of

* The estimate of tax loss was made by Mitchell Rogovin, counsel to the Internal Revenue Service, on December 28, 1962.

the medical supplies reached Cuba, the American Red Cross announced that a total of 9,703 persons (including the Bay of Pigs prisoners and the Americans) had been brought out of Cuba under the agreements negotiated by Donovan.

The staggering figure of nearly 10,000 persons rescued by one man is not widely known, because the total figure received less public attention than did the dramatic return of the invasion prisoners.

In all of these missions, Donovan had the assistance of, and worked hand in hand with, the United States Government. But he was not formally a part of it. In each case, as a private citizen, he was breaking new ground in a form of intelligence diplomacy that is a unique outgrowth of the Cold War.

In the case of the Powers-Abel swap, the negotiations that culminated on the Berlin bridge began with a series of letters to Donovan signed "Hellen Abel." The writer of the letters claimed to be the wife of the Soviet spy imprisoned in the United States. The letters came from Leipzig, East Germany.

Donovan turned each of them over to Lawrence Houston, the CIA general counsel. The agency prepared an answer to each letter from "Mrs. Abel," and shipped them back to Donovan in New York, who sent them off to Leipzig. But when Donovan eventually went to East Berlin to negotiate the final details directly with the Russians and East Germans, he was technically on his own, a private American citizen with no diplomatic immunity or protection.

Donovan's missions, then, have defied any neat categorization. President Kennedy, in a letter to Donovan after the East Berlin mission, characterized them as "unique." Because of their very nature, there was public confusion over whether he acted as a private citizen or as a secret agent of the United States Government. The truth is that he was somewhere in between.

The government was unwilling to tell the full story of its role in the Cuban prisoner exchange, as it has been related here, because to have done so during Donovan's negotiations might have handicapped his ability to deal with Castro. And, afterward, it might have engendered too many delicate political questions. In a very real sense, the seeds of one covert operation, the Bay of Pigs, had given rise to another—the return of the invasion brigade.

Those who sought a clear, simple explanation of whether an operation was private or governmental were bound to be disappointed in the case of James Donovan.

His rescue of the Bay of Pigs prisoners was not precisely a "black," i.e., secret operation. Nor was it entirely "white." It might be most accurately described as a mixture of both—truly a gray operation.

21

Missile Crisis

In the summer and fall of 1962, as Donovan was negotiating with Castro to rescue the victims of one of the Invisible Government's operations in Cuba, another operation was being conducted in the airspace over the island. In utmost secrecy, the U-2 spy plane was photographing every foot of Cuban territory in search of Soviet missiles.

The U-2 had been flying over Cuba from the earliest days of the Castro regime. In 1959 a U-2 was sent over the Zapata swamps near the Bay of Pigs to check an erroneous report that missiles were being set up in the area. By 1962 two U-2s a month were being flown over the island.

That August photographs were taken of SA-2 antiaircraft missiles being unloaded at Cuban docks. The overflight program was stepped up and seven U-2s were sent over the island in the five weeks between August 29 and October 7. Each mission returned with new pictures of short-range SA-2 defensive missiles.

But President Kennedy, citing the information provided him by the intelligence community, insisted there was no evidence that the Russians were moving in long-range offensive missiles that could threaten the United States. Kennedy gave his assurances despite the fact that John McCone had a suspicion—never passed along to the White House—that the Soviets were deploying ballistic missiles in Cuba.

In testimony before the Senate Preparedness Subcommittee on March 12, 1963, McCone said he had reported this view within the CIA on August 10. "I couldn't understand," he explained, "why these surface-to-air missile sites were there, so useless for protecting the island against invasion. They must be there, in my opinion, to shield the island against observation from aerial reconnaissance."

McCone conceded, however, that his view was based on "intuition" without "hard intelligence." And although as Director of Central Intelligence he could have ordered that his view be made the official view and reported to Kennedy, he did not do so.

McCone left Washington on August 23 to marry Theiline McGee Pigott, the widow of a rich Seattle industrialist and an old family friend. During his honeymoon cruise to Europe and his three-week stay on Cap Ferrat on the French Riviera, he received daily briefing telegrams. They deepened his apprehension, and on September 7, 10, 13 and 20 he responded with telegrams expressing his mounting concern. But, again, he did not direct that the "honeymoon telegrams" be passed along to the President. They were treated as "in-house" messages and were not circulated outside the CIA.

During McCone's absence, the Board of National Estimates was asked to assess the possibility that the Soviets would station offensive missiles in Cuba. And on September 19 a National Intelligence Estimate was produced. It conceded that the Russians might be tempted to introduce the missiles for psychological reasons, particularly to impress the Latin Americans. It also alluded to the possibility that the Soviets might wish to strengthen their position in Cuba as a prelude to a move against Berlin.

Nevertheless, the Estimate stated that it was highly unlikely that offensive missiles would be sent in, because the Soviets would be deterred by their awareness of the violent reaction which such a move would provoke on the part of the United States. The chief Kremlinologists in the State Department, Charles E. (Chip) Bohlen and Llewellyn E. (Tommy) Thompson, Jr., both former ambassadors to Moscow, concurred with the Estimate.*

However, on September 20, the day after the Estimate was handed down, a reliable eyewitness report of an offensive missile reached Ray Cline, the CIA's deputy director for intelligence. A CIA sub-agent had spotted a missile part on a highway on September 12, but had experienced delay in getting his information out of Cuba. Missile experts in Washington, who had rejected hundreds of prior reports by Cuban refugees, concluded that the sub-agent's description checked out against the known features of Russian offensive missiles. In retrospect the CIA decided the missile part had arrived in a shipment of Soviet cargo on September 8.

McCone returned from his honeymoon on September 26, and on October 4 an urgent meeting of the United States Intelligence Board was called. The members took a look at the "mosaic"—a photographic panorama of the entire island of Cuba pieced together from the latest U-2 pictures. There were still no photographic indications of offensive missiles. But McCone noted that there had been no pictures of the western sector of the island since September 5. He ordered that overflights be further stepped up and concentrated on that section of Cuba.

Until that time all U-2 flights had been made by civilian CIA pilots. Now, however, the risks would be greatly increased by the expanded schedule of missions and by the presence of the anti-aircraft missiles. The CIA had concluded that an SA-2 had downed Francis Gary Powers over the Soviet Union in 1960, and that another had accounted for a Nationalist Chinese U-2 over Communist China on October 9, 1962. Rather than risk another U-2 incident involving the CIA, McCone agreed to McNamara's recommendation that the overflight operation be transferred to the Strategic Air Command.

During this interval, on October 10, Senator Kenneth B.

---

* After the October crisis McCone was urged to make Sherman Kent, of the Board of Estimates, the scapegoat for the bad guess. But McCone refused to fire him, despite repeated reminders from the White House that the Estimate was wrong.

Keating, the New York Republican, announced that he had confirmed reports of intermediate-range missile sites under construction in Cuba.

Four days later, early on the morning of October 14, SAC flew its first U-2 mission over Cuba and returned with photographs of mobile medium-range ballistic missiles (MMRBM) at San Cristobal, 100 miles to the southwest of Havana.

The pictures were analyzed by the photo-interpreters in Washington all the next day, and late in the afternoon the findings were reported to General Carter, McCone's deputy (McCone had left Washington earlier in the afternoon for Los Angeles to take the body of his stepson, Paul J. Pigott, who had been killed in a sports-car crash, to Seattle).

General Carroll, the director of the DIA, was next to be informed. Then Carroll took two civilian photo-interpreters to dinner at the home of General Maxwell Taylor. Joining them were Carter, and Roswell Gilpatric and U. Alexis Johnson, both members of the Special Group. When the officials had been convinced that Soviet missiles were in place in Cuba, McGeorge Bundy was notified at his home. He arranged for the photo-interpreters to report to him at the White House the following morning.

Shortly before nine o'clock on the morning of October 16 Bundy took the pictures to President Kennedy, who was in his bedroom in pajamas and robe, reading the newspapers. Kennedy quickly indicated those officials who were to be called to the White House.

At 11:45 the group, which was later to be named the Executive Committee (Excomm) of the National Security Council, gathered in the Cabinet Room for the first of a running series of meetings during the following two weeks. Present were Kennedy, his brother Robert, Lyndon Johnson, Rusk, McNamara, Gilpatric, Bundy, Taylor, Carter, Theodore C. Sorensen, the presidential adviser, Secretary of the Treasury Douglas Dillon, Under Secretary of State George Ball and Edwin M. Martin, Assistant Secretary of State for Latin American Affairs. Adlai Stevenson joined the group that afternoon. McCone was brought in immediately upon his return from the West Coast. And two Truman Cabinet members were called in later in the week: Dean Acheson, former Secretary of State, and Robert Lovett, former Secretary of Defense.

Kennedy entered the first Excomm meeting with the feeling that two choices were open: knock out the missiles with an air strike or make representations to Khrushchev.

During the next four days the Excomm weighed the alternatives, moving gradually toward a consensus that the safest course was to take the middle way: to set up a blockade and insist that the Soviets withdraw, or direct military force would be applied.

In coming to this decision the Excomm was strongly influenced by Robert Kennedy. Recalling Pearl Harbor, he opposed an air strike against the small island of Cuba. He argued that the nation might never recover from the moral outrage of the world and the shock to its own conscience.

At first, the discussion centered on the immediate problem of getting the missiles dismantled or removed. There were detailed technical analyses of what kind of surveillance and inspection would be necessary to make sure the missiles were rendered inoperable.

Stevenson was troubled that the discussion would bog down in details and that the larger problem of eliminating the Soviets from Cuba would be obscured. He reminded the Excomm that a long period of negotiation would probably follow the removal of the missiles. And he recommended that some thought be given to possible United States proposals during that period.

Stevenson suggested that once the missiles were out, the United States might propose this deal: a pull-out of all Soviet troops from Cuba in return for a promise by the United States that it would not invade the island and would withdraw its missiles from Turkey. Stevenson was aware that the administration had decided the previous year to remove the missiles from Turkey (they were Jupiter IRBMs, obsolescent, clumsy liquid-fuel rockets. The plan was to replace them with missile-bearing Polaris submarines stationed in the Mediterranean. Turkey announced on January 23, 1963, that it had agreed to removal of the Jupiters)..

As the Excomm deliberated, the President went through with two scheduled campaign trips, lest their cancellation betray the secret maneuvering. On October 17 he kept speaking engagements in Stratford and New Haven, Connecticut, and on October 19 he campaigned in Cleveland, Springfield, Illinois, and Chicago. He was supposed to go on to St. Louis and Seattle that weekend, but on Saturday morning, October 20, Pierre Salinger announced that the President would return to Washington immediately because he had a cold and was running a slight temperature.

At the White House that afternoon the secret meetings continued. Kennedy approved the Excomm's recommendation that a blockade be imposed around Cuba. The decision was ratified the next day by the National Security Council. (Up to that point the Excomm had been operating without formal, statutory authority. To make its actions official, it was necessary to include the Office of Emergency Planning, one of the five statutory members of the NSC. The Office had been excluded from the previous deliberations.)

The President also arranged to go on television Monday night, October 22, to inform the nation that offensive missiles had been discovered in Cuba and that a blockade would be imposed.

All weekend long, starting the previous Thursday and continuing until the afternoon of the President's speech, the Defense Department had repeated: "The Pentagon has no information indicating the presence of offensive weapons in Cuba." *

In his TV address the President emphasized that the blockade was only an "initial" step and indicated strongly

---

* In a speech on March 22, 1963, Salinger insisted that during the Cuban crisis "We did not lie to the American people." He went on to explain that the Pentagon spokesman who issued the denials "was not lying. He was communicating the information as he knew it." By implication, Salinger excused his own statements about Kennedy's "cold."

that direct military force would be employed if necessary to get the missiles out.

"It shall be the policy of this nation," Kennedy added, "to regard any nuclear missile launched from Cuba against any nation in the Western Hemisphere as an attack by the Soviet Union on the United States, requiring a full retaliatory response upon the Soviet Union."

For the next four days the world balanced on the brink of war, watching fearfully to see if the Soviets would continue work on the missiles, attempt to run the blockade, or otherwise defy the President's ultimatum.

Finally, late in the night of October 26, a message was received from Khrushchev. It suggested he was ready to withdraw his missiles under United Nations supervision in return for a lifting of the blockade and a pledge by the United States not to invade Cuba.

The Excomm convened the next morning in a hopeful atmosphere. But the optimism was quickly shattered by a second Khrushchev message, which was made public in Moscow. It offered to swap the Soviet missiles in Cuba for the U.S. missiles in Turkey.

The members of the Excomm knew that President Kennedy would not accept such a deal. As Kennedy was later to explain privately, he felt it imperative to reject the missile swap in order to preserve the Western alliance. The Turks had opposed the removal of the Jupiters during 1962. They looked upon the missiles as symbols of U.S. determination to defend them against Russian attack.

To accept Khrushchev's deal, Kennedy reasoned, would be to confirm all the things Europe had said and suspected about the United States: that when the vital interests of the United States were at stake, Europe's interests would be sacrificed.

It was a strange and ironic situation, Kennedy conceded, since he had decided the previous year to remove the obsolescent missiles from Turkey: a future historian might question the wisdom of risking a nuclear war over missiles that the nation did not need or want.

Kennedy issued a public statement, in effect rejecting the missile swap. Then he sent off a private message to

Khrushchev, ignoring the Turkey proposal and agreeing to the terms of Khrushchev's first message.

Meantime, the Excomm's apprehension deepened as reports came in, first, that an SA-2 had opened fire in Cuba for the first time, downing a SAC U-2, and second, that a U-2 had wandered over Siberia while on an "air sampling" mission near the Arctic Circle.*

The first U-2 incident that day suggested to the Excomm that Khrushchev might have reversed himself overnight and decided to defy Kennedy's demands. The Excomm also realized the second incident might have suggested to Khrushchev that Kennedy was planning some type of direct military action against Russia.

The President and the Excomm waited uneasily through the night. Then, shortly after ten o'clock on Sunday morning, October 28, Moscow released the text of another message from Khrushchev to Kennedy. The Soviet leader said he had ordered a stop to work on the Cuban bases and had directed that the missiles be crated and returned to the Soviet Union. United Nations representatives would "verify the dismantling."

Kennedy hailed Khrushchev's decision and responded with an expression of "regret" for the Siberian U-2 incident, which the Russian had complained about in his letter.

The missile crisis was over. Kennedy had won perhaps the greatest triumph of the Cold War. And in the November Congressional elections the triumph was reflected in a major Democratic victory.

The crisis had cost the Republicans as many as twenty House seats, said Representative Bob Wilson of California, the chairman of the Republican Congressional Committee. He insisted that the administration had known in late

* The Russians had charged that another U-2 flew over Sakhalin Island north of Japan on August 30, 1962. The United States replied that "severe winds" might have forced the plane "unintentionally" to violate Soviet air-space. After the Powers incident, Presidents Eisenhower and Kennedy promised there would be no more U-2 overflights of the Soviet Union. But their pledge did not rule out flights over Cuba, other Communist countries or along the borders of the Soviet Union.

September that Russian missiles were in Cuba but had delayed announcing the fact in order to go into the election in a time of crisis, when the nation traditionally rallies round the President.

Wilson said administration officials had held a secret briefing for him and other members of the CIA subcommittee in the House six weeks before the election and had disclosed that offensive missiles were then in Cuba (Wilson apparently was referring to the eyewitness report of a missile part which reached the CIA on September 20).

The administration denied Wilson's accusation, but its credibility was called into question when Arthur Sylvester, Assistant Secretary of Defense for Public Affairs, made a series of statements which suggested that the administration might have been manipulating the facts in its official announcements.

"The generation of news by actions taken by the government," Sylvester declared on October 30 in commenting upon the Cuban crisis, "becomes one weapon in a strained situation. The results, in my opinion, justify the methods we use. . . . News generated by actions of the government as to content and timing are part of the arsenal of weaponry that a President has in application of military force and related forces to the solution of political problems, or to the application of international political pressure."

Sylvester went even further in a speech on December 6: "It's inherent in [the] government's right, if necessary, to lie to save itself when it's going up into a nuclear war. This seems to me basic."

In order to keep a closer watch over government information, Sylvester directed that a representative of his office monitor each interview between a reporter and a Pentagon official. Alternately, the official could report the substance of the interview to Sylvester at the end of the day. The State Department instituted a similar practice, but withdrew it a few weeks later under pressure.

Critics accused the administration of "managing the news," using information as a "weapon," even lying to protect itself.

318

Kennedy's October triumph was further compromised when Castro refused to allow on-site inspection of the missile sites by the United Nations. The Republicans seized upon this to suggest that the Russian military build-up was continuing and that all of the offensive weapons had not been removed.

Leading the Republican attack was Senator Keating, who had gained something of a reputation as an intelligence expert by virtue of his announcement on October 10, twelve days before Kennedy's TV address, that there were offensive missiles in Cuba.

Keating issued a series of post-crisis statements, culminating in a speech on January 31, 1963, in which he said:

"There is continuing, absolutely confirmed and undeniable evidence that the Soviets are maintaining the medium-range sites they had previously constructed in Cuba . . . they may have missiles left on the island and need only to wheel them out of caves. . . . Without on-site inspection, it is hard to see how we will ever know for sure the true missile situation in Cuba."

Keating's statement drew banner headlines across the country. And the administration had difficulty gaining public acceptance of its denials. Its failure to quiet the storm over Cuba was undermining efforts to turn the October triumph into a Cold War breakthrough.

Finally, Kennedy decided he would have to overwhelm his critics with photographic proof. The original idea was to invite the small group of reporters covering Keating to view the special briefing which had been put together for several Congressional committees. At the last minute, however, the President decided that if classified material was to be released, he might as well go the whole way. He ordered McNamara to go on nation-wide television that evening—February 6—and display the aerial reconnaissance photos brought back from Cuba.

The decision was reached so quickly that there was no time to check with McCone. The CIA boss would have opposed the idea on grounds that the TV show would reveal the high degree of perfection which had been achieved with the U-2 cameras (much better than those which fell into Khrushchev's hands when Powers' plane was captured in 1960).

At the time of the decision, McCone was on Capitol Hill testifying: "We are convinced beyond reasonable doubt . . . that all offensive missiles and bombers known to be in Cuba were withdrawn."

A few hours later McNamara went on TV. For close to two hours the American people were exposed to some of the "blackest" secrets of the Invisible Government. Most of the briefing was conducted by General Carroll's thirty-four-year-old assistant, John Hughes. He displayed dozens of blowups of reconnaissance photos showing the Cuban missile sites first under construction and then in the process of dismantling, and finally he showed the missile equipment being put aboard ships and carried away from the island.

It was a breath-taking demonstration of the high degree of sophistication which had been achieved in electronic intelligence. But the presentation prompted two questions which were to prove embarrassing to the administration. First, no pictures were shown for the period between September 5 and October 14, raising the question of whether the intelligence community had neglected to conduct aerial reconnaissance during this period or whether the administration was suppressing pertinent photos. And second, the briefing added up to a tacit admission that there had been no photographic count of the number of missiles shipped to Cuba and, therefore, there could be no certainty that the number spotted going out represented the total arsenal.

McNamara sidestepped these problems in answering questions after the briefing. But the next day Kennedy admitted frankly to his news conference: "We cannot prove that there is not a missile in a cave or that the Soviet Union isn't going to ship next week." He noted, however, that the Soviets were aware that if any missiles were discovered, it would "produce the greatest crisis which the world has faced in its history."

The President deplored the "rumors and speculations"

which, he said, compelled the administration to go on TV and disclose "a good deal of information which we are rather reluctant to give about our intelligence-gathering facilities."

As to the so-called "photo gap" between September 5 and October 14, McNamara finally explained at a news conference in February that the U-2 missions during that period "didn't relate" to the areas where the Russian missiles were found. In plain English, McNamara was saying that the CIA failed to photograph the western half of Cuba during the six weeks preceding the flight which discovered the offensive missiles.

At his news conference on March 6 Kennedy argued that it really didn't matter very much because the Soviets set up their missiles so quickly, there would have been nothing to see until a few days before October 14.

"I suppose," the President remarked, "we could have always perhaps picked up these missile bases a few days earlier, but not very many days earlier . . . ten days before might not have picked up anything. The week before might have picked up something. . . . So I feel that the intelligence services did a very good job . . . I am satisfied with Mr. McCone, the intelligence community, the Defense Department and the job they did in these days, particularly taken in totality."

But many important members of the administration were not so satisfied with the Invisible Government. They suspected that someone in the Pentagon or high in the CIA had been funneling incriminating evidence to the Republicans, possibly raw intelligence which had not yet been analyzed or brought to the President's attention. On March 25, when McCone came for one of his periodic meetings with the President, a third person, McGeorge Bundy, was included for the first time. Clearly, Bundy was there to monitor the conversation.

The Invisible Government had taken great pride in its performance during the missile crisis, only to find its achievement compromised by suspicions that it was playing politics with intelligence.

There was no denying, however, that the intelligence

community had succeeded in raising the art of aerial photography to unimagined heights. The missile crisis had revealed unmistakably that automation was revolutionizing the spy business as rapidly as it was transforming American industry.

22

Electronic Spies

> *"The camera, I think, is actually going to be our best
> inspector."*
> JOHN F. KENNEDY on television,
> December, 1962
> *"That function [inspection] can now be assumed by
> satellites. Maybe I'll let you see my photographs."*
> NIKITA S. KHRUSHCHEV to Paul-Henri Spaak,
> July, 1963

THE PRESIDENT of the United States and the Premier of
the Soviet Union were referring to one of the strangest
secrets of the Cold War, a secret which was scarcely a
secret at all. Kennedy and Khrushchev were alluding to a
revolutionary tool of espionage, the camera-bearing "spy
in the sky" satellite. And it was clear that neither had been
fooled by the elaborate security precautions of the other.

The United States had been orbiting SAMOS spy satellites over the Soviet Union since 1961, and the Russians
were known to have the capacity to track them. With
similar technique and purpose the Soviets started in 1962
to send up their COSMOS satellites under the vigilant
eye of the U.S. tracking system.

By 1963 aerial reconnaissance had become the most
secretive operation of the Pentagon. Yet, ironically, when
SAMOS was first tested in 1960, its virtues were graphi-
cally described in official pronouncements. Indeed, the
electronic and optical laws upon which it was founded had

long been the property of the scientific community, Russian and American alike.

Until Francis Gary Powers was shot down in his U-2 over Russia on May 1, 1960, little had been disclosed about SAMOS. But a summit meeting in Paris was being held that month and the Eisenhower Administration was emphasizing its determination to keep the Soviet Union under surveillance despite the U-2 incident. Suddenly, from the depths of the Pentagon, came a spew of previously highly classified details. By following the official disclosures over the next several months, a diligent Russian analyst could easily have pieced together the following description of the remarkable satellite:

SAMOS, the name of a Greek island, was a contraction for Satellite and Missile Observation System. The project was in an advanced state of development and the White House had given it a "DX" rating, which meant it was one of the handful of Pentagon programs with the highest national priority. Still, it was to be pushed even faster on a budget of just under $200,000,000 a year.

SAMOS was designed to be operational by 1962 and to take photographs with detail equal to what the human eye could see from a hundred feet. The satellite was launched * by an Atlas-Agena rocket, standing ninety-five feet high, or a Thor-Agena rocket, with a height of seventy-eight feet.

The Agena, or second stage, was made by the Lockheed Aircraft Corporation, designers and producers of the U-2. It was that part of the rocket which went into orbit. The satellite weighed 4,100 pounds and was twenty-two feet tall and five feet in diameter. It circled the earth upright like a giant cigar, carrying a 300-to-400-pound gold-plated instrument package.

SAMOS was launched from Vandenberg Air Force Base, California, into a polar orbit from which it could photograph every nation in the world as the globe rotated under it. The camera could be shut off when the satellite was off target, thereby conserving power.

(By 1964 reliable reports indicated that a SAMOS was

* SAMOS I failed to achieve orbit on October 11, 1960. SAMOS II was a success on January 31, 1961.

passing over the Soviet Union eight to twelve times, and over Communist China two to four times, every day.)

Orbits varied: some carried the satellite around the earth at an equal altitude of 300 miles; others were purposely egg-shaped so that the satellite dropped as close as 150 miles. From this height a telescopic camera with a focal length of 120 inches could photograph objects two and a half feet wide.

In April, 1959, Amrom H. Katz of the RAND Corporation, a semi-official research group for the Air Force, wrote that camera lenses with a 240-inch focal length had already been developed.

In April, 1960, Howard S. Stewart, a University of Rochester optics expert, indicated in *International Science and Technology* that it was possible to develop satellite cameras capable of "resolving two objects three inches apart from 125 miles up."

In February, 1964, the Air Force's Aerospace Medical Division reported that astronauts could readily spot missile bases, encampments and troop movements from 100 miles in space.

There were four types of SAMOS satellites: one carried television cameras for transmitting simultaneous pictures back to earth; a second carried conventional cameras for producing more detailed photographs that could be ejected on command and recovered in big nets strung from aircraft; * a third carried both types of cameras; and a fourth incorporated eavesdropping equipment.

The fourth version was known as the "ferret." It could pick out radar and communication centers, and pinpoint missile sites by their radio guidance signals. It could also tap microwave telephone links. The SAMOS photographs could locate enemy military targets and provide instantaneous indications of troop or supply build-ups.

The reconnaissance satellite would be subject to some of the limitations of the U-2. It could be frustrated by

* In July, 1963, the Outstanding Unit Award was presented to the 6593 Test Squadron at Hickam Air Force Base, Hawaii. The Air Force said the squadron had achieved 70 percent success in its capsule recoveries.

clouds which cover 60 percent of the earth at all times. But it could provide pictures of the northern stretches of the Soviet Union that were beyond the reach of the U-2. And it would be much less vulnerable to defensive measures. SAMOS' orbit could readily be determined by Russian tracking stations, and theoretically the satellite could be destroyed by an anti-satellite missile (the United States began experimental tests with such a system in 1963). But if it were hit by a rocket, it would burn up on re-entry into the earth's atmosphere and the evidence would be destroyed. And it would be a considerably more difficult target than a U-2 flying ten times lower.

Besides, SAMOS could carry a rocket motor which, on command from the earth, would enable it to move evasively. On the assumption that Soviet spy satellites would incorporate similar devices for evasion, the Air Force started work in 1960 on SAINT (Satellite Intercept). It was to be a maneuverable satellite which would rendezvous with an enemy vehicle in orbit and inspect it by electronic means such as television. Ultimately, it was to have the capacity to neutralize or destroy an enemy satellite.*

Another reconnaissance system also came into view during this period. It was MIDAS (Missile Defense Alarm System), designed to detect missile launchings with infrared sensors. MIDAS' weight and dimensions were virtually identical to those of SAMOS. It was fired into orbit by the same rocket and it was also produced by Lockheed.

By detecting the intense heat given off by rocket exhaust during take-off, MIDAS was to provide a thirty-minute warning of enemy attack. This would double the fifteen-minute alert of BMEWS (Ballistic Missile Early Warning System), a massive radar in Thule, Greenland, which would pick up an incoming ICBM halfway between launch and impact. MIDAS' infrared instruments were so sensitive that they could detect a lighted cigarette from a distance of eight miles. During one test launching the heat

* The project proved much more complicated than SAMOS, however, and in 1962 its operational date was extended to 1967 at the earliest.

sensors sent out signals set off by a coffee pot on the firing pad. (MIDAS encountered a series of difficulties which ran the research and development bill up close to $500,-000,000. But in May and July of 1963 the satellite succeeded in detecting missiles launched from Florida and California.)

Another satellite launched with much public fanfare in 1960 was TIROS. Its cameras were to televise cloud cover and storm conditions in order to promote better weather prediction. Such surveillance obviously could be of great value in timing SAMOS launches for moments of minimum cloud cover over the Soviet Union.* But in Senate testimony in July, 1961, James E. Webb, NASA's director, denied Soviet charges that the weather satellites were for purposes of espionage. He asserted that it was perfectly lawful for satellites to be flown over foreign territory just as ships freely sail the high seas. National sovereignty extends only to air space, Webb contended, and "as to outer space where there is no air, this is a completely open field."

The head of NASA was betraying the fears of the administration that U.S. satellites operating over Russia would be shot down by Soviet propaganda. When President Kennedy took office, he was faced with three alternatives: (1) to continue the semi-public practices of the Eisenhower Administration; (2) to shut off all official discussion and disclosures about the espionage satellites; or (3) to make the program "overt" by proposing a new "open skies" plan and submitting all satellite photographs to the United Nations.

The last recommendation was privately proposed by a group of prominent scientists at the outset of the Kennedy Administration. They argued that there was a presumption of guilt in surreptitious activities and that the Soviet Union could play upon this as justification for shooting down a SAMOS or securing a UN resolution condemning the practice. On the other hand, they con-

---

* Dr. S. Fred Singer, director of the National Satellite Weather Center at Suitland, Maryland, declared in a speech on February 20, 1963 that TIROS had been so used to plan U-2 flights over Cuba during the missile crisis in October, 1962.

tended, if the operation were placed under the UN, the Soviets would be hard-pressed to destroy SAMOS either with rockets or words.

The Kennedy Administration quickly decided that secrecy was a safer course. When SAMOS II was successfully launched on January 31, 1961—eleven days after Kennedy took office—the Pentagon prohibited the release of any details about it. This prohibition soon developed into an absolute ban on any discussion of the satellite, even in areas of prior official revelation. It was thereafter impossible to obtain official confirmation that in fact SAMOS existed. Future announcements were restricted to such words as: "A satellite employing an Atlas-Agena B booster combination was launched by the Air Force today. It is carrying a number of classified test components."

Since security, if any, had long since been breached by the original SAMOS disclosures, it was clear that the administration had international political purposes in mind in its new crackdown. The likeliest explanation was that it hoped to avoid provoking the Russians into countermeasures against SAMOS. Khrushchev had known for years that the U-2 was flying over Russia, but he said nothing until his hand was forced by the Powers incident. Might he not be inclined to maintain a similar silence on SAMOS, particularly since his own satellites were the first to fly over the United States and other nations?

The answer was quick in coming. SAMOS II was hardly off the pad before the Russians protested. Their complaint, which was formally carried to the United Nations in March, 1962, was summed up on December 3 of that year by Platon D. Morozov, the Soviet delegate to the UN Committee on the Peaceful Uses of Outer Space.

"Such observation," he said, "is just as wrong as when intelligence data are obtained by other means such as by photography made from the air. The object at which such illegal surveillance is directed constitutes a secret guarded by a sovereign state and, regardless of the means by which such an operation is carried out, it is in all cases an intrusion."

The standard reply of the United States was that a nation's sovereignty extends only to the air space above it. Officials noted that in the first three years of the space age neither the United States nor the Soviet Union had claimed its territorial sovereignty was infringed by satellite overflights. In the absence of protest or international agreement to the contrary, these officials maintained that a common law had been established, giving any nation the right to orbit satellites over another.

On January 13, 1962, the United States asserted formally that this freedom of movement in space had been endorsed by the UN General Assembly in its unanimous resolution the previous month on "international co-operation and the peaceful uses of outer space."

The resolution stipulated that international law and the United Nations Charter were to apply to outer space and that celestial bodies were not to be subject to national appropriation. The United States interpreted this as a contradiction of the Soviet argument that SAMOS violated national sovereignty.

To demonstrate its sincerity in subscribing to UN supervision of space, the United States pledged, shortly after the *UN Space Registry* was established in February of 1962, that it would list all of its satellites.

From time to time knowledgeable space watchers in the United States and Europe noted, sometimes in print, that more objects were in space than had been reported to the UN. Playing upon the deep secrecy surrounding the SAMOS program, the Russians alleged that the United States was concealing some of its launches.

These allegations imposed a nasty dilemma upon the United States Government. If it were to dispose effectively of suggestions that it was cheating, it would have to open up the SAMOS firings to much greater publicity. But this would run counter to the basic policy decision not to provoke the Russians.

Or the United States could publicly produce evidence that the unlisted objects in space were of Soviet origin. But this would expose the fact that the United States possessed a vast electronic network which kept a precise watch on all Soviet space operations. And the CIA and the

Pentagon were opposed to providing the slightest help to the Russians in compromising the network.

Their opposition was twofold. First, if it were officially admitted that the United States was eavesdropping along the Iron Curtain, nations providing the clandestine facilities might be subjected to severe Russian pressure, as they were after the U-2 incident.

The second argument was expressed in a news conference on December 6, 1962, by Arthur Sylvester: "We are trying to keep intelligence [secret], not only what we gather but how we gather it. . . . We know that lots of things that two years ago we assumed our adversaries had, they did not have. We know this by what they're spending money to get. What we are trying to do in this field is to make it as difficult as possible for them. We are trying not to wrap it up, put it on a silver platter and hand it to them. We are trying to make them spend as much time and effort as we have to."

Defense Secretary McNamara was particularly jealous of the secrecy policy. He was incensed when Hanson Baldwin, the military-affairs analyst of the *New York Times*, disclosed in June, 1962—clearly on the basis of SAMOS reports—that the Soviets were erecting concrete storage "coffins" for their ICBMs. McNamara was disturbed that Baldwin's report might have given the Russians an indication of the excellence of SAMOS. He apparently did not comprehend that he himself had exposed SAMOS' effectiveness when he announced the month before that the United States was in a position to locate and destroy Soviet missile sites.

Arrayed against McNamara and the secrecy policy were those in the State Department who saw great propaganda value in destroying the myth that the Soviets could do no wrong in space and that they had suffered fewer failures than the United States. This viewpoint prevailed in September, 1962, when the government claimed that in the two previous years the Russians had failed in five attempts to reach the planets—two to Mars and three to Venus.

In trying to substantiate the claim, the fears of the CIA and the Pentagon were realized. A Pandora's box of black electronic arts was opened. Out of it came revelations of a world that was unknown to the vast majority of Americans, if not to the Soviet leaders.

The United States had detected the Russian space failures through a surveillance system known as SPADATS (Space Detection and Tracking System). It was a complicated network of electronic fences, stretching across the United States, and sensitive radios and radars hidden along the perimeter of the Soviet Union. The network was so effective that no Soviet rocket could get off the ground without its being known within a few minutes at the North American Air Defense Command in Colorado Springs and at the CIA and the White House.

The first point of detection was a radar and communications system in the Middle East. It was centered in Turkey at small Black Sea towns such as Zonguldak, Sinop and Samsun. There, powerful radars and listening gear monitored the countdowns and rocket launchings at the main Soviet missile sites near the Aral Sea.

The radars, which went into operation in 1955, could reach at least 3,000 miles. The scope of the listening gear was suggested by an advertisement which slipped uncensored into *Aviation Week* on February 25, 1963:

> Modern electronic counter-measures are an important deterrent and intelligence tool for the military services. "Ferreting" ECM systems—for the detection, location and analysis of foreign electromagnetic radiation associated with radar, missile command and communications—are a demonstrated capability of Babcock's military products division, where operational ferreting systems are in production. . . .

Another indication of the potential of the eavesdropping equipment got out the following month. Senator Barry Goldwater, a general in the Air Force Reserve, disclosed that an "electronic ear," operating in planes off Cuba, was so sensitive that it could pick up the sound of various machines to the point of detecting a small generator in operation.

At the same time, the Pentagon was perfecting super-range "over the horizon" radar and the Air Force had installed highly sensitive atmospheric pressure gear which could provide instantaneous indications of a Soviet missile launching.

After a rocket had been detected by the Middle East system, it would next be picked up by the BMEWS radar in Greenland, which kept watch over the Arctic, or by the large saucer-like radar at Shemya in the Aleutians, which tracked Soviet test rockets as they flew out over the Pacific.

The third point of detection and the most precise was NAVSPASUR (Naval Space Surveillance System), an electronic fence stretching from Georgia to Southern California. Transmitters in Alabama, Texas and Arizona created the fence by sending out a beam of radio signals which were deflected back to one of four receiving stations when an object passed through them.

By running the angles of deflection through a massive computer at Dahlgren, Virginia, it was possible to determine a satellite's orbit, position, size and weight (NAVSPASUR was so sensitive that a piece of wire one-sixteenth of an inch in diameter was detected in 1960 when it separated from a U.S. satellite). It was also possible to calculate the exact time and place of launch and predict the future path of the satellite.

Many officials felt that too much was being revealed about these secret electronic systems. Nevertheless, NASA continued until April, 1963, to list Soviet launchings in the Satellite Situation Reports it issued twice a month.

Then there was an abrupt and unexplained return to the previous practice of secrecy. The House Information Subcommittee sought an explanation, but NASA spokesmen said all they knew was that the tracking system was controlled by the Pentagon, which refused to release the information.

This prompted the subcommittee's chairman, John E. Moss, the California Democrat, to observe: "The taxpayers certainly should not be called upon to spend billions of dollars on our space programs without being given all the facts necessary to make an intelligent judgment as to whether we are behind, ahead, or at least keeping pace with, Russian space efforts."

Despite the fact that the policy of secrecy was perpetuating a false image of United States inferiority in space, the administration held to its practice of suppressing the truth about Soviet failures. Despite the fact that nuclear test-ban negotiations were threatened by public ignorance of the elaborate array of U.S. detection devices, the administration refused to embark upon even a modest program of education.

It was a strange anomaly, indeed. The United States was seeking to hold its tongue about secrets that were no longer secret to the Russians. In November, 1962, the Soviets, indicating their complete awareness, dropped their long-standing demand for a ban on spy-in-the-sky satellites. This opened the way to a United States–Soviet agreement on the peaceful uses of outer space. Why the Russian about-face? Electronic experts suggested the Russians were developing a spy satellite of their own and did not wish to be inhibited by international prohibitions on such devices.

Khrushchev's son-in-law, Alexei Adzhubei, the editor of *Izvestia*, seemed to substantiate this theory in a speech in Helsinki, Finland, on September 2, 1963.

"One Western paper," Adzhubei said, "has published a picture taken of Moscow by a satellite from a height of 750 kilometers [about 465 miles] in which the *Izvestia* building is plainly discernible. We do not publish pictures of this kind, but I believe that we could print a similar picture of New York taken by one of our satellites."

23

Black Radio

THE EMERGENCE of the transistor radio in the 1950s has intensified one of the most shadowy, elusive and least-known electronic aspects of the Cold War. This is the war of words, conducted on the airwaves by combatants who are thousands of miles apart—and who will never meet.

Daily, East and West beam hundreds of hours of propaganda broadcasts at each other in an unrelenting babble of competition for the minds of their listeners. The low-price transistor has given this hidden war a new importance. Millions of people in the Middle East, Latin America and Asia who cannot read, can nevertheless be reached by the propaganda of both sides.

The Invisible Government is heavily engaged in "black radio" * operations of every conceivable type. So is the Communist bloc.

United States radio activities have ranged all the way from overt, openly acknowledged and advertised programs

---

* To intelligence officers, the term "black radio" can have a specialized meaning, to describe a radio that is captured and then operated as if all were normal in order to deceive the opposition. The Germans successfully undermined the British Operation Northpole during World War II by using this technique. Parachutists dropped by British Intelligence were lured into traps by Dutch underground radios that had been captured by the Nazis. In this chapter, however, the term is used in its broader sense, to describe radio operations in general where they are controlled directly or indirectly by an intelligence apparatus.

of the Voice of America to highly secret CIA transmitters in the Middle East and other areas of the world. In between is a whole spectrum of black, gray, secret and semi-secret radio operations. The CIA's Radio Swan, because it became operationally involved at the Bay of Pigs, never enjoyed more than the thinnest of covers. But Radio Swan was a relatively small black-radio operation. Other radio operations, financed and controlled in whole or in part by the Invisible Government, are more skillfully concealed and much bigger.

Some are hybrids—broadcasting organizations that solicit funds from business corporations and the general public but also receive secret funds from the CIA. While allegedly "private" organizations, they receive daily policy direction from the State Department and take orders from the CIA.

In some cases, it is possible, indeed probable, that lower-level employees of such an organization are unaware of the true point of control of the particular activity. A secret CIA transmitter in Lebanon, to take a random example, would be run directly by CIA officers. But in a larger, hybrid operation, knowledge of financing and control by Washington might be limited to a handful of top executives.

For purposes of this book, it is sufficient to note that an inevitable by-product—as in clandestine operations generally—is that the American public has been beguiled by some of this allegedly "private" broadcasting work. It has contributed its gift dollars to such "private" activity, entirely unaware that it is already supporting the same broadcasting operation with its tax dollars, through the CIA.

Black-radio operations fall into two categories—transmitting and receiving. Besides broadcasting, both sides carefully monitor each other's broadcasts to learn what the opposition is saying.

For the United States, the task of monitoring and recording foreign radio broadcasts, by friendly as well as unfriendly countries, is performed by the CIA. The intelligence agency's listening posts all over the globe capture every major broadcast of a foreign nation on tape. Daily, this extremely valuable foreign broadcast information is edited, correlated, mimeographed and distributed to a wide list of consumers from a CIA office in downtown Washington.* The consumers are asked not to mention the name or initials of the arm of the CIA which performs this work. However, this broadcast monitoring service, which is more or less openly acknowledged by the CIA, is about the most "overt" operation the agency conducts.

Some idea of the magnitude of the CIA's task, in monitoring Communist bloc broadcasts alone, can be gained from a speech made on January 30, 1963, by John Richardson, Jr., the president of the Free Europe Committee, which operates Radio Free Europe.

Radio stations of thirteen Communist countries, he said, "transmit more than four thousand hours of radio programming abroad every week in sixty-three languages. Leaving nothing to chance, the broadcast languages include even Esperanto. . . . The Soviet Union leads this radio propaganda parade with some thirteen hundred weekly hours of radio propaganda directed abroad. Red China comes second, with almost seven hundred hours weekly, followed by East Germany . . . with little Cuba in fourth place." [1]

Surprisingly, the fact that black-radio operations are conducted by the United States was indirectly admitted by President Eisenhower in his Middle East speech to the UN General Assembly on August 13, 1958:

"The United Nations Assembly has on three occasions, in 1947, 1949 and 1950, passed resolutions designed to stop the projecting of irresponsible broadcasts from one nation into the homes of citizens of other nations . . . we all know that these resolutions have been violated in many directions in the Near East. If we, the United States, have been at fault, we stand ready to be corrected."

For the background to this unusual passage in the President's speech, one must look to 1956 and Suez. In the aftermath of the abortive Anglo-French-Israeli invasion of

* Less well known are the CIA's mimeographed summaries of the foreign press.

Egypt, Nasser increased his efforts to bring the entire Arab world under his domination. A major weapon in this campaign was Radio Cairo.

Up until 1956, the British-controlled Near East Broadcasting Station at Zyghi, on the south coast of Cyprus, was the most powerful propaganda voice in the Middle East. NEBS was a British black-radio operation, ostensibly under private ownership.

Beginning in 1956, Nasser's radio supplanted NEBS. Cairo spread the most violent sort of propaganda against its Arab neighbors and the United States. Its "Voice of the Arabs" was on the air from 6:30 A.M. to 1:15 A.M. the next morning, broadcasting throughout the Middle East and as far south as the Belgian Congo from two seventy-kilowatt transmitters on the Mokattam Hills overlooking Cairo, and from two other transmitters on the Nile Delta.

By 1958 Radio Cairo was openly urging bloody revolution in Iraq, Jordan and Lebanon. In February of that year Nasser had seized power in Syria and proclaimed the United Arab Republic. Iraq's King Feisal II countered by joining with his Hashemite cousin King Hussein of Jordan to form the Arab Union.

On May 2, 1958, as an example, Radio Cairo broadcast to Baghdad: "Arise, my brethren on the police force and in its army in Iraq! Stand side by side with your brothers and your people against your enemies! The freedom of Iraq is in your hands."

Since Iraq was the world's sixth largest oil producer and the only Arab member of the pro-Western Baghdad pact, the CIA felt this kind of talk from Radio Cairo could not go unanswered. As a result, by 1958 the CIA had set up a series of clandestine radio stations in the Middle East and along its fringes to counteract the influence of Radio Cairo.

Meanwhile, a crisis was brewing in Lebanon over the selection of a successor to President Camille Chamoun, whose term was expiring. The CIA had helped elect Chamoun, then turned against him.

On July 14 Brigadier General Abdul Karim el-Kassem took over Iraq in a pre-dawn coup which had not been "clearly predicted"[2] by the CIA, according to Allen Dulles. In the coup, twenty-three-year-old King Feisal and his uncle, the crown prince, were murdered. Premier Nuri as-Said, captured while trying to escape dressed as a woman, was also killed.

The next day Eisenhower, in Operation Blue Bat, sent the Marines into Lebanon to shore up the Chamoun government. Two days later the British airlifted 2,000 troops into Jordan.

Radio Cairo exulted in the bloodshed in Baghdad and urged the people of Jordan to rise up and butcher King Hussein. But now, as the CIA transmitters got busy, new voices were heard on the airwaves.

This obscure dispatch appeared in American newspapers on July 23, 1958, for example:

BEIRUT, July 23 (UPI)—A second mysterious Arab radio station went on the air yesterday calling itself the "Voice of Justice" and claiming to be broadcasting from Syria.

Its program heard here consisted of bitter criticism against Soviet Russia and Soviet Premier Khrushchev. Earlier the "Voice of Iraq" went on the air with attacks against the Iraqi revolutionary government.

The "Voice of Justice" called Khrushchev the "hangman of Hungary" and warned the people of the Middle East they would suffer the same fate as the Hungarians if the Russians get a foothold in the Middle East."[3]

On August 14 Egyptian officials charged that seven secret radio stations were operating in the Middle East, attacking the UAR and Nasser personally. Cairo said two stations were transmitting from the French Riviera, and said others were in British Aden, Jordan, Lebanon, Cyprus and Kenya. Before the revolt in Iraq, there had been another in Baghdad, the statement said. The carefully worded announcement stopped barely short of mentioning the CIA.

The Egyptian spokesman said the Voice of America was heard regularly in Egypt also, but added: "The Voice of

America is not in the same category with clandestine stations." Asked if there was any evidence of who was behind these secret stations, the official replied laconically: "There is no way to be certain. Certainly they are too expensive for any small nations or groups to maintain without help." [4]

The Egyptian official had put his finger on one of the soft spots in black-radio operations. These operations are indeed expensive, and one of the most nagging problems for such radio stations is to explain the source of funds.

One short-wave radio station in the United States with an interesting history is WRUL, with offices in Manhattan as the World Wide Broadcasting System, Inc. In his fascinating book about Sir William Stephenson, the head of British Intelligence in the United States during World War II, H. Montgomery Hyde maintains that WRUL was penetrated by British Intelligence in the war years and subsidized by it through intermediaries.

In more recent times, WRUL has taken a more overt part in Cold War operations. As will be described, it joined with Radio Swan in broadcasting the programs of "Havana Rose."

In 1954 WRUL received a letter of commendation from the Castillo-Armas government of Guatemala, thanking the station for its services during the revolt against Arbenz. The letter was from Jose Toron, who had operated a clandestine "Free Guatemala" radio station before the Communist government was overthrown.

Thus, WRUL has been linked with at least two CIA operations—the Bay of Pigs (through Radio Swan) and the Guatemala coup in 1954.

Not long after Cairo complained about clandestine transmitters in the Middle East, Konstantin Zinchenko, the head of the press department of the Soviet State Committee for Foreign Cultural Relations, told a news conference in Moscow that the United States had set up a whole series of secret radios aimed at making trouble for the Soviet Union. Among those he mentioned was Radio Liberation.

Radio Liberation, which changed its name to Radio

Liberty in 1959, is an avowedly private organization with offices at 30 East 42d Street in New York. It broadcasts exclusively to the Soviet Union, twenty-four hours a day, from seventeen transmitters in three locations—Lampertheim, West Germany; Pals, near Barcelona; and Taipeh, Formosa.

Its programing center is a rebuilt former airport building near Munich at Oberwiesenfeld, which was once Hitler's airfield. An official of Radio Liberty said the majority of its 1,200 employees are in Munich, but that the organization also has offices in Paris and Rome, as well as New York, Formosa and Spain.

Radio Liberty does not go to the public for funds. It says it is supported by foundations but does not list them anywhere. It insists that it receives no government funds, directly or indirectly, but says its budget is "classified."

"We do not advocate revolution," the official said, in explaining why Radio Liberty had changed its name from the more controversial Radio Liberation. "When the revolution comes, it will have to come from within. In the meantime, we can feed them ammunition."

According to its official booklet, "Radio Liberty is supported by the American Committee for Liberation, founded in 1951 by a group of private Americans who formed a working partnership with the free emigration from the USSR." It first went on the air on March 1, 1953. The American Committee for Liberation also supports the Institute for the Study of the USSR, Mannhardtstrasse, 6, Munich, which describes itself as a scholarly organization that puts out a number of publications on Russia, including *Who's Who in the USSR.*

Radio Liberty broadcasts a heavy diet of news to its Soviet audience. In 1956 it broadcast the text of Khrushchev's secret speech to the 20th Communist Party Congress. In 1961 it broadcast the fact that the Russians had resumed nuclear tests. Neither event, of course, had been disclosed to the Russian people by the Soviet government. The Russians, in turn, have tried hard to jam Radio Liberty.

Possibly, they have taken other steps as well. In 1954

two Radio Liberty employees died under mysterious circumstances in Munich. In September, Leonid Karas, a writer on the radio's Byelorussia desk was found drowned. In November, Abo Fatalibey, head of the Azerbaijan desk, was murdered and stuffed under the sofa in the apartment of a Russian named Mikhail Ismailov.

Police assumed the body was that of Ismailov, a fellow émigré. At the last moment the coffin—which someone noticed was too short for the six-foot Ismailov—was opened. The body was definitely identified as that of Fatalibey, the Radio Liberty official. Ismailov had vanished. Radio Liberty does not discount the possibility that the drowning and the murder were the work of the KGB.

Another interesting case was that of Anatoli Skachkov, a Russian émigré who joined Radio Liberty on January 1, 1957. Skachkov died on July 22, 1959. On November 5, 1962, *Izvestia* carried an article which accused Radio Liberty of being staffed by CIA men. It listed eight alleged agents by name. In the course of the article, *Izvestia* said Skachkov had fallen from favor with American intelligence:

"He was seized at his place of employment and sent to a mental hospital. The next day two Americans, Valerio and Sanker, bearing flowers and a bottle of cognac, visited Skachkov. After their visit, he died. The physicians attributed his death to poisoning."

The tale of poisoned cognac is colorful, but Radio Liberty tells a different story. According to the radio station, Skachkov was an alcoholic who developed a persecution complex. As a result, he was committed to the State Institute for the Mentally Disturbed. He died, said Radio Liberty, of "a heart attack." Radio Liberty employed a Joseph Valerio and a Paul Sanker in its news department, but "neither Valerio or Sanker ever visited Skachkov, so the whole premise is a fabrication."

But the continuing Soviet attacks on Radio Liberty and its present and former employees provide some indication that this radio station "supported by a group of private American citizens" is reaching the Russian people in sufficient numbers to be irritating to the Soviet leadership.

341

By far the biggest, and from time to time the most controversial, of these radio operations is Radio Free Europe, which says it is a "private non-profit, non-government network broadcasting through the Iron Curtain to eighty million captive people in Poland, Czechoslovakia, Hungary, Romania and Bulgaria."

One distinction between Radio Free Europe and Radio Liberty is that RFE broadcasts exclusively to the five satellite nations, while Radio Liberty broadcasts exclusively to the Soviet Union.

Radio Free Europe was born in 1949, with the formation of the National Committee for a Free Europe. In 1950 the committee's Crusade for Freedom fund drive was launched by General Eisenhower and General Lucius D. Clay, the hero of the 1948–49 Berlin airlift. The purpose of the fund drive was to raise money for RFE.

"We need powerful radio stations abroad," Eisenhower said in launching the crusade, "operated without government restrictions."

Clay struck the same theme. He praised the Voice of America but said: "There seemed to me to be needed another voice—a voice less tempered perhaps by the very dignity of government; a tough, slugging voice, if you please."

In 1950–51, the directors of the National Committee for a Free Europe * included Clay, Allen Dulles, C. D. Jackson, who became Eisenhower's psychological warfare adviser, and A. A. Berle, Jr., who participated in the Bay of Pigs operation a decade later.

RFE has twenty-eight transmitters at three sites. Two locations are in West Germany, at Biblis, near Frankfurt, and at Holzkirchen, near Munich. The third site is at

* The committee is now known as the Free Europe Committee, Inc., 2 Park Avenue, New York. The Crusade for Freedom is now the Radio Free Europe Fund. The Committee engages in a multitude of other activities. It publishes *East Europe* magazine (22,000 copies a month) and works with Eastern European exile groups "engaged in the struggle for eventual freedom of their countries." The Committee has five operating divisions: RFE, Communist Bloc Operations, Exile Political Organizations, Free World Operations and West European Operations.

Gloria, near Lisbon. RFE headquarters, like Radio Liberty, is at Munich. The organization employs about 1,500 persons.

"We're supported by contributions from the American people, mainly from the Radio Free Europe Fund," a spokesman said. He added that RFE is "privately managed and privately financed." However, he said "we work within the published policy of the United States Government."

Asked how it went about making sure that its broadcasts were consistent with United States foreign policy, he replied: "We read the *New York Times*."

Are any government funds behind RFE? "No," was the reply, "but I prefer to put it positively—we are supported by voluntary contributions." RFE's budget figures, however, are not published anywhere.

For a time, RFE dabbled in some intriguing balloon operations. In 1953 it set up something called the Free Europe Press, which began wafting rubber and plastic balloons filled with propaganda materials to Eastern Europe. For a time the balloon barrage went under the code name "Operation Prospero."

In February, 1956, the Czech Government charged that a balloon released by RFE had caused the crash of a Czech airliner on January 18 of that year in the Tatra Mountains of Slovakia. The crash killed twenty-two and injured four.

Moscow also protested the balloons, and Hungary chimed in that American balloons had caused three Hungarian air crashes. RFE replied that the balloons were not dangerous, that the "captive nations" had "attempted to shoot down balloons by aircraft and ground fire" and that Czech intelligence had tried twice "to blow up our balloon sites in Western Germany."

RFE called in its balloons during the Hungarian revolt. The program was not revived.

RFE figured in another cloak-and-dagger episode in December, 1959, when it charged that "a Communist diplomat" had put lethal amounts of atropine in the salt shakers of the radio station's cafeteria in Munich.

If taken in sufficient quantity, atropine can cause

343

delirium, convulsions, coma or death. The U. S. Army Counter Intelligence Corps investigated and charged that Jaroslav Nemec, the vice-consul of the Czech consulate in Salzburg, Austria, had given the spiked salt shakers to a Communist agent "for placement in the Radio Free Europe cafeteria in Munich." The case was quietly dropped the next month, when the Munich public prosecutor said the amount of poison in the salt cellars had not been sufficient to cause serious harm.

At times, RFE has come under critical attack for the content of its broadcasts to Eastern Europe. On July 9, 1959, for example, there were news reports from Warsaw that the United States Ambassador to Poland, Jacob D. Beam, had protested RFE's broadcasts because he felt they contained misinformation and too blatant a propaganda line. At his press conference the same day, Secretary of State Christian A. Herter appeared to confirm the reports; he said any recommendations from Beam "will be very carefully studied."

But it was RFE's role in the Hungarian revolt of 1956 that brought the most criticism and controversy upon it. At the heart of the issue was the extremely touchy question of whether United States foreign policy should be aimed at the "liberation" of Eastern Europe.

"In thirteen years," an RFE executive explained, "Radio Free Europe has incurred a heavy moral responsibility. We must be extremely careful that what we say cannot lead to an ineffective uprising." Obviously, he had Hungary in mind.

Nevertheless, a recent RFE fund-appeal booklet, *Your Money's Worth*, illustrates that the radio station still speaks with a militant voice. "The captive people," the appeal said, "desire freedom and do everything reasonable in their power to obtain it. . . . Radio Free Europe helps the East Europeans resist Communism . . . helps them keep alive their faith in freedom. . . . Support Radio Free Europe . . . it is one of the few ways *you* as a private citizen can take an *active* part in the fight against Communism . . . bring the battle to the Kremlin's doorstep."

344

The Soviet role in Hungary was a sickening spectacle to civilized men everywhere. In the first phase, Moscow seemed willing to grant Hungary a measure of freedom. Then Russian tanks rolled into Budapest and brutally crushed the Hungarian patriots.

In the aftermath of the blood bath, questions were widely raised about RFE's role. Had it incited the Hungarians to revolt? Had it held out false promises of Western aid, knowing that this aid would not come? Was RFE, to put it bluntly, partly responsible for the carnage in Budapest?

Various tribunals examined this question, but little was said publicly about some more subtle and basic underlying questions.

These questions began with the Voice of America, the official voice of the United States Government. It is an organ of the United States Information Agency, and it broadcasts around the globe in thirty-six languages.

The Voice spends $22,000,000 a year. Forty percent of its programing is aimed at Communist countries. (In West Berlin, a huge 300,000-watt station called RIAS—Radio in the American Sector—broadcasts around the clock to East Berlin and East Germany. It is said to be under the USIA.) In 1963 work was completed on a gigantic transmitter complex at Greenville, North Carolina, giving the Voice the most powerful long-range broadcasting station in the world.

From all this, it should be obvious that news and propaganda broadcasts across national boundaries to other nations, particularly behind the Iron Curtain, are among the mechanisms of United States foreign policy. On the face of it, therefore, it would seem logical that the United States Government could scarcely allow a competing organization to broadcast, as it pleased, material that might affect relations between governments, incite to revolt, or even involve the United States in military action. It did not seem likely, in other words, that it could allow a "private" broadcasting organization to conduct the foreign policy of the United States.

Consequently, lying ominously just below the surface

345

of the various inquiries into RFE's role in the Hungarian revolt was the larger question of whether the United States Government had erred in permitting RFE to broadcast any degree of encouragement to the Hungarians that could not be backed up by U.S. military assistance.

However, the post-Hungary inquiries were not conducted in these terms. To do so would have opened up the entire sensitive question of whether and/or to what extent RFE received policy guidance, funds and direction from the CIA and the State Department.*

The charges against Radio Free Europe began in Moscow and soon spread to the free world, where they were picked up by *Freies Wort*, the organ of West Germany's Free Democratic Party. They were aired further when three revolutionary leaders who had escaped from Hungary said at a press conference in Bonn, on November 19, that RFE had broadcast "more than the truth." On November 29 Anna Kethly, the Hungarian Social Democratic leader who had escaped to the West, dealt RFE another blow when she said of its broadcasts: "The intentions were good but the results were not always happy."

In New York, RFE countered by calling Miss Kethly's statement "utterly without foundation and wholly incorrect." A spokesman said broadcasts promising Western military aid to Hungary were the work of a "Communist radio located in East Germany. These Communist programs were broadcast in the name of Radio Free Europe."

There were then three inquiries into RFE's role. The West German Government set up a commission to study the charges (since RFE was headquartered in Munich on West German soil). RFE turned over to it three miles of tape containing all its broadcasts to Hungary before, during and after the revolt.

On January 25, 1957, Chancellor Konrad Adenauer reported the results of this inquiry at a press conference.

* About the furthest anyone went was Edwin A. Lahey, a veteran Washington correspondent, who said in a December 15, 1956, dispatch from Munich in the *Chicago Daily News*: "The United States Government probably supports RFE with 'unvouchered funds' but this has never been officially established."

346

Charges that RFE had promised the Hungarians armed assistance by the West "do not correspond with the facts," he said. "Remarks, however, were made that were subject to misinterpretation. The matter has been discussed and personnel changes have resulted. I believe we can consider the matter closed for the time being."

Adenauer's report seemed internally contradictory. On the one hand, it found the charges to be incorrect. On the other hand, it said there had been a shake-up at Radio Free Europe.

A second inquiry was conducted by a special committee of the Council of Europe, an organization of Western governments formed in 1949 to deal mainly with social problems. In its report on April 27, 1957, the committee said the charge that RFE had promised "military aid from the West was proved to be without ground." But it said one RFE news broadcast "could easily have led to misunderstandings."

The report added it was "regrettable that Radio Free Europe is still entirely financed by the U.S.A. . . . Radio Free Europe depends entirely on American funds and is consequently a purely American affair . . . actual political leadership and the last word rest with the American management."

In June, 1957, a United Nations special committee on Hungary came in with its verdict on RFE:

"Listeners had the feeling that Radio Free Europe promised help . . . the general tone of these broadcasts aroused an expectation of support. . . . In a tense atmosphere such as that prevailing in Hungary during these critical weeks . . . the generally hopeful tone of such broadcasts may well have been overemphasized in the process of passing from mouth to mouth. . . .

"The attitude of the Hungarian people towards foreign broadcasting was perhaps best summed up by the student . . . who said: 'It was our only hope, and we tried to console ourselves with it.' It would appear that certain broadcasts by Radio Free Europe helped to create an impression that suppot might be forthcoming for the Hungarians. The Committee feels that in such circumstances the greatest restraint and circumspection are called for in international broadcasting."

The three cautiously phrased reports, in other words, found in varying degree that RFE's broadcasts, while they did not promise aid in so many words, "helped to create an impression," as the UN put it, that assistance might be on the way.

One RFE broadcast that might have contributed to this was a news report of Ambassador Henry Cabot Lodge's words in the UN. Lodge said the Hungarian resistance had given the UN "a brief moment in which to mobilize the conscience of the world on your behalf. We are seizing that moment and we will not fail you."

Another RFE broadcast during the revolt gave instructions on how to blow up attacking Soviet tanks.

While none of the inquiries produced any evidence that RFE actually promised military aid, there is no doubt that it encouraged the revolutionary fighters. For example, one script broadcast to Hungary by RFE on November 3, as Soviet tanks ringed Budapest, said:

"The Soviet monster stands at our gates . . . the eight days' victorious revolution have turned Hungary into a free land. . . .Neither Khrushchev nor the whole of the Soviet army have the power to oppress this new liberty. . . . What can you do against Hungary, you Soviet legions? It is in vain to pierce Hungarian souls with your bayonets. You can destroy and shoot and kill: our freedom will now forevermore defy you. . . ." [5]

In his book *The Bridge at Andau*, James A. Michener said that RFE did not incite the uprising "but this radio did broadcast messages of freedom and is presumably still doing so. Are we now prepared to assume direct responsibility for these messages? How long can we broadcast such messages without assuming direct responsibility for our words?" [6]

Michener's question is well worth pondering. The effect of RFE's words is nowhere more heartbreakingly recorded than in the broadcasts from inside Hungary in the dying hours of the revolt. Better than any UN or other investigation, they reflect how the men and women inside Hungary, whether rightly or wrongly, regarded the role of RFE.

On the afternoon of November 5, Radio Free Rakoczi broadcast this message from inside Hungary at 13:48 hours: [7]

"Attention, Radio Free Europe, hello attention. This is Roka speaking. The radio of revolutionary youth . . . continual bombing. . . . Help, help, help . . . Radio Free Europe . . . forward our request. Forward our news. Help! Help!"

November 6, 13:52 hours:

"We appeal to the conscience of the world. . . . Why cannot you hear the call for help of our murdered women and children? Peoples of the world! Hear the call for help of a small nation! . . . This is Radio Rakoczi, Hungary . . . Radio Free Europe, Munich! Radio Free Europe, Munich! Answer! Have you received our transmission?"

15:05 hours:

". . . Attention, attention, Munich! Munich! Take immediate action. In the Dunapentele area we urgently need medicine, bandages, arms, food and ammunition! Drop them for us by parachute."

And, finally, on November 7 at 09:35 hours:

"Must we appeal once again?

"Do you love liberty? . . . So do we.

"Do you have wives and children? . . . So have we.

"We have wounded . . . who have given their blood for the sacred cause of liberty, but we have no bandages . . . no medicine. . . . And what shall we give to our children who are asking for bread? The last piece of bread has been eaten.

"In the name of all that is dear to you . . . we ask you to help. . . . Those who have died for liberty . . . accuse you who are able to help and who have not helped. . . . We have read an appeal to the UN and every honest man. . . .

"Radio Free Europe, Munich! Free Europe, Munich!"

24

CIA's Guano Paradise

"THERE ARE THREE coconut palm trees on Great Swan Island at the present time," the State Department brochure discouragingly told Americans who inquired about retiring to an island paradise in the Caribbean. "There are no poisonous snakes, but the islands are infested with hordes of lizards ranging in size from only an inch to over three feet."

The vision of thirty-six-inch lizards slithering underfoot would likely deter any potential visitor who had written to the State Department for travel information about the little-known Swan Islands, which, on the map, beckon attractively as a speck in the western Caribbean near Honduras.

But the department's brochure, prepared for just such inquiries, had even more hideously disenchanting news. "It has been necessary," it said, "to construct the few houses on the island on piers and to take other steps to keep the lizards from overrunning them."

The water, the brochure added, "is exceptionally clear and blue and abounding in different types of fish. Ocean bathing is considered dangerous as a constant watch must be kept for shark and barracuda."

The State Department's disheartening travel folder might, just possibly, have been prompted by the fact that Great Swan Island, as late as 1964, was the site of a covert CIA radio station broadcasting to Cuba, Mexico, Central America and the northern tier of South America.

Not that any prospective tourist would have been likely to stumble on the island. There is, naturally, no commercial airline service to the CIA's airstrip. The only boat takes five days to ply between Tampa and the island and carries a pungent cargo of bananas and fertilizer.* And normally anyone visiting the island must have a secret clearance.

Despite these precautions, the story of the bedeviled efforts to conceal the CIA's hand on Swan Island provides an episode of comic relief.

The Swan Islands are really two islands, Great Swan (usually known simply as Swan Island), which is a mile and a half long and half a mile wide, and Little Swan. There is also a reef, called Bobby Cay. The islands are due south of the western tip of Cuba, and ninety-seven miles north of Punte Patuca, Honduras. They are said to have been named for a seventeenth-century pirate who used them as a base.

Like the lair of Ian Fleming's nefarious Doctor No, the CIA's Caribbean isle is made entirely of guano, the accumulated droppings of sea fowl. The United States has claimed the islands since 1863, but then, so has Honduras.

When the CIA received approval to mount the operation against Cuba that grew into the Bay of Pigs, it was decided first to soften up Castro's island psychologically by means of radio broadcasts.

By 1960 Radio Swan was on the air. Initially, its mission was confined to propaganda broadcasts designed to undermine the Castro regime. Gradually, as the Bay of Pigs invasion planning progressed, the radio station was assigned a more militant role. During the invasion, as has been seen, Radio Swan broadcast coded messages, appeals for uprisings among the Cuban populace and armed forces, and instructions in the art of sabotage. But back in May of 1960, there had to be some public explanation for the mysterious new fifty-kilowatt station that suddenly began to broadcast from Swan Island.

And so it was that something called the Gibraltar Steam-

* The boat service is operated by Hamilton Bros., Inc., a Honduran company, according to the State Department brochure.

ship Corporation, then of 437 Fifth Avenue, New York, announced publicly that it had leased land on Swan Island to operate a radio station. (Officials of the line said that the Gibraltar Steamship Corporation had not owned a steamship for ten years.)

Horton H. Heath, who described himself as "commercial manager" of the station, explained that Radio Swan would broadcast music, soap operas and news. "It is strictly a commercial venture," he announced to the press. "We plan to get advertisers. We haven't got any yet, but are negotiating."

But who owned Gibraltar Steamship?

Walter G. Lohr, of Baltimore, who said he was a stockholder, identified the president of Gibraltar as Thomas Dudley Cabot, of Weston, Massachusetts, a banker and the former president of the United Fruit Company, and the director, in 1951, of the State Department Office of International Security Affairs. Appropriately, considering his new capacity, Cabot was also president and director of Godfrey L. Cabot, Inc., the world's largest producer of carbon black.

Another stockholder was publicly identified at the time as Sumner Smith, a Boston businessman who claimed that his family owned Swan Island. Horton Heath explained that the Gibraltar Steamship Corporation was leasing the land for the radio station from Sumner Smith, who was chairman of the board of Abington Textile Machinery Works, 19 Congress Street, Boston.

When a reporter for the *Miami Herald* reached Smith in Boston in June, 1960, he fended off questions about Radio Swan by saying: "Speak to the government."

But the government professed ignorance of the radio station. In answer to a question at the time, a State Department spokesman had replied: "The only station that I know anything about on Swan Island is a United States Weather Bureau station." (And it was true that the United States had operated such a station on Swan Island intermittently since 1914.)

The United States Information Agency did go so far as to say it had planned a project similar to Radio Swan but had abandoned the idea because of "interference and licensing problems."

Peculiarly, the Federal Communications Commission, which is required by law to license all radio stations operating from United States territory, did not license Radio Swan or the Gibraltar Steamship Corporation.

"We don't know who owns the island," an FCC spokesman explained lamely.

The State Department suffered no such doubts. It firmly listed * Swan Island as a "possession," and had consistently rejected Honduran claims.

And so Gibraltar Steamship and Radio Swan were in operation. It did not take long for Havana, stung by the propaganda broadcasts, to bark back. As early as June 21, 1960, Castro's Radio Mambi, in Havana, complained that "a counterrevolutionary radio station, supported by U.S. dollars, is now active on Swan."

Things were going reasonably smoothly for the CIA, however, until the Hondurans began to get fidgety over the funny business taking place on what they insisted was *their* mound of guano.

The trouble had its roots in the fact that a 1960 U.S. census had been taken on Swan Island. In March of that year, a two-star admiral had been piped ashore to count noses on Great Swan. (Only birds lived on Little Swan). Rear Admiral H. Arnold Karo, the director of the United States Coast and Geodetic Survey, stopped off to take the census during a voyage of the survey ship *Explorer*.

In April, with much fanfare, it was announced in Washington that the population of Swan Island was twenty-eight, a drop of four since 1950. In Tegucigalpa, Honduras, a group of students reacted indignantly to the claim of sovereignty implied by the taking of the 1960 census. They

---

* Most recently in *Geographic Report*, No. 4, February 7, 1963, The Geographer, Department of State. It should be understood that the State Department claimed U.S. *sovereignty* over the Swan Islands; this did not mean private individuals could not own property on the island, as the Smith family claimed it did. The State Department brochure on the islands said that a letter from Sumner Smith, dated February 19, 1956, "states that he, as agent, represents certain owners."

353

announced plans to organize an expedition to plant their country's flag on Swan Island. And in July, thirteen armed Hondurans arrived off Swan Island. The invaders were repulsed single-handedly by John Hamilton, a Cayman Islander who was the Weather Bureau's native cook.

From their boat, the Hondurans shouted that they were coming ashore to place a marker on the beach claiming Swan Island as their own. "Leave your guns in the boat," the intrepid cook ordered. The Hondurans meekly complied. They came ashore, unarmed, sang the Honduran national anthem, took their own census and planted their flag.

In Washington, the State Department announced solemnly that the government was awaiting a report from its embassy in Tegucigalpa on the illegal landing by the Hondurans.

On Swan Island, the CIA took direct action to smooth things over. It invited the Hondurans to lunch. Horton Heath announced that all was well.

But in October the dispute got into the United Nations. Francisco Milla Bermudez, the permanent Honduran representative to the UN, told the General Assembly, on October 3, that the United States had occupied Swan Island "against the right and will" of his government. "Historically, geographically and juridically," he declared, "the Swan Islands are and always will be Honduran territory."

But the United States claim to the islands was solidly based on guano, specifically the Guano Act of 1856. Under it, the President could issue a certificate when an American citizen discovered guano on an unclaimed island. This gave the discoverer the right to collect and sell the guano, a valuable fertilizer rich in phosphates. The President, at his discretion, could then designate the island as United States territory.

In 1863 such a certificate was issued for Swan Island to the New York Guano Company by Secretary of State Seward, who acted for President Lincoln. Shortly after the turn of the century, the company abandoned the islands. They were claimed in 1904 by Captain Alonzo Adams, an old salt who sailed out of Mobile, Alabama.

354

In the 1920s Honduras made several passes at the islands, but Washington warned Tegucigalpa to keep off and sent along a copy of Seward's Guano Certificate to back up its territorial claim.

For a time the United Fruit Company harvested coconuts on the island, but the 1955 hurricane swept away all but the three trees alluded to in the State Department travel brochure.

The CIA shared Swan Island with two other branches of the Federal Government: the Weather Bureau and the Federal Aviation Agency. The Weather Bureau maintained a station, staffed by eight men, to take wind direction, wind speed, temperature and humidity pressure. The FAA maintained a high-powered radio beacon as a navigational aid to pilots.

The Weather Bureau people were rotated every three to six months, since they were not allowed to bring their wives and children to Swan Island. A favorite pastime of gourmets among the government men was clonking lobsters over the head with stones in the shallow water.

The CIA set up shop in lizard-proof Quonset huts half a mile from the Weather Bureau compound. They installed their radio equipment in big trailers slung with awnings to protect the delicate electronic gear from the broiling Caribbean sun. The Cayman Islanders, imported as a labor force, lived nearby with their families in a compound called Gliddenville.

In September, 1960, Walter S. Lemmon, the president of the World Wide Broadcasting System, announced that his station, WRUL, would co-operate with Radio Swan in broadcasts to Cuba. World Wide, besides its Manhattan office, had a short-wave station at Scituate, Massachusetts. Since April, WRUL had been broadcasting to Cuba. The programs featured Miss Pepita Riera, a Cuban exile billed as "Havana Rose." Lemmon said Radio Swan would tape and rebroadcast WRUL's programs.

At the same time, Representative Roman C. Pucinski, Chicago Democrat and sponsor of an organization called Radio Free Cuba, announced that his group would also co-operate with World Wide and Radio Swan. Pucinski described Radio Free Cuba as a privately owned group that had six radio stations in Florida, including the Florida Keys, and Louisiana.

During this period, Radio Swan's programs were for the most part recorded in the New York office of the Gibraltar Steamship Corporation. Some prominent Cuban exiles taped programs for the CIA station, including Luis Conte Aguero, a former Havana radio and television commentator.

Havana Radio kept up its counter-barrage. On October 24 Castro's radio attacked the "miserable curs who speak over Radio Swan." In January, 1961, it said: "Radio Swan is not a radio station but a cage of hysterical parrots."

During the invasion, the CIA station was on the air twenty-four hours a day, transmitting romantic-sounding messages in code. At 10:57 P.M. on April 18, for example, the CIA broadcast this cryptic message in Spanish over Radio Swan: "Attention, Stanislaus, the moon is red 19 April."

Even after the invasion had collapsed, Radio Swan continued to broadcast mysterious orders to nonexistent battalions. On April 22 three days after the end of the invasion, Radio Swan ordered various detachments not to surrender—help was on the way. Orders went out over the air to "Battalion Three" to advance. "Battalion Four and Seven" were told to "proceed to Point Z."

"Mission Alborada," which means reveille in Spanish, was ordered to commence, and Squadrons Four and Five were told to protect it. At the same time, "Air Group Pluto Norte" was told to cover position "Nino Three N/S."

In the swamps and forests around the Bahia de Cochinos, some of the weary brigade survivors who heard the broadcasts as they tried to evade capture by the militia were bitter at what they felt was false encouragement by Radio Swan.

By this time, Radio Swan's cover as a private station owned by the Gibraltar Steamship Corporation had worn perilously thin. A private station that had broadcast messages in code and instructions to troops during a clandestine invasion—well, it seemed to be time to get out of town.

And that is just what Gibraltar did. It kept an office in Manhattan, but moved the entire operation to Miami in September, 1961. The "steamship" executives moved into rooms 910, 911 and 912 of the Langford Building in downtown Miami. Fred Fazakerley, a spokesman for the Gibraltar line, told a newsman that Horton Heath would be moving to Miami to take over the office. Several pieces of luggage being moved into the suite were marked with the name "George Wass," who was identified as an official of Radio Swan. Gibraltar took this listing in the Miami telephone book: *

Gibraltar SS Corp. Langfrd Bl 371–8098.

Then, silently, by a process akin to alchemy, Gibraltar Steamship faded away and was metamorphosed into a brand-new identity—the Vanguard Service Corporation, "consultants." Radio Swan fluttered into a CIA Valhalla, only to emerge as "Radio Americas."

Oddly, the Vanguard Service Corporation did not bother to move out of Gibraltar's quarters or to change its telephone number. The 1963–64 Miami telephone book still carried the same listing for Gibraltar, but it also carried this listing:

Vanguard Serv Corp consltnts Langfrd Bl 371–8098.

With a whole new *dramatis personae*, Radio Americas, now managed by one Roger Butts, continued to broadcast from Swan Island.

In 1962 an elderly New England couple, Mr. and Mrs. Prince S. Crowell, decided to visit Swan Island. Mr. Crowell's father had been a chemist for a guano company, and the adventurous couple occupied their leisure time with visits far and wide to the scene of bygone guano operations. "Mr. Crowell had set his heart on going to Swan to continue the guano investigation," Mrs. Crowell wrote later in the *Falmouth* (Massachusetts) *Enterprise*.[1]

The couple would not be put off. They contacted Sum-

* There was no listing for Radio Swan.

ner Smith, who agreed to write to "his caretaker, Captain Donald E. Glidden, to make plans for us. . . . The captain had given us into the care of Mr. Roger Butts, an executive of Vanguard Service Corporation, which manages the commercial station, Radio Americas, on the island."

The Crowells were, apparently, innocently unaware of what they had stumbled into.

Once a week, a CIA plane would leave Miami for Swan Island, and it was the only air link with the United States.

"At last arrangements were made for us to be among the few recent visitors to Swan," Mrs. Crowell wrote. "We flew from Miami in a DC-3, twenty-four-passenger plane with two pilots, the mail, medical supplies, weekly food, several wares for the store, etc. We learned later that we presented some problem. About one half-hour before we were to land, the island found out that no preparation in the line of ramp or ladder had been made to get two aged passengers from the high door of the plane. After much scurrying around and various suggestions, a solution was found. They drove a tractor with a scoop up to the door, raised the scoop, led us onto it, backed away a bit and lowered us. Every available man, woman and child was down to greet us. I was a curiosity indeed, the only female citizen of the United States on the Island."

What happened next was like a scene straight out of a Margaret Rutherford–Alistair Sim film comedy, as the charming couple was turned loose on the CIA's guano island.

"Mr. Butts gave up his home for us, a Quonset hut, five rooms and a bath with hot and cold water," Mrs. Crowell continued.

"The radio station and weather bureau were carefully explained to us, but not comprehended. We were taken swimming in the loveliest water I ever saw . . . my especial joy on that trip was the birds; at least one hundred frigate birds, one hundred brown boobies, and twelve red-footed boobies. . . . Palm warblers . . . were around our house all the time and I had an excellent view of a vittelina warbler, Nelson's (*denolroica vittelina nelsoni*) named for

Mr. George Nelson and found only on Swan, I believe. On the runway we enjoyed daily a flock of twenty little blue herons in all stages of color, a few white ibis and one cattle egret. It seemed like home to hear and see one catbird, also one tree swallow.

"One of the technicians led us to a young white booby in its nest. We had to pick our way several hundred yards over jagged sharp coral with great cracks to be crossed."

There was no question that the CIA had gone above and beyond the call of duty to be hospitable to the delightful Massachusetts couple. "When we reluctantly left for home," Mrs. Crowell concluded, "the pilot flew low over and around the islands as a farewell treat. We realized with grateful appreciation that no stone had been left unturned to make our unusual adventure a reality."

A year later, Radio Americas was still on the air from Swan. It called on Cubans to burn cane fields, and to carry matches to be ready for sabotage at all times. It instructed them to go into offices and telephone booths and take the receivers off the hooks to tie up communications. And it urged the people of Cuba to smash as many bottles as possible. The CIA's reported plan was to curtail the island's beer supply by creating a bottle shortage.

In Boston, Sumner Smith maintained he was not sure whether or not he was still a director of the Gibraltar Steamship Corporation. Smith, explaining his family's ownership claim, said that he had foreclosed a mortgage on the island that had been acquired years ago by his father, the late Charles Sumner Smith. Smith said he had since transferred ownership of the island to his four children, and that they in turn had leased the land to Gibraltar for operation of the radio station.

A telephone call was placed to the Vanguard Service Corporation, consultants, in Miami late in 1963. "Vanguard Service," said the girl who answered. Roger Butts then came on the line. Mr. Butts explained that Radio Swan was now Radio Americas and was "currently in operation."

"It is a privately owned commercial station operating on Swan Island," he said.

359

"What happened to the Gibraltar Steamship Corporation?"

"Vanguard is leasing from Gibraltar Steamship on a profit basis. Gibraltar leases from Sumner Smith."

Mr. Butts identified himself as the "vice-president" of Vanguard. "The president and treasurer is Mr. William H. West, Jr. Mr. James Hollingsworth of Palm Beach is the vice-president and Richard S. Greenlee is the secretary."

Mr. Butts was asked how the station was supported. After a long pause he replied: "By income from sponsors."

A call to George O. Gillingham, the public information chief for the Federal Communications Commission, brought this response to an inquiry about the Swan Island station: "It's still operating. We do not license this station. Try the State Department."

Gillingham said yes, the FCC does license stations broadcasting from the United States or its possessions. That is the law of the land. "We don't license government stations," he added.

Was he saying that this was a government station then?

"No, no, no!" the FCC man said. "We don't know what it is. All we know is that it's operating."

25

The 1960 Campaign—and Now

UNKNOWN to the American people, the Bay of Pigs invasion plan played a crucial role in the 1960 presidential campaign.

Despite the fact that millions of persons watched the four televised debates between Richard M. Nixon and John F. Kennedy, the voters went to the polls without knowing the secret reasons for the public positions the candidates took on Cuba. Behind the scenes, on both sides, there was deep concern over the pending CIA invasion.

To understand the secret drama that unfolded inside the Nixon and Kennedy camps in 1960 over the planned invasion, one must go back to a tradition that began in 1944.

In that year, wartime intelligence reports were made available to Thomas E. Dewey, the Republican presidential candidate, by President Roosevelt. Mr. Dewey received similar information in 1948. In 1952 President Truman made CIA data available to General Eisenhower and to Adlai Stevenson.

In 1956, following what by now had become an established custom, Eisenhower arranged CIA briefings for Stevenson. And in 1960 Eisenhower sent identical telegrams on July 18 to Kennedy and to Senator Lyndon Johnson, the Democratic vice-presidential candidate, offering them "periodic briefings on the international scene from a responsible official in the Central Intelligence

Agency. . . . Because of the secret character of the information that would be furnished you," said Eisenhower, "it would be exclusively for your personal knowledge." [1]

Kennedy and Johnson accepted Eisenhower's offer. On July 23 Allen Dulles, then Director of Central Intelligence, flew to Hyannis with two aides, James Brooke and Gates Lloyd. The CIA men arrived in an Aero Commander that had the markings of a private plane. Brooke and Lloyd carried secret papers in two slim dispatch cases.

In a two-and-a-half-hour conversation at Senator Kennedy's summer home, on the brick terrace overlooking Nantucket Sound, Dulles briefed the Democratic presidential candidate on what Kennedy described afterward to reporters as "a good many serious problems around the world." Kennedy said these had been discussed "in detail" and indicated particular emphasis had been placed on Cuba and Africa.

On July 27 Dulles flew to the LBJ Ranch in Texas and remained overnight to brief Johnson. Dulles briefed Kennedy once more during the campaign, on September 19.

A few days after this second briefing, in a reply published on September 23 to a series of questions from the Scripps-Howard newspapers, Kennedy said: "The forces fighting for freedom in exile and in the mountains of Cuba should be sustained and assisted. . . ." [2]

Then, on October 6, in Cincinnati, Kennedy delivered his major speech on Cuba. "Hopefully," he said, "events may once again bring us an opportunity to bring our influence strongly to bear on behalf of the cause of freedom in Cuba." Meantime, he called for "encouraging those liberty-loving Cubans who are leading the resistance to Castro." [3]

These sentiments were making the Nixon camp increasingly edgy. Nixon and his aides did not know exactly how much, if anything, Kennedy knew about the invasion plan. They did not know if Dulles had told him about it. They certainly did not want the Democratic candidate to be able to claim credit for an invasion that might be

362

launched by a Republican President. It was President Eisenhower, after all, who had ordered the CIA to arm and train the exiles in May of 1960. Nixon and his advisers wanted the CIA invasion to take place before the voters went to the polls on November 8.

A top Nixon campaign adviser later privately confirmed this. He explained that Nixon was hoping for an invasion before the election because "it would have been a cinch to win" the presidency if the Eisenhower Administration—in which Nixon was the Number 2 man—had destroyed Castro in the closing days of the campaign.

The best documentation of this is an article by Herbert G. Klein, press secretary to Vice-President Nixon during the 1960 campaign. On March 25, 1962, writing in the *San Diego Union*, of which he was the editor, Klein revealed what had been going on behind the scenes in the Nixon camp in 1960. It was a candid and most interesting news story that did not gain the wide national attention it merited:

"From the start of the 1960 campaign many of us were convinced that Cuba could be the deciding issue in a close election. Certainly, in retrospect, it was one of the decisive factors in what was the closest presidential election of modern history. . . .

"Only four of us on the Nixon staff shared the secret that refugees were being trained for an eventual assault on Castro and a return to Cuba. We had stern instructions not to talk about this, and, despite many temptations, we protected security by remaining silent.

"For a long time, as we campaigned across the country, we held the hope that the training would go rapidly enough to permit the beach landing. The defeat of Castro would have been a powerful factor for Richard Nixon. . . .

"But the training didn't go rapidly enough for a pre-election landing. . . ."

Klein also wrote that a pre-election Cuban invasion would have made it possible to reveal during the campaign that Nixon had written a confidential memo in 1959, analyzing Castro as "either incredibly naïve about Communism or under Communist discipline." * Klein added that Nixon had urged a tough policy on Cuba "which led to the training of refugees."

While the Nixon people were hoping the invasion would take place any day, that was exactly what the Kennedy strategists hoped would *not* happen. They were receiving persistent, and disturbing, reports that some kind of Cuban exile operation was in the works. The reports of invasion training were picked up from several sources, including alert members of the press.

In mid-October, Andrew St. George and Hank Walker went to Florida to shoot pictures for *Life* magazine of Cuban exiles training to invade their homeland. The Kennedy campaign staff heard about this assignment. While in Miami, St. George received several telephone calls from William Attwood, a member of Kennedy's speech-writing staff.†

Attwood was calling St. George for information on the state of training of the Cuban exiles. According to St. George, Attwood expressed concern that the Republicans would try to launch an invasion of Cuba before election day. St. George said the question, apparently, in the mind

---

* In April, 1959, after a long meeting with Castro in his office in the Capitol, Nixon drafted a confidential memo for the White House, the CIA and the State Department. Key excerpts said: "As I have already indicated, he was incredibly naïve with regard to the Communist threat and appeared to have no fear whatever that the Communists might eventually come to power in Cuba. . . .

"My own appraisal of him as a man is somewhat mixed. The one fact we can be sure of is that he has those indefinable qualities which make him a leader of men. Whatever we may think of him he is going to be a great factor in the development of Cuba and very possibly in Latin American affairs generally. He seems to be sincere, he is either incredibly naïve about Communism or under Communist discipline—my guess is the former and as I have already implied, his ideas as to how to run a government or an economy are less developed than those of almost any world figure I have met in fifty countries. But because he has the power to lead to which I have referred we have no choice but at least to try to orient him in the right direction."

† After the election, Attwood was named Ambassador to Guinea, and in February, 1964, he became Ambassador to Kenya.

of the Kennedy aide was not whether there was to be an invasion, but when.

St. George told Attwood that there seemed little possibility of an immediate invasion, judging by the state of readiness of the exiles. This word was passed on to Robert Kennedy, who was managing his brother's campaign. At one point, there had been discussion among Kennedy strategists of the possibility of the candidate's giving a speech anticipating the invasion that seemed to be brewing, and thereby neutralizing its political effect. The idea of a formal speech was dropped, however, when investigation showed there was little possibility that an invasion could be launched before election day.

However, the Cuban issue was not dropped completely. On October 20 the Kennedy and Nixon campaign trails crossed in New York City, where both were preparing for their fourth and final televised debate the following night. That afternoon, newsmen accompanying the Democratic candidate were alerted for an important statement by Kennedy. The release was delayed, and when mimeographed copies finally arrived at the pressroom in the Biltmore Hotel, it was after 6:00 P.M. On the very last page these key words appeared:

"We must attempt to strengthen the non-Batista democratic anti-Castro forces in exile, and in Cuba itself, who offer eventual hope of overthrowing Castro. Thus far these fighters for freedom have had virtually no support from our government." [4]

At the Waldorf-Astoria, eight blocks away, the effect on Nixon was immediate and explosive.

A year and a half later, in his book *Six Crises*, Nixon wrote that when he read Kennedy's Biltmore statement, "I got mad." Nixon went on to say that the "covert training of Cuban exiles" by the CIA was due "in substantial part at least, to my efforts," and that this "had been adopted as a policy as a result of my direct support." Now, Nixon felt, Kennedy was trying to pre-empt a policy which the Vice-President claimed as his own.

Nixon wrote that he ordered Fred Seaton, Interior Secretary and a Nixon campaign adviser, "to call the

White House at once on the security line and find out whether or not Dulles had briefed Kennedy on the fact that for months the CIA had not only been supporting and assisting but actually training Cuban exiles for the eventual purpose of supporting an invasion of Cuba itself.

"Seaton reported back to me in half an hour. His answer: Kennedy had been briefed on this operation."

Kennedy, Nixon continued, was advocating "what was already the policy of the American government—covertly —and Kennedy had been so informed . . . Kennedy was endangering the security of the whole operation. . . .

"There was only one thing I could do. The covert operation had to be protected at all costs. I must not even suggest by implication that the United States was rendering aid to rebel forces in and out of Cuba. In fact, I must go to the other extreme: I must attack the Kennedy proposal to provide such aid as wrong and irresponsible because it would violate our treaty commitments." [5]

The next night, during their fourth debate from the ABC-TV studio in Manhattan, Nixon hopped on the Kennedy proposal as "dangerously irresponsible." He said it would violate "five treaties" between the United States and Latin America as well as the Charter of the United Nations.

The Nixon camp was elated. All the next day, as the Republican candidate barnstormed through eastern Pennsylvania, members of the Nixon staff let it be known that they felt Kennedy had finally made a serious error.

That night, October 22, in the crowded gymnasium at Muhlenberg College in Allentown, Nixon attacked:

"He [Kennedy] called for—and get this—the U. S. Government to support a revolution in Cuba, and I say that this is the most shockingly reckless proposal ever made in our history by a presidential candidate during a campaign—and I'll tell you why . . . he comes up, as I pointed up, with the fantastic recommendation that the U. S. Government shall directly aid the anti-Castro forces both in and out of Cuba. . . .

"You know what this would mean? We would violate right off the bat five treaties with the American States, including the Treaty of Bogota of 1948. We would also violate our solemn commitments to the United Nations. . . ." [6]

Kennedy was campaigning in Missouri and Kansas that day. By the time he reached Wisconsin the next day, he was feeling the heat of the Nixon attack.

In North Carolina, Adlai Stevenson, campaigning for Kennedy, was alarmed at Kennedy's stand on Cuba. Stevenson had spoken at Duke University on October 21, and now he was at his sister's plantation in Southern Pines, North Carolina. He placed a long-distance call to Kennedy in Wisconsin. When he got through, Stevenson warned that the statement urging aid to the exiles could develop into a political trap for Kennedy if he were elected. He expressed strong opposition, and urged the Democratic standard-bearer to back off slightly from his New York statement.

In their conversation, Kennedy seemed embarrassed about the statement and implied it had been issued without adequate clearance. He told Stevenson he would pull back from it, and regain a safer position. Accordingly, Kennedy dispatched a telegram to Nixon that day in which he said he had "never advocated and I do not now advocate intervention in Cuba in violation of our treaty obligations." And he said no more about aiding Cuban exiles.

Three days later, the October 31 issue of *Life* appeared with St. George's and Walker's pictures of Cuban exiles in training.

The campaign was now rushing to a climax. On November 2 Kennedy had his last CIA briefing, this time from General Cabell, rather than from Dulles. Kennedy had requested this briefing in order to be brought up to date on any last-minute international developments.

The CIA deputy director flew to Los Angeles and talked with the candidate aboard the *Caroline*, Kennedy's Convair, during a flight from Los Angeles to San Diego. The two men were alone in the rear compartment of the plane. Cabell left Kennedy at San Diego.

In March of 1962, when Nixon charged in his book

that Kennedy had been briefed about the Cuban invasion and had deliberately endangered its security, the White House issued an immediate denial, which was backed up by Allen Dulles. Pierre Salinger said Kennedy "was not told before the election of 1960 of the training of troops outside of Cuba or of any plans for 'supporting an invasion of Cuba.'" Nixon's account was based on a "misunderstanding," Salinger said. Dulles' campaign briefings had been general in nature, he added. He said Kennedy was first informed of the Cuban operation when Dulles and Bissell came to see him in Palm Beach on November 18, 1960, ten days after the election.*

Dulles, too, attributed Nixon's version to "an honest misunderstanding. . . . My briefings were intelligence briefings on the world situation," he said. "They did not cover our own government's plans or programs for action, overt or covert." [7]

And in fact, Nixon did not explain how Seaton, by telephoning the White House, had learned what had transpired between Kennedy and Dulles. He did not say to whom his adviser had talked. Seaton has declined to shed any further light on this. "It was an appropriate White House official, a man who would be in a position to get the answer," was all that he would say. "It certainly was not the White House janitor." [8]

In fact, Seaton talked to Brigadier General Andrew J. Goodpaster, the White House staff secretary and President Eisenhower's link with the CIA. But there is no indication that Goodpaster checked with Dulles, or that Nixon or Seaton ever checked with Dulles directly.

Exactly what transpired during Dulles' briefings of Kennedy—the nuances, the inflections, Dulles' precise words when the question of Cuba arose—these will never be known for certain, since the meeting was top-secret and

---

* Immediately after the election, Dulles went to Eisenhower and urged that the full details of the Cuban invasion plan be laid before the President-elect. Eisenhower authorized Dulles to do so, and the CIA chief, with Bissell, flew to Palm Beach for the November 18 meeting.

unrecorded. The same applies to General Cabell's briefing aboard the *Caroline* November 2.

But there is some evidence that Kennedy did not want to be told about operational matters—such as the Cuban invasion—because of the very fact that this might limit his freedom of action.

In any event, Nixon's dispute with Kennedy and Dulles over who told what to whom missed the point. Regardless of the content of the CIA briefings, the Kennedy camp had learned informally from other sources that an exile invasion was hatching.

The candidates for President of the United States were allowing their campaign strategy and public positions to be influenced by a secret operation of the Invisible Government. (All three major issues debated in the closing days of the 1960 campaign were related to clandestine operations. First, there was Cuba. Second, there was the issue of Quemoy and Matsu. Third, the question of whether President Eisenhower should have "apologized" to Khrushchev after the U-2 flight of Francis Gary Powers in order to save the Paris summit meeting.)

The point is that as a by-product of operations of the Invisible Government the electoral process—the very heart of democratic government—was being confused and diluted.

In the case of the Cuban invasion, both candidates were concerned about a secret plan of which the electorate knew nothing. In choosing the man to fill the most powerful elective office in the world, the voters were basing their decision, in part, on misleading statements.

As has been noted, one candidate, Vice-President Nixon, confessed considerably later that he took a false public position during the campaign, exactly the opposite of his true feeling, in order, he said, to protect the CIA invasion plan.

But the millions who watched Nixon and Kennedy argue the Cuban issue on television had no way of knowing that the facts were being distorted or suppressed.

This is not to suggest that the invasion plan should have

been announced on nation-wide television. But it does seem reasonable to ask how the voter can make an informed choice when a candidate is not telling the truth, for whatever laudable patriotic motivation.

Those who argue against tighter controls over the secret branches of the government are fond of making the case that the American system already has enough built-in safeguards. The people elect a President and place their faith in him. During his term in the White House, he is free to run the government, including its secret machinery, as he sees fit. But if the voters dislike how he is running the country, they can turn him out of office in four years. For during every presidential election campaign, the great issues are debated, there is a full public accounting and the people can look, listen and make their intelligent choice.

So the argument goes. What happens to this theory, however, when the electoral process becomes so enmeshed in the tentacles of the Invisible Government that a candidate tells the voters he stands for one course of action, when he really believes just the opposite? Obviously, the electoral process itself is fundamentally weakened. That is what happened in 1960, and there is no reason to think it could not happen again.

When the public positions of candidates for President are shaped (or reversed) by secret operations which the voters are not entitled to know about, something has happened to the American system, and something for ill.

The Invisible Government participated in the presidential campaign of 1960. It was unseen, but there. It provided a valuable lesson for future presidential campaigns.

26

A Conclusion

THE PRIMARY CONCERN of the men who drafted the Declaration of Independence was the consent of the governed. By the mid-twentieth century, under the pressures of the Cold War, the primary concern of the nation's leaders had become the survival of the governed.

The Invisible Government emerged in the aftermath of World War II as one of the instruments designed to insure national survival. But because it was hidden, because it operated outside of the normal Constitutional checks and balances, it posed a potential threat to the very system it was designed to protect.

President Truman created the nucleus of the Invisible Government when he signed the National Security Act of 1947, giving birth to the CIA. He has asserted that he conceived of the CIA primarily as a co-ordinating and intelligence-gathering aid to a modern President who needed concise, centralized information on which to base national policy. But by 1963 the intelligence apparatus had taken on dimensions which Truman said he had never anticipated.

"With all the nonsense put out by Communist propaganda . . . in their name-calling assault on the West," he wrote, "the last thing we needed was for the CIA to be seized upon as something akin to a subverting influence in the affairs of other people. . . .

"There are now some searching questions that need to be answered. I . . . would like to see the CIA be restored to its original assignment as the intelligence arm of the President, and whatever else it can properly perform in that special field—and that its operational duties be terminated or properly used elsewhere.

"We have grown up as a nation, respected for our free institutions and for our ability to maintain a free and open society. There is something about the way the CIA has been functioning that is casting a shadow over our historic position and I feel that we need to correct it." [1]

In effect, Truman was lamenting the damage to national prestige caused by such special operations as the U-2 affair of 1960, the Bay of Pigs, and the episodes in Indonesia, Burma, Laos, Vietnam and elsewhere.

Yet the Plans Division, which conducts the CIA's special operations, was established in 1951 under President Truman. And it was under Truman that Allen Dulles came to Washington to be the first director of that division. Since Truman could not have been unaware of these events, the real question is whether the operational activities of the CIA have grown to a size and shape that Truman had not intended when he signed the 1947 Act.

Has the dagger, in short, become more important than the cloak? Certainly, in the years since 1951, secret operations have grown greatly in size and number. When they have gone awry—and some have gone sensationally awry— they have brought notoriety to the CIA.

Nevertheless, CIA officials have insisted that the majority of these operations have been successful. However, there have been a large number of known failures. There is only one logical conclusion, if one is to accept the CIA's claim to a high percentage of success: that the total number of secret operations has been much greater than is supposed even in knowledgeable circles.

As in the case of the Bay of Pigs, some of these operations have become so big that they cannot be practicably concealed or plausibly denied. In other instances, clandestine activity has turned loose forces which have proved uncontrollable. Around the world, the CIA has trained and supported elite corps designed to maintain internal security in pro-Western countries. But these police units have sometimes become a source of acute embarrassment to the United States, notably in Vietnam, where CIA-financed special forces raided the Buddhist pagodas.

Despite these wide-ranging clandestine activities, and despite the importance, the power and the vast sums at the disposal of the CIA and the other agencies of the Invisible Government, there has not been enough intelligent public discussion of the role of this secret machinery.

In general, critics of the CIA have been hobbled by a lack of sure knowledge about its activities. By and large, their criticism falls into three categories: that the CIA conducts foreign policy on its own, that it runs its affairs outside of presidential and Congressional control, and that it warps intelligence to justify its special operations.

There is a sophisticated notion that the problems raised by a hidden bureaucracy operating within a free society can be resolved by limiting the CIA to intelligence-gathering and setting up a separate organization to conduct special operations. The argument is that when the two functions are joined, as they are now, the intelligence-gatherers inevitably become special pleaders for the operations in which they are engaged.

There is little question that this has happened in the past and that it poses a continuing, basic problem. But the difficulty is that an agent who is running a secret operation often is in the best position to gather secret information. A CIA man involved in intrigues with the political opposition in a given country will very likely know much more about that opposition than an analyst at Langley or even the ambassador on the scene.

If the CIA were to be prohibited from carrying out secret operational activity and that task were to be turned over to another agency, it might be necessary to create another set of secret operatives in addition to the large number of CIA men already at work overseas. Such a situation would probably reduce efficiency, raise costs and increase the dangers of exposure. The Taylor committee grappled with the problem after the Bay of Pigs and came to the conclusion that the present arrangement is the lesser of two evils.

This problem, as important and complex as it may be, is secondary to the larger question of whether the CIA sets its own policy, outside of presidential control. While this accusation contains some truth, it, too, is oversimplified.

There are procedures which call for the approval of any major special operation at a high level in the executive branch of the government. The public comments of Eisenhower on Guatemala and Kennedy on the Bay of Pigs demonstrated that they not only approved these operations, but took part in the planning for them.

However, many important decisions appear to have been delegated to the Special Group, a small and shadowy directorate nowhere specifically provided for by law. But because the Special Group is composed of men with heavy responsibilities in other areas, it obviously can give no more than general approval and guidance to a course of action. The CIA and the other agencies of the Invisible Government are free to shape events in the field. They can influence policy and chart their own course within the flexible framework laid down by Washington.

In Costa Rica, for example, CIA officers did not see fit to inform the State Department when they planted a fake Communist document in a local newspaper. In Cairo, "Mr. X" slipped in to see Nasser ahead of the State Department's special emissary. In the Bay of Pigs planning, the CIA men selected the political leadership of the Cuban exiles.

Yet because of the existence of the Special Group and a generalized mechanism for approving operations, intelligence men have been able to claim that they have never acted outside of policy set at the highest level of the government. In short, even when a clear policy has been established, a President may find it difficult to enforce. Presidential power, despite the popular conception of it, is diffuse and limited. The various departments and agencies under his authority have entrenched sources of strength. They cannot always be molded to his will.

In his relations with the Invisible Government, the President's problems are compounded. He cannot deal with it openly and publicly. He cannot bring to bear against it the normal political tools at his disposal. He cannot go over the heads of the leaders of the intelligence community and appeal to the people.

A President operates under a constant awareness of the capacity of disgruntled members of the Invisible Government to undercut his purposes by leaking information to Congress and the press. During the deliberations leading to the Bay of Pigs, Kennedy obviously realized the political dangers of canceling a plan to overthrow Castro which had been brought to an advanced stage by a Republican administration. Similarly, during the Cuban missile crisis in 1962, White House officials suspected that someone high in the CIA was attempting to undermine the President by providing the Republicans with information.

This suspicion reflected the fact that the Invisible Government has achieved a quasi-independent status and a power of its own. Under these conditions, and given the necessity for secret activities to remain secret, can the Invisible Government ever be made fully compatible with the democratic system?

The answer is no. It cannot be made fully compatible. But, on the other hand, it seems inescapable that some form of Invisible Government is essential to national security in a time of Cold War. Therefore, the urgent necessity in such a national dilemma is to make the Invisible Government as reconcilable as possible with the democratic system, aware that no more than a tenuous compromise can be achieved.

What, then, is to be done?

Most important, the public, the President and the Congress must support steps to control the intelligence establishment, to place checks on its power and to make it truly accountable, particularly in the area of special operations.

The danger of special operations does not lie in tables of organization or questions of technique, but in embarking upon them too readily and without effective presidential control. Special operations pose dangers not only to the nations against which they are directed, but to ourselves. They raise the question of how far a free society, in attempting to preserve itself, can emulate a closed society without becoming indistinguishable from it.

The moral and practical justification for secret operations has been stated simply by Allen Dulles, who said the government felt compelled to "fight fire with fire." The implication was that the CIA could justifiably respond in kind to the unscrupulous practices of the Soviet espionage machine. It could mirror the opposition.

"Today," Dulles has observed, "the Soviet State Security Service (KGB) is the eyes and ears of the Soviet State abroad as well as at home. It is a multi-purpose, clandestine arm of power that can in the last analysis carry out almost any act that the Soviet leadership assigns to it. It is more than a secret police organization, more than an intelligence and counter-intelligence organization. It is an instrument for subversion, manipulation and violence, for secret intervention in the affairs of other countries. It is an aggressive arm of Soviet ambitions in the Cold War." [2]

A free society has difficulty in adopting such practices because of its moral tradition that the end does not justify the means. It must proceed with caution, alert to the danger of succumbing to the enemy's morality by too eagerly embracing his methods.

Special operations should be launched only after the most sober deliberation by the President, acting upon the broadest possible advice. This counsel should come not only from those within the intelligence community, but from responsible officials with a wider viewpoint. Operations such as those at the Bay of Pigs and in Indonesia involved the potential overthrow of a foreign government. They amount to undeclared war. They should be launched only when the alternative of inaction carries with it the gravest risk to national security.

If, nonetheless, it becomes necessary to undertake a secret operation, it is imperative that the long-range repercussions be weighed fully in advance. The consequences of failure must be faced. Was it worth running the risk of national humiliation in attempting to overthrow Castro? Was it worth running the risk of permanently alienating Sukarno by supporting his enemies?

Equal consideration must be given to the problems that would result from the success of a special operation. Is the United States prepared to assume responsibility for the economic and political conditions growing out of a successful CIA-supported revolt? How much is really accomplished, in such cases as Guatemala and Iran, if a pro-Communist government is removed, but the conditions which permitted Communism to make inroads in the first place are restored?

It is a delusion to think that the problems of United States foreign policy in a complex world can be resolved by the quick surgery of a palace coup. The intelligence and espionage technicians, who have a natural affinity for such activist solutions, should never be allowed to dominate the deliberations leading to secret operations. Nor should they be permitted exclusive control of the conduct of operations in the field.

Both Eisenhower and Kennedy directed that the ambassador be in charge of all United States activities in a foreign country. It is essential that this theoretical supremacy become a reality. An ambassador should never be put in the position of a William Sebald in Burma. If he is to maintain the respect of the government leaders with whom he is dealing, he must be kept informed about American clandestine activity. If circumstances dictate a covert policy that conflicts with the avowed policy of Washington toward a given country, the ambassador must know about it.

Congress should also be kept informed. Under the Constitution, Congress is supposed to act as a check upon the activities of the executive branch. Traditionally, the Senate has given its "advice and consent" to major commitments in the sphere of foreign affairs. But in its relations with the Invisible Government, Congress has all but voted away its rights. It knows relatively little about what goes on in the $4,000,000,000-a-year intelligence complex for which it appropriates the money.

The CIA subcommittees in the House and Senate are controlled by the most conservative elements in Congress, men who are close personally and philosophically to those who run the Invisible Government. These subcommittees are now heavily weighted with legislators whose field of competence is military affairs. They should be reorganized to encompass men with a wider view and expert knowledge of foreign affairs. Men such as Senator Fulbright (who foresaw the perils of the Bay of Pigs with such clarity) should not be purposely excluded from Congressional surveillance of the intelligence apparatus.

The shadowy subcommittees should be replaced by a joint committee, including men from both the House and Senate. There is no reason why secrets should leak in any greater degree from one formal committee than from the present group of informal subcommittees. There has not been any leak of classified data from the Joint Committee on Atomic Energy.

Although the need for greater Congressional control is apparent, both President Eisenhower and President Kennedy resisted it as an infringement upon their executive power. They established a veneer of outside control by creating advisory boards of private citizens. This produced an anomalous situation. Selected private citizens are privy to secrets of the Invisible Government, but the elected representatives of the people are denied any meaningful knowledge of the intelligence machinery.

Congress is not only ignorant of operations overseas, but it has been denied information about the increasing involvement of the Invisible Government in domestic activities. The mandate to gather and analyze intelligence has been broadened into a justification for clandestine activities in the United States.

Clearly, some foreign intelligence can be gathered at home, but no rationale has been offered for a broad spectrum of domestic operations: maintenance of a score of CIA offices in major cities; the control of private businesses serving as CIA covers (such as the Gibraltar Steamship Corporation and Zenith Technical Enterprises, Incorporated); academic programs (such as the Center for International Studies at MIT); and the financing and control of freedom radio stations, publishing ventures and of exile and ethnic groups.

There should be a thorough reappraisal by private organizations and by the universities of the wisdom of their ties to the Invisible Government. There is a real danger that the academic community may find itself so closely allied with the Invisible Government that it will have lost its ability to function as an independent critic of our government and society. The academic world should re-examine its acceptance of hidden money from the CIA.

These unseen domestic activities of the CIA have become disturbingly complex and widespread. To the extent that they can be perceived, they appear to be outside the spirit and perhaps the letter of the National Security Act. No outsider can tell whether this activity is necessary or even legal. No outsider is in a position to determine whether or not, in time, these activities might become an internal danger to a free society. Both Congress and the Executive ought to give urgent attention to this problem.

In a free society attention should be given as well to the increasing tendency of the American Government to mislead the American people in order to protect secret operations. For example:

U-2: "There was absolutely no—N-O—no deliberate attempt to violate Soviet airspace. There never has been." —Lincoln White. State Department spokesman.

Bay of Pigs: "The American people are entitled to know whether we are intervening in Cuba or intend to do so in the future. The answer to that question is no."—Secretary of State Dean Rusk.

Indonesia: "Our policy is one of careful neutrality and proper deportment all the way through so as not to be taking sides where it is none of our business."—President Eisenhower.

Missile crisis: "The Pentagon has no information indicating the presence of offensive weapons in Cuba." —Department of Defense.

Guatemala: "The situation is being cured by the Guatemalans themselves."—Secretary of State John Foster Dulles.

Bay of Pigs fliers: "Unfortunately, at present neither CIA nor any other government agency possesses the slightest pertinent information on your son's disappearance."—The White House.

Misleading statements related to covert operations have even distorted the electoral process, as was demonstrated in the presidential campaign of 1960.

It seems reasonable to suggest that there be fewer righteous declarations and less public misinformation by the government and, perhaps, more discreet silence in difficult circumstances.

The secret intelligence machinery of the government can never be totally reconciled with the traditions of a free republic. But in a time of Cold War, the solution lies not in dismantling this machinery but in bringing it under greater control. The resultant danger of exposure is far less than the danger of secret power. If we err as a society, let it be on the side of control.

"It should be remembered," Thomas Jefferson wrote in 1819, "that whatever power in any government is independent, is absolute also."

Notes

1. *The Invisible Government*
1. Speech by Allen W. Dulles at Yale University, February 3, 1958.

3. *Build-Up*
1. The entire text of the memorandum was published for the first time in *Fulbright of Arkansas*, a collection of speeches and papers by Senator J. W. Fulbright. Robert B. Luce, Inc., Washington, 1963.

5. *The Case of the Birmingham Widows*
1. Interview with Robert F. Kennedy, in *U.S. News & World Report*, January 28, 1963.

6. *A History*
1. Article by Harry S. Truman, syndicated by North American Newspaper Alliance, in the *Washington Post*, December 22, 1963.
2. Memorandum by Allen W. Dulles, contained in Hearings, *National Defense Establishment*, pp. 525-28; Senate Committee on Armed Services, 80th Congress, 1st Session on S. 758, 1947.
3. *New York Times*, May 28, 1949.
4. Interview with Allen Dulles, "Meet the Press," National Broadcasting Company, December 31, 1961.
5. *New York Herald Tribune*, April 16, 1948. See also *New York Times* of the same date.
6. *New York Herald Tribune*, June 27, 1950.
7. Truman, Harry S., *Memoirs*, Vol. II, p. 331. Doubleday & Company, Inc., New York, 1956.
8. *Ibid.*, p. 372.
9. Dulles, Allen W., *The Craft of Intelligence*, p. 166. Harper & Row, Publishers, Inc., New York, 1963.
10. Interview by Eric Sevareid, "CBS Reports: The Hot and Cold Wars of Allen Dulles," Columbia Broadcasting System, April 26, 1962.
11. Dulles, Allen W., *The Craft of Intelligence*, p. 224. Harper & Row Publishers, Inc., New York, 1963.

12. Hearings, *The President's Proposal on the Middle East*, p. 446; joint meeting of the Senate Committee on Foreign Relations and Senate Committee on Armed Services, 85th Congress, 1st Session, February 1, 1957. See also pp. 174-75. January 15, 1957.
13. Dulles, Allen W., "The Craft of Intelligence," article in Britannica Book of the Year, Encyclopaedia Britannica, Inc., Chicago, 1963.
14. The report cited by Mansfield had appeared in an editorial in the *Washington Post*, January 9, 1953.
15. Hearings, *Events Incident to the Summit Conference*, p. 124; Senate Committee on Foreign Relations, 86th Congress, 2nd Session, testimony by Secretary of Defense Thomas S. Gates, June 2, 1960.
16. Television interview with Allen Dulles by David Schoenbrun, Columbia Broadcasting System, August 18, 1963.
17. Hearing, *Francis G. Powers, U-2 Pilot*, Senate Committee on Armed Services, 87th Congress, 2nd Session, March 6, 1962. The interview cited in the footnote was taped by Mr. Clarke on March 12, 1962, during the home-town reception for the U-2 pilot in Pound, Virginia.
18. *Statement Concerning Francis Gary Powers*, Central Intelligence Agency, March 6, 1962. This document was made public by Representative Carl Vinson, D., Ga., chairman of the House Committee on Armed Services, in advance of Powers' public testimony the same day before the Senate Committee on Armed Services.
19. Dispatch by Walter Sullivan, *New York Times*, July 23, 1954.

10. *Vietnam: The Secret War*

1. State Department situation paper, April 11, 1963.
2. White House statement, October 2, 1963.
3. Fifth Report, Senate Study Mission, February 24, 1963.

11. *Guatemala: CIA's Banana Revolt*

1. From a speech to the American Booksellers Association, Washington, D.C., June 10, 1963. The former President later related the incident in the first volume of his presidential memoirs. See Eisenhower, Dwight D., *Mandate for Change*, Vol. I, *The White House Years*, pp. 420-27. Doubleday & Company, Inc., New York, 1963.
2. Hearings, Part 13, pp. 865-66; Senate Internal Security Subcommittee, Committee on the Judiciary, 87th Congress, 1st Session, testimony by Whiting Willauer, July 27, 1961.
3. Ydigoras, Miguel y Fuentes, with Mario Rosenthal, *My War with Communism*, pp. 49-50. Prentice-Hall, Inc., Englewood Cliffs, N.J., 1963.
4. Speech to the nation by John Foster Dulles, June 30, 1954. *New York Herald Tribune*, July 1, 1954.

382

12. The Kennedy Shake-Up

1. Interview with Robert F. Kennedy, in *U.S. News & World Report*, January 28, 1963.
2. Interview with Robert F. Kennedy by David Kraslow, in *Miami Herald*, January 21, 1963.
3. *Ibid.*
4. Interview with Robert F. Kennedy, in *U.S. News & World Report*, January 28, 1963.

13. The Secret Elite

1. Senate Committee on Armed Services, Hearings on the nomination of John A. McCone, January 18, 1962.
2. *Ibid.*
3. *Ibid.*
4. *Congressional Record*, January 30, 1962.
5. House Subcommittee on Appropriations, testimony by J. Edgar Hoover, January 24, 1962.

15. The Defense Intelligence Agency

1. Dulles, Allen W., *The Craft of Intelligence*, p. 47. Harper & Row Publishers, Inc., New York, 1963.

16. CIA: "It's Well Hidden"

1. "Issues and Answers," American Broadcasting Company, June 30, 1963.

17. CIA: The Inner Workings

1. Kirkpatrick, Lyman, *Military Review*, May, 1961.
2. Memorandum by Allen W. Dulles, contained in Hearings, *National Defense Establishment*, pp. 525–28; Senate Committee on Armed Services, 80th Congress, 1st Session on S. 758, 1947.
3. Television interview with Allen Dulles by David Schoenbrun, Columbia Broadcasting System, August 18, 1963.

18. The Search for Control

1. Dulles, Allen W., *The Craft of Intelligence*, p. 189. Harper & Row Publishers, Inc., New York, 1963.
2. *Intelligence Activities*, A Report to the Congress by the Commission on Organization of the Executive Branch of the Government, June 29, 1955.
3. *National Security Organization*, A Report to the Congress by the Commission on Organization of the Executive Branch of the Government, January, 1949.
4. Report to President Eisenhower by a special study group, October 19, 1954. The group included William D. Franke, Assistant Secretary of the Navy; Morris Hadley, New York attorney; William D. Pawley, former Ambassador to Brazil.

5. *Congressional Record*, March 10, 1954.
6. *Ibid.*, April 11, 1956.
7. *Ibid.*
8. *Ibid.*
9. *Ibid.*, April 9, 1956.
10. Dulles, Allen W., *The Craft of Intelligence*, p. 261. Harper & Row Publishers, Inc., New York, 1963.
11. *Compilation of Studies on United States Foreign Policy*, 86th Congress, 2nd Session, prepared under the direction of the Committee on Foreign Relations, United States Senate.

23. *Black Radio*

1. Speech by John Richardson, Jr., the president of the Free Europe Committee, to the New York State Publishers Association, Albany, N. Y., January 30, 1963.
2. Dulles, Allen W., *The Craft of Intelligence*, p. 155. Harper & Row Publishers, Inc., New York, 1963.
3. *St. Louis Post-Dispatch*, July 23, 1958.
4. Associated Press dispatch filed by Relman Morin in Cairo, in the *Washington Post*, August 15, 1958.
5. Broadcast by Miklos Ajtay, by Radio Free Europe to Hungary, November 3, 1956. This is one of several scripts of broadcasts during the Hungarian revolt made available to the authors by RFE.
6. Michener, James A., *The Bridge at Andau*, p. 257. Random House, Inc., New York, 1957.
7. All of these excerpts are from *The Revolt in Hungary*, A Documentary Chronology of Events Based Exclusively on Internal Broadcasts by Central and Provincial Radios. Pamphlet published by Free Europe Committee, New York.

24. *CIA's Guano Paradise*

1. Mrs. Crowell's account, from which this and the following quotations are taken, appeared in the *Falmouth Enterprise*, July 6, 1962.

25. *The 1960 Campaign—and Now*

1. *New York Herald Tribune*, July 19, 1960.
2. *Freedom of Communications*, Part III, p. 432; The Joint Appearances of Senator John F. Kennedy and Vice-President Richard M. Nixon, Presidential Campaign of 1960, Senate Committee on Commerce, 87th Congress, 1st Session.
3. *Freedom of Communications*, Part I, p. 515; The Speeches of Senator John F. Kennedy, Presidential Campaign of 1960, Senate Committee on Commerce, 87th Congress, 1st Session.
4. *Ibid.*, p. 681.
5. Nixon, Richard M., *Six Crises*, pp. 354–55. Doubleday & Company, Inc., New York, 1962.
6. *Freedom of Communications*, Part I, pp. 710–11; The Speeches

of Vice-President Richard M. Nixon, Presidential Campaign of 1960, Senate Committee on Commerce, 87th Congress, 1st Session.

7. Both the Salinger and Dulles quotes are from the *New York Herald Tribune*, March 21, 1962.

8. *New York Herald Tribune*, March 25, 1962.

26. A Conclusion

1. Article by Harry S. Truman, syndicated by North American Newspaper Alliance, in the *Washington Post*, December 22, 1963.

2. Dulles, Allen W., *The Craft of Intelligence*, p. 86. Harper & Row Publishers, Inc., New York, 1963.

Index

Doster, General G. Reid, 40, 72, 80, 83, 84, 85n.
Double-Check Corporation, *see* Double-Chek Corporation
Double-Chek Corporation, 79, 80, 86–89, 93–95, 156, 263
Douglas, Senator Paul H., 123n.
Downey, Mrs. Claudia Edwards, 240
Downey, John Thomas, 112–115, 242
Dulles, Allen Welsh, 2, 9, 19, 24, 33, 41, 49n., 50, 59, 60, 66, 100–107, 105n., 111, 119, 120, 125, 128, 129, 130n., 132, 169, 178–180, 183, 184, 189, 191, 199–203, 209, 210, 219, 223, 226–231, 232, 236, 237, 243, 246–248, 248n., 250, 252, 269–273, 279, 281, 284, 285, 291, 293, 338, 362, 368, 368n., 369, 372, 376
Dulles, John Foster, 103–105, 105n., 121, 122, 125, 126, 140, 143, 149–152, 156, 169, 187–189, 194, 209, 379
Dunlap, Sergeant Jack E., 223
Dwiggins, Don, 34
Dynamics of Soviet Society, The, 260

East Berlin, 133, 135
East Europe, 134
Eberstadt, Ferdinand, 281
Echols, Emmet, 246
Edmundson, Charles, 115
Egorov, Alexsandra, 257n.
Egorov, Ivan D., 257n.
Egypt, 121–126, 137, 338
Eisenhower, Dwight David, 5, 17, 24, 24n., 33, 36, 49, 79, 103, 124, 126, 128n., 130, 131, 145, 146, 154, 161, 167, 167n., 168, 175, 176, 177–179, 182–184, 189, 191, 198, 199, 209, 214, 219, 223, 233, 234, 248, 280, 287, 301, 317n., 324, 336, 338, 342, 361–363, 368n., 374, 377, 378
Eisenhower, Dr. Milton S., 184, 233

El Salvador, 183, 185, 188, 193
El Tamarindo, 185
ELINT missions, 225
Escambray, 31, 32, 34, 36, 76
Esquipulas, 189, 192
Essex, aircraft carrier, 71
Executive Committee (Excomm), of National Security Council, 313–318

Falmouth (Massachusetts) *Enterprise,* 357
Farias, Matias, 60
Fatalibey, Abo, 341
Fecteau, Richard George, 112–115
Federal Aviation Agency (FAA), 85, 355
Federal Bureau of Investigation (FBI), 1, 3, 212, 214–217, 218, 264, 265
Federal Communications Commission (FCC), 353, 360
Feisal II, King, 337, 338
Felfe, Heinz, 133–137
Felt, Admiral Harry D., 173
Fernandez, Jose A., 60, 66
Fernandez Mon, Daniel, 8, 10, 66
54/12 Group, *see* Special Group
Figueres, Jose (Pepe), 127, 128, 128n., 186
Folres, Lieutenant Fernando, 275
Ford, Representative Gerald, 285n.
Ford Motor Company Fund, 304
Foreign Aid Act, 1951 Amendment, 259
Formosa, *see* Nationalist China
Forrestal, James V., 98, 100, 103n.
Fort Matamoros, 193
Fort Meade, Maryland, 220
France, 125, 126
Frankel, Rear Admiral Samuel B., 229
Free China Relief Association, 143
Free Europe Committee, Inc., 336, 342n.

391

United States Immigration and Naturalization Service, 11, 47

United States Information Agency (USIA), 251, 251n., 279n., 345, 352

United States Intelligence Board (USIB), 102, 211, 212, 218, 226–230, 252, 253, 278, 312

United States neutrality laws, 14, 15, 44, 47, 47n.

United States Weather Bureau, 352, 355

U.S. Government Organization Manual, 219

U.S. News & World Report, 91, 201

U-2, 25, 51, 130–132, 132n., 214, 225, 227, 228, 240n., 299, 310, 312, 317, 317n.ff., 369, 372, 379

Valdes, Ramiro, 12

Valerio, Joseph, 341

Vandenberg, General Hoyt S., 98

Vandenberg Air Force Base, 324

Vanguard Service Corporation, 263, 357–360

"Vaquero," 27

Varela, Joaquin, 60–63, 66

Varona, Manuel Antonio de, 26, 26n.

Vega Vera, Oscar, 63

Venezuela, 295

Vianello, Raul, 61, 62, 66

Vieques Island, 50

Vientiane, 157, 160–164

Vietnam, 166–176, 267, 372, 373

Vietcong, 169–172

Villafana Martinez, Manuel, 40, 69

Villoldo, Gustavo, 69

Vinson, Representative Carl, 285n.

Voice of America, 335, 338, 342, 345

"Voice of Iraq," 338

"Voice of Justice," 338

"Voice of the Arabs," 337

Von Broekhoven, Harold, 191

WRUL, 339, 355

Walker, Hank, 364, 367

WALNUT, 239, 240

Walz, Skip, 242

Washington Post, 235

"Wass, George," 357

Watson, Thomas J., Jr., 210

Webb, James E., 327

Weber, Judge Kurt, 134

West, William H., Jr., 360

West Berlin, 136, 136n.

West German Federal Intelligence Agency (FIA), 133, 136, 136n.

West Germany, 133–136, 343, 346

West Irian, 147, 150

Western Enterprises, Inc., 115

Wheelon, Dr. Albert D., 250

Whelan, Tom, 180

Where-to-Go Travel Agency, 264

White, L. K., 236

White, Lincoln, 34, 109, 149

White, General Thomas D., 37n., 71

Who's Who in the USSR, 340

Willauer, Whiting, 44, 179

Willis, Representative Edwin E., 222

Wilson, Donald M., 251n.

Wilson, Representative Bob, 285n., 317, 318

Wisner, Frank G., 100, 184, 193, 247, 250, 267

Woodbury, Mr. and Mrs. James A., 246

Woods, George D., 209

Woodward, Robert F., 128n.

World Wide Broadcasting System, Inc. (WRUL), 339, 355

Wynne, Greville M., 269

Wulfbrook, 188

Yalu River, 111, 111n.

Ydigoras Fuentes, Miguel, 22, 23, 28, 33, 35, 41, 183, 185, 189, 190, 195, 196

Ydigoras, Miguelito, 28

Your Money's Worth, 344

War Photographers and Writers

Picture of Raw War as never before!

EYEWITNESS HISTORY
OF WORLD WAR II

- **EYEWITNESS PHOTOS BY PRIZE-WINNING WAR PHOTOGRAPHERS!** See the war through the dramatic on-the-spot photographs of Robert Capa, Edward Steichen, Joe Rosenthal—plus hundreds of dynamic war photos culled from private and public collections the world over.

- **EYEWITNESS ACCOUNTS BY WORLD LEADERS!** Go behind the battle lines with Churchill, Roosevelt, Stalin, Hitler, Rommel, for a fresh new insight into the massive holocaust.

- **EYEWITNESS STORIES BY COMBAT JOURNALISTS!** Feel the pile-driving power of the written word as you tour the battle grounds with Ernie Pyle, William Shirer, Cornelius Ryan, Alan Moorehead, S.L.A. Marshall, and other famed war reporters.

Now see the first terrible months of the blitzkrieg! Join the evacuation at Dunkirk! Feel yourself catapulted into the fury of the fight on the beaches of Normandy. Sit in at the Yalta conference with Roosevelt, Churchill, Stalin and other world leaders.

This four-volume EYEWITNESS HISTORY unfolds World War II in 500 monumental war photographs and 100,000 gripping words. Each volume is packed with rare photos—confidential reports—historic revelations. A priceless addition to your library! Treasured gift!

In a hard-cover edition, you'd expect to pay over $20.00, but this handsome Bantam gift set is yours for only $5.95, complete. Get yours today!

AT YOUR BANTAM DEALER OR MAIL HANDY COUPON TODAY